The How-To Book of International Dolls

Also by Loretta Holz

Make It and Sell It: A Young People's Guide to Marketing Crafts
Jumping Jacks: 16 Easy to Assemble, Full Color Toys That Move
How to Sell Your Art and Crafts: A Marketing Guide for Creative People
Mobiles You Can Make
Teach Yourself Stitchery

The How-To Book of International Dolls

A Comprehensive Guide to Making, Costuming, and Collecting Dolls

Loretta Holz

CROWN PUBLISHERS, INC., NEW YORK

To Sybil Harp who got me started in writing
and who also loves fine, handcrafted dolls

Printed in the United States of America
Published simultaneously in Canada by
General Publishing Company Limited

Library of Congress Cataloging in Publication Data

Holz, Loretta.
   The how-to book of international dolls.

   Bibliography: p.
   1.   Dollmaking.   2.   Doll clothes.   3.   Dolls—
Collectors and collecting. I. Title.
TT175.H67   1979   745.59'22   79–14212
ISBN 0–517–53053–8
ISBN 0–517–53054–6 pbk.

Designed by Rhea Braunstein

Contents

Acknowledgments

I am deeply grateful to all the dollmakers and doll owners who shared with me their knowledge and their dolls. Without them this book could not have been.

Special thanks to Doris and Fred Hupp, Halina Hercek, Lorraine Wood, Ann Weiner, Jean Groszmann, David Stuehler, Germaine Reusch, Lisa and Amy Schichtel, Alice Miller, Marguerite MacNeer, Peggy Cassott, Loretta Stukas, Mr. and Mrs. R. W. Fisher, Mrs. L. Urdang, Anne Hulsizer, Adele Moore, Nancy Ann Melik, Sosaia Foukimaoana, Charlotte Decker, Peg Parsons, Nancy Luisi, Helene and Fred Vosburgh, Helen O'Gara, and Susan Grant.

Thanks also to Barbara Ferguson of the International Craftsman in Flemington, New Jersey; Edwina Mueller, editor of *Doll Castle News*; Sybil Harp, editor of *Creative Crafts*; Muriel Adams and Stanley Greenberg of the Forbes Library, Northampton, Massachusetts; Charles Darby of the White Star Trading Company, Northampton, Massachusetts; Herbert Travis and Miss Bacala of the United Nations Gift Shop, New York City; Peg Cullen of My Irish Cottage of Murray Hill, New Jersey; Joan Pinney of Dolls International of Kingston, Ontario, Canada; William Nyce of SERRV; Ruth Green of the Children's Museum, Boston, Massachusetts; Myles Libhart of the Department of the Interior, Indian Affairs Bureau; Judy Laversons of Mohawk Crafts; Kathy Manning of the North Plainfield Library, and Terri Dominici of the Somerset County Library.

Many thanks also to my husband and sons who endured my many trips out to see "doll people," my cartons of dolls constantly opened and packed away again, the many hours I spent "down cellar" developing film and printing photographs, the weeks and weeks I spent in my workroom making dolls and in my office and at the computer typing away at the manuscript. Special thanks to my husband George, my film-loader and constant critic. Grateful thanks to my mother who typed most of the final manuscript. Thanks also to Brandt Aymar, my editor, who was so patient and encouraging over the two years it took me to put this book together.

1
Introduction: Why Dolls?

A doll is basically a representation of the human form. Because it is the image of a person, a doll has a special magic, a personality of its own to an amazing degree.

There is something very potent and compelling about the images people make of themselves and their fellow human beings. Not only dolls but portraits, puppets, idols, and statues retain and project something of the personality of their maker—and yet they have a separate and distinct personality of their own. In the case of an old doll the aura of personality surrounding it can be not only that of the personality given to the doll by its maker, but that acquired from the owner who cherished it.

Somehow even if we are alone with dolls, we don't feel quite alone. Perhaps that is why some people collect them and keep them on display. Dolls can bring back memories of childhood. They have a strange power to fulfill the need for companionship even though they are inanimate objects. We can talk to them without feeling foolish, confident that what we whisper to them won't be repeated.

DOLLS OF MANY PURPOSES

Dolls have been used for many purposes. Today people think of them mainly as playthings for children. Traditionally they have been girls' toys, but with the advances in women's equality they have become accepted as toys for boys too. Though many dolls are made as playthings, others are created solely as display items—to be looked at and touched only cautiously. Since the 1920s dolls have been popular as collectors' items, especially antique dolls and contemporary dolls handmade by doll artists.

We think of dolls mainly as toys, display or collectors' items, but in the past they have had far more serious purposes. Dolls were made before man began recording his history, so nobody really knows when they were first created. They have been found in the tombs of ancient Egypt, and no one knows how long ago they were first made in the Orient.

Dolls had religious significance in ancient times. In the Stone Age small images were carved as charms and fetishes or as ritual images or idols and used in religious worship. Archeologists can only guess at the meaning of some of the ancient figures, but many are thought to have been cult objects. Most of the dolls created by primitive man were miniatures, but later larger human representations were made.

Among primitive people, children did not have dolls because dolls were religious or magical objects to be used by the medicine man or sorcerer. They were sacred idols and not to be touched by children.

Later, dolls were created as ancestor figures and might be set up in a shrine that was the sacred center of the family life. They were treated with great respect and on feast days special offerings of food and drink might be set before them. This custom was observed by some European peasants and is still practiced in the more remote parts of Africa. Today religious figures are still made in many countries, not to be worshipped but to inspire religious feelings or thoughts.

Dolls have been involved in a variety of strange customs and dark rites. They have been found beneath old buildings. Originally a living child might have been interred to propitiate the earth gods, but later the doll was used as a substitute for the human sacrifice.

Dolls have been an integral part of primitive man's

Dolls have their own personalities. This doll, named Cora, is a study in black and white. Made by Ellen Campbell, she has a trapunto face, a life-size cloth body, and an authentic Victorian costume. (*Photo courtesy of the dollmaker, photo by David L. Kramer*)

Dolls have been used to inspire religious worship. These figures of the Holy Family by Robert Morrison of Billings, Montana, are made of cloth, paper and clay. (*Photograph courtesy of the dollmaker*)

burned so that the spirit of the harvest residing in the old doll could enter the newly made one.

Dolls were also used as "changeling dolls." In England and Germany, for example, these dolls were put into babies' cradles to deceive witches and fairies so they would not foist changelings on parents.

Dolls were even used as shop signs; for example, Indian dolls indicated the sale of Virginia tobacco. Dolls were also a part of evil rites celebrated to wreak vengeance on an enemy and this use did not cease in ancient times. Spite dolls appear in the folklore of many countries and are an integral part of voodoo, a

effort to control a world beyond his control. They have served to protect people from disease and to help them recover from illnesses. Dolls have been used as charms against misfortune. In Japan children who played with special clay dolls were supposed to grow up healthy and wealthy. A doll might also be given to a sick child as a scapegoat, supposedly causing the disease to pass from the child into the doll.

In parts of China and Japan paper dolls were made to represent each member of the family. They were then inflicted with every possible disease and tossed into the fire in order to ensure that the illnesses so inflicted on the dolls would never come to the living family members.

Dolls have been and are still made today in primitive societies to ensure fertility and to encourage the birth of a healthy child. They have been put into tombs to represent the slaves and servants that should accompany an Egyptian nobleman to the underworld.

Dolls have been made to celebrate the harvest, to ensure next year's crop, and to beg for rain. In England, especially in the West Country, the last gleanings of the field were used to make harvest dolls. These were hung in homes in the hope of a good harvest next year. Before the new doll was put into place, last year's doll was taken down and

Dolls have functioned in superstitious rites. This contemporary voodoo doll handmade in Haiti of modern materials such as paper ribbon has a primitive look with its feather headdress and strange shape. (*Author's Collection*)

religious cult of African origin that is characterized by a belief in sorcery, rituals, and fetishes in which participants attempt to communicate through trances with ancestors, saints, or animistic deities. In Devonshire, England, crude dolls almost black in color were fetishes made to represent the despised person. Pins and nails were inserted into the doll's body to inflict pain in the corresponding parts of the victim's body.

In some areas of the world dolls were used as talismans. For instance, when a girl wished for a lover she would make a doll of wax and throw it into the fire so that the youth might similarly melt with love for her.

Dolls have functioned not only in love affairs but in death rituals as part of the rites of a tribe of Indians of British Columbia. If a dead person is buried near water, a spirit canoe is made and set afloat carrying a doll that represents his spirit.

Among the Ojibwa Indians of Lake Superior a doll representing a dead child might be made of feathers. Their belief was that a dead child was too young to look after itself in the next world, so to assist it the mother would wrap the doll in a bundle of the child's clothes and toys so that her child might feel cared for.

Dolls were also useful objects in spreading the latest ideas in fashion. The French clothing designers dressed dolls in the latest fashions long before the age of the mass media, and used the dolls to show women what they should be wearing.

In England, Japan, and other countries pin-

Some dolls are both decorative and functional, such as these egg-warmer dolls of European origin. They have crocheted woolen skirts, and over them white aprons of crocheted cotton. They have yarn arms and faces with yarn features and hair. Each one has beads at the neckline. (*Hupp Collection*)

cushions have been made in the form of dolls. The "worktable companion" was a popular Victorian-type doll, which usually had a pincushion hat and carried a tape measure, thread, scissors, a thimble, and a package of needles, as well as other sewing items, and kept them conveniently at hand for her owner. Such dolls could be bought made up, and for those who wanted to make their own, magazines of the day in England and the United States told the Victorian ladies how to turn an ordinary doll into a useful companion.

In Japan dolls have been put to another use. In the poor families a child carried a doll on his or her back. The size of the doll would be increased until the child was strong enough to carry his baby brother or sister. Dolls were also put to illegal use in smuggling goods. They were made with hollow heads in which contraband goods were concealed to evade customs duties.

Dolls also play a part in psychotherapy. Doctors have observed in children playing with dolls the expressions of repressed emotions and impulses, for example, aggressive feelings toward parents or siblings.

Dolls have also been used in cultural exchanges as ambassadors of friendship. In 1927, 11,000 dolls were sent to Japan from the United States by the Committee of World Friendship for the Doll Festival on March 3. In return a contingent of Japanese dolls were sent to the United States.

Dolls have been used to educate the child at home. In Japan a girl learned the intricacies of traditional ceremonies through her dolls. The Victorian mother in England taught her daughter how to run a house using dolls. A rich girl might have had a complete household of dolls and become aware of social class distinctions through them. Her wax dolls would be dressed as gentlemen and ladies, the leather dolls might be middle-class people, and the wooden dolls might represent the common folk.

Dolls have been used to teach children about people of other lands by showing them how the people of a certain country look and dress. Dolls take only a small amount of room but they are very effective teaching tools. Museums, libraries, and sometimes schools have collections of dolls to teach children about people from other lands.

A teacher could base a lesson on showing dolls and talking about their costumes. She could, for example, show a woolen-clad doll made in Guatemala and explain why it has the clothing of the people who live in the highlands. She could explain why those who live in the hot coastal lowlands, in contrast, would be dressed in cotton. If a doll has a huge basket on her head or if she is wearing a large backpack, the teacher can show in a dramatic way that transportation in Guatemala is very primitive.

Collectors' dolls show in detail regional folk costumes and are very valuable in keeping alive folk traditions. Part of a collectors' series, these 9" dolls are dressed in the folk costumes of Krakowiak, Poland. This costume is still used today by the dancers of Krakow when they perform the regional dance that is one of the most well known in Poland. Ordinary citizens wear this costume only on important holidays.

The figures have wire frames covered with fabric, and their faces are made of a claylike substance and hand painted. Both have red hair, a physical trait that is not common among the Polish people, but as dancers they may be wearing wigs. The girl has long braids that extend below her waist and she wears a white blouse with full sleeves edged in white lace. Her black velvet vest has tube beads sewn on it, and she wears seed beads at her neck. Long colorful streamers printed with a rose design dangle behind her from her flower headdress, and printed on her red skirt is a rose design characteristic of the Krakowiak region.

Her partner wears the typical male costume of the region. His traditional long dark blue vest is decorated with sequins, beads, and embroidery stitches. He wears a white shirt with full sleeves and red-striped pants with red tassels. In his four-cornered hat is the traditional feather and flowered ribbon.(*Hercek Collection*)

Many museums use displays of dolls to show period costumes and to complete period settings. Dolls provide authentic records of a culture and so are valid as items for the museum to collect. Old dolls vividly show what clothes were worn, what fabrics were used, and how the clothing was constructed.

Dolls have been used to commemorate events and to benefit charities. Special editions of dolls might be made to sell for a specific fund-raising purpose. This was done in England, for example, during World War II to raise money for war widows. Dolls have also been sold to raise money to help the fledgling State of Israel and for many other causes.

Dollmaking, which is a cottage industry in places like Hong Kong, has given refugees and other people the means of supporting themselves.

Dollmaking is part of the peasant tradition of folk art in many countries. Dolls have traditionally provided work for farm people in otherwise slack periods. Dolls made from locally available materials might be made by the peasants to earn some extra money during the winter months. The Russian moss men and the prune people of Germany are just a few of the dolls made by idle farmers.

Dolls have also functioned as remembrances of places visited. The souvenir doll is a product of the eighteenth and nineteenth centuries and became especially popular because of the World Expositions of the nineteenth century. Once the possibility of travel for pleasure opened up to the middle class, the market for inexpensive souvenir dolls boomed. Many of the dolls in this book could be considered souvenir dolls.

In the late eighteenth century in Europe there was a growing interest in costume, especially native peasant costumes. Dolls dressed to show these costumes became popular as the costumes themselves fell into disuse. As tourists increased in number they created a greater demand for these costume dolls. Many cities, towns, and regions had their own special dolls, and collectors could amass large numbers of such dolls. Today collecting dolls is mainly an adult hobby, though children are often given, as presents, dolls meant to be added to their collections.

DOLLS AND THEIR MAKERS

In creating dolls, the makers are creating images of themselves or of the people around them as they see them. The doll then can be an object charged with social, ethnic, and even didactic implications. People all over the world have created dolls in their own image, and a study of these dolls can tell quite a bit about how their makers view themselves.

A great variety of materials, usually those indigenous to the area, are used in making dolls. Sometimes these materials are taken directly from nature and sometimes they are altered by spinning, carving, or whatever, using the traditional craft skills of the area. Dolls thus show what their makers have taken from their environments and learned to use, and they can often be dated by these very materials.

Dolls also tell much about the everyday clothing or traditional costume of their makers. The dollmaker, especially one whose contact with the world at large is limited, would naturally create a doll using the clothing within his own experience. Dollmakers of different countries naturally present their heritage to the world.

Dollmaking is a good craft, a "small industry," for people in poor countries because it is so labor intensive, that is, the labor that goes into making the handmade doll is usually what makes it valuable. Dollmaking does not require a large capital investment; in fact, for many types of dolls the investment in materials is low or nonexistent if natural materials are used.

Impoverished craftsmen can use materials at hand and produce dolls investing what they have in the project—their time. If a good market is available to them, dollmaking can be a way to earn extra money. The basic problem is to get the dolls from these dollmakers to the many doll collectors all over the world who are interested in adding handmade dolls to their collections. Often volunteer organizations help in the marketing effort.

One such organization is SERRV, which is part of Church World Service. This nonprofit organization works with religious and nonsectarian volunteer groups all over the world, mainly in the underdeveloped countries. It provides a nonprofit marketing service giving the participants in the various programs a chance to help themselves. The Mennonite Central Committee runs a similar program.

ORGANIZING THIS BOOK

Categorizing dolls from all over the world and presenting them in a logical manner is difficult to do. It might be done geographically, chronologically, according to the material used, according to the purpose of the doll, and so on. I chose to arrange the dolls geographically and for the most part this arrangement has worked well.

Arranging them geographically has allowed me to show the worldwide range of the dollmaker's craft and also the nearly universal appeal of the doll itself. But in a way this arrangement is a compromise as just about any arrangement would be.

Dolls are taken from one place to another so in some cases it was difficult to figure out under which country to include a specific doll. The penny wooden, or Dutch, doll is a primary example. This type of doll was made in great numbers in Germany during the nineteenth century. It was exported through the ports of Holland and hence the name "Dutch doll." The dolls went to England, the United States, and many other countries, and in their new homes many received elegant new wardrobes. These dolls—which are discussed in the section on Germany—were often dressed in their final country of residence.

2
Materials and Basic Techniques

This is an incomplete book. No book on handmade dolls from all over the world could possibly be complete unless it was an encyclopedia of many volumes. It would certainly take a large set of books to show all the different types of dolls made. Rather, this book represents a sampling meant to show the diversity of methods and materials used. Sometimes the same methods or materials are used in countries geographically far apart. Sometimes this can be accounted for by migration and sometimes not. The origins of dolls can pose some very interesting questions.

This is meant to be a looking as well as a doing book. It aims to show you dolls from all over the world to give you ideas for the types of dolls you can make. It presents many different methods of making dolls as well as details about costuming. You might make dolls like the ones you see here, or you might instead use these to inspire your own creations, adapting the methods shown here to your own ideas and taking the suggestions for using materials given here and adapting these to your own methods.

In choosing dolls for this book I tried to select only handmade ones. In the instructions I explain how to make dolls without using elaborate equipment and using easily available materials. For dolls requiring elaborate equipment or hard-to-get materials I have suggested alternatives. I have tried to give full instructions mainly for dolls that the beginning dollmaker could make, with step-by-step photographs showing how it is done, and with any required patterns. These dolls can be made by beginners, but they should also be of interest to experienced dollmakers because they show a variety of techniques, some of which may be new even to a very experienced doll artist. I have also included photos of completed dolls that are the work of experts. These should inspire both the beginner and the experienced dollmaker.

I hope this book will inspire its readers to experiment with dollmaking. Today a large market for handmade dolls exists because there are so many people interested in them. Miniature dolls especially are in demand because so many people are interested in miniatures and want dolls to people their dollhouses. Also there is a resurgence of interest in dollmaking itself, especially in applying the traditional and new crafts to the art of making dolls.

This chapter will discuss some of the commonly used materials for making dolls and how to work with them. Since many of the dolls in this book have wire frames, the general directions for making such dolls will be given here. Looking through the geographically arranged dolls you can see how dollmakers in many lands used this method of dollmaking.

Both stuffed dolls and wire-frame dolls often have fabric heads with features that are either painted on or embroidered. Since quite a number of the dolls in this book have embroidered features, a section on how to embroider them is given here.

Next to fabric, wood is probably the most popular material worldwide for dollmaking. Basic instructions will be given in this chapter on carving and on turning wood, which can be applied to dolls throughout the book.

Another popular material for dollmaking is clay. Natural deposits are found in many areas and dollmakers often take advantage of these. Some dollmakers use substances similar to clay in forming their dolls and dolls' heads; these are discussed. Another material that is used for dollmaking on a universal basis is paper; a section on working with this material is included.

MATERIALS

Dolls can be made from so many different materials it is almost impossible to list them all. Natural materials such as grass, fruit, nuts, flax, wax, pinecones, raffia, cane, and bone have been used for dollmaking, but probably the most popular of the natural materials is wood.

Dolls can be made from almost any kind of material. Fabric, papier-mâché, china, and bisque are among the materials that have been used. Primitive man used crude natural materials. Today natural materials are still being used, but synthetic fabrics, polyester-fiber filling, and many other manufactured materials, even recycled ones, are popular for dollmaking.

Leather, too, has been used for making dolls and one of its advantages is that it is unbreakable. The whole doll could be leather, or the head might be made from another material and the body made from

People make dolls from all sorts of strange materials. This 5" grotesque skier doll, made in the United States, was created from plastic knives, forks, and spoons that were heated and twisted into shape. (*Weiner Collection*)

Recycled materials can be made into dolls. In a handcraft instruction class at school in West Berlin, this boy used cans and metal bottle caps to make fascinating, futuristic dolls. (*Photo courtesy of the German Information Center*)

leather. Some of the North American Indian tribes used leather to make dolls, as have dollmakers in Morocco.

The dollmaker might work with prepared leather or instead prepare it himself from killing the animal onward. In making leather dolls the rawhide is cured in the usual way and steamed to make it flexible. Then it can be modeled and perhaps reinforced with plaster.

Metal is another material used for dollmaking. Tiny figures in gold and silver were made centuries ago for wealthy Europeans. The most universal type of doll made from metal is the toy soldier that first appeared in Europe in the Middle Ages. These figures were eventually made to a standard height and used by officers to carry out military maneuvers in miniature.

For centuries edible dolls from flour, sugar, and other foodstuffs were also made. During the Middle Ages bread dolls were made to represent saints and were eaten on their feast days. It is thought that the people believed that by eating these dolls they might

Rope of various kinds is used in making dolls. In this photo a man in Ibarra, Ecuador, is spinning sisal, a plant fiber, into rope. (*Photo courtesy of World Neighbors*)

gain some of the saint's good qualities. The dolls were made in molds, which had to be carefully greased before the dough was pressed in. The molds were handmade so no two were ever exactly alike. The saint's day was celebrated by giving the saint dolls to friends. The likenesses of famous people were also made into edible dolls; the Duke of Wellington dolls, for instance, were made of gingerbread.

The custom of making edible dolls at Christmastime was transplanted from Europe to the United States and in some areas still lives on. The Moravian settlers brought their tin cookie cutters and use them every Christmas. Today inedible bread dough dolls coated with lacquer are made in Ecuador.

WORKING WITH FABRICS

Many dolls are made from fabrics because they are so easy to work with. Dolls have been made from

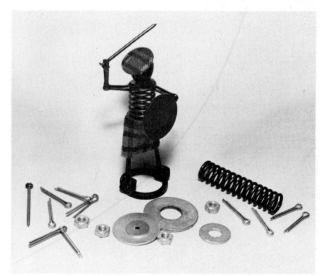

Washers, cotter pins, springs, nails, and nuts are the metal pieces used to construct this delightful warrior from Scotland. His hat is a washer covered with a bit of plaid fabric, and he wears a matching plaid kilt. (*Author's Collection*)

Flax is a plant whose fibers can be made into linen. The plant is shown here in the center. To the left is dew-retted, hand-dressed flax, and to the right is water-retted hand-dressed linen. (*Photographed at Frederick J. Fawcett, Inc., Boston, Mass.*)

fabrics for centuries, probably from the time they were first available. Today many dolls are still made of fabrics, ranging from the primitive hand-loomed ones to modern synthetics. Cotton, wool, and linen have been used for weaving fabrics, and these materials also are used before they reach the woven stage. Cotton has been used for stuffing, and unspun wool for doll's hair. Flax has also been used before it was woven into linen.

You can use almost any kind of fabric for doll-making, but choose yours carefully, keeping certain requirements in mind. First the fabric should not be too thick. In making doll bodies and clothing you are working generally in small sizes. If the fabric is too thick you will have material bunched at seams and clothing that looks too heavy for the doll.

If you are using printed fabric, choose the print according to the size of the doll. Small prints are usually best. Also choose the colors of your fabrics so that they blend well together. Keep in mind also that you want fabrics that do not ravel and are easy to finish.

For dollmaking you generally need only small amounts of fabric. Save scraps from other sewing projects. Buy remnants at fabric stores. Usually shops will cut as little as ¼ yard for you. Stockpile fabric so that when you are working on a project, you will have a choice of color and can easily gather what you need.

Here are some of the fabrics you might consider using for dollmaking together with some of the advantages and disadvantages they offer:

Cotton and cotton blends: These tightly woven fabrics are probably the most useful and versatile fabrics you can find. Available in a variety of weights, textures, colors, and prints, they are colorfast and washable. The cotton blends usually wash better and wrinkle less than 100% cotton and so are excellent for making dolls that will be played with.

Knit fabric: Rather than being woven, this type of fabric is made from interlocking loops, so therefore it is stretchy and flexible enough to take on the contours you desire. Knits are available in a wide range of textures, prints, and plain colors and are good for dollmaking. Nylon-stocking material cut from dis-

Flax before it is woven into linen is the material used to create this doll. Flax dolls, such as this one, are made in northern and eastern European countries. This 7″ doll has arms of flax tied at the ends with red embroidery cotton. The skirt is a bell shape of flax, decorated with red rickrack. The head is a wooden ball with features painted on it and a wooden dowel sticking down from it into the body. Her hair is long braids of flax. On her head is a crown of braided embroidery cotton with long strands going down her back. (*From the Collection of Nancy Ann Malik*)

carded pantyhose or stockings, and lightweight knit fabric from underwear are often used in making stuffed and wire-frame dolls.

Corduroy: This fabric does ravel a bit, and you must be careful to cut all parts in the same direction because the fabric has nap.

Felt: A pressed fabric, felt will not ravel, so it does not need to be finished around the edge. It is useful for doll clothing and accessories that have edges, such as vests, shoes, and hats, but it can be too thick for making certain kinds of clothing. It cannot be washed and in working with it you must also be careful because if it is stuffed too tight or pulled at a seam it will give. In cutting pieces from this fabric you can lay them in any direction.

Specialty fabrics: Linen, terry cloth, velvet, taffeta, satin, silk, and brocade are some of the other fabrics you may use for special effects in making dolls and their clothing.

Finishing details are very important when you are making fabric dolls. Many of the dolls in this book are beautifully finished by dollmakers who take great pride in their work. Others, especially dolls that were made in quantity for quick cheap sale, are poorly finished.

Since doll clothing is usually small, finishing is often done by hand stitching. Though you may prefer to use a sewing machine for long straight seams, hand sewing is more convenient for short seams and for hemming. Felt need not be hemmed, but most other fabrics should be. Any edges left raw tend to ravel somewhat and look poor. You can take some shortcuts in working with fabric, but be sure that these shortcuts do not adversely affect your final product.

EMBROIDERING FEATURES

Features of stuffed dolls are embroidered or painted on, or they are made with bits of fabric, felt, or other material glued in place. To make effective embroidered features you need to know only a few embroidery stitches. Some of those you may want to use are described and illustrated here.

The face should be symmetrical and the features carefully placed, so plan the features carefully. Draw them directly on the fabric, or plan them on scrap paper and transfer them to the fabric with dressmaker's carbon. Probably the most useful stitches for embroidering features are the outline, satin, and French knot. These are quite easy to learn.

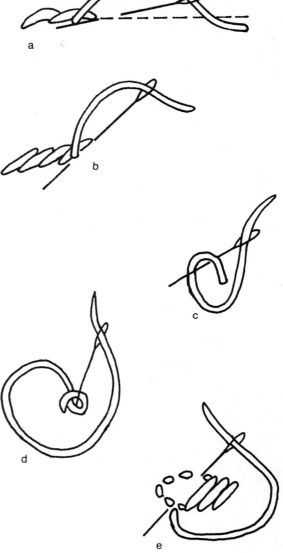

a. To do the outline stitch, bring the needle to the surface of the fabric. Put it in a little further along the guideline, bring it back to the surface between these two points and pull through. Repeat along the line.

b. To make a thicker outline stitch, for eyebrows perhaps, slant your stitches. Put your needle in at an angle to the guideline each time.

c. To make a French knot, bring the needle to the surface near the spot where you want the knot to be. While you hold the thread with your left hand, with your right hand put the needle against the thread just above the place where it came out of the fabric. Bring the thread around the needle with your left hand.

d. Keep the twist of thread on the needle and put the needle into the fabric, close to where it came out. Draw the thread so it is fairly snug around the needle while you push the needle through the fabric.

e. To do the satin stitch, you can begin by making a row of small stitches around the shape you wish to fill in (optional). Bring the needle out through the fabric at the lower edge of the form you are filling. Insert the needle at upper edge and then out again beside the point where the thread is coming out of the fabric. Pull it through and continue to work in this manner until the shape is filled.

The features of this stuffed fabric doll from Pakistan are hand embroidered. She wears black cotton pantaloons and the rest of her costume is fine chiffon. (*Photo courtesy of Dolls International, Kingston, Ontario, Canada*)

THE STUFFED DOLL

A doll made completely of fabric might be called a fabric doll, a stuffed doll, or a rag doll. The word rag usually refers to a piece of old, worn, or throwaway material, but a rag doll can be made of the finest new silk, satin, brocade, or velvet, as well.

Stuffed dolls run the gamut from the simplest homemade rag dolls of scrap materials to those of finely modeled felt and stockinette, the productions of accomplished dollmakers. Fabric is one of the least complicated materials from which to create a doll, so it has been used by people all over the world; in fact, almost every country has fabric dolls in some form or other.

Rag dolls are probably as old as man's ability to make cloth. Early examples are those found in children's tombs in ancient Egypt, Rome, and Peru. Among the earliest stuffed dolls now in museums are those dating from the sixth and seventh century A.D., which were discovered in the Coptic graves in Upper Egypt. Some are made of colored wool and others have painted wooden heads and colored woven clothing.

For centuries rag dolls were made without patterns. In the nineteenth century occasionally patterns for rag dolls were given in magazines like *The Delineator* along with instructions on how to sew them. In the twentieth century some famous rag dolls were created and even patented. Among the famous ones were Rose O'Neill's Kewpies (1909), the Katherine Kruse dolls (1912), Raggedy Ann and Andy (1919), and the beautiful Lenci felt and pressed-cloth dolls (1921).

In addition to these patented dolls many other rag dolls were made and continue to be made at home. Though some of these dolls are original creations, patterns were and are available for dolls designed by doll artists. Patterns can be obtained in magazines, books, through pattern companies, and through dollmakers who specialize in creating dolls and selling patterns for their creations.

Early rag dolls had flat faces and even today many are still made this way. However, many are also made with needle-sculpted faces or have faces made with multiple pieces of fabric to make them three-dimensional. You will see examples of all these types when you leaf through this book.

One special type of stuffed doll familiar to almost everyone is the printed rag doll. These dolls became available in the latter part of the nineteenth century. They were printed on fabric, ready to cut out, sew together, and fill with stuffing. Hundreds of designs were produced in both the United States and England, by such companies as the Arnold Print Works and Dean's Rag Co. Soon they became available in other countries also, and though some were sold all made up, most were sold as pieces of fabric with the doll sections printed on them.

These printed dolls were successful because they were inexpensive, easy to make up, and, when finished, took lots of hard use from the children who played with them. Printed rag dolls were discovered by manufacturers anxious to make their products "household names." They were adopted as an advertising promotion by makers of cereal and grain products as well as other commercial companies. Some of these famous character dolls were Aunt Jemima (pancake flour), the Cream of Wheat chef (cereal), Buster Brown (shoes), and Puffy of Quaker Oats (oatmeal).

These printed advertising dolls were given as premiums with flour, soap, coffee, and so on. Along with the stamped fabric came directions for cutting out the dolls, sewing, and stuffing them. Printed rag dolls ready to be cut, stitched, and stuffed at home are as popular today in many countries as they were in the 1890s when they were introduced. Some are still made for advertisers, but many others are available where fabric is sold, in a huge variety of designs from cartoon characters to nineteenth-century Victorian ladies.

Stuffed dolls are made as advertising promotions. Today's children get to hug the bright red and yellow Burger King if they frequent his chain of fast-food restaurants.

The method for completing these printed dolls is very similar to making original stuffed dolls. The main difference is that the features and the clothing are already on the printed doll whereas for the traditional stuffed doll these must be supplied.

For making a stuffed doll choose a soft, pliable, lightweight fabric like broadcloth—in flesh color, cream, tan, or brown rather than white. If you have only white available, tint it with dye or strong tea or coffee. Remember the fabric looks darker when wet but will dry lighter.

For stuffing use cotton batting, shredded foam

rubber, or similar material. The most popular type of stuffing used today is polyester-fiber filling, which is easy to handle and will avoid the lumpiness so common in many other types of filling.

Put a piece of tracing paper or other lightweight paper over this pattern and draw around it. Fold the paper in half and cut a full pattern. Or use scrap paper to work out your own simple doll outline. Cut out the pattern.

The printed fabric doll, one of the simplest for a dollmaker to complete, remains popular. It is a good project for a novice dollmaker, who by making one such doll can learn the basic technique of making stuffed dolls. Printed fabric dolls are sold in yard-goods stores ready for the customer to sew and stuff according to the directions printed right on the fabric. Cartoon characters, such as Elmer Fudd, appeal to children.

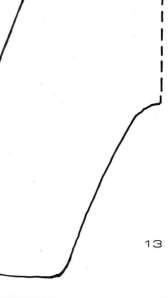

13

1 Pin the pattern to a double thickness of fabric in order to make the front and back of the doll exactly alike. With a pencil or tailor's chalk draw around the pattern.

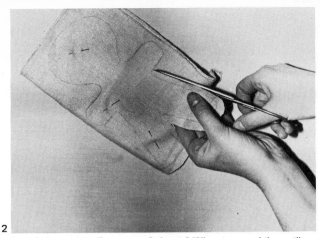

2 Leaving a seam allowance of about 3/8", cut around the outline. You can if you wish put on the features at this point, drawing them freehand or transferring them from your paper using dressmaker's carbon paper. Paint them on with liquid-embroidery tube paints or embroider them as described earlier in this chapter.

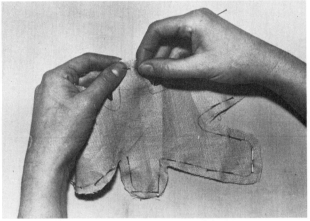

3 Pin the layers of fabric right sides together. Sew all around leaving an opening along one side.

4 Clip all of the curves, cutting not quite to the stitching line.

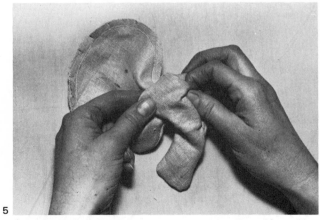

5 Turn the body right side out. Push out the hands and feet with a chopstick, knitting needle, or other similar tool. Press all the seams.

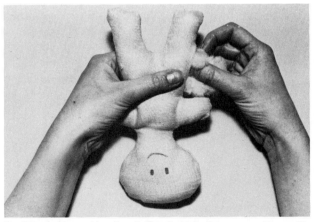

6 Stuff the body pushing the stuffing first into the arms and legs with a chopstick or similar tool. Stuff firmly and evenly.

7

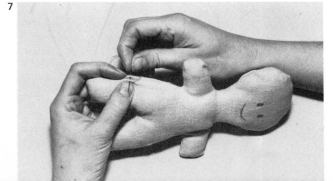

With hand stitches, close the seam you left open for turning.

8

If you wish to make yarn hair, cut a piece of cardboard 4″ x 10″. Make a slit at the center, not quite to the edges, and cut out a narrow rectangle. Wrap the yarn around the cardboard at least a dozen times making sure that the yarn stays over the rectangular cutout. Sew across the yarn at the opening. Cut the yarn off the cardboard at each end. Stitch the yarn to the doll's head at the center and at each side. Trim as desired.

9

Your completed doll, once you have made her a very simple dress, should look something like the authentic Czechoslovakian doll at the left. Made from unbleached linen, with black yarn hair, she wears a dress with a pink and maroon woven design. Her partner also was made in Czechoslovakia. He has a bleached linen top and unbleached linen bottom. His hair is made of flax, and he has a piece of cord sewn at his neck and looped at the front. Her body is a very simple outline; his is even simpler—the arms have been eliminated. (*Photographed at the United Nations Gift Center*)

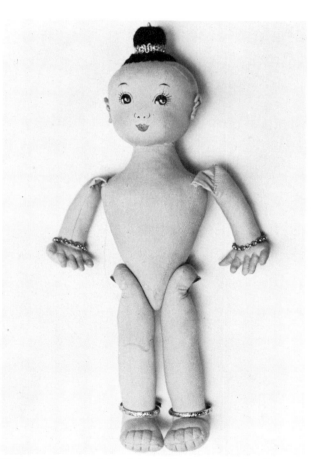

Fabric dolls often have painted features. Painting on attractive ones takes practice and some artistic skill. With a very fine, good-quality brush, and acrylic paint aim for an appealing face, such as this stuffed doll's from Thailand.

Stuffed dolls can be flat and simple like the Czechoslovakian one at top right. Or they can be very complicated, of many different pattern pieces of fabric, with darts or folds sewn in to give them contour. The basic method, however, remains pretty much the same—sew, trim, turn, and stuff. The head can be made three dimensional rather than flat by using multiple pieces. Even the fingers can be delineated with pieces of fabric that are sewn together and stuffed, as on this doll from Thailand. Arms and legs can be made separately and with multiple pieces so they, too, are three dimensional. Note how the head and body of this doll are shaped using different pieces of fabric with darts in them. (*Urdang Collection*)

NEEDLE-SCULPTED FACES

Many fabric dolls have flat faces, their features indicated only by paint or embroidery, but some of the most effective dolls have features that are sculpted by using a needle and thread. As you flip through this book you will see that this technique of making molded fabric faces is used in many countries with a variety of results.

To make a needle-sculpted face you will need stuffing and a piece of knit fabric or nylon stocking. Though it may be possible to use a woven fabric in making the faces, you will find it is much easier to work with a knit fabric because it will mold without much effort and form the features you want.

The basic technique of using thread to pull the stuffed fabric into shape is given here. The technique can be used to create more complex faces by making larger ones and using more stitches.

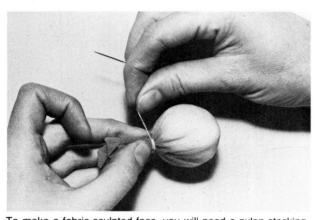

To make a fabric-sculpted face, you will need a nylon stocking, polyester-fiber filling, thread, and embroidery floss or crewel yarn. Take a small amount of polyester filling and roll it into a ball less than 2" in diameter. Cut the stocking into a 4" to 5" square (if you want the skin to look darker, use two or more layers of stocking), then fill it in the center with the polyester-fiber and pull the stocking around it. Tie or sew it securely with a piece of thread.

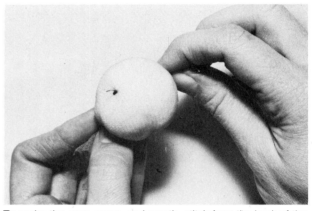

To make the eyes, nose, and mouth, stitch from the back of the head through to the front with satin stitches. Make the eyes just above the center of the face. If you pull the thread, the eyes will be indented just a little.

Make the nose and mouth below the eyes, then poke and pinch with your fingers to shape the face as desired. You can add color to the face using lipstick, rouge, chalk, pastels, and so on.

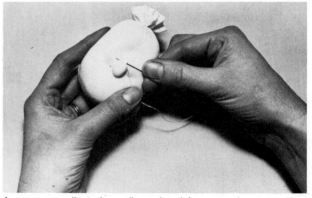

A more complicated needle-sculpted face may have separate parts sewn on. Shown here is a nose being added on. If you wish, a layer of flesh-colored nylon can be added over the white knit base after the part or parts are sewn on.

The same method of using a needle and thread to contour the doll's face can be applied in making even more complicated faces, such as that of this Elisa Lotter doll. (*Photo courtesy of the doll-maker*)

MAKING PRESSED FABRIC FACES

Some of the fabric dolls in this book have what I call "pressed fabric faces"; that is, their faces were made by pressing fabric against a mold. These types of faces are not really difficult to make—they can be created mainly with things you have around the house. The challenge is to find the proper mold. Such objects as a bisque or vinyl doll's head or a plaster figurine can be used for a face mold. Look around for a molded face that is the size and type you need. If you cannot find what you need, you might consider making your own mold.

To make the mask you start with a knit fabric (an old T-shirt will serve the purpose). First you stiffen the fabric using plaster of Paris or flour paste. Of the two, plaster is the more difficult to work with because it begins to harden within a short time and you must work quickly with it. You will find flour paste easier to use, especially if you are a beginner.

An alternative and probably the easiest stiffener to use is starch. Sold in a liquid form, it can be used right from the bottle with or without some water added. I have experimented using the starch full strength and it seems to work fine.

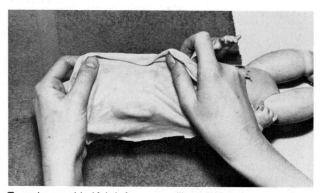

To make a molded fabric face, you will need a face to copy, a piece of knit fabric, and a stiffening solution. Cut the knit fabric large enough so that it extends beyond the face to be copied. Prepare the mold by coating it with some dishwashing detergent or similar liquid soap. This will help the molded fabric slip off the face more easily. Dip the fabric in a stiffening solution, leaving it there until it is thoroughly saturated. Hold the fabric above the solution and let the excess drip off. Lay the fabric on the face mold centering it carefully.

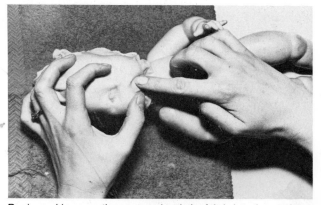

Begin working over the nose and tuck the fabric into the crevices, pushing it outward toward the edges of the face. A small pointed tool, such as a toothpick, may help you get the fabric into the small crannies. Work over the fabric with your fingers, making sure you have pressed out all the air pockets.

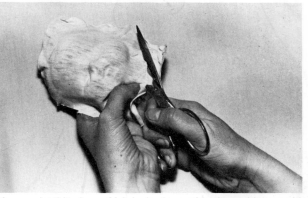

You can let this piece of fabric dry thoroughly, then add a second layer. You might prefer to add a second layer ever before the first one is dry. When the fabric is thoroughly dry, remove the mask carefully from the mold. Cut off any excess fabric. The mask can be reinforced by putting papier-mâché or plaster under it. It can then be colored as desired with pastels, eye makeup, face powder, felt-tip pens, or whatever coloring medium is desired.

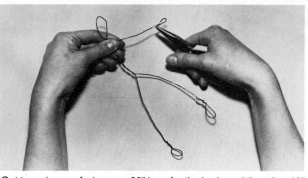

THE WIRE-FRAME DOLL

Many of the dolls in this book have wire-frame bodies. This means that there usually is a wire going through their arms and legs as well as through the body itself. Usually the wire is covered by padding with fabric over it. Sometimes a wire frame is wound with yarn or other materials, even banana leaf as in the case of the doll from Kenya.

A wire frame is helpful because it allows you to pose the doll. The arms and legs as well as the torso are flexible so you can make the doll take lifelike poses. The wire frame allows the doll to stand up or sit down as you prefer.

In choosing wire for the frame, look for wire that will make the doll stiff enough to pose but not so stiff that the wire is hard to bend into shape. You can use just about any type of wire you have available or you might purchase it from a hardware or electronic supply store. Some dollmakers use 18-gauge copper wire, while others prefer 10 or 12 gauge or any number in between. Choose your wire depending on the size of the doll you wish to make. The larger the doll, the thicker the wire you should choose. You could even use pipe cleaners if you prefer.

Dollmakers use different ways to bend the wire and wrap it. Experiment with the general method shown here to find the method you like best. Begin by wrapping the arm and leg wire segments with filling, or yarn, or whatever, and then attach them to the body. Or join the wires together first, then start wrapping them.

As far as the head is concerned, decide what it will be, and if possible make it before you make the body. If you make a needle-sculpted head as described above you could have a stick coming out of it to which the wire body is attached. For an applehead doll you can insert a wrapped wire into the dried apple. If you are using a different method to make the head, consider how you will attach it to the body.

Cut two pieces of wire, one 22″ long for the body and the other 10″ long for the arms. Take the 22″ piece of wire and bend it in half. Leave a round circle at the top for the head, and below this twist the wire for the body. Below the body form the legs with circular feet. For the arms, twist small circles at the end of the 10″ wire, then twist this wire around the top of the body wire under the head. You can twist the wire with your fingers or use a pair of needlenose pliers to help you.

Cover the wire frame with polyester-fiber filling and wrap it with thread to hold it in place. Keep adding more filling encircling it with thread until you are pleased with the result.

Before you begin wrapping the arms, you will have to decide how to finish the hands. You might make felt hands or dried apple hands for an applehead doll. Or you might cover the loop of wire with pieces of nylon stocking. Padding can be put under the fabric, if desired.

You can make the doll's skin by wrapping the fiber filling with strips of nylon stocking. Cut off the top and feet of the stocking and then start cutting a strip at the top. Continue to cut around and around to make a continuous piece with which to wrap.

The wire frame of the doll need not be wrapped with nylon stocking. Sometimes other fabrics are used. For example, these Slavic dolls have arms and legs wrapped with silk. Probably made in the early 1900s, these 5″ dolls with delicately painted features have crocheted shoes with the ties wound up their legs. He wears a turban-like black velvet hat, green silk shirt, and dark green velvet pants. She wears a burgundy red velvet blouse, beige skirt, and head scarf. (*Wood Collection*)

The first wrapping on the doll can be done rather quickly, but the last wrapping should be done carefully so that the top layer is as smooth as possible. Wrap until the whole doll is covered. You can wrap the head part or not, according to how you plan to finish it.

Instead of wrapping the doll with nylon stocking, you can cut a piece of stocking or flesh-colored woven fabric and stitch body sections out of it. The wire frame can then be inserted into these custom-made sections. If desired, the sections at the hands and feet can be sewn with small stitches to delineate the fingers and toes.

Once you have made your wire-frame doll you can dress it any way you like. This drummer doll clothed in cotton is from Sri Lanka (the former Ceylon) and has a body of contoured fabric sections that are firmly stuffed. Notice that the fingers and toes are separated with tiny stitches. (*Photo courtesy of Dolls International, Kingston, Ontario, Canada*)

A dollmaker might choose to make a wire-frame doll by covering it with yarn. This small yarn doll was probably made in Portugal. (*Hulsizer Collection*)

You can even use pipe cleaners to make the wire frame of your doll. This 8″ doll has a pipe cleaner base with pieces of natural sponge attached to it. Her face is white yarn wound around the wire, and her features are indicated with red yarn. Her feet are decorated with wool, and her legs are cross-gartered with red thread. (*MacNeer Collection*)

WORKING WITH WOOD

Wood has been used by dollmakers all over the world for centuries, not only for very inexpensive turned and carved European folk dolls but also for expensive dolls like the Queen Anne type and the American Schoenhut. Though nature and man have destroyed any evidence of prehistoric wooden dolls, such dolls are probably as old as carving itself. The museums of Europe and America have many old ancestor dolls, votive figures, and talismans of wood. Well before the eighteenth century wooden dolls were made in quantity both in England and in France and distributed by enterprising peddlers in the Middle European countries.

Probably the most famous wooden dolls are the penny woodens, which were made in Germany start-ing in the seventeenth century. Queen Victoria spurred the popularity of the wooden doll. She had 132 dolls which she dressed and played with as a child. Most of them were inexpensive wooden jointed dolls and they are preserved today in Kensington Palace.

In the United States kachina dolls were carved from cottonwood by the Pueblo Indians. Wooden dolls were made at home by the early New England colonists, but it was not until 1873 when Joel Ellis invented and patented his wooden doll that they were made commercially.

Wooden dolls are made today all over the world especially in Germany, Scandinavia, and the United States as well as in Italy, India, the South Pacific,

Holland, Japan, Mexico, and so on. Wooden dolls are probably the most common type made in Africa. Tribal craftsmen use local indigenous woods to carve dolls for many different purposes.

Wooden dolls are sometimes made from found wood but are often made by carving or wood turning. Sometimes the dolls are left untouched after they are carved or turned, but often they are painted or adorned with beads or feathers or whole outfits of fabric clothing.

When you are carving a head for your doll, you can hold it steady by putting it into a vise.

Dolls are sometimes made from pieces of "found wood" (wood exactly as the doll artist found it) as in this wooden fence doll with stuffed arms and legs made by Lois Morrison. (*Photo courtesy of the dollmaker*)

CARVING WOOD

Wooden dolls have a very long history because one of the earliest arts was that of carving. Whittling and carving are often used as interchangeable words to mean shaping wood with tools. Whittling is a term commonly used in the United States to mean shaping using a knife only, and carving usually means using carving tools such as gouges. The piece of wood is always held in the hand when whittling, whereas the wood may be put into a vise when carving.

Many different kinds of wood have been used to carve dolls. What is needed is a wood that is fairly soft and has a straight grain so that it will cut easily. Expert carvers all have their favorite type of wood that they like to work with. Start out with pine, which is a good choice. Other woods to experiment with are balsa, basswood, cedar, birch, juniper, cherry, maple, hickory, mahogany, and poplar.

Each wood has its own advantages and disadvantages. Some are easier to carve, while others take a finish better. Balsa wood, for example, is easy to carve and readily available in hobby shops in an assortment of sizes, but it does not take a finish well and the final product is easy to damage.

You may be able to buy suitable pieces of wood at your local lumber company or you may have to order from a mail-order company specializing in wood. Remember when you are buying pieces of wood that the measurement given is the rough not the finished size. When you buy what is called a 1″ piece it usually measures about ¼″ less than that.

If you want to whittle parts for your doll, all you need is a good knife—a common pocketknife or jackknife is fine. A good blade is essential to a good knife. You can tell that you have a good steel blade if it stays sharp a long time when you are using it on soft woods. The edge of the blade should not bend or chip when you hit a knot in the wood. Also, the knife should have strong rivets to prevent the blade from becoming wobbly and a good spring to keep it from closing when in use. In addition to the knife itself, you need a way of sharpening it—with an oil- or a whetstone.

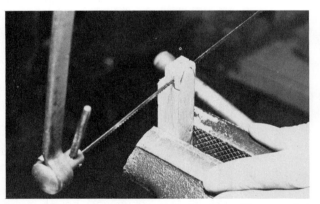

To begin carving wooden parts for your doll, cut a piece of wood to the approximate size you will need using a coping or jig saw. For an arm you might use a piece ½″ × ½″ × 3″. Copy the pattern given here or design your own on a piece of scrap paper and cut out the paper shape. For the lower arm you might have two drawings like these showing the front and side views.

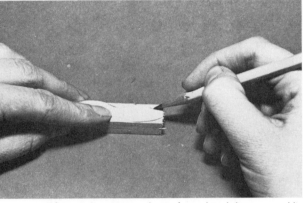

Lay the paper pattern on your piece of wood and draw around it, then outline the same pattern on the back or opposite side of the piece of wood. Copy the second pattern on the two remaining sides of the wood.

With a coping saw, cut away the largest portions of the unwanted wood.

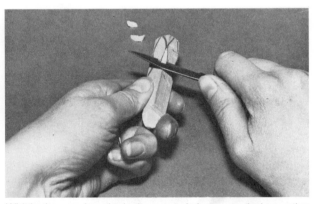

Whittle the wood to obtain the general shape you desire, cutting away corners and roughing out your design. Always work from high places to lower ones, and where slopes meet in the low places take care not to split the wood.

Whittle away the wood until you have the final shape you desire. Work in one direction and then the other, turning the wood in your hand.

Once you are pleased with the shape, sandpaper it to make it as smooth as you desire.

To begin your carving project draw onto the wood the basic lines of the design you want to carve. To save time cut away the largest portions of the unwanted wood by using a jigsaw, band saw, or coping saw, making the silhouette block. Next mark off further cutting that you want to do. With your knife cut away the corners and rough out your design. Finally whittle away the wood to the shape desired.

Whittle with the knife going the way of the grain. Go from high to low places. Where slopes meet in the low places be careful not to split the wood. Instead, make delicate gradual mergings, first favoring one direction and then the other. Take down the highest ridges working over the whole piece and gradually rounding out the shape with short, light strokes. When you have the general shape you can carve the details.

Sharpen the knife as soon as it seems to be less than very sharp. A dull knife can easily slip and ruin your work. When you are finally satisfied with the carving, sandpaper it to make it smooth. Finally, paint or lacquer your wood to protect it.

WOOD TURNING

One way for craftsmen to produce dolls quickly and in quantity is to use a mechanical lathe. In many countries dolls are made with turned wooden parts. Because they can be made so quickly these dolls are usually inexpensive and therefore easily within the budget of the average person.

Wood turning has been used in dollmaking for a long time. In the nineteenth century, with the introduction of the mechanical lathe, the work of dollmaker was greatly speeded up. It became possible to make 100-dozen dolls in 24 hours with a mechanical lathe.

Once the turner's art was introduced to toymaking, wooden dolls were mass produced, and dollmaking became specialized. The turner could produce large numbers of attractive dolls and toys with versatility and skill. The turner created the basic part for the dolls, and other workers took over the job of painting and completing them.

The making of dolls through wood turning is a German specialty, but it is also found in other countries with national and geographic variations in ornamentation and shape. In Sweden, for example, nine-pin-shaped dolls were made from birchwood. Today many wooden turned dolls are made there. Another turned wooden doll, the matroyshka of Russia, is almost a symbol of folk art in that country. Kokeshi dolls, which have become almost a symbol of Japan, are also made through the art of the wood turner.

Some home workshops are equipped with wood-turning lathes. Small ones for craftwork are available also. If you wish to make your own wood-turned parts for dolls, you will have to learn to operate a lathe, which is fairly easy to do. However, it will take time and experience to learn to operate it well and to learn to obtain the shapes of wooden pieces you need.

In addition to the lathe, you will need special gouges, which are available in sets with each one having a different tip. Some are flat and others curved but each one is used to shape the wood a little differently. You will also need a piece of hardwood such as cherry, maple, or walnut.

Begin by inserting the wood securely into the lathe according to the requirements of your machine. Select the gouge you want to work with. The lathe should have a rest against which you hold the gouge. Rest it there as you bring it in contact with the revolving wood. Experiment with the various gouges to see what each one will let you do to the wood. Learn to hold the gouge at the proper angle as you learn the art of wood turning by experimentation. Once you have the feeling of how these gouges work, you can work toward making the wooden shapes you need.

As an alternative to making the wooden turned pieces yourself, you can buy many different shapes of wood all ready for use. These are sold in hardware stores ready to be used in making bookcases and other projects. You can also find wooden balls and other wooden shapes in craft shops that specialize in macramé.

Very simple dolls can be made with wood turnings. Just add features and wire earrings, if desired. (*Wood Collection*)

Insert the wood into the lathe, according to the requirements of your machine. Select the gouge you want to use, hold it on the rest, and move it toward the wood as it rotates.

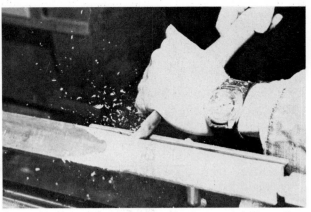

Scraps of wood will fly as your gouge begins to round off your piece of wood.

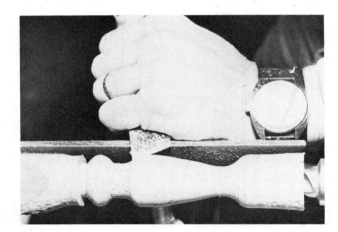

By using a variety of gouges you can create different contours on your wood. Experiment with different gouges holding them at different angles.

You can use a miniature craft lathe instead of a shop lathe for shaping wood. This small lathe by Dremel accepts stock up to 6″ long and 1½″ wide and will perform both spindle and face-plate turnings. (*Photo courtsey of Dremel Manufacturing*)

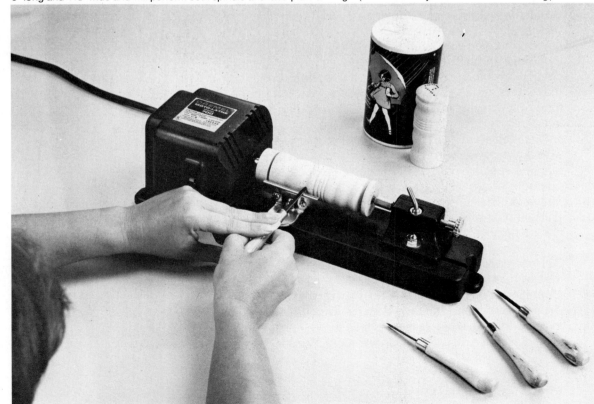

WORKING WITH CLAY, WAX, AND OTHER MODELED SUBSTANCES

Clay and similar substances are often used in doll-making. The doll can be made completely of clay or it can have just a clay head. The doll can also have clay hands and feet, as well as a clay head, and a body made from fabric with a wire frame. Or the doll can have a wooden body. Many different combinations are possible and you will find many variations as you thumb through this book.

Dollmaking with clay has a long history. In Egypt, Greece, and Rome, clay and terra-cotta dolls were made for children, and such dolls have been found in

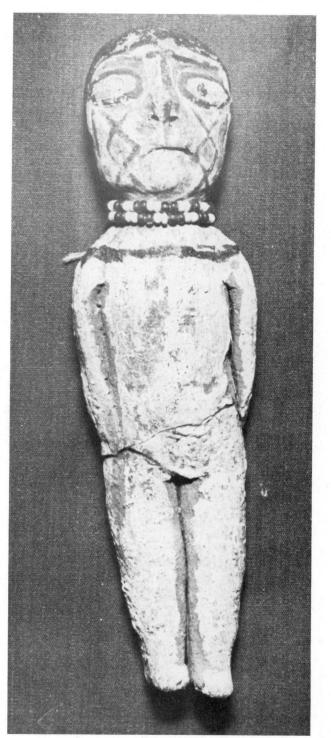

These dolls look like images made by a primitive tribe, perhaps as idols or fetishes. Actually they were made by a contemporary American collector and dealer in such treasures. He enjoyed creating his own "primitive" figures using clay, paint, seed, beads, scraps of fabric, and his own hair. You can have fun doing the same thing. Look at the photos of the clay dolls shown in this book to give you inspiration.

This 5½" primitive American Indian doll was made from clay. Parts of the figure are painted white, and on the face are some red marks indicating features. Around the neck of the doll are blue and white beads. (*Hupp Collection*)

The whole doll might be of clay or another modeling substance, or only the head might be of clay as is this doll's. Made in Israel, with hand-painted features, she has a wire-frame body, braid-trimmed dress, and hands and feet of leather. (*Photo courtesy of Doll, International Kingston, Ontario, Canada*)

Sometimes dolls are made with clay heads, feet, and hands and a wire-frame body. Wendy Ellertson used the same materials in making this 13″ doll. She first sculpted the head, hands, and feet from stoneware or porcelain clay, then fired and glazed them. She linked them with wire and wood for stability, then wrapped this armature with polyester-fiber filling secured with thread. She covered the body with muslin, applied the hair from a Briard dog, and dressed the doll. (*Photo courtesy of the dollmaker*)

their tombs. Clay continues to be used for dollmaking by both adults and children even in the present century. American Indians of the Southwest used clay for making dolls, and in Mexico doll artists specialize in hand-forming clay dolls and baking them in crude outdoor ovens.

In working with clay two basic methods are used for making dolls and doll heads. The easiest method for making just one or a few dolls is to hand-build the doll, that is, form it with the fingers and some simple tools. The alternative is to make and use a mold.

Many different materials have been used besides clay in hand-building dolls and in making them from molds: baker's clay, bread dough, papier-mâché, plastic wood, cold-water putty, and plaster of Paris. Various mixtures have also been used including sawdust clay (fine sawdust plus flour) and white clay (salt and cornstarch). Some dollmakers equipped with kilns make bisque heads. Most are not so equipped so they have sought other alternatives.

Dollmakers have experimented with various substances, looking for one that would take the detailing required for the project and yet at the same time be easy to work with and produce a lightweight product. Since most dollmakers do not have access to a kiln, they choose a material that air dries and does not require firing. A popular contemporary choice is bread dough. Instructions for making and working with bread dough appear on page 249.

Another material that has been popular in making dolls' heads is composition, which is a mixture of resin, wood flour, starch, and water, or a combination

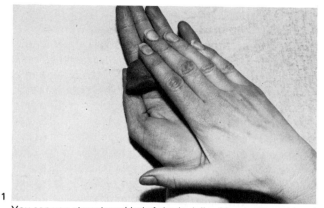

1

You can use almost any kind of clay in dollmaking, but it must be of the right consistency. If the clay is too soft, your doll will not hold its shape, and if it is too dry, it will not be plastic enough; hence the coils you make will break when you bend them. Begin by working the clay with your hands to obtain the proper consistency. To soften it add moisture by wrapping it in a damp cloth. If it needs to be firmer, spread it out on your work surface and let some of the moisture evaporate. Knead it a little at a time.

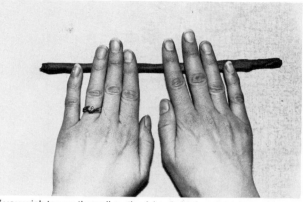

2

If you wish to use the coil method, begin by forming a long snake of clay. Work the clay back and forth with your fingers and palm to make a thinner and thinner snake.

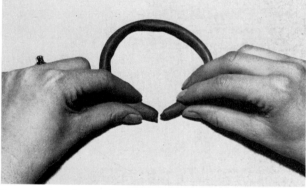

3

If your doll is to have a closed base, make a flat round circle of clay and build up on that. If it is to have an open base, begin by bringing your snake around in a circle and pinching the ends together. Add a little water to bind them better.

4

Continue to add smaller snakes building higher on your base. Wet the lower level before adding another snake to bind them better.

5

When the skirt or bottom section of your doll is done, rub a wet finger over the coils to smooth over the indentations from the separate pieces used to form it.

of bran, sawdust, glue, and perhaps some special ingredients that are the secret of the dollmaker. Formulas varied, and some were even patented.

Another modeling material used in dollmaking is wax. This has been used for a long time in making dolls—sometimes very beautiful and elaborate, with wax skin that looks very realistic. Some of the oldest dolls in the world were made of wax; for instance, in ancient Rome the children played with wax dolls. In the funeral rites of Egypt, wax figures were used.

During the Middle Ages craftsmen made wax images that were used for religious purposes and sometimes for black magic and revenge. In Spain and Germany modeling in wax attained a very high standard of workmanship. Dolls representing saints and angels were made in various sizes from that of a tiny matchstick to one that would burn for a year.

Build up the doll's upper body by forming coils with your fingers and attaching them, always binding them with a little water. With this method, you can make dolls like these Dymkovo clay dolls made in Russia. (*Photo by Lawrence Crump*)

Wax was used as a modeling material, especially in the last half of the sixteenth century. Doll heads were made extensively of wax during the eighteenth and nineteenth centuries in Germany, France, and England.

In Austria workmanship of a high level went into the making of wax figures, particularly portraits. The doll-makers in the nineteenth century took great care in the details of making wax dolls. For instance, they even embedded separate hairs in the wax for a very realistic appearance.

In this century dollmakers in Mexico have also produced beautiful wax dolls. These dolls portray different characters and are usually dressed in clothes that were dipped in wax to produce a modeled effect.

Three different methods were commonly used in making wax heads: the solid, the molded, and the dipped. The early wax dolls were made of poured wax. Later they had a metal or papier-mâché base. And finally they were made with a coating of wax over composition.

Solid heads might be carved from a block of wax or modeled by hand when the wax was warmed. To make molded heads, wax would be melted and poured into molds forming multiple layers. Wax heads made by the dipped method had a base of a material such as plaster, wood, papier-mâché, metal, or composition. The head then would be coated with melted wax. Naturally wax dolls are very fragile because they soften if exposed to heat and their coloring fades if exposed to strong light. Their restoration is a delicate operation. Making wax dolls is less popular today than it was in the past probably because there are so many other available materials that are easier to work with and more durable.

WORKING WITH PAPER

Paper was invented by the Chinese. Hence the first paper dolls may have been made in China long before the Western world was exposed to paper. In Europe paper was made in the twelfth century, and perhaps one early use of it was making dolls.

No dolls survive from the early days of paper-making, but among the earliest surviving ones are the animated paper dolls made in the seventeenth century. This movable type of jointed doll was called a *pantin* in France, a jumping jack in England, and a *Hamplemann* in Germany.

Pantins were completely made by craftsmen and they were also printed on sheets and sold to be made up by the customer. Some were in color and some in black and white so that the customer could do the coloring. They were printed in quantity in many different costumes. More information on these dolls is in the section on France.

Printed paper soldiers, which also became popular, were first made in the province of Alsace in France. Typically they were about 5 ″ tall and were made to be slipped into wooden bases to hold them upright. The older ones were printed in black and white, with some hand colored. In the United States paper soldiers of various sizes were printed and often used as premium inserts in packages of cigarettes and candy.

Another type of paper doll made for adults was the mannequin, which was used to show off the new fashions in women's clothing. These were not meant for children because they were delicate and expensive. Perhaps because girls liked these mannequins so much, special paper dolls began to be made just for them. These paper dolls were often of famous

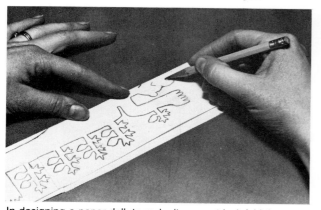

In designing a paper doll, to make it symmetrical, fold the paper and draw so the center of the doll is along the fold. Use a pencil so you can erase and redraw as necessary. Cut it out while it is still folded and you will have a pattern ready to use. If you have left too much space between the parts, try to take up the slack by making a small pleat in the paper.

When you are cutting layers of paper to make dolls, the easiest way to hold the layers together is to staple them in the areas of the paper that will be cut off.

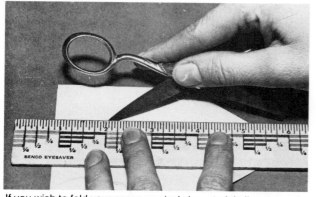

If you wish to fold your paper precisely in a straight line, score the line by holding a ruler on it and running a scissor blade or knife along the line.

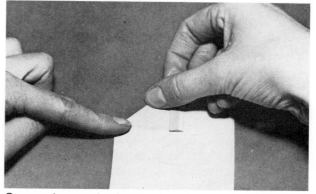

Once you have made a fold in a piece of paper, rub your thumbnail alongside it to make it sharp.

women of the time—actresses, singers, and ballet dancers—and their costumes were copies of the clothing worn by these women.

Paper dolls with separate paper clothing were first sold in Germany, France, and England around 1790. The early dolls were colored by hand. They were bound together like the paper doll books of today and because they were hand colored they were expensive.

Fashion magazines soon had paper dolls for the customer to color and cut out, and of the paper dolls that were commercially printed, those made by Raphael Tuck and Co. of London, England, were among the finest made. Not until about 1880 was an economical process of color printing invented that made colored paper dolls much less expensive. Many advertising dolls were also printed and given as premiums.

Another famous type of paper doll was that intro-duced in the United States by the Dennison Company around 1889. The customer was given printed dolls as well as crepe paper to make up costumes for the dolls.

Today manufacturers print paper dolls in great number. Paper doll artists design their dolls and often have them privately printed. Paper is probably the most popular material for young dollmakers because it is so inexpensive and readily available to them.

Paper is cut, folded, and printed by hand or machine. For dollmaking at home the equipment for working on paper is simple, usually consisting of scissors, ruler, and coloring equipment like crayons, paint, colored pens, or pencils.

Cut paper dolls are still being made today in Mexico while in Japan paper dolls are created from folded paper. See specific instructions for cutting and folding these two types of paper dolls under the respective countries.

3
Dolls of Africa and the Near East

The dolls of Africa and the Near East have served a variety of purposes. Some are playthings, but many have been influenced by the religious and superstitious practices of the people who made them.

DOLLS OF BLACK AFRICA

In the predominantly black countries of Africa dolls have been made of wood, though occasionally clay, fabric, and other materials have been used. They are often figures of idols or ancestors, or representations of family members and are unadorned or dressed in beads, feathers, or pieces of fabric.

Many dolls made in Africa are very primitive in appearance, but others are quite modern. Some dolls are traditional in style, but some show a European influence—depending on which part of Africa they are made in.

Africa has a rich variety of trees that supply wood for native handcrafts, The African wood carver knows well the different kinds of wood growing in his area and can choose the one that would be best for making a house, a wooden bowl, or a doll. For carving dolls the African craftsman often uses ebony, which is a very heavy black wood capable of holding sharp detail. Or he might use the striking zebrawood, a striped wood, mahogany, or other wood.

African wood carvers use a variety of knives as well as the adze, a tool with an arched blade that is at right angles to the handle and is used for shaping wood. The carvers are not confined to conventional proportions so they might make the head of the doll half as big as its height. Many African wooden dolls are tall and slender with shortened arms—influenced by the shape of the piece of wood from which they are carved.

Some of the wooden dolls of black Africa are very sophisticated and intricately carved but many are quite simple—sometimes starkly so. For an African child a doll could be just a straight piece of wood, perhaps with a bit of hair attached or maybe a small amount of rough carving to differentiate the head from the body.

Some African dolls are made for children showing them how they will look as adults. In the northern frontier district of Kenya, the Turkana people who live in the Lake Rudolf area make dolls for little girls that show how they will look as young women. The father

The African woodcraftsman knows the types of wood that grow in his area and which of these is best suited for making dolls, carved animals, and other items. He usually sits outdoors and works on the ground. This wood carver from Kenya is working on an animal, cutting out the large areas with a saw. Using his carving knife, he will soon do the finishing work on this project as well as on the dolls to his left. (*Photo courtesy SERRV*)

For a child, very little is needed to create a doll. This primitive African doll is a 10″ piece of wood with some coarse brown animal hair attached to the top and braided. To a child this represents a human image. (*MacNeer Collection*)

women who carry them until they bear a child. Sometimes dolls are associated with living children. Among some tribes the belief exists that harm will come to the owner of a doll if the doll comes to harm. Therefore in case of a fire or other emergency, the doll is the first item to be rescued from the home.

Among the Ovambo people the husband-to-be names his future mate's doll and the same name is given to the first child of the marriage. In West Africa dolls are often used as tokens of love and affection. When a child is sick, the mother puts a doll in a place indicated by the medicine man along with a gift to speed the child's recovery.

On the Ivory Coast and in Senegal, girls wear large dolls on their backs to indicate they are ready for marriage or, if married, that they desire children. In some areas, if no child arrives, the doll is thrown away or given away to be used as a plaything. If the woman does have a child, she will consider the doll valuable and use it again.

The Ashanti people of Ghana make a flat wooden doll called an *akuaba*, which has a moon- or disc-shaped head representing a woman as the mother-creator, since the moon is viewed by the people as the visible symbol of the mother-goddess. The tradition of making these dolls started when barren women went to the priest at the shrine of the mother-goddess. The priests gave them the akuaba as a fertility symbol to carry while they waited to have a child. Such dolls later came to be made for little girls who carry them in order that they might grow up attractive. They may continue to carry them when they marry and become pregnant, hoping through the influence of the doll to bear attractive children. They carry the dolls tucked into wide waist cloths designed to carry babies. They play with them, bathe, and even dress them.

The Ashanti dolls with their spoon-shaped, carved features, round faces, tiny mouths, long necks, and high smooth foreheads represent the local idea of beauty. Some have bead hair but most are plain or have holes pierced at the sides of the head for earrings. They might have strings of beads at the waist and neck. They have long necks that are smoothly finished or carved with rings. The arms of the doll are extended to each side to form a cross with the short cylindrical body.

Dolls are also carved as ancestor figures. At the time of a man's death his relatives might have the wood carver make a doll. They believe that the soul of the man enters this figure for a while before it passes to the beyond.

carves a doll of wood from Ethiopia. The mother dresses it in tanned goatskin; then using brass wire she decorates the arms; taking beads she makes from ostrich-egg shell, she strings and winds them around the doll's neck. These beads represent the many strings of beads that Turkana women wear continuously around their necks and which are known to stretch their necks from 3″ to 5″.

In black Africa dolls have been connected to a number of superstitious practices. A tribe from the Ivory Coast used dolls to drive witches away.

Dolls have also been used to ensure fertility. Tribes in Transvaal in South Africa make pairs of fertility dolls, called *Ndebele*, which are 3″ to 4″ high and carved from wood. Later ones were made from wire and beadwork. These dolls were fetishes used not only for ensuring fertility but also to ensure the growth of crops. Among some tribes dolls are given to

This 20″ finely finished wooden figure is typical of the work done by artists of the Baule tribe of the Ivory Coast region. It is an ancestor figure made to represent a specific deceased person. The figure is meant as a dwelling place for the spirit of that person who is watching the fortunes of his descendants and listening to their prayers. The figure is not intended to be a portrait showing the person old and wrinkled, but instead the ancestor is always shown as wise, quiet, dignified, and strong. On the chest of the figure is a pattern of cuts like those made by the tribesmen on their own skin for the sake of beauty. The markings are also on the neck and cheeks of the figure. (*Photographed with permission of the White Star Trading Co.*).

This black wood-carved doll with beads at its base is an Ashanti fertility doll, called an *akuaba*. Girls and women carry around flat dolls like this one tucked into their wide waistcloths, which are designed to carry babies. They play with these dolls, bathing and dressing them. The dolls, which are considered religious objects, are worn by the women in hopes they will have beautiful children. The doll shows the Ashanti ideal of beauty with its round face, high smooth forehead, small mouth, and long neck. (*Photographed with permission of the White Star Trading Co.*)

Black, wooden carved male figure made around 1900 by an artist of the Bakongo tribe of Zaïre. A fetish or magical figure, it was carved to achieve some good or evil purpose. Around the neck of the doll is a snake skin that contains a magical substance. The eyes of the figure are small pieces of mirror. (*Photographed with permission of the White Star Trading Co.*)

This 6" wooden figure was carved in Dahomey (now called Benin) by the Yoruba tribe. (*Photographed at the Primal Arts Center, New York City*)

This hand-carved figure is 6″ tall and was made by an artist of the Sanufo tribe of Upper Volta. It certainly relates to woman's fertility and might have been meant as an ancestor figure. (*Photographed with permission of the White Star Trading Co.*)

This 18″ wooden doll is an ancestor figure from the Cameroons. (*Photographed at the Primal Arts Center, New York City*)

This 2′ doll was made from wood by the Luba tribe from the Congo (Zaïre). It is a royal figure surmounted by a leopard totem. (*Photographed at the Primal Arts Center, New York City*)

This 10″ doll carved from wood was made by the Lega tribe of the Congo. The arms are decorated with fur and the chest with a series of holes. (*Photographed at the Primal Arts Center, New York City*)

This 12″ hand-carved wooden doll was made on the Ivory Coast. The doll has a long neck and wears beads. (*Photographed at the Primal Arts Center, New York City*)

This 5″ Baule doll has a pot for a body, and his head is a stopper that can be removed. (*Photographed at the Primal Arts Center, New York City*)

This 10″ doll made in Nigeria by the Yoruba tribe is an *ibeji*, or "twin spirit." This type of doll is made when a twin dies and is looked after by the surviving twin. The living twin took such good care of this doll, washing the face so often, that it is literally washed away. (*Photographed at the Primal Arts Center, New York City*)

This 18″ modern-looking wooden-carved doll bought in Tanzania (Tanganyika) is a woman holding her baby. (*Photographed at the International Craftsman, Flemington, N.J.*)

Many of the West African tribes make these wooden ancestor figures as permanent dwelling places for the spirits of the dead who are watching over their descendants and listening to their prayers. The dolls are not intended to be portraits and are never made to look old and wrinkled. Instead they are shown to be strong, quiet, thoughtful, wise, cool, and dignified.

Closely related to the ancestor dolls are the twin dolls made when a twin dies. The living twin washes and cares for this doll as if it were a living person. Sometimes this is done over such a long period of time that the carved face is worn completely smooth.

Wood is used for carving ancestral figures and other dolls connected with tribal beliefs, and in black Africa it is also used for carving modern secular dolls.

These 3″ figures from Nigeria are hand-carved natural wood. The hands and faces are darker wood glued in place. One doll is reading and the other is making a basket. (*Photographed at the United Nations Gift Center*)

In Nigeria members of the Yoruba tribe make dolls combining their native skill with interesting indigenous woods. They combine light and dark woods to make the various parts of the doll, making maximum use of the natural grain of the wood.

Sometimes wood is combined with other materials like wire, feathers, grass, and so on. In Zaïre, Bapende dance fetishes are made by first carving a wooden base and then weaving straw over it. Wood also provides the base for ancestral figures made by the Bamoun tribe of the Cameroon. These large dolls have wooden frames and are covered with fabric, with shells and beads then sewn on them.

Though many of the dolls in black Africa are made of wood, various other materials are also used. In some areas dolls are made from metals. In the Cameroon they are made from wood, seeds, beads, cowrie shells, wax, corncobs, leather, nuts, fur, fabric, and other materials. There dolls play an important part as ancestor figures and also as gifts or tokens of friendship. The friendship dolls are carefully taken care of so that the friendship will be preserved.

These 3½″ dolls from Nigeria show two women and illustrate further typical Nigerian characters. The one on the left is sitting in the marketplace selling her fish while the one on the right is stirring food for supper. The carver made good use of the natural grains of his woods in making these dolls. (*Photographed at the United Nations Gift Center*)

These carvings made in Nigeria were probably done by the Yoruba tribe. The dolls representing royal retainers are carrying (*left to right*) a bell, maraca, staff, and staff and spear. (*Photographed at the Primal Arts Center, New York City*)

These 8″ wooden dolls are Bapende dance fetishes from Zaïre. They have hand-carved wooden bodies that have been covered with woven straw that is fringed at the wrists, waists, and ankles. The circle eyes and other details on the masks are painted with white paint. (*Photographed with permission of the Primal Arts Center, New York City*)

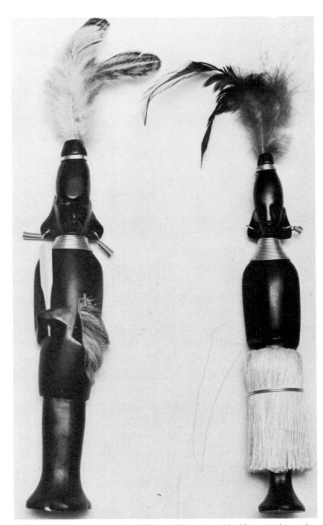

These 8″ dolls were carved from ebony wood in Kenya where the wood carvers combine their native skill with the interesting indigenous wood to do the traditional African woodwork, which is increasingly popular. They are decorated with feathers in their heads and wire earrings, collars, and headpieces. He carries a wooden spear and a shield made from a piece of animal hide with the fur left on it. She wears a fiber skirt held in place with wire. (*Imported by SERRV, Author's Collection*)

These 4½″ (8″ to the top of the hair) musicians were made in South Africa using a variety of locally available natural materials. The heads and bodies are made from seed pods. The feet and arms are sections from pinecones. The eyes are nails painted half black and half white, and the legs are wooden dowels. They wear skirts and belts that are strips of hide and around their heads are further strips of hide with long white hair on them. (*Author's Collection*)

These bronze figures from Bogon, West Africa, range in size from 3¾″ to 5″ high. (*Photographed at the Primal Arts Center, New York City*)

This 4″ high doll from Kenya is a warrior with a shield and spear. It shows a very interesting use of a natural material, the leaves of the banana plant. The doll has a wire frame wrapped with long strips of leaf. Extra pieces are added as a sort of jacket and waistband. (*Author's Collection*)

This doll from Nigeria represents the king seated on the ceremonial chair. Both he and his elaborate chair are made from iron. As early as 2000 B.C. iron smelting was known in Africa, and it reached peaks of technical and artistic accomplishment in Benin and Ife in Nigeria. (*Photographed at the Primal Arts Center, New York City*)

Some African dolls are made from stuffed fabric. In some parts of Africa, weaving is still done on primitive looms. This woman in Bomborokuy, Upper Volta, is weaving very long strips of material that can later be sewn together to make blankets, clothing, or even dolls. (*Photo courtesy of World Neighbors*)

In Kenya rope and banana leaves are among the interesting materials used to make dolls. In Lesotho dolls are made and dressed exactly like the natives. These fabric stuffed dolls wear the distinctive conical straw hat with a topknot worn by the people of this small country. Other fabric dolls are made in Africa, some using local materials made on primitive looms, others using modern manufactured fabrics like felt.

This 7" stuffed fabric girl doll was made by a member of Lesotho Cooperative Handcrafts. Lesotho is one of the smallest political units in Africa which, until independence, was known as Basutoland. It is a landlocked country, an enclave, in South Africa. Remote and difficult to get to, this country exists in a world of its own. On the flag of the country is the Basotho people's original cone-shaped straw hat with its unusual topknot. The type of hat shown on the doll is still worn by many men and women of this country where hats are a must to keep off the hot sun and swirling dust. Many people wear Western clothes, such as the simple cotton fabric dress worn by this doll. In the winter, however, instead of wearing coats they wrap themselves in blankets. These blankets have unique patterns that show the Basotho love of color and design. In fact, it is a matter of pride for a native to wear a blanket that has a pattern that no one else has. But since blankets are made not by hand but by machine this is not always possible. The doll's blanket is held in place with a safety pin decorated with beads and typical of those worn in Lesotho. Her mouth is a scrap of red felt, and her eyes small pieces of white fabric held on with French knots. (*Imported by SERRV, Author's Collection*)

SISAL ROPE DOLL FROM KENYA

In Kenya on the outskirts of Nairobi, the Christian Council of Kenya has a development program to help underprivileged people improve their lives. Administered by a trained social worker, this diversified program includes a craft project working with wood and also making dolls with wooden heads and braided sisal rope bodies.

To make your own rope doll you can purchase sisal rope in hardware and other stores. Though it is stiff, it is not difficult to work with. The same braiding technique used on this rope doll can be used to make dolls from yarn, which is easier to braid than sisal.

To make a rope doll, in addition to the sisal rope or yarn, you will need a 1½" macramé bead for the head, scraps of cotton-print fabric for the dress, snap fasteners, thread, black felt tip pen, and white paint.

Cut six 14" pieces of rope. Fold them in half and begin braiding all six together. Work for only 2". Divide the strands and bring six to each side. Braid each group of six together to form the two legs. Braid until the whole braid measures about 3½", then wind thread around to secure the rope in place. Cut off any excess rope, so the whole braid measures 4". Repeat for the second leg.

Cut three 7½" pieces of rope. Wind a piece of thread around to hold the ends of the rope pieces together and tie securely in place. Braid the yarn until the piece measures 5". Wind another piece of thread around the ends and cut off the excess. Use a needle and thread to attach the short braid across the top of the wider braid.

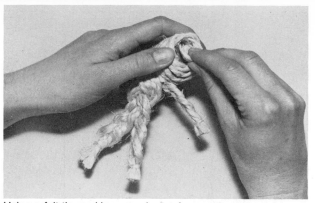

Using a felt-tip marking pen, draw a face on the macramé bead. Add a dot of white paint at the center of the eye, using the end of the paintbrush. Put glue on the head and wind the rope around and around making the doll's hair.

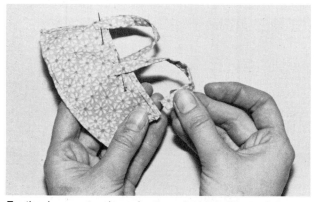

For the dress, cut a piece of cotton print fabric 5" × 7½". Cut two shoulder straps 4" × 1" of the same fabric or a contrasting plain color fabric. Turn up a narrow hem all around the skirt piece. Fold the straps in half the long way, then turn in and sew the raw edges to make finished strips about ⅜" wide. Find the middle front of the skirt and sew the two shoulder straps there. Sew the other ends of the shoulder straps near the edges of the fabric.

Sew a snap fastener where the edges of the skirt overlap at the back to keep the dress on the doll. Put on the dress and your doll is complete. The authentic doll made in Kenya is at right, and the author's version is at left.

BEADED DOLLS

Beads are used all over the world to decorate dolls. Especially popular are seed beads. Nowhere are beads used as extensively on dolls as in black Africa, Among African tribes beads are universally prized both as a convenient and ready item to be used as a medium of exchange and as a means of personal adornment. Colorful beads play an important part in the tribal dress of the Zulus, Ndebeles, Zhosa, Bantus, and other tribes.

Researchers have investigated the sources of beads used in Africa and have been interested particularly in those found before the Europeans made settlements there. Beads have been found dating as early as 960 to 1200. These included a celadon glazed ceramic bead from China, but most of the earliest beads found in Africa were evidently Arab trade beads from Ptolemaic Egypt.

Glass beads have been made in Africa for centuries in centers like Breda, using glass from bottles and trade beads. Beads are still made there using ancient techniques with the glass still being melted in charcoal fires pumped with bellows. Once the glass is melted, it is formed into beads and shaped with metal pincers and other tools. For multicolored glass beads several pieces of colored glass are melted together. To make the hole in the bead a thin iron rod is pushed into the glass while it is still soft.

At the beginning of the sixteenth century the Portuguese who landed in East Africa brought red beads. These replaced the less striking native-made beads that had been in use. For the first twenty years of that century shiploads of trade beads poured into Africa in exchange for gold, ivory, and slaves. Two hundred years later the beads were still pouring into Africa; the explorer Livingstone in his journal commented on the long lines of porters carrying them.

Beads that traders brought to Africa came first from the Arab countries, and then from England, France, Italy, Austria, Germany, the Netherlands, and other European countries. Even today beads for export to Africa are still made in Europe.

African dolls are often made using beads. While some just have a few beads added as eyes or as decoration, others wear one or more strings of beads around their necks, wrists, or ankles. Still others are heavily covered with beads.

The Ashanti add strings of beads and sometimes bead earrings to the flat wooden dolls they make. *Basuto* dolls, also made of wood, are wound with

These beaded Cameroon dolls are about 4" to 5" tall. They have stuffed fabric bases covered with beads, and their feet are Jacob's tears, which are natural seeds. The faces are covered with seed beads, and the features indicated with different colors of beads. Their chests are covered with beads. Each figure has a black fabric belt, and below it a piece of bright red/orange fabric. (*Photographed with permission of Banboula Associates, New York City*)

This doll, which stands about 5' tall, is an ancestral figure made by the Bamoun tribe of Cameroon. It has a wooden base that has been covered with fabric. Cowrie shells were then sewn on the body. The face, features, hands, and so on, were completed with trade beads. (*Photographed with permission of the Primal Arts Center, New York City*)

This spectacular 5' doll is a Bamoun beaded ancestor figure found in the Bamede area of Cameroon. It has a wooden base decorated with thousands of beads. (*Photographed at the Primal Arts Center, New York City*)

fabric and many strings of beads. Tribes of Northern Rhodesia make wooden dolls ornamented with strings of beads. In the Cameroons beads are used extensively in making dolls.

The Zulus also make very extensive use of beads —not only in making dolls but in decorating their native dress. Today most Zulu men wear Western clothing but others, mainly the women, wear the tribal clothes, or at least a modern version of them. They are especially fond of colored fabric that contrasts vividly, and of course beads. The Zulus wear necklaces, head circlets, earrings, bracelets, anklets, and so on.

The patterns of color in which the beads were arranged on these items had meanings as clear as words to the Zulu. Through bead symbolism, for instance, lovers could convey their meanings to each

other. Today, however, many Zulus do not understand the language of beads.

The Zulus make interesting beaded dolls. Typically, they are about 3″ high, have wooden bases, and are dressed in rows of beads. They also make larger ones with fabric bases, and both these types are made strongly in the native tradition.

Beaded dolls showing European influence have also been made in South Africa. Felt dolls made in the Red Cross Rehabilitation Project in Durban show the beautiful beadwork done by the natives on accurate reproductions of themselves. Fabric stuffed dolls made in Transkei reflect accurately native costume and show beaded necklaces and pins as they are worn by the women.

This 11″ fabric stuffed doll made in South Africa has arms but no legs, and her features are embroidered as are the hair and features of the baby on her back. She is dressed exactly like the woman who made her. She has a wraparound skirt made with orange homespun and decorated with black strips. She has a strip of the same fabric hanging down in the front and a shawl of the same with an X at the center of her back. She wears a cotton-print apron under the orange strip. The baby is held in place on her back by a piece of blue homespun, which is under the shawl. The doll was made by a member of All Saints Home Industries, Transkei, South Africa. (*Author's Collection*)

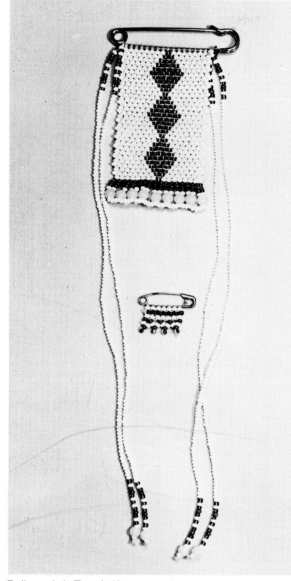

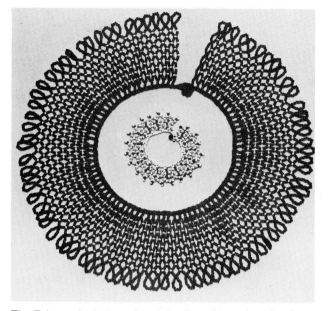

The Zulus make intricate beaded collars. Shown here is a large collar made from blue and white beads; the doll's collar is at the center. (*Author's Collection*)

Dolls made in Transkei have a small version of the pins decorated with beads. Here is the small doll-size one along with an elaborate one made for an adult to use. (*Author's Collection*)

In this back view of Nomusa (front view on page 46) the detailing on the child can be seen. He (or she) has the same felt features as his mother, and rows of beads decorate his ankles and wrists. He has beadwork earrings and a necklace, and his hair is black seed beads sewn onto his head. The detailed beadwork on the back of his mother's headpiece is also visible in this photograph. (*Weiner Collection*)

These beautiful felt dolls were made in South Africa. Their tags say: "This is a product of the Red Cross Rehabilitation Centre, Durban." They are all about 15″ high. Each part of their bodies is made from firmly stuffed felt. The dolls have features of felt, lips of light brown felt, and white felt eyes with black circles of felt as pupils. The nose and eyebrows are painted on, and the dolls are magnificently dressed in seed bead costumes. They have ears, which are separate pieces of stuffed felt sewn into the seam at the sides of the heads. The figure on the left has strands of beads crossed on her chest as well as in the back. Another strip of beading goes from the neck down to the waist. She has black yarn hair, elegant earrings with dropping strands of seed beads.

The woman on the right is called Nomusa or Kindness. She is wearing a black felt skirt, decorated with rows of colored beads in blue, green, white, and purple. On her back she has a baby in a felt backpack. On her head is a magnificent headpiece of beads. She has circle earrings of blue and white seed beads, and she wears bands of beads at her ankles and her wrists. Crossing her chest are blue and white bands of beads. (*Weiner Collection*)

These handsome 15″ felt dolls show off the beautiful beadwork done in South Africa. All three have wide bands of seed beads as well as strings of seed beads hanging from their waists. The man on the left is called Mandle, or Strength, and he is lavishly dressed in beads of green, blue, orange, and yellow. He has a black yarn beard and hair. He wears green and white earrings and black and white anklets, knee and wrist bands. On his head is a circlet of beads, and in it are some colorful feathers. He is carrying an animal-hide shield and wooden spear.

The doll in the center is Sanyamma, the witch doctor. He has a string of bones around his neck separated with seed beads, and pieces of animal hide across his chest and around his wrists. He is wearing an elaborate headdress of strings of white and black beads. He has bands of seed beads crossing his chest, and a square piece at his neck with beads in black, blue, red, and white. He holds a wooden stick that is covered with cloth and rows of seed beads, and out of the top come pieces of yarn.

The third figure on the far right, called Mngani, or friend, is dressed in green, blue, red, white, and black beads. He wears star seed-bead earrings and carries a wooden spear and shield. He has beads at his wrists and ankles, as have the other figures, and the same rows of beads and feathers around his head. He has bands of beading crossing his chest and his back. He has some larger beads at the back of his head. (*Weiner Collection*)

MAKING A ZULU DOLL

The form of this doll is extremely simple, just a pillar with a head and body and no arms and legs. The feature of the doll is the hair, which imitates in a simple form the elaborate hairstyle of the Zulu woman, whose hair is sometimes piled high on her head and dressed with reddish clay. The style of the headdress varies from tribe to tribe. In some tribes the women spend many hours perfecting a hairdo that will last a long time.

The most convenient beads for making a Zulu beaded doll are those sold in craft shops for making beaded flowers. You can use the seed beads sold unstrung in vials, or you can buy them already strung on pieces of thread, which is much more convenient.

For the base, use a piece of wood about 3″ high and about ⅞″ thick. You can obtain a wooden dowel of this thickness, cut it to size, and round off the top. Or if you have an old broom or mop with a wooden handle rounded at the top, you can saw it off 3″ from the top and your wood will already be rounded.

To cover the wood you will need black fabric. A knit fabric is convenient because the knit will more easily conform to the rounded top of the wood than would a woven or pressed material. You will also need black thread and a needle.

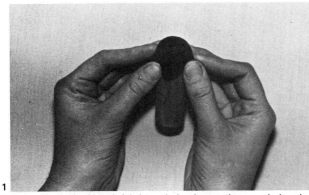

1
Cut a 3″ circle of black fabric and glue it over the rounded end of your wood. Make small cuts around the edge of the circle if necessary to get it to fit onto the wood. Glue it in place and hold the fabric there with a rubber band while it dries.

2
Cut a strip of black fabric about 2½″ x 3½″ (depending on the size of your wood) and bring it around the body of the doll crossing the end over at the back and stitching them in place. Cut a circle of black felt the exact size of the base of your doll and secure it there with a bit of glue. For the features, sew on two beads for the mouth and one white bead for each eye. Bring two short strands of beads over the head and sew the ends in place at the sides of the face. Take a few stitches at the top of the head, securing the beads in place there. Attach the end of a long strand of beads at the bottom of the face. Bring the strand around and around the doll. Make stitches here and there to hold the beads in place.

3
Continue to add more beads, bringing strands of them around and around the doll, securing them as necessary and changing colors as you wish. Continue to add beads until you are within about ⅜″ of the bottom of the doll.

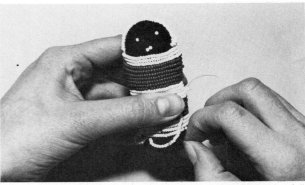

4
Secure a string of beads at one side of the doll. Let the string fall down in a loop to almost touch the bottom of the doll and secure the string about an inch further along. Repeat around the doll making a looped border.

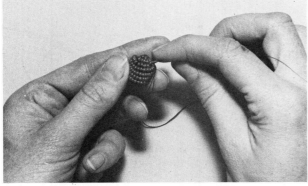

5
For the beaded hair, make a base by cutting a strip of black fabric ½″ x 3½″. Bring the fabric around and around to make a small coiled pillar and stitch the end to hold it secure. Attach the end of a string of beads at the base of the hair. Stitching it as necessary, bring the string of beads around and around to cover the whole base of the hair.

6
Stitch the beaded hair in place at the back of the doll's head.

These 3″ Zulu dolls were bought before 1932, in Johannesburg, South Africa. Note that the doll on the right has a baby on her back, which is just visible. The baby is also made of fabric and beads. The beaded sections coming up from the doll's head are made with red beads and represent the elaborate hairstyles of the Zulus who may dress them with reddish clay. (*From the Collection of the Forbes Library, Northampton, Mass.*)

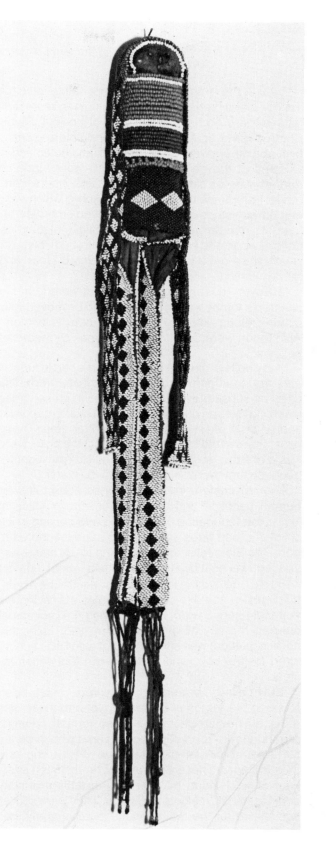

This spectacular Zulu doll from South Africa is 18″ long. It is similar to the one at the left shown with a wooden base, but it has a fabric base covered with rows of beads. The face is black fabric with just a few beads sewn on to represent the eyes, nose, and mouth. Strands of beautiful beadwork hang down from the doll. (*Photographed with permission of the White Star Trading Co.*)

DOLLS OF THE ARAB COUNTRIES

Though the Arab countries are not outstanding for the number or variety of their dolls, human representations there go back to the time of ancient Egypt. Some of these early dolls were very simple and primitive, and others were more complex and advanced.

Some of the early Egyptian dolls were made of earthenware or blue glazed porcelain. Others were made from limestone, bronze, or linen, which was stuffed with strips of papyrus and given embroidered features and thread hair. The Egyptians also made dolls of wood and wood combined with cloth, some of which were quite large and had painted faces and fabric clothing.

In Egypt, too, among the dolls that were found in children's tombs were dolls that could be moved with a string, along with tiny clothes and utensils for them. Also found were dolls that could speak by means of bellows.

Many dolls of ancient Egypt played a part in funeral rites and in superstitious practices. They were also used as substitutes for children who in earlier times would have been offered to the Nile River in supplication when it did not rise at the proper time. These dolls, thrown into the water instead of the child, were made of straw or reeds and were quickly put together because they would soon sink into the water.

Another custom involved dolls as substitutes for human sacrifice and evolved from the practice of laying the foundation of a building and burying in it a child who had been sacrificed to appease the earth god. The Bible tells how, according to Joshua, when Jericho was built by Hiel, the Bethite, about the year 1450 B.C., he laid the foundation by sacrificing Abrim, his firstborn son. He set up the gates sacrificing his youngest son, Segub, and so during the process of building the city all of his children died. Later this horrible custom was altered so that a doll was substituted for the child and buried in the foundation instead.

Dolls called *Ushabti,* or "Answerers," have been found in the tombs of ancient Egypt and these also replaced human sacrifice. These funeral offerings are thought to represent the servants who in earlier times might have been buried alive with the bodies of their masters. These dolls of clay represented every kind of work done by servants, including farming, cooking, music making, and so on. They were sent as substitutes for the real servants to accompany their master and serve him in the other world. Some of these early dolls are thought to be figures of concubines whose legs were joined together to keep them from running away.

Among the oldest wooden dolls that can be seen in museums are those from Egypt dating roughly from 2000 B.C. They were cut from thin pieces of wood and their bodies covered with geometrical designs suggesting clothes. They wore wigs made with strings of

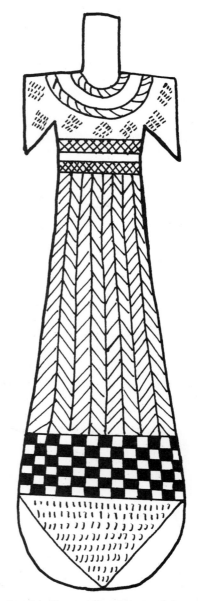

A replica of an Egyptian paddle doll can easily be cut in this shape from balsa, plywood, or similar wood. Decorate the wood with felt-tip pen in red, black, and browns. Add beads for hair if you wish.

clay or wooden beads to look like hair. The wigs were attached to the dolls' heads with wax; the wooden arms and legs were sometimes movable. These wooden figures were buried in tombs in the Nile River Valley. As befitting his station, an Egyptian nobleman, who often had many wives, would be buried with a paddle doll representing each one of them beside him in his tomb so the women could be with him forever.

These figures are called paddle dolls because their bodies are made in the form of a flat paddle with very simple arms and head. On the doll's head is a wig made from thousands of tiny beads made from black mud from the Nile River. The beads were rolled and threaded, and each strand was often finished off with a bright bead at the tip or an elongated gray one.

The body itself was made from wood about ⅛" thick. The head was often left flat, but sometimes it was given a protruding clay face. The wooden body was painted with typical Egyptian geometric motifs— triangles, and other decorative lines, and colored in earthy ocher, black, and red.

The sixth-century Arabs did have dolls, but many Mohammedan superstitions about dolls discouraged them from having many, even though it is recorded that Mohammed himself was persuaded to play with dolls by his second wife, the nine-year-old Ayesha. Parents were afraid that a too realistic doll might come to life and harm a child, or the doll might become a ghost. The Moslem religion forbad the reproduction of the human face, so the dolls remained featureless.

In recent times dolls were made in the Sudan with wooden bodies and heads, limbs of clay, and woolen hair. They were dressed in cloth ornamented with coins or beads. Witches made special dolls, which they sold to childless women who carried the dolls around on their backs until they had a child of their own or gave up and sold off the dolls cheaply. These dolls, which were 10" to 15" high, had crude shapes and very long necks and were draped with jewelry. They wore ornaments, bracelets, necklaces, and cotton skirts that reached to their feet.

In the last few decades dolls have been made in the refugee camps on the banks of the river Jordan. The YWCA has centers there offering services to Palestinian Arab refugee women and girls. In Aqabat Jaber near Jericho, for example, the Y offers programs in home economics, literacy classes, dollmaking, and embroidery. The women make dolls and the sale of these provides them with some income while they are receiving training at the center.

This 11" Sudanese doll was bought in 1925. She has a white skirt with red fabric trim. She has embroidered features and human hair on her head. Her clothing and hat are elaborately decorated with round and tube beads sewn in place or dangling in strands. (*From the Collection of the Forbes Library, Northampton, Mass.*)

The refugees make dolls from wire with hands looped around. The heads and bodies are made of fabric, and the faces of nylon stocking. Their features are simply made with straight stitches. Black wool thread is used for the eyes and eyebrows, and red wool for the mouth. Two stitches are made for the nostrils and pulled tight to simulate a nose. Some of these dolls have real hair attached.

These dolls are also dressed in accurate copies of the clothing worn in the area. The doll representing the costume of the women of Jericho, for example, has a heavily embroidered dress with long sleeves tied across the shoulder as a protection from the sun. The doll representing the dress of the women of

The tag on this 7" pair of dolls purchased in the early 1960s says: "World YWCA Center, Aqabat Jaber Refugee Camp, Jericho, Jordan." The dolls have wire-frame bodies and faces of stuffed stocking fabric with embroidered features. The woman's dress is beautifully embroidered. The man wears a black aba with gold trim sewn on it. Under the aba he has a long blue and white caftan. The woman wears the costume of Bert Dojan, with a shorter dress that shows the embroidery on her trousers. Her head scarf is edged with a green crocheted border. Her black caftan is beautifully decorated with tiny red cross-stitches in a repeat pattern. Most likely the embroiderer used a piece of needlepoint canvas over which she did the stitches, and once completed the canvas was carefully cut strand by strand and removed. (*Weiner Collection*)

This 11" woman doll was bought in Algiers in 1922. She has a fabric stuffed body, a composition material face, and on her feet are soft leather babouches. She wears strings of beads and has beads on her headpiece. In public the haik, a long piece of cotton or woolen cloth, envelops the Algerian woman. (*From the Collection of the Forbes Library, Northampton, Mass.*)

Bethlehem wears a tall headdress, supposedly a tradition from the days of the Crusades; her dowry coins are sewn on it. The doll copying the dress of the women of Bethany has a small cap on the side of her head with dowry money sewn around the edge, and so on.

Other types of wire and fabric stuffed dolls have been made in Arab countries. These costume dolls often accurately portray local dress. Some of these have hand-formed clay faces and hands and others have pressed fabric or needle-sculpted faces.

Another type of doll for which the Arab countries

are known is the leather doll. Leather is used, for example, in making figures of camels, some of which come equipped with riders. The leather is stitched with thread along the seams on the outside of the rider and camel, and both are stuffed with sawdust. The camel is typically decked out with sequins and fringe, and the rider is dressed in fabric clothing.

The dollmakers of Morocco also use leather to make dolls. However, instead of stitching the seams of their dolls they moisten and mold the leather into faces, hands, and feet. They then paint on features and dress the dolls in authentic costumes.

A pair of 6" dolls made in Jordan. They have wooden bodies and clay heads with hand-painted features. Their arms and legs are wooden pieces attached with pieces of elastic to the straight piece of wood that serves as a body. He wears a brown houndstooth knit fabric caftan, a black taffeta aba, and a white kaffiyeh with an agal of gray yarn. She is wearing a blue velvet vest and a black-and-red caftan decorated with embroidery and with a gold coin sewn on her front. She has a tarboosh of red paper, decorated with gold sequins to represent the gold coins usually sewn on this headgear. Over the tarboosh is a white veil indicating that she is a married woman. (*SERRV import, Author's Collection*)

These 14" cotton stuffed dolls from Egypt have pressed fabric faces with painted features. He has a bit of wool for a mustache and is wearing a white strip of fabric wound around his head over a red velvet hat which is decorated with a black tassel. He wears a long caftan made of a shiny twill-like fabric in black and yellow and has blue-and-white libas, or pantaloons, underneath. His paper shoes are covered with velvet. In his hands he has some blue beads on a string, and over his shoulder is a strip of white fabric, an aba.

She is wearing a blue taffeta dress with gold coins sewn on the front and a blue print tabe underneath. A black yashmak is over her face, and she has a ring in her nose and a gold coin sewn to the green head cover over her forehead. She wears earrings of blue beads and gold coins and has blue line markings on her forehead between her eyebrows. (*From the Collection of Nancy Ann Malik*)

These 9½" dolls from Lebanon are mounted on wooden stands, which have the name A. Chilinguriian on them. They have clay heads, hands, and feet, and their bodies are stuffed fabric. He wears a black kaffiyeh with a rope agal on his head, and also a gold shirt and brown jodhpurs both made from a shiny taffeta-like fabric. Around his waist is a blue cummerbund, and he holds a white pottery water jug in his hand. She has black vinyl braids and wears a print blouse and skirt. On her head is a yellow head scarf and a red pottery waterjug. (*Mueller Collection*)

53

This couple from Lebanon was bought in Beirut in the 1950s. The bodies are fashioned of wood. The heads were made of clay or similar modeling material, and the features were painted on. Their shoes were cut from a rubbery material perforated on the bottom. He has a red fez painted on his head and wears a salmon-colored satin shirt, black cotton pants, and a maroon cummerbund. She has a long pink satin skirt with long red pants underneath. Her jacket was made from a red-and-pink brocade. Her hair is a piece of twisted ropelike material, the type sometimes used on draperies. The ends are frayed to represent the ends of her hair. (*Weiner Collection*)

The Bedouins are nomads living mainly in the desert. This 10" Bedouin man was made in Palestine and bought from Kimport Dolls before 1939. He is a beautifully detailed fabric stuffed doll. His face is painted and he has a mohair yarn beard. His clothing is embroidered, and he is wearing a black wool vest with gold thread embroidery. Over this is a lighter cotton coat. His tunic is black-and-white cotton fabric, and he has a red cummerbund. On his head he wears a white cotton kaffiyeh with a black agal. (*From the Collection of the Forbes Library, Northampton, Mass.*)

This 11″ Water Seller was bought in Morocco in the early 1950s. He represents a merchant who was once a common sight in North Africa before waterworks supplied the homes with running water. This doll has a stiff wire frame, which is wrapped with a dark brown yarn built up in certain areas, for instance, to show the muscles in the legs. The elbows are indicated by knots in the yarn. The doll has leather sandals and a short unfinished caftan of red fabric over a white undergarment. On his head is a white cotton turban wound around with brown yarn. His eyes are stitched with white yarn, his nose is more brown yarn sewn in place, and his mouth is indicated with black yarn. He is carrying a black fabric water bag to represent the goatskin once used by his human counterpart. A squeeze from the Water Seller's elbow would send a jet of cool water from the shining nozzle. The doll also carries a bell, brass cups, and a piece of vinyl painted gold and silver. (*Weiner Collection*)

This Arab riding on a camel was bought in the 1950s in the U.A.R. Made out of leather, they are sewn all around with a blanket stitch and stuffed. The man's features are inked on his face, and over his leather body he is wearing white breeches, and a blue and white gingham shirt. On his head is a kaffiyeh of sheer red fabric held in place with an agal (a piece of white braid). The camel has an elegant saddle decorated with braid and sequins with tassels hanging down. The figures measure about 9″ from the top of the rider's head to the camel's feet. (*Weiner Collection*)

Three 8½″ leather dolls bought in Tangiers, Morocco, in 1934, representing, *from left to right,* a laborer, a countryman, and a water carrier. They have stuffed leather bodies with features drawn on their molded leather faces and wear coarse-fabric clothing. The laborer is carrying a fabric bundle, the countryman has a wooden gun in his hand, and the water carrier has a leather water bag and a bell to let everyone know he is coming. (*From the Collection of the Forbes Library, Northampton, Mass.*)

These 8″ leather dolls bought in Tangiers, Morocco, in 1934 have fabric clothing. They represent, *left to right*, the countrywoman, the city gentleman and his buxom wife. Their bodies are stuffed leather, and their faces are leather that has been moistened, shaped, and later painted. The countrywoman under her huge straw hat has a heavy red-and-white woven skirt. She wears a mandell, or face veil, of sheer white lawn. The city man with a large black shawl has a string of beads hanging at his side. His wife wears a white brocade dress with a green belt and beads. (*From the Collection of the Forbes Library, Northampton, Mass.*)

These 8½″ all-leather dolls with painted faces were bought in Tangiers, Morocco, in 1934. The figure on the left is a *furnowie*, a Sudanese dancer. He has shells glued to the leather strips criss-crossing his leather shirt. The figure on the right is a wood carrier. The lines on his coat were drawn on the leather, and even the wood in the pack on his back is leather. (*From the Collection of the Forbes Library, Northampton, Mass.*)

Traditional dolls in China are the paper and fabric Immortals representing figures from Chinese mythology. *(Wood Collection)*

Making cornhusk dolls is a traditional folk craft of the United States. *(Mueller Collection)*

Made in South Africa, these stuffed felt dolls have handsome beaded costumes. *(Weiner Collection)*

Authentic peasant costumes are worn by these stuffed fabric dolls from Russia. *(MacNeer Collection)*

Made in Toluca, these Mexican dolls have faces made with cloth treated with glue. *(Decker Collection)*

Made from prunes and figs, dolls like these are sold in Germany's Christkindl Market. *(Author's Collection)*

This wire-frame pair was made in the studio of Charlotte Weibull of Sweden. *(Weiner Collection)*

These dolls with flax hair have clothing made of the hand-loomed fabrics for which Lithuania is known. *(Stukas Collection)*

This fabric stuffed doll from the San Blas Islands off the coast of Panama wears a costume like that of the Cuna Indian who made her. *(Author's Collection)*

Dressed in detailed, authentic costumes, these dolls were made in Argentina. *(MacNeer Collection)*

East Indian stick dolls dressed with bright fabrics are much loved by Hindu children. *(Author's Collection)*

Japan has become famous for her *kokeshi* dolls made of turned wood. Today's versions often have fabric covering the wood. *(MacNeer Collection)*

Kachina dolls are carved from cottonwood root and painted by the Hopi and Zuni Indians of the south-western United States. (Fisher Collection)

This French fisherman and his wife have sculpted fabric faces and stuffed fabric bodies. (MacNeer Collection)

This fisherman with his hand-knit sweater hails from Denmark, a great seafaring nation. (Urdang Collection)

Yarn is the basic ingredient used to make these Portuguese dolls. *(MacNeer Collection)*

This handsome stuffed fabric doll from Thailand wears a costume of fine-quality Thai silk. *(Urdang Collection)*

Made in Italy, this Pinocchio has a wire frame wrapped with yarn. *(MacNeer Collection)*

The rabbi and his family are portrayed in this set of dolls made in Israel from wood trimmed with printed paper and fake fur. *(Weiner Collection)*

Yarn wrapped over a wire frame makes the body of this Moroccan water seller with his waterbag, brass cups, and bell. *(Weiner Collection)*

In Yorkshire, England, dolls are made from the bobbins of the old spinning mills. *(Author's Collection)*

These three wire-frame Irish dolls are dressed women from Gaeltacht, Sligo, and the West. *(My Irish Cottage)*

Made in Grenada, one of the Windward Islands of the Caribbean, this stuffed fabric stump doll is dressed in the typical manner of dolls from this area. *(Author's Collection)*

Applehead dolls often have wire-frame bodies and sometimes hands made from dried, carved apple. *(MacNeer Collection)*

ISRAELI DOLLS

The earliest dolls belonging to Jewish children, unearthed from ancient graves, are often headless or featureless because the Mosaic law forbad the representation of the human face.

After the State of Israel was founded, dollmakers started producing character dolls, each one representing an occupation or a costume either modern or traditional. These dolls illustrate typical Israelis: the Orthodox rabbi, the people of the kibbutz, and so on. Some of these dolls were sold as part of fund-raising projects by Jews all over the world to raise money to help the newly reestablished homeland. Today many dolls are made in Israel for sale to natives and also to the many tourists who visit the country.

The contemporary population of Israel is very varied, including not just Jews but Christians, Moslems, and others. Even among the Jews there are many divisions. Hence the dolls of Israel reflect a great diversity. Such dolls as the Hasidic rabbi with earlocks and a woman carrying a water jug on her head represent the traditional and conservative types; a soldier in the Israeli army and immigrants from the United States and other countries in contemporary dress represent modern types.

Some of the dolls made in Israel show different aspects of Jewish religious life: the rabbi carrying the Torah, the family at a Passover meal, rabbis performing a brith, the woman lighting the Friday candles, and so on. These dolls are often made with wire frames and modern fabrics and finishings.

This delightful set of dolls made in Israel at the Studio of Frank Meisler have wooden bodies decorated with paper and fur. Clever and very modern looking, they represent traditional figures in Israeli society. The rabbi has *pais* or earlocks of hair, showing that he is Hasidic. His eyes, hands, shirt, and jacket lapels with buttons are pieces of paper glued in place on the wood. His head is made up of several different pieces of wood, one for his face, another for his nose, and two circles for his hat, which is decorated with fake fur. The rebbitzen, his wife, has fake-fur trim on her hat and coat collar. Her brooch and coat buttons are circles of metallic paper. The daughter attached to her mother is just two pieces of wood with glued-on eyes and collar. The rabbi's son, who also has earlocks, has a leather circle between the pieces of wood representing his face and hat. He carries a prayer book made of printed paper with a Star of David on it glued to the front of him.

The detailing on the dolls is carried out in the back. The rabbi's hand and his buttons, as well as the buttons on the back of the son's coat, are paper. A small strip of fake fur completes the rebbitzen's costume.

These 7″ dolls, made in Israel, have wooden bodies with wooden legs attached with elastic cord. They have wire arms, and their faces are of clay or similar molding material with painted features. On her head is a coiled sisal basket with lentils in it. Both figures have poorly finished knit-fabric clothing. She wears a purple veil on her head, and her orange caftan is decorated with cross-stitches of embroidery cotton. He wears a wide-belted brown caftan with a cream-colored kaffiyeh. (*Weiner Collection*)

Both these dolls of women carrying water jugs were made in Israel. The woman on the left bears the label "Pisantry-Jerusalem." She has a wire-frame body, her face is made of a claylike substance, and her water jug is wooden. Her caftan is a blue, red, and green cotton fabric, and she has a yellow head scarf. The 7½″ standing woman is similarly made. She wears a yellow blouse, over which is a yellow-and-brown length of woven fabric, called a barracan, wound around her body and drawn over her head and shoulders. Her hands are made from crepe paper. (*Weiner Collection*)

This 6″ girl in a swing was handmade in Israel. She has the typical wire-frame body covered with cloth. She has a painted clay face and brown yarn hair. She wears a white cotton shirt, blue pants, and a red head scarf. (*Weiner Collection*)

A wire-frame 8″ doll, handmade in Israel, representing an Israeli soldier, probably Moishe Dayan, since he is wearing an eye patch. The figure, with its painted face made of a claylike substance, leather hands, and gray cotton-fabric uniform, bears the label "Sabra." (*Weiner Collection*)

These 7″ dolls from Israel—representing kibbutzniks—have painted clay bodies and fabric clothing. He is dressed in coarse-weave green pants, a blue cotton striped shirt with a red jersey vest over it. She is wearing a long pink dress with yellow pants underneath. She holds a scythe in one hand and a bag with cut grass in the other. *(Hupp Collection)*

A pair of dolls from Israel bearing the label "Hand made by Sabra." Both figures have wire-frame bodies covered with fabric tubing. Their hands and feet are made from leather. Their heads, made of clay or similar molding material, have hand-painted features. They are dressed in cotton-fabric clothing. She wears a blue head scarf and pants and a white blouse. She has blond hair painted on her head and yellow yarn braids coming out from under her scarf. The knitting needles she holds in her hands are toothpicks. Dressed in a brown hat and pants and wearing a blue jacket and a white scarf, he plays on a wooden stick flute. *(Weiner Collection)*

Two wire-frame dolls with leather hands, made in Israel, both bear the label "Sabra." The woman, probably a rebbitzen, wears a black skirt and maroon blouse and carries a leather prayer book. She covers her head with a head scarf, meaning she is a Hasidic. Standing behind a wooden table with a white scarf and two white candles on it, the man wears a black satin robe and a fur hat and holds a wine cup in his hand. He is a Hasidic rabbi as indicated by his earlocks and is blessing the Sabbath candles. (*Weiner Collection*)

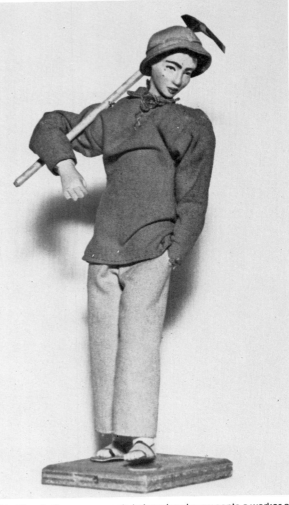

This 9" male figure was made in Israel and represents a worker on a kibbutz. The figure has a wire-frame body wrapped with fabric. His face, hands, and feet were made of clay or similar material and hand painted. He wears a blue cotton shirt and brown pants and carries a wooden hoe. (*Weiner Collection*)

Made in Israel, this 8" doll represents a Hasidic rabbi in black caftan and earlocks. Wearing the traditional black fur hat (shtreiml), he has a white prayer shawl (tallis) draped round his shoulders. He holds in his leather hands the sacred scrolls (Torah) covered in red with a gold Star of David. He has a typical wire-frame body and a wax face. Under his wooden base is the label "Sabra." (*Weiner Collection*)

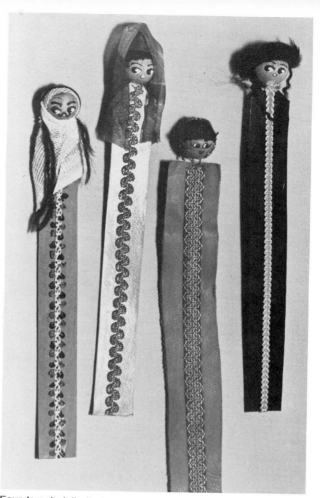

A 10″ female figure made in Israel. Standing behind a wooden table covered with a white piece of fabric, she is blessing the two Friday candles on the table. The woman has a wire-frame body with hands and face formed from a claylike substance. Her features are hand painted. She wears a brown taffeta blouse and black skirt. The shawl over her head is brown lace, and she wears a golden necklace. (*Weiner Collection*)

Four Israeli dolls that function as bookmarks. They are 9″-long strips of leather, each having a strip of decorative trim glued on it. The heads of the dolls are wooden beads with faces painted on them and yarn and fabric hats on them. (*Weiner Collection*)

The four heads of the Israeli bookmarks are representative of the different types of people in Israel. *From left to right*: The first one may be a shepherd. He wears a kaffiyeh, a cotton headcloth, with an agal holding it in place. This agal is often goat's hair, but on this doll it is represented by a piece of yarn. The second face is that of a Jewish rabbi with his fur cap and earlocks indicating he is Hasidic. The third head is that of a woman wearing the headgear of the Bethlehem costume, a tall bonnet called a *shatweh* with a veil called a *khalak*. Gold and silver coins are often sewn on this hat. The fourth face is that of a young girl, perhaps an American, who does not wear the typical Israeli headgear but instead has fluffy hair and a simple band as a head scarf.

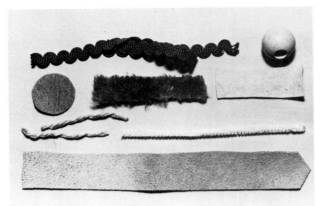

To make the Hasidic rabbi bookmark doll, you will need an 11″ piece of fabric trim, a 1″ wooden ball, a piece of fake fur about ¾″ × 3¼″, a 1¼″ circle of felt to match the fake fur, a piece of light brown felt 2½″ × ¾″, a 3″ piece of rug yarn split into two pieces so that each piece of the yarn looks like a long curl, a 6″ pipe cleaner, a strip of leather or suede 9″ × 1″ cut to a point at one end.

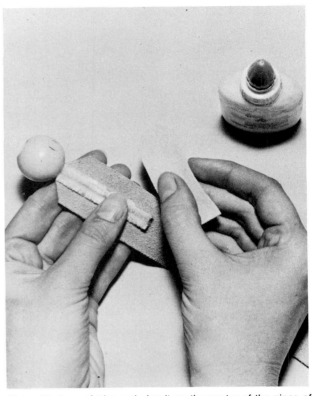

Cut a 9″ piece of trim and glue it up the center of the piece of leather. Paint a simple face on the wooden ball with acrylic paints. Bend the pipe cleaner in half and put glue on the top part and slip it into the wooden ball. Lay the ends of the pipe cleaner on the back of the suede strip and glue in place so that the wooden head is exactly at the top point of the suede. Trim the piece of light brown felt to match the pointed end of the leather. Glue it in place to hide the ends of the pipe cleaner.

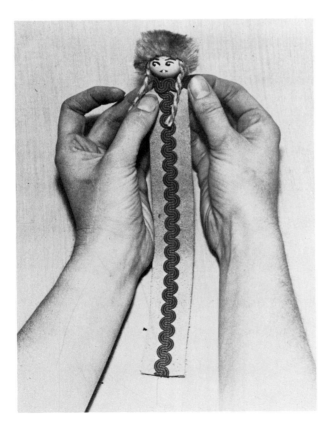

Glue the pieces of rug yarn at the sides of the head, the fake fur around the head, and the felt circle on top of the fur hat. Cut a piece of trim to go around the neck and just overlap at the back and glue it in place.

4
Dolls of Asia and the Pacific

In some countries of the world dolls are particularly cherished and dollmaking is an important craft. Japan is one of these countries, and is perhaps *the* foremost country in the number, variety, and beauty of its dolls. In fact, whole books have been written on just the handmade dolls of Japan, and even on one specific type of Japanese doll.

Other countries of Asia and the Pacific also have interesting dolls, some of them similar to the dolls of Japan. Both India and China have long traditions of dollmaking. The Immortals, made as paper dolls in China are world famous, as are the tilting dolls made there and in Japan.

DOLLS OF INDIA

India has a very strong tradition of dollmaking. Dolls have been made there for many centuries, and in fact, Sanskrit, the ancient language of that country, had a word for doll meaning "little daughter." The ancient Indian dolls were made of ivory, wool, buffalo horn, and wood.

In India dolls have long been connected with superstitious ritual. Primitive tribes of central India used to make human sacrifices during fertility rites, but later wooden or straw dolls were substituted. In order to get revenge, wooden figures were pierced with nails to bring injury to the enemy where the nails entered. Small hollow clay figures have been made in India by the thousands for the souls of Brahmans to reside in after death.

Young girls played with dolls up to the time of their marriage. The *Vatsyayana*, in fact, advises boys, if they wish to win the favor of maidens, to join them in playing with dolls.

Dolls were treated as members of the family, and in some homes they were even given a room of their own. Parties were given in honor of dolls and even public celebrations with feasting and processions were held for doll weddings.

Dolls are highly prized as gifts by the Hindus. When infant marriages were common among both the Hindus and Moslems, elaborately dressed dolls were among the presents given to a girl at marriage.

Dolls have been closely associated with various Indian festivals. During the Sassiva Festival, which lasts for nine days, girls throw clay dolls into the river and for three months go without dolls. These clay dolls are a substitute for human sacrifice. The river Ganges in India was offered human sacrifice just as the river Nile was in Egypt. The substitutes were at first life size, but gradually they became smaller so that eventually dolls were used.

At various other Indian festivals throughout the year toys and dolls are sometimes bought as presents for children. Dolls have a part in the annual ceremonies held for girls before they are ready for marriage, and dolls are customarily included in the bride's dowry.

Like China, India had doctor dolls. In both these countries the doctor was not allowed to touch the woman so these dolls were used to indicate where on the patient's body she was having pain. The doctor would see only the doll and not the woman herself and had to prescribe on this basis.

Today India exports beautiful handcrafted items to many countries, and dolls are among them. Traditional potters of Madhya Pradesh make beautiful authentically dressed dolls. Painted dolls of papier-mâché and of wood are made in southern India. Fabric stuffed or rag dolls are made all over India, often using fine hand-loomed and hand-silk-screened fabrics. Women wearing saris, dancing girls, and men in traditional attire are popular subjects for these costume dolls.

The potters of Bhopal in Madhya Pradesh make dolls 2′ to 4′ high and decorate them realistically with genuine clothes, hair, and other accessories. These two figures represent a Bhandara girl and a Bhilai woodcutter. He wears a white cotton turban and breechcloth, and she a skirt, blouse, and headdress of figured fabric. (*Photo courtesy of the Information Service of India*)

Wooden dolls, 7½″ tall, hand carved in India. They have dark painted faces and clothing painted in bright colors, such as red and gold on a white background. (*Hupp Collection*)

Spectacular and somewhat gaudy witch and wizard dolls from India, about 16″ tall. Their heads and arms are fabric stuffed, but below the waist they have a wooden base. Their faces are made from starched and folded fabric, and their features are painted. The costumes are a combination of beads, paper, and fabric. They have tinsel on their heads. Both wear seed bead earrings, necklaces, and bracelets; the female doll has beads on her nose. (*Photographed at the United Nations Gift Center*)

The stuffed dolls made in India often have pressed fabric faces, sometimes with embroidered features, but often with hand-painted ones. Usually care is lavished on dressing the dolls. Their clothing might be made from hand-loomed and hand-silk-screened fabrics and trimmed with braid and embroidery.

The female stuffed dolls made in India usually wear a *cholee*, a short cotton blouse, and a sari that is often embroidered or woven with metal thread and sometimes decorated with pieces of sparkling glass. These dolls often have bracelets, armlets, and anklets, and rings worn on their fingers and sometimes on their toes as well. They may also have gems on their forehead, nose, or ears.

If the male doll is dressed as a Hindu, he usually wears a *dhoti* of white cotton. It is wrapped around his hips and the ends are passed between the legs and tucked in at the waist. He might also wear a turban, which is a strip of fine cotton. In turbans worn by Hindus this strip measures from 10 to 50 yards long, and fabric is wound and wound around the head in various ways with one end hanging down the back.

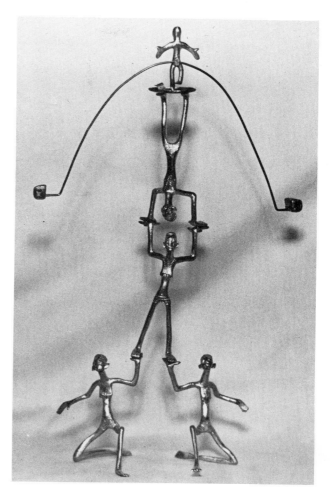

These brass figures from India are balancing dolls. The two lower figures stand on the base of the feet of the lowest two. The small figure at the top is attached to the balancing rod with weights at the ends. He is balanced with one foot touching the pan held up by the lower figures. (*Photographed at the United Nations Gift Center*)

India is known for her beautiful textiles, some of which are handloomed. These sumptuous fabrics are often used in saris and other pieces of clothing for the rag dolls made there. Here, in Kerala, India, a woman is being trained in weaving. (*Photo courtesy of World Neighbors*)

In India handwoven fabrics are used for many purposes, including dollmaking. These fabrics, woven by hand, may also be silkscreened by hand. These men in Kerala, India, are applying the second color to the design on some handwoven fabric. (*Photo courtesy of World Neighbors*)

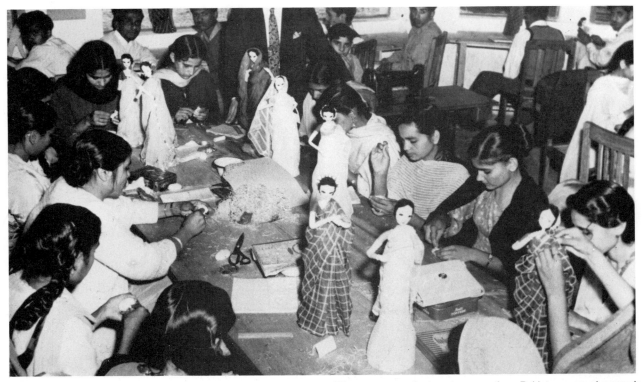

These women, displaced persons from Pakistan, were given work in a textile dollmaking center set up by the Ministry of Rehabilitation in a township near Delhi. (*Photo courtesy of the Information Service of India*)

Refugees from Pakistan learn to make dolls at the Uday Villa, a Women's Co-operative Industrial Home in India. The woman, shown here, is carefully hand painting the doll's eyes. Some of the graceful dolls made at the center can be seen in the background. (*Photo courtesy of the Information Service of India*)

This 10" wire-frame doll from India has a molded-felt face. He is elegantly garbed in a white turban decorated with sequins and a long elegant orange-satin coat trimmed with white felt. (*Hupp Collection*)

An 8" doll from India made of fabric and stuffed. The face is needle sculpted, and the features are embroidered. The doll is wearing a pink blouse, called a choli, and a white sari with a metallic ribbon edge. (The sari is the most important piece of clothing in the wardrobe of the Hindu woman or girl from the age of thirteen up and consists of a piece of cloth about 40 inches wide and six yards long, of cotton, silk, or both, and handloomed, embroidered, or printed. It is worn in folds as a skirt, tucked into a drawstring worn around the waist, then draped up the front and over the left shoulder. The end may be left hanging or it can be draped over the head as a hood.) (*MacNeer Collection*)

Three female figures from India, each standing about 12″ tall. All three have wire-frame bodies with pressed fabric faces. The one on the left wears a white outfit with silver trim and blue shoes. She bears the label "Parsi." The woman in the middle wears a green sari decorated with metallic trim. The woman on the right has a blue sari printed with a gold paisley design. (*Weiner Collection*)

A fabric stuffed doll, 11″ tall, has a pressed fabric face and painted features. She is from India and wears a purple sari drawn up over her head. She wears plastic bracelets and balances a bundle on her head. (*MacNeer Collection*)

Indian character dolls (*from left to right*): a drummer, sitar player, singer, and harmonium player. From Poona, India, they are home industry products by Sont Nathu. (*Photo courtesy of Information Service of India*)

These 7" dolls from India are made with firmly stuffed fabric bodies and pressed fabric faces. The figure on the left, playing a harmonium, a piano-like instrument, has a gold turban, white linen trousers, and a high-collared buttoned-up choga (the contemporary Indian man's outfit). The choga is blue, decorated with sequin buttons. The figure on the right, playing the sitar, a stringed instrument, wears a green velour cap, a white skirt, and a gold vest (*Weiner Collection*)

These dolls from India have the typical fabric stuffed bodies with pressed fabric faces and painted features. The maharaja wears a gold choga, or jacket, and carries a metal dagger. The woman is elegantly dressed with pearls on her ears, neck, wrists, and in her hair. She wears a full blue silk skirt and a peach blouse. (*Weiner Collection*)

This elaborately decorated 12" doll was made in India. She has a pressed fabric face and wire-frame body, and the gold satin skirt with her dress is adorned with pearls, sequins, seed beads, embroidery stitches, and sisha mirrorwork. (*Hulsizer Collection*)

69

A pair of 11″ dolls from India with bodies of white stuffed cotton fabric. Their faces are stitched in profile, and the features are embroidered in black thread. The top of the man's body is wrapped with metallic ribbon and his turban is created with strands of metallic cord. The bottom half of his costume is pink fabric decorated with metallic braid and ribbon. The woman wears a pink veil and a yellow dress elaborately decorated with metallic ribbon and braid. (*MacNeer Collection*)

A 10″ doll from India with a pressed fabric face and painted features has a body of a stiffly stuffed fabric. Her hair is of black mohair falling in a single braid down her back. She wears pearls on her headband and several bracelets on each arm. (*Author's Collection*)

This 7½″ doll, made in India from jute, has a skirt made with a paper-cone base. The jute is tied at the waist, wrists, neck, and so on, with red and black string, and her features are embroidered with the same material. (*Imported by SERRV, Author's Collection*)

These fabric stuffed dolls from India are dressed in typical fashion. She wears a sari and has bracelets and earrings. He is wearing a choga (jacket), a turban, and beads around his neck. He also has a sword attached to his choga. (*Photo courtesy of SERRV*)

These 5½″ dolls have carved and painted wooden heads and trunks. Their arms are stuffed fabric, and they have bands of metallic ribbon crisscrossing their chests. They dangle on long pieces of cord. (*Author's Collection*)

An 11″ female doll made in Pakistan from stuffed fabric with painted features. Her fingers are indicated by stitches, and her fingernails are painted red. Her black string hair is braided, and she wears a black veil with silver circles sewn on it. Her dress is a green taffeta with a silver bodice. At the cuffs and at the bottom edge of the skirt are strips of black trim with a gold flower design woven into it. She wears long black pants and has beaded jewelry. (*Weiner Collection*)

These rag dolls of a Hindu man and three women are each about 12″ tall and were made about 1875 by schoolgirls in Ceylon (now Sri Lanka) when it was a colony of England. Their bodies are fabric stuffed, and the noses and ears are separate pieces of fabric, which are stuffed and stitched onto the head. The eyes and mouths of the doll are embroidered. Their costumes reveal the Indian influence on style and in the use of beautiful silk and fine cotton, for example, for the draped sari on the woman in the center. The man wears a beret, pants, and a bolero. Both sexes wear jewelry including earrings, bracelets, and necklaces. When the Ceylonese go visiting, they commonly borrow jewelry not only from their families but also from friends. The *comboy,* part of the national dress of Ceylon, is worn by both males and females. The length and width of the cloth indicate a person's class. A man wears it wrapped around his body and gathered above the belt in front. The woman uses the comboy as a skirt, with pieces that come up over each shoulder. The woman's comboy is often two different pieces of fabric woven together, one plain white and one designed, as can be seen on the woman at the far right. (*From the Collection of the Forbes Library, Northampton, Mass.*)

piece for the arms. You will also need ¼ yard of yellow cotton fabric, small pieces of red, black, and rose colored fabric, cotton balls or fiber filling, and single-fold bias binding in gold, green, and purple, as well as matching thread, red and black thread or embroidery cotton for completing the features, and seed beads for the woman's earrings.

EAST INDIAN STICK DOLLS

In India dolls are made from sticks and dressed with brightly colored fabrics. These cloth-and-wood dolls are much loved by Hindu children.

To make your own East Indian stick dolls you will need wooden dowels that are ½″ in diameter. For each doll, cut two 10″ pieces for the body and one 5″

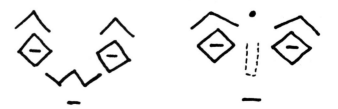

Transfer these features to your doll's face copying them freehand. If you prefer, you can trace them on scrap paper and transfer them using dressmaker's carbon.

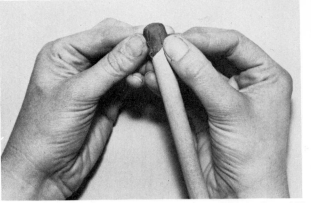

1

Cut four 1″ squares of red fabric. At one end of each of two 10″ dowels and at each end of the 5″ dowel, glue a small amount of cotton. Glue a square of red fabric over each padded area to make the hands and feet.

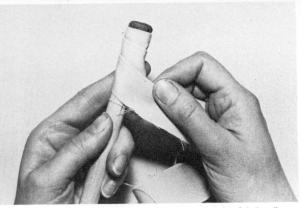

2

Cut 1″ wide strips of yellow fabric as long as the fabric allows. Lengthwise, turn under one side of each strip ¼″ and press with an iron if necessary to hold in place. Then start near the end of one of the 5″ dowels and wrap the fabric around the stick with the turned edge downward so that no raw edge can be seen. Use a bit of glue to hold the first winding in place. Keep winding the fabric around the stick covering the whole length.

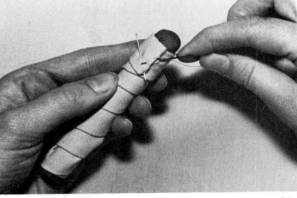

3

At the other end of the wooden dowel, tuck in the raw edges of the fabric so that no raw edge shows. Glue or stitch down the end of the wrapping fabric to hold it firmly in place. Repeat this process for each of the 10″ dowels, wrapping for about 7″ and finishing off the end of the fabric in any convenient way because it will not show.

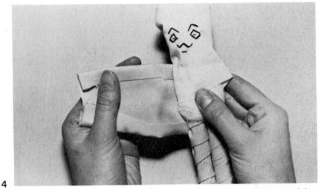

4

Hold the two 10″ dowels together and glue cotton balls around the upper 5″ of both sticks to make the trunk and the head of the doll. Cover the ends of the sticks also with padding. Cut a 6″ square of white fabric. Fold it in half, and in the middle of one half, copy the actual-size features onto it and embroider them. Put the white fabric over the ends of the sticks, placing the face in front and making it smooth. Fold and pleat the fullness in the back of the head and take a few stitches to hold the fabric in place. Next cut a piece of yellow fabric 3″ × 5½″. Fold it under both top and bottom and bring it around the doll fitting it over the padding and having it just under the chin. Turn under the end, taking a few stitches in back to hold it in place.

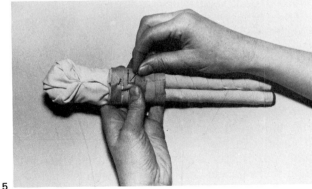

5

Cut five 5½″ pieces of bias tape. Starting just below the chin at the top of the piece of yellow fabric, bring the tape around the body of the doll to the back. Turn under the end and stitch in place. Continue to add pieces of bias binding to cover the body section.

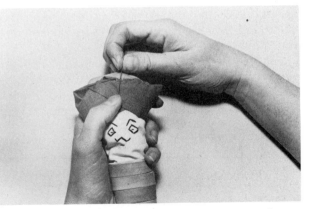

6

To make the man doll's turban, cut a 4″ × 11½″ piece of rose-colored fabric. Fold under the raw edge ¼″ along both long edges and iron down. Wrap the fabric around the doll's head, crossing the ends in the front and tucking them in so that the fabric looks like a turban. Take a few stitches to hold the turban in place. Sew the arms to the center back of the doll about 5½″ from the top of the head.

7

Make the woman doll in the same way you would make the man doll until you come to cutting the pieces of bias tape for the chest area. At this point, cut four pieces of bias binding 5½" long, two purple and one each in yellow and green. Sew together two pieces of purple bias binding for her bust. Stitch this in place on the yellow fabric front of the doll with extra padding under it. Put a piece of green binding above it and a piece of gold below it, stitching these in place. For her skirt, cut a piece of yellow fabric 7" × 20". Open a piece of green bias binding and sew it to the back of the skirt, stitching along the fold in the bias binding. Bring the binding to the front of the skirt and sew it in place so that it makes a finished edge on the bottom of the skirt. Fold the skirt in half and sew the back seam. Turn down the top of the skirt ¼" and run a gathering stitch at the waistline. Put the skirt on the doll, pull the gathering thread, and slip-stitch the skirt to the body. Sew the arms in place. For the hair, cut a 6" square of black fabric and fold it in half. Slip-stitch the folded edge over the forehead. Pleat the fabric to fit the head in back and tack in place. Sew small strings of beads to the sides of the head where the hair ends for earrings.

8

You can make the dolls larger by using thicker dowels and cutting them longer.

DOLLS OF CHINA

Dolls have been made for many centuries in China, and archeologists have discovered clay and wooden dolls in ancient graves. Before 550 B.C. in China, death sacrifice was practiced as it was in ancient Egypt. Finally the offering of living people was abolished and their places were taken by wooden dolls with movable limbs.

For hundreds of years images in vast numbers were made as grave offerings, which were exhibited before the funeral. The rich began to have dolls made of gold, silver, copper, and tin, and carried the practice to excess. The emperor, as a consequence, issued an edict limiting the number of grave offerings for each class of people, and only clay dolls were allowed. But this rule too was abused and finally everyone was limited to one clay doll.

For the richer people the clay grave dolls were made from finely granulated clay, baked and glazed. The poor had only rough unglazed dolls. Both types were formed using molds, and while both male and female dolls were made, many more women dolls have been found. Some of the earlier graves had hundreds of female figures, including dancing girls, harem women, and servants, often dressed in imaginative costumes and headdress. Besides men and women, there were also dolls representing divinities who were to protect the grave from demons. These guardian gods were usually grotesque.

The words "doll" and "idol" have the same root in the Chinese language, and for centuries the dolls were thought to have magical powers and many superstitions were connected with them. For example, to wreak vengeance on an enemy a straw doll was made with a head of cotton and dressed in blood-stained paper. The doll was pierced through with needles to the accompaniment of incantations. In Canton in the Temple of Unfortunate Women many paper figures of men once hung. They were hung there upside down by wives who wished their husbands would reform.

Simple plaited-straw dolls were used in China in prehistoric times for sacrifice. These were burned at funerals and placed in the grave. In ancient times every house had a small shrine of dolls, representing titular deities, which were carved from soapstone. The people brought presents to the dolls believing that by doing so they would gain health and fortune for themselves. Though the figures were originally looked upon as gods, after a while they became amulets and good-luck symbols.

In making dolls Chinese dollmakers have used ivory, soapstone, marble, metal, wood, silk, lacquerware, and other materials, along with their own ingenuity and gentle humor. A unique type of doll they made was a piano doll of sticks and paper that sat on a piano and reacted in a sort of dance to the vibrations when the piano was played.

Among the most famous Chinese dolls are the "doctor dolls," which were handed down from one generation to the next as family heirlooms. These dolls were made of ivory, carnelian, jade, or transparent rhino tusk. They were used by highborn Chinese ladies who had little contact with the world outside their own homes. Up to the time they were married the only men they saw were their fathers and brothers.

When a noblewoman married, her mother gave her a doll, a recumbent female figure. Whenever the woman became sick, she would have her maid take the doll to the doctor and point out exactly where she was having pain and explain the symptoms. The doctor, who was never allowed to personally examine the patient, prescribed treatment according to what the maid told him.

Made in China, this 2½" wire-frame doll is undated, but according to the appearance of her dress, it must have been made in the early 1900s. The doll has a fabric face with delicate features painted on it, and her feet and hands are fabric covered. She is wearing striped-black pants tied at the waist with a knotted belt. Her blouse is folded over in front like a kimono, and she wears a bandana of unfinished fabric on her head. On her back she carries a bundle of twigs tied with a string, which is brought around to the front of her body to hold the bundle in place. She stands on a slice of birchwood. (*Hercek Collection*)

A pair of 3" dolls from China made of silk and brocade. Their faces are circles of stuffed silk with embroidered features and hair. Their kimonos were made from brocade glued over a stiffening card. (*MacNeer Collection*)

Because of the superstitions connected with dolls, children in China never used them as playtoys until the last century. In recent times Chinese dollmakers have made dolls using a great variety of materials, including paper, clay, wax, wood, composition, and fabrics. Dolls made of fabric today are firmly stuffed, and are dressed very carefully, usually in traditional costumes with fine colorful materials and skillful stitching.

Dolls made in the far north of China are dressed in fur and skins, while those from the south wear silk, cotton, and other light fabrics. Rag dolls are made to represent figures from daily life—perhaps members of a family. There are also dolls representing figures from the Peking opera, with colorful costumes and highly stylized masks.

In China, as in Japan, tumbling Daruma dolls are made from papier-mâché and weighted so they cannot be knocked over. These dolls represent the ascetic priest Bodhidharma who came from Ceylon to China in 520 and founded Zen. They are made without legs, in imitation of this holy man, who is said to have lost his legs through meditating so many years. Children are supposed to learn endurance and patience from his example.

Dollmaking has provided work for the thousands of refugees who fled into Hong Kong when the Communists took over their country. Cottage industries were set up; that is, the people were given work to do at home. One product they made was the fabric stuffed doll, which not only gave the refugees work but also recorded the rural Chinese costume for posterity. Today handmade rag dolls are still being made in Hong Kong in a program sponsored by the Lutheran World Federation and are exported to the United States by SERRV, of the Church World Service.

To help support her family, this young dollmaker of Hong Kong, with the baby strapped on her back, works on a man doll to be sold through the Lutheran World Federation. In the United States these beautifully handcrafted dolls are sold through SERRV, a self-help program of Church World Service. (*Photo courtesy of Lutheran World Federation and SERRV*)

A beautifully detailed pair of 8″ dolls made in China. Both have wire-frame bodies covered with stuffed fabric. Their faces are pressed fabric with painted eyes and mouth. The woman carries a basket on her arm and wears a blue brocade waistcoat and black taffeta breeches. The man's brocade waistcoat is the traditional dark blue and his ankle-length silk robe is brown. The garments are fastened with loops and buttons and are in the subdued muted and artistic tones traditionally worn by well-dressed Chinese. (*Weiner Collection*)

Hong Kong is a densely populated city crowded with many poor refugees who fled mainland China when the Communists took over. In the early 1960s they were pouring into Hong Kong at the rate of one thousand a day, bringing only what they could carry. Many of these people could not find jobs so groups such as the Lutheran World Federation created self-help projects, whereby these people could work at home. One such project is the making of fabric stuffed dolls, which are sold through the Lutheran World Federation, and through SERRV, which is part of the Church World Service. Through this dollmaking project, a mother can stay home with her children while earning money making dolls. Shown here is a mother sewing a doll while her daughter holds two beautiful dolls already completed. (*Photo courtesy of Lutheran World Federation and SERRV*)

These dolls were bought in Kowloon, China, in the 1950s. They have painted white papier-mâché faces and painted carved wooden feet. Their bodies are of wood, and they are dressed in elaborate multicolored clothing stitched with designs and edged with fake fur. The man has black pants, the woman pink, and on a panel over the pants they each have an apron-like piece edged with fur with a dragon design sewn on it. (*Weiner Collection*)

The detailing on the costume of the man doll is marvelous. His black satin hat is completely and neatly lined with white fabric. His satin slippers, less than 2″ long, are neatly made with no waste of fabric.

Both the ankle-length robe and the sleeveless brocade jacket worn by the man doll are completely lined and are fastened with miniature buttons and loops made from tiny braid. Under the robe the doll has long pants, and each item of his attire is so well made that it can easily be taken off and put on again.

These 7″ Chinese actor dolls with white faces have wire-frame bodies mounted on wooden bases. They are gorgeously arrayed in tinsel, vivid silks, braid, wires covered with silver paper, bits of painted paper, sequins, cutout patterns from silver paper, and ribbons. (*Weiner Collection*)

A family of fabric stuffed dolls made in Hong Kong and sold through the Lutheran World Federation Project. The dolls, which range from 10″ to 6″, are beautifully detailed. They have stiffly stuffed fabric bodies, embroidered features, and yarn hair. Their clothing is made of brocades and other fabrics. (*Author's Collection*)

This 13″ Chinese boy doll was bought in 1928. He has a cotton stuffed body with embroidered features and black yarn hair. He is wearing blue fabric shoes, gray, black, and pink cotton pants and an orange silk top with a mandarin collar fastened with small buttons and loops made from braid. (*From the Collection of the Forbes Library, Northampton, Mass.*)

All that can be seen of these two sleeping dolls made in China are their heads, popping out of a 5½″ slipper. The slipper is made with a piece of cardboard covered in red flannel. The dolls' heads are fabric-covered balls, their features are painted, and their hair is black yarn. (*Author's Collection*)

THE IMMORTALS

A unique type of doll that has been made in China for hundreds of years is the set of dolls called the Eight Immortals and Lao-tzu, founder of Taoism. These classic dolls made from thinly padded silk are classified as paper dolls, but paper is only one of the materials used in making them. They have paper backing and paper feet and some paper accessories, but their garments are made from thinly padded fabric and their beards are real hair.

These dolls have been made in China for hundreds of years and currently are being made in Hong Kong in refugee projects and exported to the West. The quality of the sets has gradually declined over the years. Originally the faces were individually hand painted on padded silk, but today's versions are printed on paper. The paper accessories and feet were also once hand painted, but again today's are printed. The earliest sets were made with thickly padded silk sections for their costumes, but later sets had only slight padding, and today's have little or no padding at all. The fabrics used today are usually Oriental looking, but they are not the high-quality silk and brocade of the earliest sets.

The Immortals, as padded dolls, were used as decorations for the home, not as playtoys. Today they are available on eight-sided containers made with fabric-covered panels. Each panel has one of the Immortals on it, and when not in use the container folds flat. When it opens, an octagonal piece of cardboard sits in the bottom.

The baskets, which are sold in several sizes, are very inexpensive and therefore quickly made. The faces and accessories are all printed paper, and there is no padding on the fabric sections. The fabric is all inexpensive, not the rich silks and brocades used for the early dolls.

The Immortals, or Pa Hsien, represented in these padded fabric dolls, are often reproduced in Chinese art in other mediums including ivory, porcelain, painting, etc. They are legendary beings of the Taoist sect who are said to have lived at various times, and through their studies of nature's secrets attained immortality. For the Chinese they represent the eight human states of youth and age, wealth and poverty, aristocracy and plebeianism, masculinity and femininity.

Each of the Immortals has his or her own story or background, and sometimes sources of information differ as to the details. Also the names are often spelled differently in different sources. Each one of the Immortals is represented holding a specific item that has become his or her symbol. Sometimes nine rather than eight dolls form a set. Shou Lao, founder of Taoism, is the ninth figure. He is not actually one of the Immortals but is connected with them. He is called the "Star of Longevity" and he is usually represented as an elderly man with an enormous domed and bald head. The stories behind each of the Immortals are interesting:

Chung-Li Chuan is the chief of the Immortals and is said to have obtained the secrets of the elixir of life and the power of transmutation. He is usually represented as a fat man carrying a magical fan. One legend says that he met a young widow who was fanning the earth over her husband's grave because she had promised not to remarry until it was dry. She already had a new husband lined up, so Chung-Li Chuan dried the grave for her with his magical fan.

Lu Tung-pin is a scholar and recluse who is the patron of barbers and also of the sick. He wears a pleated cap and sometimes holds a Taoist fly brush in his right hand. His emblem, a sword, is usually slung across his back, with the handle just showing over his shoulder. Legend says that he was exposed to and overcame a series of ten temptations and was then invested with the sword of supernatural power, with which he traveled, slaying dragons and ridding the earth of various forms of evil for 400 years.

Lan Ts'ai-ho is sometimes shown as a young man and sometimes as a young woman. As a woman, she wears a blue gown with one foot bare. She continually chants doggerel verse denouncing the fleeting of life and its elusive pleasures. She is the patron of florists, and her emblem is the flower basket, which she always carries and from which she strews all good things.

Li T'ieh-kuai is usually pictured as a beggar carrying a gourd, standing on one leg and leaning on a crutch. He was not always a beggar, and he had the power to leave his body at will. One day he left his body in the care of a disciple who cremated it too early. Because his body was gone, Li T'ieh-kuai was forced to enter the body of a beggar who had just died and he has stayed there ever since.

Chang Kup-Hao is a bearded man carrying what looks like a golfer's bag with two clubs in it. His symbol is actually a drum made from bamboo sticks with two rods to beat it. Legend says that he had a very handy form of transportation in the form of a white mule. The mule was a paper one that was rolled up and hidden away in his bamboo tube. When he wished to go somewhere he could change the mule into a real one that could carry him for thousands of miles a day. Once he reached his destination he could change the real mule back into a paper one, roll him up, and insert him back into the tube.

Ts-ao Kuo-chiu is a bearded man, and his symbol, which he carries, is the group of tickets of admission to the Imperial Court. He wears a court headdress and official gown of a member of the court, but he is said to have given up courtly life and become a hermit. He is supposed to be worshipped by scholars and is the patron of theatrical performers.

Han Hsiang-Tzu, who is the patron of musicians, is represented carrying a flute. Legend says that he was able to spellbind animals with his music. Usually he is shown holding the flute, but sometimes he is

The immortals shown here are (*from left to right*) Han Hsiang-Tzu, holding the flute, Shou Lai, the Star of Longevity, Chung-Li Chuan holding a fan, and Ho Hsien-Ku holding a lotus blossom. This is part of a set that includes the Eight Immortals and their companion Shou Lai. It was brought by a missionary to the United States. On both the faces and the overlapping costume parts the padding is thick. The hand-painted faces are delicately done and the hair is human hair. This is a beautifully made set in the old tradition. (*Photo by Lorraine Wood*)

pictured playing it. Sometimes he also carries a broken branch of a peach tree. Legend says that he tried
to climb up the tree to immortality. Since he fell before
reaching this lofty goal, he carries the broken branch
as a symbol of his attempt.

Ho Hsien-Ku is a woman and carries as her symbol
a lotus blossom, which represents beauty and fertility. Legend says that she was forced by a wicked
stepmother into the hills. She ate powdered mother-
of-pearl, which produced immortality. She assists in
house management and is said to appear when
China is in great danger.

These 15″ padded fabric dolls represent the Immortals. Beautifully
made of exquisite satins and brocades, they are part of a set of
nine cardboard Chinese wall dolls. Each section of a doll is separately padded. The beards are of human hair, and the faces hand
painted delicately. The dolls were a gift in 1945 to the Forbes
Library, Northampton, Mass.

Here are three more members of the set of Immortals shown
on page 80. These dolls represent (*from left to right*) Lu Tung-Pin
with the sword on his back, Lan Ts'ai-ho holding a basket, and Li
T'ieh-kuai, the beggar. They are 10″ to 11″ tall, dressed in beautiful
brocades and silks. (*Photo by Lorraine Wood*)

This set of Immortals was mounted on an eight-sided fabric-covered container. Made in
Hong Kong, the set has no date. There is slight padding on the clothing and the faces
are hand painted, so the set is of fairly recent origin and is not the present-day type
made without any padding and with printed faces. The dolls, 6″ to 7″ tall, are (*from left to
right*) Ho Hsien-ku with the lotus, Chung-li Chu'an with the fan, Han Hsiang-tzu holding
the tickets. (*Photo by Lorraine Wood*)

This is a contemporary set of Immortals made in Hong Kong. The dolls are mounted on a basket, which is collapsed flat in the photo. The other four Immortals are behind those you see. The faces and accessories are all printed. The fabric-covered sections are not padded. The Immortals represented (*left to right*) are Ho Hsien-Ku with her lotus blossom, Li T'ieh-kuah, the beggar with his gourds, Chang Kup-hao with his drum, and Lan Ts'ai-ho with a basket. (*Author's Collection*)

The remaining Immortals in the set on the back of the basket shown above are Lu Tung-pin with his pleated cap and Taoist fly brush, Chung Li Chuan with his fan, Han Hsiang-Tzu with his flute, and Ts'ao Kuo-Chiu with his tickets and court headdress. (*Author's Collection*)

For each section that is to be padded and covered with fabric, cut a backing of lightweight cardboard and a piece of fabric about ⅜" larger all around. Put some glue on the cardboard and put a small amount of cotton on the glue.

Put glue around the edge of the back of the cardboard. Lay the cardboard at the center of the wrong side of the fabric. Bring the edges of the fabric around the cardboard and make small folds in the fabric as you press it against the cardboard. Check to be sure the fabric is smooth on the right side. Repeat for each section that is to be covered with fabric.

CHINESE SATIN CLINGING DOLLS

China has for a long time produced a type of satin pincushion with a row of small dolls clinging all around the edge. The dolls on these pincushions may be only an inch tall. In Hong Kong women still make pincushions as a mean of supplementing their meager incomes. They also make such items as round jewelry containers, which also have clinging dolls on them.

To make your own clinging dolls, you will need some white fabric for the heads and pieces of solid-color satin or similar material in different colors for the bodies (you can use very wide satin ribbon if this is available), a small amount of any kind of stuffing, and a needle and thread. To make a pincushion for these dolls you will need fabric and stuffing, too. The dolls can be any size you wish. Control the size by the dimensions of the square of fabric you start with.

Use this pattern to make your own Immortal. Complete the face as a painting on paper or instead make a padded fabric face and paint the features on it. For each of the body sections, continue the outline as shown by the dotted line. Cut a copy of each pattern piece from lightweight cardboard and proceed as shown in the how-to photos. For the accessories, copy each section on paper and paint.

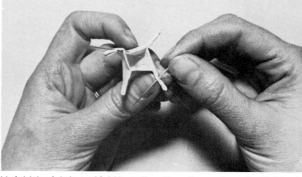

Cut a square of fabric. Fold back the edges about ¼″ all around and press with an iron so that the fabric stays in place. Fold the fabric in half on one diagonal and do an overcast stitch from the farthest point in toward the center stitching about halfway toward the center from each side. **1**

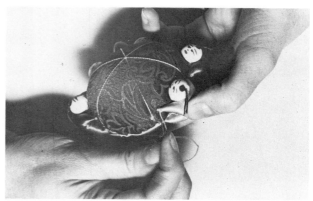

Unfold the fabric and fold in on the other diagonal, again stitching in toward the center. Fill the body with stuffing, pushing it out into the points of fabric. **2**

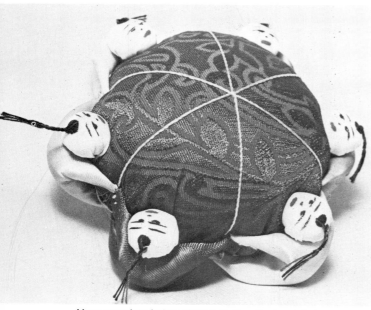

Make a small ball of stuffing and put a circle of white satin over it. Wrap a piece of thread around the fabric under the ball of stuffing. Draw on the features with marking pen. For the hair, make a circle above the features. Make a stitching into it with several pieces of embroidery cotton or heavy thread. Braid these, or if you prefer, wrap them with another piece of thread. Hold the head in place against the body and take several stitches to secure it there. **3**

Secure the doll in place by sewing the arms and legs to your pincushion or whatever you are going to attach it to. **4**

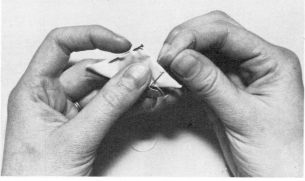

Your completed pincushion with the clinging dolls is a conversation piece and a useful sewing accessory. **5**

The dolls can also be attached to other items. This brocade covered container made in China opens at the top and has a space inside for storing jewelry or whatever. (*Author's Collection*)

DOLLS OF SOUTHEAST ASIA

Korean dollmakers use a variety of materials to make dolls, including wood, paper, and fabric. They make wire-frame dolls similar to the display dolls made in Japan. These are often figures of women dressed in kimonos made of brocade and similar fabrics. They also make stuffed fabric dolls similar to those made in China.

Korean dollmakers also make paper dolls. Some of these are just flat figures, while others are padded dolls made in a similar fashion to the figures of the Immortals made in China.

The dolls of Thailand (Siam) are often exceptionally delicate and made from baked clay and dressed with real cloth or clothing that is painted on. Silver wire is used for the jewelry. Dolls of wood, fabric, and paper are also made in Thailand.

Though a flood of cheap manufactured goods from the more industrialized nations has had a bad effect on Thai handcrafts, some crafts are still practiced, including silk weaving, making lacquerware, wood

A 4″ doll bought in Korea in 1963. This figure was carved from wood and glued on a slice of wood. His features and clothing were painted on. Holes were drilled at his armpits, and a straw carrier was added to his back. He has a white shirt and pants, a maroon vest, and a painted-on moneybag dangling from his waist. (*Weiner Collection*)

This set of carved wooden dolls was made in Korea. The figures are a musical group, with some in painted-on silk coats fastened with one-loop bowknots. The man on the far right wears a traditional Korean black horsehair hat to protect his topknot. It was the custom of married men to dress this way. Bachelors wore their hair in pigtails and went hatless. (*Weiner Collection*)

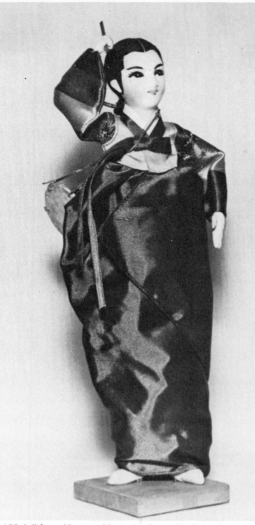

A 10" doll from Korea with a wire-frame body and a pressed fabric face. Her kimono is purple. (*Weiner Collection*)

This is the back of the doll shown in the photo at left. On her back she carries what is probably a drum.

carving, and dollmaking. Villages specialize in different crafts. Sometimes these crafts are combined, as, for example, dollmaking and silk weaving, in the creation of a beautiful handmade doll wearing a costume of beautiful Thai silk.

Dolls from Thailand often are dressed in the tradition of the old Siamese royalty whose clothing and stories are perpetuated in the Thai theatre today, for example, in a ballet of Thailand's national epic, *Ramaken*, which tells the story of the folk hero Ramaken, who rescues his abducted wife with the aid of monkey warriors.

The players in this theatre act on an unadorned stage and use the words of old Siamese dramas to enchant listeners, but the simplicity stops there. Their costumes are magnificent. Exaggerating the splendor of dress of ancient Siamese royalty, they are topped off with carved and brightly painted demon masks. Dolls from Thailand often have these de-

These 14" fabric stuffed dolls are from Korea. They have flat satin faces with painted features and human hair on their heads. The man's clothing is all white silk. The woman has braided hair and wears a white brocade dress, a green and pink shawl, and a blue brocade fur-edged vest. The baby in the woman's arms, made the same way as its parents, is dressed in a green, red, and blue outfit. (*MacNeer Collection*)

mon masks, or they may be figures of dancers without masks but wearing elaborate, pagoda-like headdresses of gilt-covered metal—decorated with sparkling stones—whose shapes suggest the spires of a Buddhist shrine.

A 9″ doll from Korea with a wire-frame body. The young woman's face was made with pressed fabric and painted. She wears a white brocade jacket trimmed with maroon brocade, decorated with metallic gold rickrack and fastened with a wide belt. Her pants are of blue brocade, and her boots of fabric over a paper base. She wears a blue-silk crown decorated with gold rickrack. (*Weiner Collection*)

A very appealing 9″ female doll made in Korea. She has a wire-frame body with a painted, pressed fabric face made from nylon stocking material. Atop her head is a metal pan that contains a piece of fabric and a bunch of plastic bananas. The woman carries another bunch of bananas in the very long fingers of her left hand. (*Weiner Collection*)

A 4″ handcrafted Korean wooden doll painted with flat paints, except for the hat which is a shiny black. The doll wears a blue overcoat, and at the chest an embroidered plastron with a stork design on it. (*Author's Collection*)

"물깃는녀자" Means of bearing. "지게군"

Padded fabric dolls from Po-Hang, Korea, illustrating ways of carrying bundles. The face on each doll is delicately hand painted on silk. (*Wood Collection*)

"신랑" New Married. "신부"

The background of these padded Korean figures was printed in black. The scene was then hand painted in colors. The woman's hat and the doves held by the man are separate pieces of hand-painted paper. (*Wood Collection*)

"소녀" Girl. "소년" Boy.

Padded dolls made in Po-Hang, Korea, at the Holy Mother's Social Charity Work Catholic Orphanage. These dolls are about 4″ tall, and each section of them has a cardboard base with some padding. Over the padding, silk and brocade are stretched. (*Wood Collection*)

Mother and baby. "아기어머니" Farmer. "농부"

The farmer, his wife, and child are portrayed in this fourth set of padded Korean dolls. The farm animals in the background are painted on.

These 6" paper dolls were handmade in Korea before 1920. Brought to the United States by a missionary in 1920, the bodies are made from heavy card, and the clothes of each figure are separate pieces of colored and printed paper glued in place. The faces are drawn in black ink. The whole family is represented, with the father and mother in the center, the grandparents to the right, and the children to the left. (*Wood Collection*)

A back view of the Korean family showing that they are two-sided dolls. The backs of each piece of clothing are fully delineated.

This 9" male doll from Thailand was made with stuffed stocking-fabric arms and legs set in a stylized gesture. The face is hand painted over the stuffed stocking fabric. The doll is dressed in the gorgeous costume of the Siamese dancer. He wears a panung, a skirt worn by both men and women. (This article of clothing is a piece of fabric about a yard wide and three yards long, which is wrapped around the figure and laid into groups of pleats held securely in place by a belt.) The panung on this doll is made of a silver-and-blue fabric and decorated with rhinestones and seed beads. The pagoda-like metal headdress, covered with gilt and sparkling stones, suggests the spires of a Buddhist shrine. (*Weiner Collection*)

This 10" palace guard with his frightening mask was made in Thailand. He has pointed epaulets, and his mask is red with green and orange designs painted on it. His clothing is made from fabrics woven with metallic threads. The top is green with a silver design, and his panung (skirt) is red and green with a gold design. (*Weiner Collection*)

The label on this 11″ male doll says "Bangkok Doll, Handmade in Thailand." He has a hand-painted, pressed-fabric face and wears golden slippers. He has golden, painted epaulets at the shoulders topped off with bits of yarn. His shirt and panung are green, and the elegant red sashes hanging down in the front are decorated with many seed beads, rhinestones, and tube beads. (*Weiner Collection*)

An 8″ beautifully dressed female doll from Thailand. She wears a red cape, a green skirt, and a flame-shaped headdress decorated with rhinestones and artificial flowers. (*Weiner Collection*)

A 6″ demon-masked doll from Thailand dressed in white and wearing a sparkling outfit. (*Weiner Collection*)

From Nepal, these 6″ dolls have carved wooden bodies with fabric clothing. They both carry wooden hammers, each made from separate pieces of wood and inserted into a hole in the wooden hand. On his back he has a wooden pack and she a wooden jug, both attached by strings to the dolls. He is wearing a gray top and pants, a black-and-white dotted hat, and a white cummerbund around his waist. She has a red-dotted blouse, black-dotted skirt, and a wide cummerbund at her waist. Both have painted black hair and features, and each has a red dot at the middle of the forehead. She has wooden earrings painted gold. (*Weiner Collection*)

This beautiful stuffed doll made in Thailand is wearing a costume of fine-quality Thai silk. After World War II an American, Jim Thompson, who had been stationed in Thailand during the war, became interested in and helped revive Thai silkweaving on hand-made looms, then a dying craft. He developed a lucrative silk industry by working with household weavers, importing reliable dyes for them, and encouraging them to produce good-quality silk. He developed an export market for the beautiful silks woven with the traditional Thai motifs. (*Urdang Collection*)

Made in Thailand, these 4½″ dolls represent peasants going out to the fields, the man with a rake slung over his shoulder and the woman with a scythe in her hand. They are made of wood, except for their arms, which have folded fabric bases. Their clothes are cotton fabric unfinished at the edges and glued in place. Their shirts are blue; the woman's skirt is a striped fabric. Their features are drawn in pencil, and his hat and her head scarf are both made with glue-impregnated fabric. (*Imported by SERRV, Author's Collection*)

These 5″ wooden dolls were made in Burma. The one in the middle has separate legs nailed in place. The two dolls on the sides have heads and bodies carved from one piece of wood and separate arms and faces (or heads) nailed in place. They are all painted white and have hand-painted features and clothing predominantly in pink. (*Author's Collection*)

JAPANESE DOLLS AND DOLLMAKING

Some countries have worldwide reputations for dollmaking, and Japan is certainly one of them. The skill of the Japanese dollmakers is legendary. The dolls of this country are the products of a long tradition. Some are simple, whimsical folk dolls, and others are elegant, exquisite works of art, made with the fine craftsmanship for which Japan is famous.

Dolls reflect various aspects of Japanese culture, particularly the Japanese awareness of the beautiful. The dolls the Japanese create are so beautiful and well made that many are put under glass and kept as conversation pieces.

Japan is one of the few countries where dolls are an important part of the cultural life, and doll collections are recognized as among the nation's treasured possessions. Dolls are seen as an exquisite reflection of life, both past and present. The Japanese people appreciate them because of the craftsmanship with which they are made and the beauty of imagination, line, and color they show.

In Japanese the word for doll is *ningyo,* which is composed of two Chinese ideographs meaning "human" and "form." Dolls have had a long history in Japan. The most primitive ones were those made of shaved willow sticks that had string or shavings for hair.

Near the end of the twelfth century sculptors began making dolls in Japan. These early dolls, known as *sago ningyo,* were carved out of wood and decorated with gold foil and pigment. Japanese mothers in medieval times were very happy to receive a gift of a doll, because they believed that as long as the doll was safe and cared for, their own child would be happy.

The Japanese people made clay dolls as early as the seventeenth century and they are still made today as folk art. During the Edo period from 1615 to 1867 a popular type of doll was the *gosha ningyo,* the court or palace doll.

In the eighteenth century primitive dolls made of ivory were placed near a newborn baby's head to grant him good health and protection. Today dolls are still given to a newborn child with the idea of bringing good luck. They are also given as elegant wedding presents.

Today dolls continue to be made in great numbers in Japan and, in fact, after the United States, Japan is the largest producer of toys, and accounts for about one third of the world's production. About 50 percent of this production is carried out in very small workshops.

Dolls are sold throughout Japan, not only in souvenir stores and tourist resorts but also in toy stores, department stores, and special doll stores in cities. In small shops in villages all over Japan simple rural dolls can be found. In fact, Japan is one of the few countries that has such a rich variety of local toys.

Regional dolls are especially interesting because they carry the flavor and characteristics of each district. A doll called a *hime darma,* for example, has the face of a girl and is the souvenir of the Dago Spar in Shikoku, one of the oldest hot spring resorts in Japan.

Many different techniques are used in the production of dolls in Japan, and some are even made with a single chisel cut. The *lhobori* doll is made from Japanese cypress boldly cut with a slant knife and left unfinished. There are also other wooden dolls like the *kokeshi,* which are turned and painted.

Besides creating wooden dolls, Japanese dollmakers also make dolls of paper, terra cotta, bam-

A circular-woven basket, such as those above, is called an *izumeko* in Japanese, and a doll of this type is an *izumek-ningyo.* Such baskets were used in the past in Japan in the Yamagat Prefecture, an area of Japan with a cold climate. Originally the baskets were used to store cooked rice to keep it warm. Gradually the baskets came to be used for babies. The child, warmly wrapped in quilts, was put in the basket while his parents worked nearby. At first the izumeko dolls were crude little toys made for the family's enjoyment. They were made from the hollowed-out half of an acorn and scraps of leftover fabric. Today more sophisticated versions, such as the ones shown here, are found in department stores in Japan. The larger doll has a basket about 4″ in diameter and the small doll's basket is 3″. The heads are painted clay over papier-mâché, and the clothes and blankets are taffeta and brocade. *(Hupp Collection)*

From Japan, a 6½″ folk doll of handcarved wood. The hat is made of grass with a piece of fabric hanging down in the back. The Japanese tradition of carving such toys as this from wood goes back about a thousand years. Wood carving was a sideline of the farmers in the Sasano district during the winter when they could not work in the fields. These craftsmen used several kinds of sharp knives to whittle and carve walnut and other woods. The most popular subject for such carvings is the rooster. (*Photographed at the United Nations Gift Center.*)

Nested dolls made in Japan and ranging in size from 1¾″ to ⅜″. Even the smallest one opens. They are of lacquered natural wood with painted faces and a few lines to indicate clothing. (*Hupp Collection*)

A set of quints made in Japan. The dolls are sitting on a wooden base and are made from wood. Their heads are wooden balls with painted features, their legs are pieces of turned wood, and their bodies are wooden tubes covered with fabric. (*Hupp Collection*)

boo, stone, cloth, and so on. Clay dolls are sometimes turned out as a sideline in areas where pottery or tilemaking is a major industry, especially in the Fushimi district of Kyoto.

Though dolls are made everywhere in Japan, the center of dollmaking is Kyoto, which was the cultural center of the country from the eighth to the sixteenth century. A traditional doll made there is the *hakata*, an earthen doll.

Tokyo is another center of dollmaking. On the famous Ningyo Cho, or doll street, in Tokyo are located more than 300 shops that sell not only dolls but also doll clothing and other accessories. Certain Japanese cities are known for making special types of dolls. Tokyo, for example, makes the festival dolls. The city of Nara makes the *otsu* ornamental dolls and the *satsuma* thread dolls. Kyoto is famous for the goshi ningyo made of wood pulp and glue and covered with oyster shell powder.

Weavers in Kyoto and Tokyo specialize in making cloth for dolls. They make materials that are both beautiful in design and high in quality.

One special type of Japanese doll is the *gosho* doll, which is made of wood pulp and glue. Boys from the ages of one to five are used as models for these dolls. They are made with a 1:2 head-to-body proportion, and have white shiny skin. The white is *gofun*, a white face paint made from oyster shells, which is dissolved in glue. This solution is painted onto the dolls. Since up to twenty coats are given to the doll, making the dolls requires patience.

Another type of Japanese doll is the *yamato ningyo*, which is similar to the Western type of jointed doll as far as the separate body, head, and limbs are concerned. First, a master of the doll is carved from wood. Molds are then made from hardened resin. These molds can be used to produce hollow copies pressed out of composition, which is made of kiri wood sawdust and wheat starch.

The Oriental look of these dolls lies in the finishing process. Dark eyes are put into the eyesockets and the thick coating of gofun is applied and allowed to dry. The whole surface of the doll is then smoothed and polished. The second coating of gofun is applied, and then a final coating of fixative.

In Japan dolls are made for different and specific purposes. At one time the difference between dolls was very definite. Some were made strictly for display and some for play, but now the dividing line is less exact.

One type of decorative doll is the *sakura-ningyo,* which translates literally to "cherry doll." This type of

doll is regarded as an ornamental conversation piece and in English is usually called a "shelf doll" because it is often seen on display in Japanese homes in an alcove on a shelf in the living room. The dolls might represent characters from the Kabuki plays, often

The gracefulness of the Japanese woman in her traditional kimono is obvious in these dolls made of heavy metal. They are wearing the style of hat worn by fisherwomen. (*Author's Collection*)

These Japanese dolls of a 10″ fisherman and his wife, probably from the northern island of Hokkaido, have bodies of a poured plaster substance and painted. They are wearing fabric clothing. He has a straw hat, and around his shoulders is a raincoat made from dried grass. When it is not raining, the coat can be slipped down and worn around the waist. (*MacNeer Collection*)

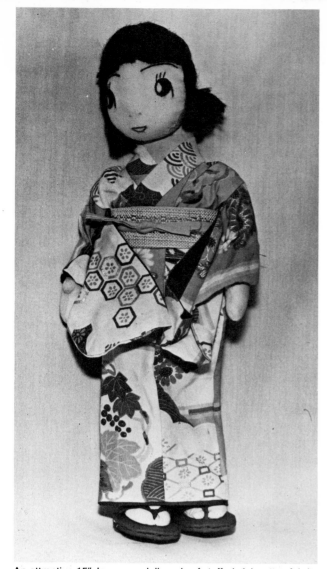

warriors or a warrior's handmaiden. They are usually made with a wire or wooden frame.

The modern artistic display type of Japanese dolls has been made since about 1927. These dolls are known for their beautiful clothing and elegant poses. They have attractive faces generally with pale yellow or pure white skin, slanting eyes with sweeping eyelashes and eyebrows made with a swift brushstroke. Some have heads made of plaster and others have heads of papier-mâché or stiffened fabric. They have black hair, which for the women dolls is usually elaborately dressed in the traditional manner. Their bodies, however, may be no more than just a slight framework of wood or wire over which the rich costumes are draped. The doll might also have a fan, parasol, or artificial flowers.

An attractive 15″ Japanese doll made of stuffed pink cotton fabric. She has embroidered features and black yarn hair. She is wearing a silk kimono printed with a bright design. She wears an obi (wide belt), and on her feet are zoris made with fabric-covered cardboard. She wears tabis (white socks) which have toe indentations so the wearer can put on her zoris. (*Weiner Collection*)

A *gosho* doll modeled on a young child with the typical 1:2 head-to-body proportion.

A beautifully made doll from Japan dressed in fabulous brocade clothing. Dressed for one of the many holidays for which the Japanese have special dolls, she is holding a drum and wearing an elaborate headdress. (*Photographed at the United Nations Gift Center*)

These 6″ Japanese dolls have faces made with a papier-mâché base with white clay over it. They have vinyl hair. The dancing girl on the left is dressed in a red silk kimono with a floral design and is carrying bells on cords. The one on the right wears a blue silk kimono and an obi woven from rich metallic thread. She is holding what appears to be a kite. (*MacNeer Collection*)

A 6″ doll made in Kyoto, the dollmaking center of Japan where making dolls is an art. The craftsmen are supported by the government and are considered a national treasure. They have apprentices who are taught the art of making dolls, such as this one. (*Hulsizer Collection*)

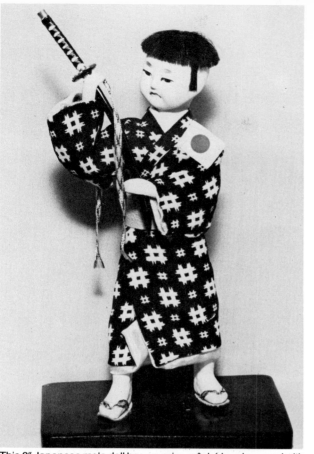

This 8″ Japanese male doll has a papier-mâché head covered with fine clay. Under his silk kimono he has a wire-frame body covered with paper. He has a sword in one hand and very patriotically carries a flag in the other. This boy is probably training to be a samurai warrior. The doll would probably be a gift to a young boy who wanted to grow up to be as brave as a samurai. (*Hupp Collection*)

Most of the display dolls, both male and female, wear a kimono, a piece of clothing that was developed from the ancient Chinese court of the P'ang period from 618 to 907. The man usually wears a dark, ankle-length kimono of blue, gray, or black. The sleeves are usually shorter than those worn by the woman. The man wears a wide sash around his waist, wound two or three times and tied in back. This is usually black or gray. Over the kimono he wears a black silk, wide-sleeved, knee-length coat called a *haori*. This is similar to a kimono but is fastened with two cords tied at the waist and is not lapped over.

On his haori the family crest may be stenciled or embroidered at the center back, at the elbows of the sleeve, and on the sides of the front at the level of the chest. On formal occasions he wears the *hakama*, very full silk trousers.

Both men and women wear tabi, white stockings that reach only above the ankle. These have a division in the front that separates the big toes from the other toes. This separation is made to make room for the cords of the zoris—sandals that pass between the first and second toes.

The woman's kimono touches or just clears the floor and is usually in a subdued and soft color. Only the geishas and actresses wear kimonos in bright garish colors. The married woman generally wears a kimono that is a quiet gray, brown, or blue, though its lining may be brilliantly colored. She also has an obi around her waist made of brocade, often in brighter colors than the kimono. It may be decorated with embroidered flowers or other graceful designs. It might be 4 to 6 yards in length and also 12″ to 15″ wide.

The Japanese woman also wears a haori, a knee-length coat similar to that worn by the man. If worn by a younger woman, it would be brightly colored. The Japanese woman usually carries a fan which, when not in use, is tucked into the folds of her obi.

Though many Japanese people have put aside

A 12″ Japanese male doll with a pressed-fabric face, painted features, and a wire-frame stuffed body. The top part of his kimono is gray silk, and the bottom is a gold-and-white brocade. His feet are in tabis, with the separation between the first and second toes so that he can wear zoris. His hair is cut in the style of the samurai and their trainees. Even though he is carrying a sword, he is not currently warring since he is not dressed as a warrior. (*Weiner Collection*)

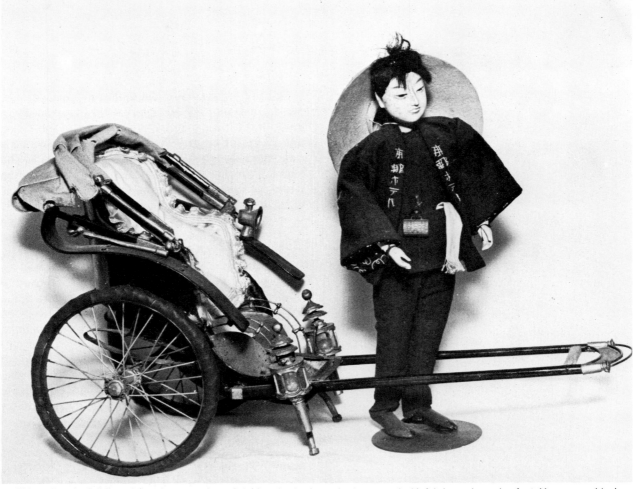

This 11" male doll from Japan has a papier-mâché head, wire-frame body covered with fabric, and wooden feet. He wears a black cotton outfit with Japanese words embroidered on his jacket. His "straw" hat is made of cardboard. A towel sticking out of his pocket is probably used for wiping up his rickshaw between passengers. The little lights at the sides of the rickshaw are powered with a battery hidden under the seat of the rickshaw. (*Hupp Collection*)

this traditional dress in favor of Western clothing, in parts of Japan the kimono, obi, and other such articles of dress are still worn. For those who have put aside this traditional clothing, the beautiful display dolls are constant reminders of their past.

One problem Japanese dollmakers have in making their dolls in the authentic costumes described above arises from the fact that the true Japanese costume with proper underclothing has many layers. Reproduced in miniature on dolls, these layers are cumbersome, and the effect is hardly like the graceful full-size costumes that are supposed to be represented.

Of course the smaller the doll the bigger the problem. To solve the problem dollmakers have reduced the doll's body to little more than a framework.

The frame of a costume doll may be chiseled wood or made from a mixture of sawdust and glue. Selecting the wood carefully is very important, because if it is of poor quality the completed doll might crack or lose its shape. The wood then is very fine-grained and it must be completely dry. To be sure that it is

naturally dried to the very center, it is cut and sometimes stored for twenty years before being used.

Another way dollmakers use to avoid the cumbersomeness of the clothing is to dress the dolls in outer clothing and attach this to incomplete undergarments. On some dolls this is carried out to such an extreme that they look emaciated. Some have become stick dolls, their bodies just a stick with a ball of padded silk for the head. The costume gracefully draped on a slender base can produce a finished doll that is quite charming.

Sometimes it takes twenty to thirty different steps to make a display doll. The Japanese feel that the most important step in making a doll is painting the eyes. They have a special word for this process, *kai-gen*. This word means not only painting or shaping the eyes but also giving the doll a soul and heart. This step decides how graceful the doll will be and the type of personality it will have. The expression of the eyes of a human being tells a lot about him or her. A healthy person will have sparkling eyes, while someone who is ill or low in spirits will show it in his or her

A 10″ Japanese doll with a papier-mâché head and hands and wearing a blue kimono. The Japanese figure wears two kimonos, both in dark muted colors. His inner kimono, of taffeta, can be seen at the neckline. The outer kimono is of silk with a feather design printed on it. The doll has a wooden body, with zoris on his feet. (*Hupp Collection*)

housewives, and career women but also men enjoy it as a relaxing hobby. Classes are held to teach people to make dolls, and much of the dollmaking goes on at home also. There are also private schools that teach such subjects as the tea ceremony, flower arranging, dollmaking, and dressmaking, and amateur dollmakers like to attend these schools in their spare time.

In 1952 the Tokyo dollmaking school was established. The school has taught many students by mail, not only from Japan but from other Asian countries as well as North America and Europe. The doll schools supply kits that contain all the materials needed for making a Japanese doll. Each kit includes a ready-made mask, with a face that was made by pressing a mixture of paper and paste into a mold covered with georgette crepe. Also included in the kit are the doll's cotton stuffed body, arms, and legs. Wires project from the arms and legs so that these sections can be inserted into the body. Special ornamental hairpins, and strings for tying and adorning the hair are also included, as well as other necessary accessories.

Doll artists of Japan create dolls of exceptional beauty and originality. Sometimes they make them to represent famous Japanese heroines in classical poses. These dolls made by traditional craftsmanship have an exquisiteness which makes them worthy of the name fine art. Authoritative art organizations have exhibitions of the work of these artists, and an entire museum in Tokyo is devoted to dolls.

Also, doll collecting by amateurs is popular, as old Japanese dolls are eagerly sought after. The Japanese people realize that their old period dolls are a fine record of costume and of the facial expressions and poses of their great actors.

To the Japanese people, although dolls are used as playthings, they have long symbolized friendship and goodwill among friends. The gift of a doll from one person to another as well as from one country to another has been a Japanese custom for many generations.

To promote international understanding, a doll mission was sent from the United States to Japan in the spring of 1927 by the Committee of World Friendship Among Children. In honor of the Japanese doll festival, 10,000 dolls were sent with a letter of friendship, and these dolls were distributed to schools throughout Japan. To promote international goodwill and return the courtesy, a society was formed in Japan. Money was raised by Japanese schoolchildren, and fifty dolls were sent to the United States.

eyes, which have lost their liveliness. Therefore drawing dolls' eyes to obtain that special sparkle is the process on which the Japanese dollmaker spends his most concentrated effort.

Dollmaking, as it is practiced by both professionals and amateurs, is considered one of the fine arts in Japan. It is a national hobby and a popular pastime among the Japanese today. Not only schoolgirls,

KAMI NINGYO

Japan is famous for her fine papers and for the many artistic uses to which her craftsmen have put these papers. Naturally this material came into use in dollmaking.

The paper dolls of Japan have basically developed in two different ways: first, as part of purification rituals and other superstitious practices, and second, as playthings for girls used by them to act out the rituals of keeping a house and entertaining guests.

In the Kyoto district of Japan, *katashiro* dolls have been made since the year 900 or even before. These little paper figures, which measure about 3″ x 5½″, have been used in the purification or cleansing ceremonies. The Shinto believer went twice a year to his shrine and for a yen bought a katashiro. On this paper doll he wrote his name, the year and the month of his birth, and his sex. He then breathed on the doll and rubbed it over his body, thereby transferring any diseases or impurities he might have to the katashiro. He returned the doll to the priest at the shrine. All the dolls thus collected were placed in a boat at the close of the ceremonial period and taken out into the deep water and thrown into the waves.

Different versions of this practice of purification were observed in different parts of Japan. In some areas the purification dolls were cut from paper by an old person, blessed by the Shinto priests, and then on March 3 taken by the Japanese family to the river. There members of the family rubbed their bodies with the paper dolls, which were supposed to take away their sins, and then threw them into the water. In some areas, rather than throwing them into the water, the people set the dolls afloat on paper boats, and as the water swept them away, it was supposed to sweep away sins.

In time the simple paper dolls made for the purification ceremonies became more elaborate, and people began to keep them as ornaments after the ceremonies were over. It is thought that the Japanese Girls' Doll Festival, which began over two centuries ago, was an outgrowth of these purification ceremonies and the dolls made for them. Legend says that an eighteenth-century *shōgun* with many daughters gave the ceremonies a new purpose, that of teaching children loyalty to the emperor, the father of the Japanese people, and love and respect for parents.

Usually the dolls made for the purification rites were single dolls made of paper, but in some areas sets of dolls were made. In the Tottori region, begin-

ning in the fifteenth century, two rows each with ten dolls, one row male and the other row female, were made of clay and paper and inserted in a slit piece of bamboo.

People in this district bought two sets for the doll festival and placed them on the display. After the festival one of the new sets, along with one old set from the previous year, was set afloat on the river. This rite expressed the hope that all accidents and bad luck would depart with the dolls. The remaining set of dolls was put away with the festival dolls as a further charm against bad luck.

Another use for paper dolls was discovered by the Japanese fishermen. A pair of paper deities were

This paper-folded Japanese doll has an exaggeratedly tall thin shape. She wears the traditional kimono and obi, and her coiffured hair is made of black crepe paper. Dolls like this are made to be seen from the back because the interest centers on the hairstyle and obi. (*Wood Collection*)

hung on vessels to pray for a big catch and a safe voyage. These dolls were usually placed at the bottom of the mast or in a room at the stern. If the ship encountered bad weather or faced other perils, the paper deities were thrown into the seas as substitutes for the lives of those on board.

Another traditional type of paper doll made in Japan is the *anesama*, or "big sister," doll which is made in various forms in different regions of Japan. These dolls are made usually with flat bodies made of colored and patterned papers folded into kimonos. The heads, which may be three-dimensional, have elaborate hairstyles.

The anesama dolls developed as play dolls, but they were also used in a girl's education. For centuries little Japanese girls took part in a game called *mamagoto asobi*, or "playing house." They used dolls to act out the courtesies of dining and entertaining guests and other rituals in imitation of the daily life of adults. The anesama dolls developed as the hostess, servants, and guests for these games.

The dolls themselves range from the very simple to the very complicated with the emphasis always put on the dolls' hairstyles and costumes. The hands and feet are ignored in making these dolls. The anesama usually has a face without features perhaps for fear a pretty face might detract from the costume or hairstyle. Actually the doll does not need a face because she is usually displayed with the back of her costume out and her face toward the wall. The anesama dolls wear different costumes and hairstyles because in Japan women wore different costumes and hairstyles according to their age and station in life. The married woman dressed differently from a young girl or a grandmother and so on.

These dolls as developed in different parts of Japan show individual differences. For example, paper dolls from the famous dollmaking district of Matsue have heads made from clay that has been mounded around a thick bamboo stick. Dolls from other regions have little paper balls as heads.

The anesama dolls were first made in the eighteenth century around the middle of the Edo period (1614–1868). At that time women put great emphasis on the beauty of their hairstyles and elaborate coiffures were popular. This explains why the dolls' hairstyling is so complicated and ornate while the body is simple and the face is usually completely blank.

Today the anesama dolls are usually made with black hair because that is what people naturally expect in Japanese dolls. Hundreds of years ago when the dolls were first made the Japanese people had only white rice paper to use for the hair because at the time it was too difficult to dye paper black. The oldest anesama dolls therefore have white hair.

The anesama dolls, which show the grace and atmosphere of the Edo period of Japanese history, have been passed down from mother to daughter and are treasured family heirlooms. Today they are made by enthusiasts of the dolls usually for display.

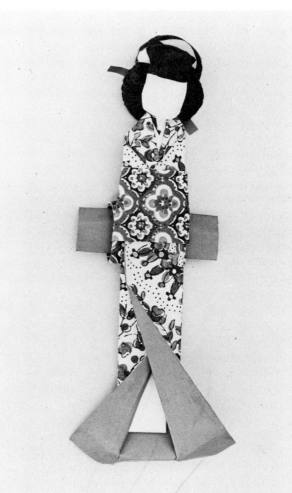

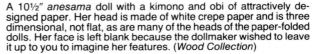

A 10½" *anesama* doll with a kimono and obi of attractively designed paper. Her head is made of white crepe paper and is three dimensional, not flat, as are many of the heads of the paper-folded dolls. Her face is left blank because the dollmaker wished to leave it up to you to imagine her features. (*Wood Collection*)

The back view of the paper doll on page 101, showing her three-dimensional obi and her elaborate coiffure of crepe-paper hair.

Paper dolls with three-dimensional crepe-paper heads are used as attractive ornaments in Japan today. This one graces a decorative panel, which has a greeting printed on it. (*Collection of Marion Albury*)

These Japanese paper dolls are 9″ and 12″ tall. They were made of paper by Ann Hulsizer according to directions she found in a book on Japanese paper dolls. Such dolls are often made in Japan as decorative items and show the costumes and hairstyles of various periods. They are all paper with a wooden-dowel core. The doll on the right represents a young girl with her hair cut to the shoulders in a kappa style, surmounted by a big bow. The doll on the left has a much more elaborate adult hairstyle.

MAKING A KAMI NINGYO

Directions are given here for a Japanese paper doll. I was taught to make this particular doll by Michiko Iizuka of Tokyo, She called the doll a *kami ningyo,* which simply means "paper doll." She had learned to make it from her mother and made such dolls for her own daughter for the Girls' Doll festival The doll represents a young girl with her hair cut to the shoulders in a kappa style with a ribbon on it. She wears the costume of the Tokagawa period (1600–1870).

This doll, which is made of folded *origami* paper, can also be made with fabric. The adding of fabric to folded paper dolls was started in the eighteenth century by wealthy, leisured ladies of Japan. They folded flat human figures, especially those of the *dairi-bina* (the royal prince and princess). When the dolls were completed they sometimes pasted them onto printed colored paper or gorgeous materials. Dolls like this are still made in Japan, and they are exhibited to illustrate the costumes worn at different periods of history in different areas of Japan. The dollmakers who create these exhibition dolls attempt to make their costumes as authentic as possible.

Cut a piece of tissue paper and a piece of origami paper each 3″ × 6″. With the origami paper white side up, place the tissue paper on top. Fold down the top ¼″. Fold back ¼″. Find the midpoint, bring the top left corner across and fold down as shown, folding from that midpoint.

Fold the right top corner to correspond to the left. Fold the left side ⅔ the way across the figure.

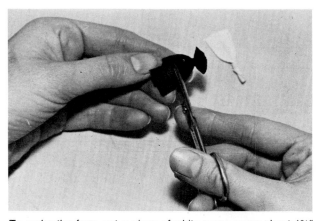

To make the face, cut a piece of white crepe paper about 1⅜″ square. Bring the left side to two-thirds across the paper. Bring the right side almost to the left edge. Hold the top half of the folded paper between the thumb and first finger of one hand. Grasp the bottom section between the same fingers of your other hand. Twist leaving the top section flat for the face. To make the hair, cut a piece of black crepe paper approximately 2⅛″ square. Bring the left side to ⅔ the way across the paper and bring the right side almost to the left edge. Fold the top edge to ⅔ the way toward the bottom. Gather and pinch together at the midpoint of the top half. Wind black thread around tightly and tie securely. Turn over. Cut the top open and spread out the layers of crepe paper. Cut out a rectangle of paper where the face will show, cutting only one layer of paper.

Bring the right side almost to the left edge. Pick up and fold back the bottom edges.

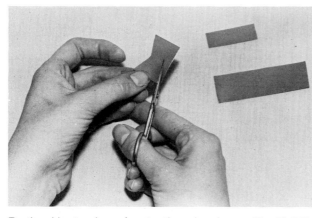

For the obi cut a piece of contrasting origami paper 1″ × 3″. With the white side up, fold each side toward the center so that the piece is now about 2″ across. Turn over and cut into a bow shape. Cut another piece of the same color paper 1½″ × ½″. Wrap the second piece of paper around the first so that it looks like a bow. For the belt section of the obi, cut a 1″ × 3″ piece from the same paper.

Insert the face into the hair section so that it is under the bangs in front, and glue in place. Cut a strip of block printed paper ⅛″ × 1¼″. Wind the band around the hair covering the thread and crossing the ends in back. Glue in place. Open the kimono temporarily, insert the head, and glue in place. Fold the belt around the body, overlapping the ends in back and gluing them in place.

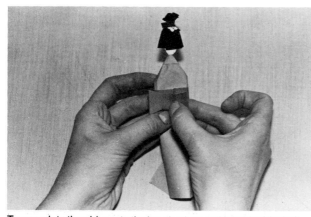

To complete the obi, paste the bow in place at the back of the belt.

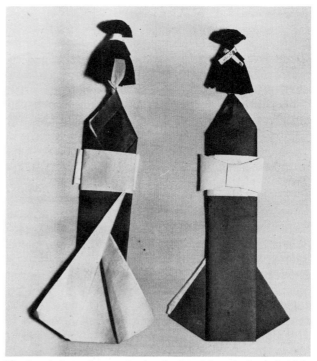

The *kami ningyo* is meant to be displayed from the back, but it is attractive from the front also, even though no features are drawn.

The daughter of Michiko Iizuka, who taught me how to make the kami ningyo, is dressed in her kimono and obi and holds a doll that is similarly attired. The child's mother made the doll from origami paper.

HINA MATSURI

On March 3, the third day of the third month, the Japanese people celebrate the girls' festival, which is called Hina Matsuri (literally "Honorable Small Dolls' Festival"), the Feast of the Peach Blossom. The doll festival is a national and traditional festival and holds a special place in the hearts of the Japanese people.

Some of the reasons given for holding the festival are showing girls the importance of tradition in marriage and family life, fostering an understanding of the history and culture of Japan, teaching reverence for the ruling house and explaining the social order. Also the day is a celebration that observes the birthdays of all Japanese girls.

An integral part of the festival is the *hina ningyo,* or festival doll. Only paper dolls were used at first, but about 250 years ago earthen and wooden dolls came into fashion. Today beautiful fabric display dolls are used for the festival and they are set up on a stand covered with a red cloth. The dolls are taken out of storage only for the duration of the festival; for the rest of the year they are safely packed away.

The dolls have been made for over 400 years and represent the emperor and his court. They are elegantly costumed in silk and brocades and are family heirlooms passed from mother to oldest daughter. When the daughter gets married her dolls go with her. Younger daughters receive the festival dolls as gifts from their relatives at the first festival after they are born.

The conventional and basic set of dolls for the girls' festival is made up of fifteen dolls in ancient costume. In addition, miniature cherry and orange trees and miniature pieces of furniture are usually part of the set. New dolls may be added to the collection each year. Most families have accumulated dolls, some of them centuries old. The older dolls, especially those representing the royal personages, are especially valued.

The custom of setting up the *hina dan,* wooden boxes in the form of steps placed in the most important room in the house, has been a custom in Japan for hundreds of years. There can be three to eight tiers, but five is the most common and seven is also popular. They are covered with a bright red cloth, and a beautiful and conventional arrangement of dolls and miniature properties is made on them.

The most important and most highly valued dolls are the *Dairi-Samia,* the emperor and empress. Since the restoration of imperial power in 1868 the dolls representing the emperor and empress have traditionally been placed at the top of the hina dan.

The emperor is wearing the old-style Japanese crown of shining lacquer and he holds a thin wooden scepter. On his left sits the empress in her elegant court dress of twelve garments over a divided skirt of red. Usually holding a fan, she wears a crown of gold filigree and jewels, or her crown may sit on a table beside her. Behind the royal couple is usually a folding green screen or several screens, and on the top shelf, as perhaps on each of the others, there are lanterns with candles to be lighted on the festival day.

On the second step are three maids of honor in red and white silk gowns. They are supposed to serve the emperor and empress with the food and drink that is put on the exquisite lacquered tables placed between them.

On the third shelf are the orange and cherry trees placed according to ancient custom, in the manner these trees are always found in the Imperial Court. On the same shelf are imperial guards and at the center are five court musicians, two playing stringed instruments, one a drum, another a flute, and the last one, holding a fan, is singing. These represent the orchestra of the famous No plays.

On the lower shelves are other dolls from the collection. Sometimes there is a set of three male dolls who represent human life. The first of these has his hands raised toward his eyes as the sign of tears, while the second is laughing merrily and the third is in a towering rage.

Another pair of dolls that might be included is a white-haired elderly couple with peaceful, happy expressions. With them might be a pine tree with a crane on a branch and a tortoise at the base. All these are Japanese symbols of long life. Some of the other characters that might be on the lower shelves include country girls with flowers or fagots piled on their heads, a peddler, a geisha and a bride. There might also be groups of dolls representing a well-known legend, a scene from a drama, a fairy story or heroic tale.

On the lower tiers are also pieces of miniature furniture, tableware and dishes, including chests, cabinets, screens, writing tables, flowers, wagons, just about any item a bride carries with her to her new home. These may be finished in black and gold lacquer and sometimes bear the family crest. In wealthier homes the family crest may appear also on the silk draperies hung around the festival room setting off the tier of dolls.

Somewhere on the lower shelves are also two of the paper dolls that have symbolic purification meaning. Almost every Japanese family, no matter how poor, owns a festival set. The wealthier the family, the more abundant their collection of dolls. The poorest families might have just simple dolls cut from paper or painted on a hanging board.

The time of the doll festival is the most exciting part of the year for young Japanese girls. For several weeks they prepare for it. Weeks before the doll festival, shops display their dolls. In olden days a special fair used to be held in every important city in Japan, but today the department stores display the dolls. New ones are bought to add to the ever-growing collections, but that is not all that needs to be purchased. Special foods must also be obtained and prepared.

The girl has certain duties to perform before the doll festival. She cleans the room in which the dolls are to be placed, and she washes and polishes all the items to be used. This gives her early training in household duties. She also helps in the planning and purchasing of all the food, for she will serve not only the dolls but all the people who come to see her display.

The marketplace is filled with miniature items before the festival. The fish market has tiny fish, the bakery shops have displays of tiny cakes, and the vegetable sellers, besides their usual stock, have small vegetables grown by gardeners specializing in this line.

During the preparation stage of the festival the mother takes the dolls and furnishings from the boxes and gets them ready. After erecting the five- or seven-tiered frame, she sets up the dolls according to custom. While setting them up, she teaches her daughter the customs of the family and of the nation.

The arrangement is done slowly, the mother taking time to explain the meaning and history of each doll as well as the old customs connected with the Hina Matsuri ceremony.

On the doll festival day, visits are made to friends' homes to admire one another's dolls, and the special food, which was prepared for the occasion, is eaten then.

On the morning of the festival the little girl of the family puts on her finest embroidered kimono and most beautiful obi (sash), because she will act as hostess to her parents and friends. She puts the food into its proper receptacles on the shelves. Ceremoniously she offers a sweet wine called *shiro gake* to the emperor and empress dolls and then gives it to the guests. Tea is offered also to the dolls, and the tea ceremony is held in the traditional and exact way it

has been in Japan for centuries.

The dolls are served a complete miniature dinner, including the traditional sweetmeats. First the girl offers food to the emperor and empress and other doll guests and then she prepares a small table for her family and friends. She serves them soup, fish, vegetables, and sweets in miniature bowls and dishes. They eat with special chopsticks that are 5" long.

After the ceremony she might visit the homes of young girl friends. All the ceremonies are scheduled to end at sunset, but they often linger on into the evening. The festival itself lasts only one day, but the dolls are often exhibited for a week and then put away for another year. Special dolls are made in Japan not only for Girls' Day but also for Boys' Day.

The boys' festival, Tango No Sekku, which is held on May 5—the fifth day of the fifth month—is celebrated by all families in which there is a son under

In Japan on March 3, the day of the Girls' Day festival, in homes where there is a girl, tiered stands, usually with five or seven shelves, are built. The little girl who helped her mother set up this stand sits on a silk pillow in front of it waiting to serve guests delicacies from her Hina Dan.

This silk-screened print made in Japan shows one girl serving her friend in front of the Hina Dan. The emperor and empress dolls can be seen on the top shelf with a folding screen behind them. The three maids of honor are below them, and on the next lower shelf are the court musicians.

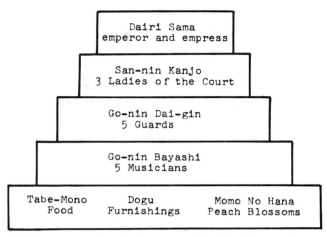

Dairi Sama emperor and empress		
San-nin Kanjo 3 Ladies of the Court		
Go-nin Dai-gin 5 Guards		
Go-nin Bayashi 5 Musicians		
Tabe-Mono Food	Dogu Furnishings	Momo No Hana Peach Blossoms

The Japanese girl typically arranges her Hina Dan as shown above. The *bonbori* (lanterns) stand at the far ends of one of the shelves, and the food, furnishings, and peach blossoms are on other shelves but mainly on the lowest.

seven. Special dolls are taken out for this celebration, ones used only on this occasion and stored away the rest of the year. Strength, manliness, bravery, patriotism, and the loyalty of the Japanese people to their rulers are the attributes that the Japanese parents want to impress on their sons, and so on this day the dolls are characters representing these qualities.

The dolls used for the boys' festival are called *gogatsu-bina,* and they represent warriors, some on horseback, and the heroes of popular tales and histories. There are armed figures of knights, fencing masters, and many figures of the samurai warrior class and sometimes even artists and scientists.

Another name for the boys' festival is the Festival of the Irises. On this day the boys take a protective bath in water in which irises have been boiled because the iris is the symbol of knighthood, and their festival has to do with the knighthood tradition.

The tiered stand that is taken out for the boys' festival is the same type of platform as the one for the girls' festival; the only difference is that it is covered with red cloth for the girls and green cloth for the boys.

In addition to the warrior dolls there are also accessories, including miniature weapons and helmets and many pieces of armor—not modern armor but the

This 5" Japanese doll wears a gray silk kimono and a taffeta obi. She has a papier-mâché face covered with clay and hand painted. Her body is a padded wire frame. She was probably one of a set of dolls for Girls' Day, a member of the court, one of the ladies-in-waiting. She is dressed finely but not royally, and in typical fashion sits on a *zebuton* cushion. (*MacNeer Collection*)

type worn by medieval Japanese warriors. Like the girls' festival, the boys' festival has traditional foods, including spiced rice cakes and rice dumplings.

This doll is typical of those sold for Boys' Day. Each year a boy might receive a new doll to add to his growing display of warriors. (*Parsons Collection*)

Kokeshi dolls range in size from less than an inch to over two feet. Those shown here are made from pieces of turned wood and are 2½″, 1½″ and ¾″ tall. (*Wood Collection*)

KOKESHI

A favorite item found in most Japanese resorts as well as many city stores is the gay wooden *kokeshi* dolls. Made of turned wood, these folk dolls have heads and bodies but no arms or legs. Flowers, perhaps chrysanthemums, are usually painted on the body section.

The kokeshi dolls were first made about 300 years ago in Tohoku, the mountainous regions of the northeast province. Wood turners there made wooden bowls and trays and other items and they started making dolls for their little daughters. These figures were playthings, although originally they might have had a religious purpose.

The old kokeshi dolls have been handed down from mother to daughter for many generations. These dolls are regarded as valuable family treasures even after they become faded in color.

The kokeshi take a bewildering variety of shapes according to where they were made. The doll may be less than an inch to two feet in height, and the true kokeshi are always made of wood. The basic shape is very stylized with a tapered cylindrical body and a round head. More modern kokeshi, however, show a much greater variation in shape and in design, and in fact the variations seem almost endless.

The early kokeshi were exclusively painted wood, but today's versions often have fabric added to the wood. Usually the head and body are made of two separate pieces of wood. The head of the kokeshi is attached by a knob into the hole made by the lathe in the body while it is still hot, so that it is automatically held when the wood cools.

Hands and feet are eliminated so that the purity of line of the doll is preserved. Since the lips, eyes, eyebrows, and hair are painted on, simplicity of the figure is maintained.

The head is usually a girl's head, and the lower part, which represents the body, has a floral or other decorative design usually painted in colors. The hair, eyes, eyebrows, nose, and mouth are usually painted in black.

Today kokeshi are made by the thousands and sold all over Japan as souvenirs and also exported. Children play with kokeshi dolls, but they have come to be used as decorative items for the home. Most Japanese houses have at least one or two of them on display, and many have more. The dolls have become collectors' items for adults, and many Japanese people collect them as souvenirs on their trips to various parts of Japan because the kokeshi is such a popular type of local doll.

Kokeshi dolls started to be sold at many hot spring resorts and became the special souvenirs of these resorts. Today they are produced in over sixty locations in Tohoku. Though they had originated in the northeast secton of Japan, they spread to other areas and are now produced in forms typical of many districts. The faces and bodies are painted in different ways in different areas of Japan.

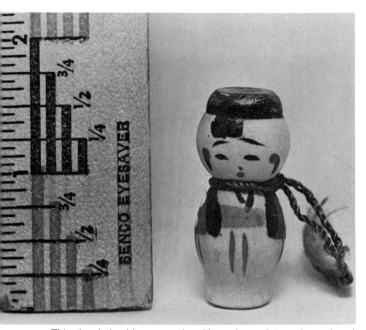

This tiny kokeshi was made with a piece of turned wood and painted in a simple design. The doll was sold as a decoration atop an oversized pencil. (*Author's Collection*)

Kokeshi dolls, 4″ and 5½″ tall, made with turned wood and painted in a very modern style. The bodies have a central panel painted black and decorated with a grain design in gold, silver, green, and lavender. (*Author's Collection*)

This 4″ tall kokeshi from Japan has a wood base with a fabric kimono. She carries a wooden shield with a flower painted on it in one hand and a stick with bells on it in the other. (*MacNeer Collection*)

Kokeshi dolls ranging from 1¾″ to 2″ tall. The two at the left are a pair as are the two at the right. Note the one in the middle has a baby on her back. (*MacNeer Collection*)

Most kokeshi dolls are wood turned, but this unusual 12″ one is carved. The cylindrical body left as natural wood is decorated with a Japanese landscape painting and a message in Japanese. (*Hupp Collection*)

These kokeshi dolls from Japan are actually wooden whistles. They measure from 3½″ to 5″ long. They are turned and carved wood and are decorated with bright paint. (*Groszmann Collection*)

Modern kokeshi dolls, 13½", with no arms or legs. They are made with turned wooden heads. Their long underkimonos are made with heavy card to which fabric is glued. There is no wood under the card. Their stylized overkimonos are made in the same way. The man's overkimono is a muted dark blue and the woman's is a brightly colored flower design. (*Author's Collection*)

MAKING KOKESHI

Make your own kokeshi dolls with pieces of wood you have turned on a lathe. Or buy wooden balls and other turned wooden pieces from the hardware store. Glue them together and paint them any way you wish. Photos of the kokeshi dolls given here will give you some ideas.

You might want to paint on just features, hair, and a floral decoration. Or you might like to add fabric over your wooden base. If you are having trouble finding the appropriate size of wooden base for the body of your kokeshi you can make your kokeshi without it. Instead, use a fabric-covered card twisted into a cone. No one will know there is no wooden base unless they pick up the doll and turn it over.

To make such a kokeshi you will need a piece of heavy card such as a file folder, an appropriate fabric, a wooden ball for the head and a thin wooden dowel to fit into the ball, single-fold bias binding for the obi, and of course glue and scissors.

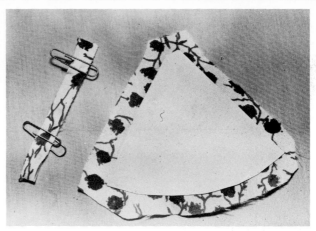

1

Draw an 8" circle and divide it into fifths. Use one of the fifths, rounding off the top for your pattern. Copy the pattern for the body of the kokeshi on a piece of index card or file folder and cut it out. Put white glue on the card and put it down on the wrong side of your fabric. Trim it, leaving ½" of excess fabric all around the edges. To make a collar, cut a strip of cardboard ¼" × 3½" and put glue on one side of the card. Put it down on the wrong side of the fabric. Put glue on the other side of the card and bring the fabric around and over it. Paper clips can hold the fabric in place until the glue dries.

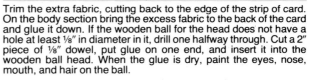

2

Trim the extra fabric, cutting back to the edge of the strip of card. On the body section bring the excess fabric to the back of the card and glue it down. If the wooden ball for the head does not have a hole at least ⅛" in diameter in it, drill one halfway through. Cut a 2" piece of ⅛" dowel, put glue on one end, and insert it into the wooden ball head. When the glue is dry, paint the eyes, nose, mouth, and hair on the ball.

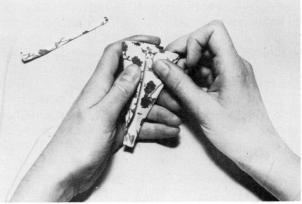

3

On the fabric-covered front, put glue along one straight edge of the body section and twist it around forming a cone and overlapping the glued section. Hold in place temporarily with a paper clip until the glue takes hold.

4 Slip the dowel into the fabric body so that the head sits on top of the body. Use a little glue to secure it there. Bring the collar strip around the neck crossing the pieces in front, letting one end slip under the other and bringing the longer end down on the body. This end will be covered later with the obi. Glue the collar in place.

6 Your completed kokeshi should look very much like these authentic kokeshi dolls made in Japan.

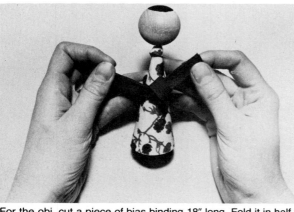

5 For the obi, cut a piece of bias binding 18″ long. Fold it in half to make it 9″ long and glue this way. When the glue is dry, bring the piece of binding around the doll at about the middle of the body, crossing the ends at the back. Make a square knot, but do not pull too tight. Cut off the excess.

DARUMA

Tilting dolls, which have been made in many countries, are weighted so that they roll back into a vertical position when they are knocked over. The ancestors of these dolls is the daruma, which was and is made in Japan. Other countries have similar toys. It is called a roly-poly in some countries, and a *pan-puh-too* in China, where tilting toys are as popular as they are in Japan.

A daruma represents the patriarch Bodhidharma who was supposed to have come from India to China during the sixth century bringing Zen Buddhism, believed to be by some the purest form of spirituality in the Far East today. Tradition says that this religious leader meditated for nine years with his face turned toward a wall. When he tried to stand up, he found that his legs had rotted away and so the daruma is an egg-shaped doll that is all head and body. It has two large, powerful eyes that look you straight in the face.

The daruma doll is said to bring good luck, and it is supposed to inspire the same confidence and determination as the master showed during his long meditation.

In Japan darumas are made differently in various parts of the country and different superstitions are linked to them. In the Kansai district, for example, the doll is made with blank eyes. When the owner makes a wish, he or she paints in one pupil. When the wish is granted, the second pupil is painted. The members of the Japanese Diet are said to celebrate their success in an election by painting in the eyes of an eyeless daruma.

Tilting darumas are made with papier-mâché with a weighted base filled with clay to keep them upright. As early as the seventeenth century papier-mâché dolls were made in Japan. This is long before the material was used for dolls in Europe. Today in Japan it is used mainly for toys, animals, and the darumas.

To construct your own daruma you will need materials for making papier-mâché, including scrap newspaper and wallpaper paste. To decorate the daruma you need paints and paintbrushes. Acrylic paints are a good choice; be sure also to have a good-quality fine brush to paint on the features as well as a larger brush for the large surfaces.

You need to make an egg shape and a good base for this is the plastic-egg pantyhose container. First coat the egg with vaseline, then cover it with papier-mâché. When it is thoroughly dried, slit it open across the middle. Take out the plastic egg and insert a weight in the bottom half of the papier-mâché egg. Put the halves together and mend the seam with additional papier-mâché, but wait until this is completely dry before you go on.

If you can spare the plastic egg, leave it right in the daruma. Before you begin, however, insert a weight into the bottom half of the egg. You can use clay, drapery weights, or lead shot, which is sold in hardware stores. Whatever you use, be sure it is securely attached to the bottom half of the egg. Close the plastic egg; it is ready to be covered with papier-mâché.

To make a daruma doll, first rip narrow strips of newspaper. Prepare a thin mixture of wallpaper paste. Soak the strips in paste until saturated. Apply several layers over the whole surface of the egg shape, working in different directions as you put on the layers of paper. To keep track of the layers, use colored comic strip, alternating with a layer of regular black-and-white newspaper.

Take a piece of newspaper about 10″ × 10″. Roll it over and over to make a tube and dip it into the paste. Put it in place on the upper part of the egg, outlining the face. (You judge where you want the face to be, then attach the rolled paper there.) Add more strips of saturated paper, working over the rolled paper. Add strips this way and that so it is no longer visible as a roll of paper but as a gradual bump. Continue working until you have built up at least six layers of paper. If you wish, the last layer can be paper toweling to give a whiter surface.

When you have finished building up the layers, let the papier-mâché dry thoroughly overnight or longer. When it is completely dry, sandpaper it to make it smooth (it does not have to be perfectly smooth). Paint the face area light pink and the rest of the doll red. Add the whites of the eyes, a red mouth, a black mustache and eyebrows, and gold-and-black brushstrokes around the face. Make a wish and paint in one pupil. Do not paint the other until your wish is granted.

DOLLS OF OCEANIA

Wood, straw, and fabric are all popular materials used in making dolls in the island countries of the Pacific. In Indonesia wood carvers turn their hands to dollmaking and create replicas of the people around them engaged in everyday activities: carrying water, playing musical instruments, herding ducks, stomping rice, and so on. Some dolls are painted white and others are left in the natural wood color.

Indonesian dolls, 6″ tall, of hand-carved wood. Though painted different, they are so similar that one is virtually the side view of the other. Each doll is carrying a wooden bucket with a wire handle and stands on a wooden base. Each one, probably on her way to the well, has a backpack filled with bottles. Each figure wears a *kabaya*, a straight jacket with long sleeves, and a brightly colored sarong, a long wraparound skirt. (*Photographed at the United Nations Gift Shop*)

Musician dolls in the lotus position, made in Indonesia. These small wooden figures are hand carved, with blue-striped jackets and brown hair. The one on the left is playing a stringed instrument made from wood and string and the one on the right is playing a piano-like instrument using a wooden mallet. (*Photographed at the United Nations Gift Shop*)

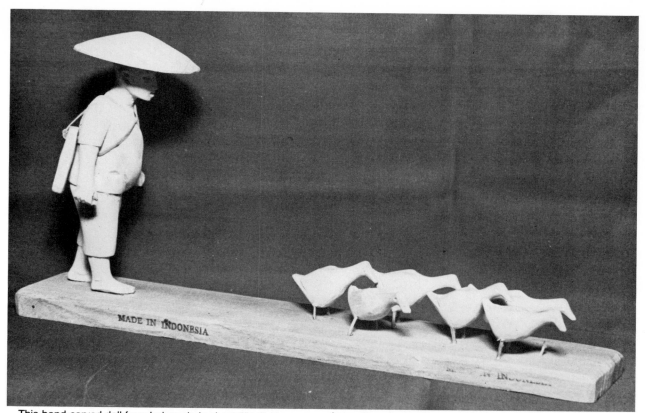

This hand-carved doll from Indonesia is about 5″ tall. He wears a shirt and trousers and an umbrella hat, or bamboo chapil. He is herding the wooden geese that flock before him. (*Photographed at the United Nations Gift Shop*)

Figures from Indonesia hand carved from wood. Each wooden section was carved separately and glued in place. The female figure on the left standing by a rice trough is about 6½″ tall. Her tag says she is stomping rice. The figures on the right, according to their tags, are a vocal group. (*Photographed at the United Nations Gift Shop*)

Palm leaves are also used by dollmakers of Indonesia who plait elaborate palm figures, which were once votive idols used in rituals to celebrate the harvest. The dolls may be made of natural palm leaf or of dyed leaves. Thread often is used to sew on decorative details and sometimes to indicate the doll's features.

Costume dolls from fabric, sometimes with wire frames, are made on Okinawa and in the Philippines and other islands.

An elaborate plaited-palm figure made in Indonesia, actually a votive idol or doll. Made from natural local materials, it may be used in a ritual to celebrate the harvest and then be given to a child as a protective plaything. (*Hupp Collection*)

Plaited-palm figures from Indonesia joined together at the base. The palm has been cut in varying widths and woven together. (*Photographed at the United Nations Gift Shop*)

A palm-leaf doll decorated with thread wound on straight and circular pieces of palm leaf. (*Author's Collection*)

116

A 10″ female figure with a wire-frame body, made in Okinawa. Her hands, feet, and face with hand-painted features are made of nylon-stocking material stuffed with cotton. Each finger and toe is defined with stitches. The doll wears a black-and-white kimono with a blue and white obi. She has a blue-and-white scarf, or kerchief, and on top of her head she is carrying a pack of small sticks with a red fabric bundle on it. (Weiner Collection)

An 11½″ doll from Okinawa made with a ceramic mold. The figure is painted white and wears an orange kimono. She holds a daruma, or tilting doll, in her hand. (MacNeer Collection)

A 14″ doll made in Manila in the 1940s. She is dressed as a bride and has a body made of composition or similar molded material. She wears a white satin dress with a train and has white paper flowers attached to her dress in front. Her veil is made from netting. (Hulsizer Collection)

This 11″ cotton stuffed doll wears an authentic replica of the costume, called "camisa China," worn by Tagalog country men of central Luzon in the Philippines. The doll is a cotton stuffed fabric doll with inked and needle-sculpted features. His jacket is made from a green filmy material called gengue, and he wears pink slippers. (MacNeer Collection)

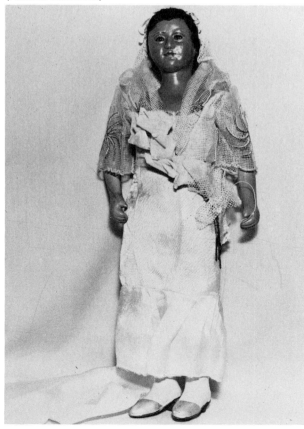

Wire-frame dolls from the Philippines mounted on circles of wood. They have pressed-fabric faces with painted features and black mohair for hair. The 9½" man on the left wears a straw hat, brown cotton pants, and a filmy fabric jacket. He has red shoes and plays a wooden guitar. The 8½" woman in the middle wears a formal yellow dress with wide arched sleeves. The filmy, stiffly starched fabric is gengue. The woman on the right wears purple satin pants and a red top. She has a wide yellow satin sash decorated with sequins and beads. She carries a basket filled with miniature fabric flowers. (*Weiner Collection*)

This doll represents a woman of the Philippines and was made there by Maria Clara Cos. Her body is made from wire and sticks covered with pink crepe paper. Her hair is made from black thread, and her face from pink crepe paper with inked features. She has a paper petticoat under her gold fabric skirt, which has panels of fancy machine-embroidered fabric. The pink flowers at the bottom of her skirt are also made from fabric, and she is carrying a gold paper fan decorated with a fabric flower. (*Mueller Collection*)

These two dolls were made in the Philippines. The one one the left represents a girl from Venezuela, and the one on the right a girl from Vietnam. They have wire bodies covered with crepe paper. Their faces are crepe paper with features drawn on them, and their hair is black string. The girl from Vietnam has a red-and-white-print fabric kimono and obi. On her head is a straw hat. The girl on the left has a red outfit made of a synthetic fabric. Her legs are of white card covered with pink crepe paper. She carries a miniature doll made of wire covered with thread and dressed in a tiny outfit of net. Her face is crepe paper with drawn features. (*Mueller Collection*)

A 10½" beautifully made Maori doll bought in Rotorua, New Zealand, in 1928. On her back is a baby with very curly hair and very red lips. She is made of wood up to her waist and above this her body is stuffed fabric. She has an exquisitely hand-painted face with blue tattooing on her chin and a blue line around her lips as well as blue tattooed lines on her nose and cheeks. Face tattooing, a common practice among the Maori, is a painful process, which involves making pinholes in the skin and inserting dye. The woman has black yarn braids and a woven band around her head with a feather stuck into it at the back (probably added by someone who thought the doll represented an American Indian). She has green earrings and a pendant made from seed beads and is carrying an embroidered bag. Her long violet skirt has a band of white trim with a red-and-black geometric design. Around her shoulders is a black-and-white shawl woven in a houndstooth design. (*From the Collection of the Forbes Library, Northampton, Mass.*)

This modern-looking 8" doll was handmade in Hawaii by Westermeyer. The main material was tapa cloth made from the bark of the paper mulberry plant, which grows on many Pacific islands. The stems of the plant, which are about 2" in diameter, are cut down and slit near the top. The bark is stripped from the stems, leaving the inner bark, which is also stripped off, then soaked in water to soften. The strips are usually about 3" to 4" wide and 7' to 8' long. They are beaten so that they are 10" to 20" wide. Strips are glued together with a paste made from boiled tapioca root and the tapa is ready for the design to be printed on it. The design is printed on the tapa by impression (as with a brass rubbing). Strips of coconut fronds are tied together and placed on a log, the tapa cloth is laid over this, and a small rag of tapa is dipped in reddish brown dye (made from the bark of the koka tree) and rubbed over the tapa. A two-toned effect may be obtained by going over the design again with dark brown dye made from the mangrove root. The doll is made from a piece of tapa cloth. Her skirt is a simple cone shape made with a stiff file card covered with tapa cloth, and her hat is molded over a nuthead with painted features. She is wearing a necklace and hat decoration of strung seeds. (*Author's Collection*)

5
Dolls of Europe

Most of the dolls youngsters of Europe play with are factory made, but some dolls are still being made by hand, mainly as collectors' items and sometimes as souvenirs.

Some European countries have one or more special types of dolls for which they are well known: Germany has the prune people, France the santons and Russia the matroyshkas. Some types of dolls, like those with stuffed or wire frames are made in many European countries and can be identified as to country of origin by their costumes.

In many European countries there is renewed interest in folk traditions and in folk crafts. Dolls are part of this tradition, and some are made according to the old ways, though many are modern-looking with wire-frame bodies and authentic folk costumes.

Sometimes the material or method used to make the doll helps determine in which European country it was made. For example, in the northern countries, especially Scandinavia and Germany, wood is a common material used by the dollmaker.

CRIB DOLLS

One type of European doll that crosses geographic borders is the crib doll. These dolls were and continue to be made mainly in the predominantly Catholic southern European countries. Legend says that St. Francis of Assisi was the first one to make a Christmas crib (crèche) but the custom is much older than the thirteenth century. As early as the fifth century there are references in recorded sermons to Christmas cribs.

During the seventeenth and eighteenth centuries in the Catholic countries of Europe, especially Italy and France, Nativity scenes were made and set up year after year in both churches and homes. In the eighteenth century in Italy presèpe-making reached its peak, but the tradition is much older, and Italian crib dolls dating back to the fifteenth century have been found.

What started as a simple manger scene with the Holy Family and a few animals evolved over a period of time into an elaborate display with deserts, streams, and waterfalls, peopled with hundreds of small animal figures and dolls. In addition to the manger and town buildings there might also be a countryside scene with the shepherds and their flocks, the kings in procession, and also the herald angels all around in a landscape more like the green Italian countryside rather than the arid Bethlehem.

The most elaborate ones were made in the area around Naples. Not only were the Holy Family and shepherds, kings, and angels represented, but also the whole village with its peasants, shopkeepers, beggars, and other characters were made part of the elaborate display. These crib figures might have terra-cotta heads with hands and feet of wood, and a wooden body wrapped with hemp, a form of straw. Such dolls were carved and painted by the men, and then dressed by hand by the women in the family.

In central Europe, especially Germany, the crèches usually had figures carved from local wood and sometimes painted. These might be simple settings with just the Holy Family, a few animals, one or two shepherds, an angel, and the kings. Oberammergau is famous for its wood-carved cribs. The craftsmen of the Grodner Tal were also famous for their religious figures. This was long before they started making the wooden-jointed dolls for which the region is so famous. The wood carvers of the Tyrol, too, made crib dolls, and some of these were as elaborate as the ones from Naples.

This 12" man doll, probably a creche figure, was made about 1845. Though his tag says he was obtained in England, it is more likely he was made in Italy. He has a terra-cotta head, wooden hands and feet, and a wooden body wrapped with hemp. His long arms and large expressive hands are typical of this type of doll. He is wearing a red silk shirt and brown silk jacket and pants and appears to be a townsman, a figure probably made for a creche in a church or wealthy home. (*From the Collection of the Forbes Library, Northampton, Mass.*)

An angel, a crib figure made in Italy in the 1700's. She has a terra-cotta head, hands, and feet. The original feathers that made up her wings have been replaced with new ones. (*Hupp Collection*)

The carvers of Oberammergau are famous for the figures they carve from wood. Here students are learning the skill in a woodcarving school in Oberammergau. (*Courtesy of the German Information Center*)

SANTONS

In France the santons, or "little saints," were made as Christmas crib dolls. They were first created several hundred years ago in Provence, in the south of France. These much-loved Nativity figures have been sold in the city of Marseilles at a santon fair held every December since 1804, and people come from far away to buy them for their crèches.

The santons were originally brightly painted clay figures from the local clay of Provence, which was especially good for modeling. These were all sizes, as small as 7⁄8" high or as large as several feet tall. The smaller sizes were much more popular because the smaller figures made it easier to collect a whole countryside scene, which was the purpose of many santon collectors.

Tiny santons from France—only 2½" tall—represent villagers who might be part of the Christmas scene. They are all clay except for the string on the bucket the woman carries. They are probably on their way to the manger with the humble gifts they carry, a duck and a pot of hot food. (*Groszmann Collection*)

This clay figure from France is a santon, made to be part of a village scene. She is painted and represents a lady going to market with her purse hanging down in the front. About 5" tall, she is all clay except for the handles of the baskets she carries. (*Groszmann Collection*)

The families of the Provence today still make the same terra-cotta figures that their ancestors made. These are molded in a primitive style and then painted in bright colors. The figures represent not only the members of the Holy Family, the shepherds, and Wise Men, but also the villagers, craftsmen, and members of the noble family of the region.

In setting up their crèches the French people had a traditional way of arranging the santons just as the Japanese have a special way of arranging the dolls on the stand for Girls' Day.

The Holy Family is of course at the center. At the left are the villagers with birds and animals. They are led by the village priest and the mayor of the town. The shepherds and the sheep are placed on the right, and fishermen come up from the harbor in the near distance while woodchoppers and gypsies come down from the hills in the back.

The angels are placed on the stable roof on Christmas Eve, and then at midnight the Christ Child is put into the manger. The Wise Men are also placed in the setting, and their procession is moved gradually each day a little nearer to the village so that by the Epiphany on January 6 they are outside the stable.

FRANCE

France is known especially for her fashion dolls, *pantins,* and her santons, or crèche dolls. Wire-frame dolls, in regional costumes also continue to be made there.

Because of its extensive seacoast, France has both dolls and doll traditions related to the sea. In past centuries when a sailor was lost at sea, a small doll was made to take the place of the body and was buried in a coffin. Fishermen and fishmonger dolls are both made in France. Also making dolls from seashells is an old traditional craft in France.

In past centuries the royalty of France—not just the children but adults as well—owned expensive

A 10″ pair of dolls of a fisherman and his wife from Brittany. They are wire-framed and have faces of stuffed stocking with expressive needle-sculpted features to which bits of paint have been added. Their hair is of gray mohair, and they wear wooden shoes formed from dough and lacquered.

The man is in the costume of a fisherman, with a blue shirt and pants, red-and-white striped dickey, and a black hat. In his arm is a bit of fishnetting. The woman wears a black dress trimmed with black fur, and a starched little white crocheted cap with lawn ties. Her white organdy apron is trimmed with white lace. She carries her knitting—yellow yarn and common pins for knitting needles. (*MacNeer Collection*)

These 9″ shell dolls were made on the French coast in the 1840s. Such dolls were often given as mementos to brides and bridegrooms. They have wooden bases, papier-mâché heads and bodies covered with shells and painted. The man wears a paper hat painted black. Sand is glued onto the shells for texture—this is especially noticeable on the woman's skirt. (*Hupp Collection*)

A French fishmonger with face, hands, and feet of clay probably molded, then hand painted. She has a wire-base body covered with a foam material and then cloth. She wears a red print dress and white bonnet and slip. She carries a cane basket filled with grass and some clay fish. (*Stukas Collection*)

dolls. Their dolls were elaborate. They were dressed in beautifully detailed costumes and sometimes equipped with toilet articles, extensive wardrobes, and even beds.

France in the latter part of the fourteenth century was already the style center of Europe. The French began to use dolls to show the latest fashions in dress, hairstyles, and millinery long before fashion magazines existed. Sometimes the dolls themselves were made in Germany but were dressed in France.

France as well as England shipped such fashion dolls to the American colonies and to India, and these dolls served the same purpose that modern fashion magazines do.

Made in the 1940s, these small French dolls, less than 2″ tall, are mainly of yarn with pipe-cleaner bases. They are attached to each end of a piece of woven ribbon and are meant to be a bookmark. The girl has gold embroidery-cotton braids and a red satin head-dress. Her apron is a small bit of woven ribbon. Dressed as a sailor, he has a base of white yarn wrapped with black. Their features are of embroidery cotton. (*Groszmann Collection*)

This 5½″ antique doll, probably made in Alsace, France, functions as a powder box. It is a round cardboard container that opens up and originally held powder. The doll has painted clay hands and face and a black ribbon on her head. Her silk shawl is blue and green, and her gray velvet skirt is covered in front by a brown flowered-cotton apron. (*Hupp Collection*)

These 8″ French dolls are made with wire-frame bodies. Their faces are made of silk, sewn along the profile, and painted in oil. They have leather hands and shoes, and knit-fabric socks cross-gartered with black thread. The man has on a beret and a gray-and-white smock with a white shirt underneath. The woman is wearing a gray fabric skirt and a blue cotton blouse with white dots. In her arms, she carries a chicken made from painted wood and wrapped in a piece of fabric. (*Hupp Collection*)

124

A 3″ elderly pair from France sit in overstuffed chairs. They were made with cardboard bases, covered with fabric, stuffed, and mounted on a piece of wood. Estimated to be over 150 years old, these dolls have finely molded face and hands made from a bread-dough-like substance and covered with lacquer. The man, reading *Le Journal*, has on a brown velvet smoking jacket and blue-and-white pants. The woman, knitting with common pins, wears a gray-and-white blouse and a green knit skirt. (*MacNeer Collection*)

This pair of 9″ wire-frame dolls is from Brittany, purchased there before 1927. Both dolls have hand-painted silk faces, yarn hair, and felt shoes. The young lady has a beige voile bonnet reminiscent of the caps of medieval days, and the same fabric was used to make her sleeves. Her dress is brown, and she wears a pink-and-blue paisley-print apron. Her wire legs are wrapped in yellow yarn, her arms in pink, and her hands are covered with pink silk. The young man wears a traditional rolled-brim felt hat and pleated breeches. His puffed sleeves are of green woolen fabric, his arms are wrapped with pink and blue yarn and his legs with blue yarn. (*From the Collection of the Forbes Library, Northampton, Mass.*)

PANTINS

The pantin is a jointed doll animated with strings and named for the little town in France where it was thought to have originated about the middle of the eighteenth century. A flat cutout figure, which could be as small as four inches or as large as two feet, the pantin became popular not only as a toy for children but also as an amusement for adults.

Some of the famous artists of that century designed pantins, creating such figures as shepherds, shepherdesses, and Harlequins. Men and women of the French court collected them and carried them about making them dance. They competed with one another in the value and size of their collections. The toy was finally outlawed in France, and the excuse given was the superstition that pregnant women who saw a pantin in action might bear a child with twisted limbs.

Though the French are usually credited with the invention of the pantin, a figure that moved by means of a thread was known in ancient Egypt and in Greece. After the French had revived, if not invented, the pantin, it was transplanted to Germany where it was called *Hampelmann* and to England where it was named jumping jack. German wood carvers also brought the Hampelmann to the New World; this figure also traveled to Russia where carvers made their own version, the jumping bear; in Mexico, jumping skeletons and witches are made.

Though pantins are no longer a raging fad, they have continued to be made in limited numbers over the centuries, often as a nursery toy. Sheets with the parts drawn out ready to be mounted on card or cardboard were once available, but are rarely found today. Instead pantins occasionally turn up in children's coloring books, and wooden ones are sometimes sold in gift shops.

Pantins have been made of different materials, some, for example, of fabric lightly stuffed. Others, like the soldier shown here, have been cut from wood and painted in bright colors. Many have also been cut from cardboard.

Directions are given here for two pantins and the necessary patterns supplied. The directions call for cardboard. However, you could adapt the patterns and make them from ¼" plywood. You would also have to string them a little differently, using small nuts, screws, and rubber bands.

To make a pantin, use any type of cardboard available, for instance, the type slipped into shirts from the cleaner's or that cut from a gift box, or poster board.

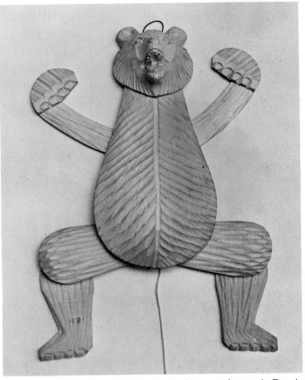

This bear pantin was carved from wood by a craftsman in Russia. (*Author's Collection*)

The parts of the Russian wooden bear are held together loosely with small nails and he is strung through holes drilled in the wood.

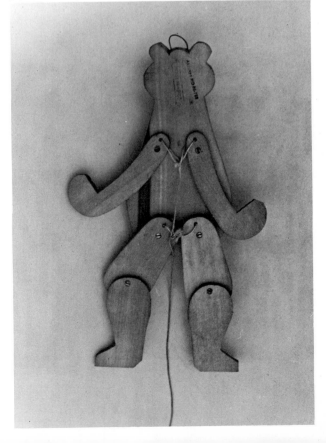

This toy soldier is a modern pantin made from plywood. (*Author's Collection*)

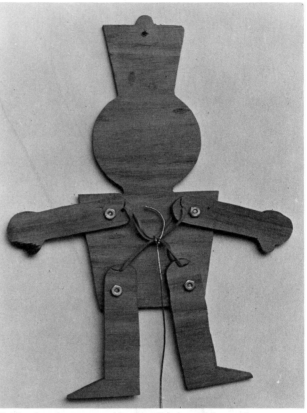

Rubber bands were used to string this toy soldier pantin.

To hold the parts of the pantin together, use knotted strings or buy ½″ brass paper fasteners, which are much more convenient. These are sold by the box in stationery and five-and-ten-cent stores and are inexpensive. You will also need very heavy thread or light string and a large needle into which you can thread the string. To make a colored pantin you will need such materials as paints, colored paper, felt-type markers, crayons, etc., as well as scissors, a pencil, tracing and carbon paper.

This chapter gives you two pantins to try. The jack-in-the-box has only three parts so it is a good project for a beginner. Most pantins, however, such as the Russian bear, have seven parts; the ballet dancer has nine.

Once you have completed the dancer, try designing your own pantin. Begin by sketching the figure on scrap paper. Copy over each section extending the arms and legs as needed so the parts overlap properly. Try a clown, owl, jailbird, policeman, elf, Santa—the possibilities are endless.

Copy these patterns on tracing paper to make your jack-in-the-box pantin. Put the tracing paper over the posterboard or cardboard with a piece of carbon paper between and trace over the patterns transferring them to the cardboard. Turn your tracing paper over to make jack's right arm. Cut the pieces out and color them as you wish, or decorate them with construction, crepe, gummed, or tissue paper. With a large needle, make a hole at each spot marked with an X.

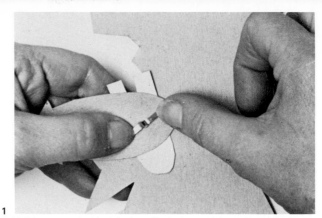

1

When you attach the pieces with brass paper fasteners, they should hang together loosely so they can be moved up with the string control and fall back easily. One way to ensure this looseness is to cut a "tool," such as this, from a piece of corrugated cardboard (or use three or more layers of thin cardboard glued together). Slip the tool in between the layers of cardboard, around the paper fastener before opening the prongs of the fastener. It should hold the pieces of cardboard far enough apart so that the pieces can swing loosely.

Hold one arm behind Jack so the holes match up. Insert the brass fastener and slip the cardboard tool between the layers. Open the prongs of the fastener and remove the tool. Move the arm back and forth and all around so the fastening is loose and the arm can swing around easily. Attach the other arm at Jack's other side.

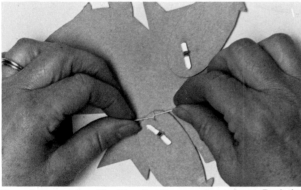

2

3

Thread the needle with string. Let the arms hang down. Push the needle through the cardboard near the top of one arm and tie it in place.

Bring the thread across and tie it to the other arm so the string is taut but the arms are still hanging down. Take a new piece of string and tie it as the control string at the center of the first string.

Now that the stringing is complete, hang the pantin from a string attached to the head or hold the head in one hand. When you pull down on the control string, the arms should move upward.

This jack-in-the-box is a simple pantin with only three moving parts (most have seven or nine). However, no matter how many parts they have, pantins all work on the same principle as this simple one.

4

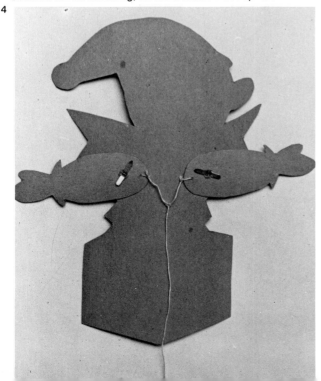

To make the ballet dancer, proceed in the same way as for the jack-in-the-box, cutting out and decorating the pattern piece, turning the right-leg and -arm pieces over to make the left-arm and -leg pieces.

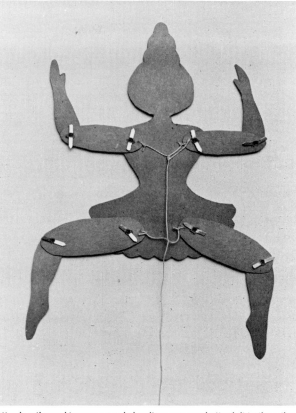

The ballet dancer is made of nine separate pieces. Using the cardboard tool, begin by attaching the right upper arm to the lower arm, the left upper to the left lower. Repeat with the legs. Attach the arms and legs to the body.

Attach a thread to one arm, bring it across and attach it to the other one. Repeat with the legs. With arms and legs in the down position, attach a control string to the center of the string holding the arms together. Bring this string down and tie it to the middle of the string between the legs. When you pull the control string, the arms and legs should go up. If they do not work to your satisfaction, cut off the string and try stringing the figure again.

Hold your pantin at the top or suspend it from a string attached to the head. Pull the control string hanging down below to make it jump.

ENGLAND

The name *doll* came into common usage in English only in the eighteenth century. Before this, dolls were called *babies* or *little ladies*. The origin of the word *doll* is uncertain. Some trace it from the Norse word *daul* which referred to a female servant; others say it was derived from the word *idol*. Still others trace it to *Dolly*, a shortened endearing form of the name *Dorothy*.

No matter what the origin of the name, the doll has been popular in England for centuries. The country claims to be the first one to produce true paper dolls. It is also known especially for its corn dollies, its historical and regional doll figures, its peddler dolls, its golliwogs, and its bobbin dolls.

In England and also in the United States and Canada, interest in dolls was stimulated by young Princess Victoria who was known throughout the

A beautifully detailed 8″ doll bought in England in 1937. Her body is of stuffed pink stockinette on a wire frame, and her hair is brown yarn. Her eyes, nose, and mouth are embroidered, and her eyebrows and pink cheeks are painted on. She is wearing tiny shoes of vinyl, a pink eyelet dress, and her bonnet is decorated with lace and satin ribbon. She is holding a yarn muff and also a yarn doll in a pink crocheted dress. The doll has brown yarn hair and embroidered features like her "mother's." (*MacNeer Collection*)

world for her doll collection. Until her era most dolls had brown eyes, but Victoria's dolls had blue eyes, so since then most dolls have had blue eyes.

Dolls made of wax, composition, and Parian were most popular at the time in Europe. However, Victoria chose wooden dolls for her collection. She dressed thirty-two of them herself, and the rest were dressed by her governess Baroness Lehzen. The dolls were dressed to represent some of the famous artists in the ballet and opera as well as court ladies.

Probably the most famous of the English display dolls was the cloaked peddler doll. Although they were made all over the world, these dolls became an English specialty.

In England during the Victorian period, peddler dolls became increasingly popular as drawing-room conversation pieces. The doll was usually covered by glass and placed in a prominent place. They were mainly figures of old women, occasionally of a pretty girl peddler and very infrequently of men. The doll traditionally wore a cloak, white cap with black bonnet over it, and white apron over a print dress.

Not only the doll itself but the many wares she carried were of interest. The customer could buy a doll with an empty basket and have the fun of collecting tiny items to go into it. If she already had a collection of miniatures, what better way to show them off than to put them in the basket of the peddler doll?

PAPER DOLLS

England claims to be the first to produce true paper dolls. Printed fashion sheets with figures meant to be cut out were sold in Europe for some time and were designed for adults. However, an English designer first produced the true paper doll, that is, the figure with sets of clothes ready to cut out and use interchangeably. These were designed for children and were quite different from the fashion sheets meant for adults.

By 1790 English firms were selling 8″ paper dolls with six sets of clothing as playthings for children. They were soon copied by the French who used paper dolls to advertise their fashions. By 1840 the paper doll had come to the United States. Paper dolls in sets were imported as well as designed and made here.

In the 1850s and 1860s, paper dolls of famous people became very popular. Soon all types of paper dolls were made—flat, cone shaped, folded and so on.

Both France and Germany began to produce paper dolls, but the most popular were still made by the English firms such as Raphael Tuck. Today, commercial publishers continue to make paper dolls, and paper doll artists work at creating original sheets of dolls and their clothes.

REGIONAL AND HISTORICAL DOLLS

England is a country very conscious of its history and its regional differences, and dolls have been made illustrating both of these. In Cornwall dolls represent local characters, such as smugglers and milk-maids, as well as mine workers (both the men and the women called the Bal-maidens who were employed above ground to break up large rocks).

In London the Pearly King and Queen are well-known Cockney characters, and dolls are made to represent them. They are dressed in black clothes lavishly trimmed with thousands of pearly buttons sewn on in interesting designs. The Pearly Queen wears a large hat covered with colored ostrich feathers and the King a spotted kerchief around his neck.

Dolls are made in Hereford to represent characters from an English village of a hundred years ago, including country girls, farm wives, farm workers, and monks.

Printed rag dolls were popular in England early in this century. These may have been actually printed on the continent and sold in England, both as made-up dolls and as printed fabric ready to make up. The strange black golliwog was one of the most popular of these doll figures.

English dollmakers have also produced stuffed dolls representing people in everyday life—children, nannies, and policemen; Scotsmen in kilts; and the Beefeaters. Beefeater dolls are very popular. These colorful figures of the uniformed yeomen who guard the Tower of London are dressed in red costumes

A 6″ pair of dolls from England representing a nanny and her charge and a bobby on his beat. Both have wire-frame bodies, and faces of fabric-covered buttons with features painted on them. The policeman wears a blue felt outfit decorated with dark blue seed beads.

The nanny wears a pink cotton-fabric dress and a white felt apron and hat, and has yarn hair. The baby in her arms has a wire body wrapped with yarn, and the same fabric face as her nanny's. She, too, has yarn hair and a pink gathered-cotton-print dress. (*MacNeer Collection*)

These 10″ English dolls bought in England in 1937 carry a Liberty of London tag. They represent King George and Queen Elizabeth, parents of Queen Elizabeth II. Fabric stuffed with needle-sculpted faces, they each have a crown of velvet with metallic trim, sequins, and seed beads.

The king wears a long maroon velvet cape, with a white felt collar stitched with black embroidery thread to make it look like ermine. He has leather hands and black felt pants. The queen wears a white brocade dress with metallic trim and sequins. She has on a sequin necklace. Her cape is regal purple with metallic trim and white felt representing ermine. At the end of the train a crown and the letters "ER" are embroidered in gold thread. (*MacNeer Collection*)

trimmed with gold-and-black braid and showing the emblems of the four countries that are part of Great Britain—the thistle for Scotland, the daffodil for Wales, the rose for England, and the clover leaf for Ireland. On the Beefeater's chest is the gold crown.

English dollmakers are also famous for the historical characters they make into dolls—Nell Gwyn, William Shakespeare, Sir Winston Churchill, and Lady Randolph Churchill, to name just a few. Dolls in period costumes, in military uniforms, and those representing royalty are typically British, and though there are many commercially made dolls on the market today, handmade dolls are also still being produced, and amateur dollmaking and doll dressing flourishes in England as it does in Japan.

Queen Elizabeth and Prince Philip were popular subjects for dolls, especially in 1977, when the queen celebrated her Silver Jubilee. The queen is usually shown in state robes with a long dress, a gold crown, blue ribbon with the insignia of the British Empire across her chest, and hanging from her shoulders a purple velvet cloak trimmed with white fur.

A 15″ doll made by Alpha Toys in England representing Prince Edward. He has a stuffed felt body and a pressed-felt face with painted features. He is dressed in traditional red-and-blue military uniform with tall black fur hat. (*MacNeer Collection*)

This Beefeater doll by Liberty of London is 10″ tall, with a stuffed fabric wire-frame body. It represents a Yeoman of the Guard and Warder of the Tower of London in the traditional uniform worn since the days of Henry VIII.

This beautifully made doll is dressed in felt. He has a bright red tunic with black-and-yellow braiding and gold emblazonry. The tunic is embroidered with the traditional crown and floral design. At his neck he has a pleated white-lawn ruff, and on his head is a black beaver hat with red, black, and white ribbon cocardes. He has red garters and black shoes with white and red rosettes. White gloves and a gold-tasseled lance complete his uniform. (*Hupp Collection*)

Made in England, a 9½″ beautifully detailed wire-frame "Liberty Doll," representing a Scotsman. The face on this figure is painted. He wears a green plaid kilt and socks and a green felt coat and vest of blue-and-pink brocade. He has a white silk shirt with a lace cravat. (*Hupp Collection*)

Among the famous English dollmakers is Norah Wellings, a craftswoman who made her reputation with velvet and cloth dolls, Many of these were sailor boys and "darkies," with pressed felt faces and painted features. Her bright stuffed British sailor dolls could be bought on cruise ships; the name of the ship was on the band of the sailor doll's cap. During World War II, she designed a parachutist doll that carried the Royal Air Force label. A percentage of the manufacturer's sales on these dolls was contributed to the RAF Comforts Fund.

Another famous English dollmaker is Peggy Nesbit, known for her handmade dolls. Mrs. Nesbit began making dolls in 1953, and her first model was Queen Elizabeth II in coronation robes. At first her sitting room served as her workroom, and her aunt helped her dress the dolls. Today she has a factory and much of the sewing is done by homeworkers in their own houses. Her many doll creations include a whole portrait series of the royal family.

BOBBIN DOLLS

Another type of English doll is that made in Yorkshire from old spinning bobbins. The textile mills of Yorkshire were once famous for their fabric, and in fact gave their name to Yorkshire dressing, a system of making striped warps from balled warps that were dyed different colors. They also gave the name to Yorkshire tweed, a type of woolen and worsted fabric made there, which differs slightly in structure, finish, texture, and other details from tweeds made in other parts of the British Isles. The wooden bobbins left from the old textile mills have been cleverly used as the bodies for dolls.

A 14″ stuffed character doll of velveteen fabric with glass eyes. He has buttons and pieces of felt sewn on his uniform. His face was made by pressing the fabric onto a mold and later painting it. He represents a black man, perhaps a policeman from the Caribbean. Souvenir dolls, like this one designed by Norah Wellings, were made in England and sold on English ships. The English sailor doll was also a popular character doll, among many others. (*Hupp Collection*)

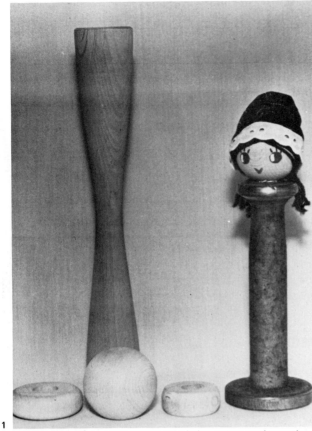

1 You can shape your own bobbin on a lathe, or you can buy a piece of wood in craft shops and other stores that sell wooden balls and other wooden forms. The one shown here can be cut in half and will make two dolls. To make a more authentic doll, you can obtain a genuine wooden bobbin at your local craft shop or directly from Gwenith Gwen, Inc.

2 Gather the wooden pieces. Paint the eyes and mouth with acrylic paints. Assemble the sections and glue them together.

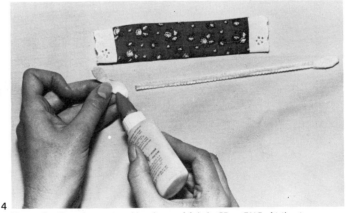

3 For the dress, cut a piece of fabric 6″ × 12″. Match the raw edges of the lace and the raw edge of the fabric right sides together, and sew the lace along both long sides of the fabric. Match the short ends right sides together and sew the seam. Turn the fabric right side out.

4 To make the sleeves, cut a piece of fabric 3″ × 5¼″. At the two short ends of the fabric, match the raw edge of the lace with the raw edge of the fabric right sides together and sew the lace in place. Right sides together, fold the fabric in half the long way. Sew along the lace and fabric. Turn right side out. Cut a piece of pink felt ½″ × 1½″. Fold each in half to make it ¾″ long. Round off the top and bottom edges to form hands. Cut a piece of pipe cleaner about 6″ long. Glue the felt hands on each end of the pipe cleaner. Slip the pipe cleaner into the fabric sleeves.

5 Slip the dress onto the doll and gather it at the neckline. Bring a piece of ribbon around the doll and tie it under the neck to hold the dress on the doll. Put the arms in place on the back of the doll, bending the pipe cleaner to bring them around to the front. Stitch them in place.

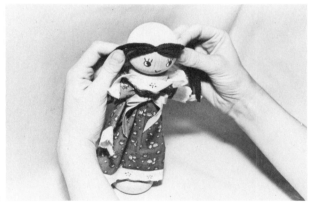

6 Cut 6 strands of yarn 11″ long. Use one of them to tie the whole bunch together at the center. Glue the center at the middle above the doll's forehead. Bring the yarn ends to the back and tie together at the nape of the neck to hold in place.

7 To make the cap, cut a piece of print fabric 6½″ × 4½″. Cut an 8″ piece of lace. Along one long edge, pin about 5 pleats. Pin one on each short edge. Pinning right sides together, matching the lace with the edge of the fabric along all three sides, adjust the pinned pleats if necessary. Sew along the edge.

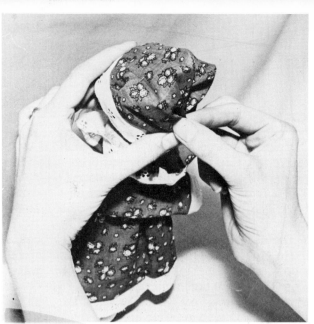

8 Put the hat on the doll's head. Pleat the fabric along the raw edge so that the hat will fit the head and stitch together the raw edges to finish off the hat.

9 The 9″ wooden-post doll on the left was made in Yorkshire, England. The body of the doll is an old spinning bobbin that was once used in the famous textile mills of Yorkshire. In the past such dolls were made by workers in the mills. Father would bring home a bobbin and attach an old wooden door handle. Mother would make clothes for the doll before giving it to her daughter. The doll on the right is the author's interpretation of this type of post doll, made with wooden pieces from the hardware store.

137

CORN DOLLIES

Making corn dollies is an old craft that has been revived in England. There is some confusion between the corn dolly and the doll made from straw. The corn dolly may not look like a doll at all and may have little in common with straw dolls other than the material from which it is made.

The use of the word corn in this context is confusing to Americans who apply it only to corn on the cob. Here it is equivalent to the more general term "grain." Corn dollies are not made with corn but instead with stalks and heads from rye and wheat straw. Oats and barley, which tend to be too soft and short, are often incorporated into the top of the corn dolly because they are decorative.

Corn dollies, which were originally made as offerings to the god of the harvest, or the "corn god," are said to go back thousands of years to pagan times when fertility rites were part of planting and harvest time. In many areas throughout Europe and the Americas part of the harvest ritual involved cutting the last sheaf of grain. Since the grain field was thought to die after the harvest, the peasants believed that the spirit of the grain field died when the last sheaf was cut. That sheaf, consequently, was made into an idol in which the spirit could rest until its rebirth in the spring.

The dollies were originally woven by the harvesters in the wagon carrying the final sheaves of grain from the field, perhaps with much singing and dancing. They were hung during the long winter, usually in a conspicuous place in the barn to guard the harvest. The following spring they were "sacrificed" by burning them or feeding them to the cows to help them produce good calves. By giving this due praise through the harvest festival the corn spirit was propitiated and the next year's harvest was ensured.

Corn dollies are made not only in England but in other countries such as Austria, Germany, Sweden, and Mexico, each country having its own traditions and shapes. Corn dollies were shaped like pillars, horns, cornucopias, human beings, and so on. In some areas the corn dolly represented the corn idol itself, the Earth Mother, in the figure of a woman.

In England where this tradition was particularly strong, there were many different designs according to the part of the country the farmer lived in. Traditional shapes included the umbrella from Cambridgeshire, the lantern from Norfolk, and the knot from Staffordshire. Corn dollies were also made for special occasions, for example, the Rattle Wattle, a fertility symbol, for a wedding. Some of today's corn dollies are figures of ancient designs while others are modern adaptations of traditional ones.

Toward the middle of this century corn-dolly weaving was a dying country craft in England, but thanks to the efforts of individuals and institutions the techniques of this manual art are now being put into practice and recorded. Lettice Sanford of Leo-

Though corn dollies need not be in the form of a doll, they sometimes are, as is this elegant corn maiden by Lettice Sanford of England. This dolly has a red bow and is carrying a bouquet of straw flowers. (*In the Collection of Terry Dominici*)

minster, among others, helped revive the interest in corn dollies in her native England as well as in the United States and other countries. A widely known authority on the craft, she is the author of *Straw Work and Corn Dollies.* Another book, *Discovering Corn Dollies,* by M. Lambeth, as well as many magazine articles, has also contributed to a renewed interest in the craft.

Natural straw and grasses have been used for thousands of years by country people for making decorative and useful items. Today natural straw is still used for making corn dollies. But because it is brittle and difficult to work with, and not readily available to city and town people, soda straws can be substituted. These drinking straws, however, are short, waxed, and harder to glue. Craft shops now carry paper straws for craftwork that are much longer and unwaxed.

Making handcrafted items from these paper straws is a modern development of the ancient and traditional craft of weaving with natural materials. Though items made with paper straws do not have the same appearance and texture as those made from natural straw, they have an aesthetic quality of their own.

This corn dolly looks like a woman carrying a bouquet of dried flowers. It was made by Lettice Sanford, Eye Manor, Leominster, England, who appeared at the Second International Crafts Exposition held at Busch Gardens, in Williamsburg, Virginia, in 1977. (*Weiner Collection*)

To make a doll like that shown at the left, you can use real straw or soda straws, as shown here. Tie together a small bundle of straws at the center and fold them in half, then tie them together at the head. Add a few folded straws at each side for arms and tie at the waist.

To make the arms and the piece for the head, do the "cat-step" using two straws, crossing them alternately. Add a bunch of flowers and your straw doll is complete.

If you wish to make corn dollies with real straw, obtain wheat from a farmer. You need pieces as long as possible, so the best time to obtain them is during July and August (spring wheat is generally too short). Before you begin working with the wheat, put it in a 200-degree oven for five minutes to kill the moths and other insect eggs that might be in it.

For weaving corn dollies, you will be using the part of the straw from the head to the first nodule. Break the pieces there and clean them pulling off any extra strands. The pieces of natural straw are hollow inside, and the smaller end of one piece can be inserted into the wider end of another.

If you are working with paper straws, attaching a new piece to one already woven in, crush the end of the used straw a little, put a small amount of white glue on it, and slip it into the end of the new straw.

Before working with real straw, soak it ½ to 1 hour to make it more pliable, and while you are working with it, keep it moist by rolling it up in a towel. Wet only the amount you will use. Any straw left wet for a long period of time may mold.

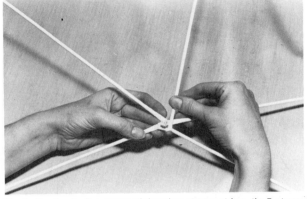

1

To do the basic five-straw plait using strong string, tie 5 straws firmly together at one end, and spread them out. If you want the ends hidden inside of the dolly, hold the ends upward as you begin to plait. Take one straw in your right hand and move it over the next two straws in a counterclockwise direction. Continue in this fashion, giving the whole piece a quarter-turn clockwise each time you move a straw.

2

Before folding over the straw each time, crease it sharply with your thumbnail to get a good sharp fold.

After creasing the straw, bring it over the last straw worked and across to the opposite side of the figure you are shaping. As you continue to work, if you look down on your work you will see that it forms almost a square.

3

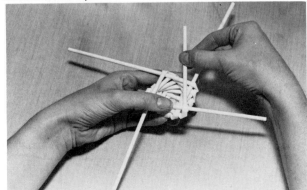

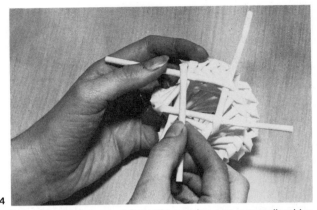

4

As you become more proficient in weaving, you can easily widen out or narrow down your figure, forming the shape desired. To narrow it, bring the straw close to the center of the figure as shown here. If you were widening the figure, you would have to put the straw more toward the edge of the figure.

These corn dollies made by Lettice Sanford of Leominster, England, are 10″ long. They show the completed form of the five-straw plait. (*Weiner Collection*)

IRELAND, SCOTLAND, AND WALES

Wire-frame and stuffed fabric dolls continue to be made in Scotland, Ireland, and Wales, often as collector's items, in traditional costumes.

Dolls made in Wales often wear the Welsh beaver hat, a tall black felt hat, now a feature of the Welsh costume doll, that first became popular in the seventeenth century. Under the black hat a snow-white bonnet usually frames the face.

In Scotland dolls are dressed in tartans representing the various clans. The origin of the Highland dress has been lost in obscurity. It is believed Scotsmen started wearing kilts about the end of the sixteenth century. Women did not traditionally wear kilts, but today they wear skirts and other pieces of clothing with the traditional plaids. Scotch dolls of

About 14" tall, this pair of dolls from Scotland bears the label "Barleycorn, Craftmade symbol made in the Highlands and Islands of Scotland." These stuffed fabric dolls have yarn hair, and the man has a delightful woolly yarn mustache besides. Both the woman and man have matching Scotch wool-plaid outfits, with her dress and his kilt of the same plaid. He wears a blue-felt jacket with sequin buttons and a lace cravat, and has woven ribbon criss-crossing on his legs copying typical Scottish cuarans of deerskin with leather thongs cross-gartering over woolen hose. (*Photographed at the United Nations Gift Center*)

A tiny 3" leprechaun made in Ireland with a pipe-cleaner body wrapped with red yarn. He has a felt head with embroidered features and a red felt cap. His beard is a bit of white wool. (*Photographed at My Irish Cottage, Murray Hill, N.J.*)

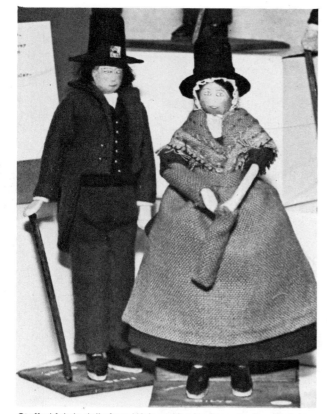

Stuffed fabric dolls from Wales with wire-frame bodies. Both have fabric faces with hand-painted features. The woman wears a tall black beaver hat over a frilled white lingerie cap. She has on a long tweed skirt and apron, and her woolen shawl is decorated with embroidery stitches. The gentleman with his beaver hat carries a walking stick and wears buckle-trimmed shoes, tweed breeches, vest, and jacket.

Stuffed dolls from Scotland measuring from 21″ to 24″ in height. These tall lanky girls are made with white stockinette bodies, brown yarn hair, and drawn-on features. Each one wears a hand-knitted hat with a large tassel and a hand-knitted sweater with an open-weave design down the front. Their color-coordinated neck scarves, skirts, and pants are Scotch plaids. Their tags say they are from Karen Krafts of Scotland.(*Photographed at the United Nations Gift Center*)

both sexes today often wear the traditional plaids in both traditional and modern costumes.

Dolls from Ireland may represent women, fishermen or leprechauns, and colleens. Both male and female dolls are dressed in regional costumes, with attention to authentic detail and good workmanship. They are often dressed in handloomed traditional tweeds. The men might have on hand-knit fishermen's sweaters, and the women hand-crocheted or -knitted scarves, hats, or shawls.

From Ireland, a peasant girl 5½" tall. Her body is a wire frame with felt covering it. Her pink felt face has embroidered features, and on her head is some human hair. Her skirt is felt with embroidered yarn trim. Her apron is made from a scrap of blue-print fabric, and over her head is a woven woolen scarf. She carries a miniature straw basket, and her label states she is "Slieve Bawn, Made in the Republic of Ireland." (*Weiner Collection*)

An Irish colleen, 13" tall, with a stuffed felt body. Her boots are black felt attached to her legs. Her eyes are circles of black felt glued in place, and her mouth and nose are drawn on her pink face. She has red woolen yarn hair, and her clothes are handloomed tweeds, her skirt in maroon, her shawl in yellow. She has a white cotton blouse, slip, and apron edged with white eyelet lace, and is carrying a little wicker basket. (*Photographed at My Irish Cottage, Murray Hill, N.J.*)

This 9" Irish doll has a stuffed cotton body and painted features. Dressed in green, he has a felt jacket and hat and boots of a vinyl material. (*MacNeer Collection*)

Made in Ireland, these are "Collector's Character Dolls Handmade by Joy," according to their tags. These 8" dolls with wire-frame bodies have felt-covered arms and legs and hand-painted, molded faces. They are figures of a man and woman from Connemara. The man is wearing a dark blue hand-knit sweater, which is traditional in Connemara, and a handwoven bainin jacket. He also has a bone-white crocheted cap. Around his waist is a crios, a special belt, in purple, blue, and green, and around his neck is a yellow felt scarf.

The Connemara woman is dressed for working in the fields. She wears pampooties—shoes from rough rawhide and worn to protect the feet from the rocky land—and so does her partner. She is wearing a light blue flannel underskirt, a dark blue handloomed skirt, a red-and-white cotton apron, a red blouse, a red hand-knitted shawl, and a red handloomed head scarf. (*Photographed at My Irish Cottage, Murray Hill, N.J.*)

A 14" leprechaun with a body made of stuffed fabric. His face and arms are felt, and his legs are handloomed fabric. He is wearing a handloomed blue-and-green tweed outfit with red-felt boots and pointed cap. He has button eyes, a red felt mouth, and his nose is a little piece of stuffed pink felt. His sleeves and pants are bainin wool, a special Irish handloomed off-white fabric. Under his belt he has a shillelagh—a protection stick shaped something like a mallet, cut from the blackthorn tree—for which the Irish are famous. The doll was made in a hospital rehabilitation program and exported to the United States. (*Photographed at My Irish Cottage, Murray Hill, N.J.*)

An Irish couple from Aran. The man is dressed somewhat formally, that is, in the way he might dress, when he is not fishing or taking care of the cattle. He wears the traditional bainin jacket, homespun tweed pants, and a hand-knit sweater. Around his waist is a crios, and on his feet are pampooties.

The woman wears flannel pantalets and a slip under her red petticoat or underskirt and black overskirt, both of handloomed wool. She has a blue handloomed head scarf and black crocheted shawl. Women of Aran in the early eighteenth century wore colored cloaks, but later these were replaced by shawls and head scarfs. The women spun and dyed the wool for themselves and their families. They used black dye extracted from logwood and red dye from madder. (*Photographed at My Irish Cottage, Murray Hill, N.J.*)

These Irishwomen are in the traditional costumes of three different areas of Ireland. The woman on the left is from Gaeltacht. She has on a red bainin skirt with a black band (the band is covered up by her big white cotton apron). A single band means that the woman is single, two bands means she is married, and three means she is a widow. She is also wearing a blue-and-white gingham blouse, a black hand-knit shawl, and blue handloomed head scarf.

The woman of Sligo, in the middle, is dressed in the mode of the 1830s. She has on a homespun skirt, tucked up in the front, showing a fancy petticoat underneath. Or she might have had, in that day, a fancy skirt on top, which would be tucked up on each side, showing a homespun skirt underneath. This figure wears a black lace mop cap and a red knit shawl.

The woman of the West, on the right, wears a red homespun skirt with a white cotton apron. She has a shawl, a white hand-knit beret, and a flannel slip with pants underneath. (*Photographed at My Irish Cottage, Murray Hill, N.J.*)

From Ireland, a shepherd and his sheep made of wood. Each piece is sawed separately from wood, stained, finished, then glued and fitted together as with a jigsaw puzzle. The shepherd, for instance, is five separate pieces of wood. (*Photographed at My Irish Cottage, Murray Hill, N.J.*)

145

This 7" figure of St. Francis was hand carved by Fergus O'Farrell, who is famous for his work in wood. The face and arms are separate pieces, and the little bird that St. Francis is holding is made from a darker wood. The doll is all natural wood with a low-shine finish. (*Photographed at My Irish Cottage, Murray Hill, N.J.*)

Some of the white-clay dolls from as early as the fifteenth century were probably christening gifts. They were very simple figures with a flat hollowed circle in the front where a coin could be put as a gift from the godparents to the child at baptism.

Another early type of German doll was made of flax, sometimes in pairs. These good-luck dolls were hung on the spinning wheel. The forests of Germany provided wood for her carvers to make wooden objects for churches. When the demand for these decreased, the carvers turned to making household objects and toys for children. Each wood-carving district originally had its own specialty, but later the traditions of making wooden dolls became merged.

A 7" hand-carved wooden doll made in Germany. It was painted and stained. (*Stukas Collection*)

GERMANY

Germany, especially the city of Nuremberg, has for centuries been considered the toymaking center of the world, and dolls have been an important part of that toy production. Germany is famous for its wooden dolls, especially the penny wooden, or Dutch dolls, and unique to this country are the prune people, special dolls sold at Christmas.

Clay dolls were probably one of the earliest types made in Germany. Dolls have been found from as early as the thirteenth century. These were molded from clay and fired in kilns.

This 5″ doll from the Black Forest region of Germany is carved from wood. She has a painted face, brown thread hair, a blue cotton dress with black twill decorations, and white cotton sleeves. On her head is the traditional hat worn by the women of the Black Forest, a straw hat with six huge woolen pompons (red ones for single girls and black for married women). (*Hupp Collection*)

A 15″ nutcracker doll made in Germany. This soldier doll is made from pieces of turned wood and brightly painted. Many of these nutcrackers are still made every year and sold all over the world. (*Photographed at United Nations Gift Center*)

These small German dolls are made of wooden balls, pieces of sawed wood, and pieces of turned wood. The figures are personifications of the sun and the stars. They are painted in bright colors, mainly yellow, and have a shiny finish.

The early German wooden dolls were shaped like bowling pins with no arms or legs, but later on limbs were added. The peasants began carving these wooden dolls during the winter months when they could not work in the fields. Known as "Tocke," and later "Docke," these dolls were made especially in the areas around Nuremberg and Sonneberg. They are believed to date back to the twelfth century because someone recorded that a preacher of that period commented on them. Martin Luther, too, in the fifteenth century, scolded women for dressing up like pretty "Tocken." The same idea is present in the English expression "she was dolled up."

Germany also has delicious edible dolls like those made for St. Nicholas's Day, December 6. On that day German children were given gingerbread figures of the saint. This custom was brought by the Germans to the United States. I remember as a child getting a St. Nicholas doll, perhaps 8" tall. He was decorated with white icing and a printed sticker with a Santa face was on the gingerbread face. He was always tied with a red ribbon to a piece of cardboard covered with white paper. I still remember eating him very slowly from the bottom up until the last bit of cookie eaten all around was the part with the sticker still on it.

Though Germany is especially famous for wooden dolls, fabric ones are also made there. These stuffed dolls are often dressed in local peasant costumes, and nearly every valley in Germany has its own style of traditional costume. One well-known type of German soft doll is the Kathe Kruse doll. Mrs. Kruse began in 1906 to experiment in making a doll that would both look and feel like a baby. She created dolls that had a childlike posture and appeal and were both durable and washable. She used a specially prepared muslin head, which was stiffened and painted. Her dolls started to be produced in quantity just before World War I, and she supervised every step of the process. The business still goes on today under the management of her children.

Wooden dolls from Germany with articulated arms and painted faces and shoes. The girl has yellow embroidery-cotton braids and a satin ribbon on her head as a head scarf. She wears a white puffed-sleeve blouse, black skirt, and bodice laced with embroidery floss. The boy's black felt pants with suspenders are styled like lederhosen. (*MacNeer Collection*)

A 5½" incense burner from Germany made from wood. This toy peddler doll has dolls, trumpets, hearts, balls, and other items in his tray and a little doll dangling in front. He is made of pieces of turned wood as well as sawed pieces and is brightly painted. His hair is fake fur. (*Groszmann Collection*)

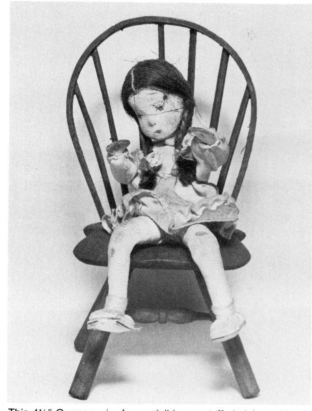

This 4½" German wire-frame doll has a stuffed pink-stockinette body. Her features are delicately painted on her stuffed fabric face. Her hair is flax, and she wears a pink organdy dress. (*MacNeer Collection*)

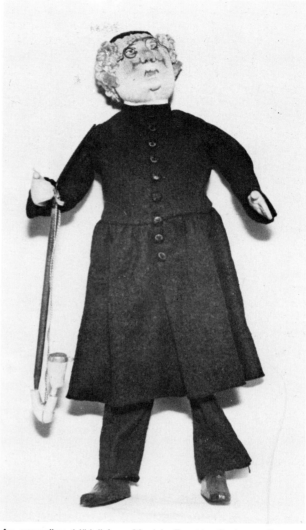

An appealing 14"doll from Munich, Bavaria, Germany, the predominantly Catholic region of the country. This figure of a monk, a symbol of this region, has a stockinette face that is needle-sculpted and painted. His body is stuffed, and his feet are of carved and painted wood. He has a black felt cassock and white yarn hair and carries an elaborate wooden pipe. (*Hupp Collection*)

This 7" whimsical goose boy appears to have been made in Germany. He is made of stuffed fabric with pink cotton fabric for his body and pink knit fabric for his face. His hair is fuzzy yellow mohair, and his delicate features are painted on. He wears a white cotton shirt, leather shoes, leather suspenders, and pants (lederhosen), which are decorated with embroidery cotton. Under his arm he carries a goose. (*Hupp Collection*)

These 7″ dolls from Austria have wire-frame bodies and wooden balls for heads. The features are painted on their wooden heads. They have arms and legs of stuffed stockinette and black felt shoes. The girl has flax hair and wears a blue-and-white apron and a maroon brocade dress with gold trim. The boy is wearing black pants, blue suspenders, a small red tie at the neck, and a gray wool jacket with green edging. His black hat has feathers and gold trim on it. (*Mueller Collection*)

A beautiful Swiss doll in the peasant costume of the Wehntal Valley in the canton of Zurich. She is wearing a black bodice, red stomacher, blue silk apron, white linen blouse with crocheted collar adorned with small roses and forget-me-nots, a black cap with folded border, and a neck streamer with ribbons. Her head is shaped and painted by hand, and her body is stuffed fabric. She was made by the artist Clair Wettstein of Zurich. (*Photo courtesy of the Swiss National Tourist Office*)

In Switzerland on December 6, St. Nicholas's Day, professional bakers as well as many amateurs make "Grattimannen." The origin of these traditional pastry dolls, and how they got their name is uncertain. The dolls probably evolved from the old man of the Christmas season who is identical to the German Father Christmas, a holdover from pagan times. The term may have come from the Bernese dialect in which the word for an old man who stumbles along is a "Gritti." (*Photo courtesy of the Swiss National Tourist Office*)

The children of Switzerland enjoy making *Grattimannen*. They form amusing figures, out of sweet dough with eyes of raisins and decorative vests and caps of dough. When the dolls come out of the oven, they are ready to admire, play with, and ultimately eat. Baking these little bread dolls is a tradition in many Swiss German families. (*Photo courtesy of the Swiss National Tourist Office*)

These clay dolls doing calisthenics were purchased in Belgium. The longest one is 3½". Their bodies are of a darker brown clay than their hair, which is blond. (*Hercek Collection*)

THE DUTCH DOLLS

Germany is renowned for its peg dolls. These dolls, which were made of wood with their joints held in place with little wooden pegs, were made in different sizes, but looked very much alike. Variously called "pegged woodens," "Nürnberg Filles," "Wooden Bettys," "Flanders babies," "penny woodens," and "peggitys," they are most famous as "Dutch dolls." They were probably named Dutch dolls because they were exported to the rest of the world through the Dutch merchants in such ports as Amsterdam.

Originally made in the seventeenth century by the carvers of religious statues in Bavaria, Sonneberg, Thuringia, and the Grodner Tal, these Dutch dolls satisfied a demand for cheap wooden dolls with shiny black hair and pegged joints. In the Tryrol, making these dolls was a cottage industry. The carvers used local pinewood; in Bavaria it was linden or lime.

The dolls ranged in size from ½ " to 24", and their bodies were made in sections with the head and torso in one piece. The arms and legs were fastened in place in such a way that they would be movable. The smaller dolls were fastened with wooden pegs; the large ones had ball joints. They had rosy cheeks and shiny black hair painted on.

By the end of the nineteenth century these little dolls were very crudely made. They were pegged with tiny splinters of wood, and rather than having their stylized black hair, red shoes, and red cheeks painted on, they were merely daubed with paint.

The legs of the Dutch doll are made in a similar fashion to those for the jigger (see page 328). The lower section is made with a tenon that fits into a mortise in the upper section. A drill is used to make an ⅛" hole through both, but the hole in the tenon should be just a little larger. A piece of wooden dowel is then pushed through and cut off at the side of the leg. The lower section should hang loosely so that the leg can move.

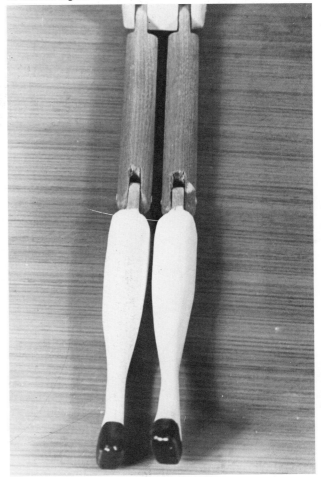

To make a Dutch doll, you need a piece of wood, a jigsaw or coping saw, and sharp jackknife. Use a piece of soft pine, balsa, or any other wood you prefer. Balsa is easy to carve, but pine or a similar wood is usually better because it will not splinter as easily and will hold the nail or pin joints more firmly than balsa.

The wooden Dutch doll is made in a similar fashion to that used for making a jigger, which is shown in a step-by-step photograph on page 326. After carving out each piece, sandpaper it. Using white enamel, paint the wood. Add extra coats until the grain of the wood is covered completely. With a small brush, paint on the features, using red paint for the lips, blue for the eyes, and black for the hair.

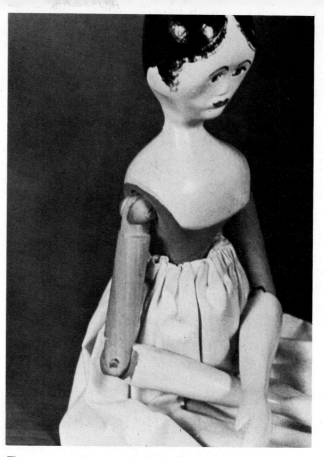

The arms are made in a similar fashion to the legs and are also pegged with 1/8" dowels. They are connected with a piece that goes through the center of the body.

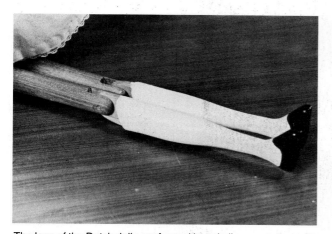

The legs of the Dutch dolls are formed in a similar way to those for the jigger, and the sections are pegged together. The difference is that there is more carving to shape the lower leg of the Dutch doll, and the feet are carved as part of the lower leg rather than being separate pieces attached by a peg.

The body of the Dutch doll is more shapely than the jigger's and is cut in one piece with the head. The body is shaped by turning the wood on a lathe. If a lathe is not available, the body can be carved. Each piece of the Dutch doll should be sandpapered very smooth before the doll is painted. The hair and features are carefully painted on. Areas not painted should be protected with polyurethane satin-finish interior varnish. (*Wood Collection*)

As time passed the penny woodens were made more crudely, with the arms and legs being dowels pegged together with splinters of wood. The painting was also done in a more haphazard fashion as this later 12″ penny wooden shows. (*Wood Collection*)

This small wooden Dutch doll was made about 1830 and imported to the United States. It is still in the original fabric dress. (*Photographed at Children's Museum, Boston, Mass.*)

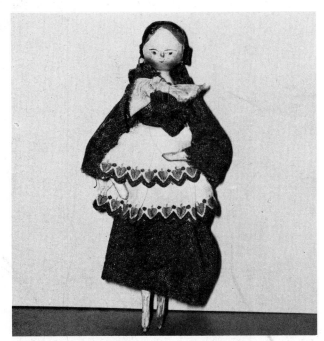

This penny wooden imported to the United States from Germany is dressed in a poorly finished homemade costume. She has a woolen dress with raw edges at the cuffs and hemline and a bow pinned under her chin. Her apron was cut from a piece of machine-embroidered, scalloped-edge fabric. (*Photographed at Children's Museum, Boston, Mass.*)

This jointed wooden Dutch doll has a brown moire silk dress with white lawn sleeves. Her white satin bonnet is decorated with forget-me-knots. She was dressed about 1860 by Mrs. Benjamin Curtis of Wellesley Hills, Massachusetts, who made the dress from fabric from her own mother's wedding dress. The bonnet is an exact copy of the one her mother wore on her wedding day and is made from fabric from her wedding dress. (*Photographed at Children's Museum, Boston, Mass.*)

This 14" wooden Dutch doll has its original old wig. The doll was restored and the clothing made from antique fabrics and laces by Doris Hupp. (*Hupp Collection*)

PRUNE DOLL

Making dolls from dried fruits threaded onto wire frames is an old craft in Southern Germany. These prune dolls, called "Pflaume Maennchen," "Zwetschgen Mannerle," or little prune people, are supposed to bring good luck and a good harvest in the year ahead.

In Nuremberg every year in December the Christkindlmarkt is held in the open square of the city. Toys of every description are sold, but the specialty of the market is the little prune people. The prune doll figure can be of a lady dressed in a kerchief, dress, apron, and shawl, or of a man with a jaunty hat carrying a walking stick, or a chimney sweep, or even an old-fashioned St. Nicholas in a red robe. No matter what figure the doll represents, it always has a walnut head and a body of dried fruit—figs, prunes, and sometimes raisins.

In the early 1800s in rural America and England as well, peddlers carried their wares sometimes fastened to their own clothing but usually in a hand-carried basket. They wore typical calico dresses and full-length capes that helped protect the merchandise from rain and snow.

The wooden Dutch dolls were sometimes dressed by their owners as peddler dolls. This 17" doll has a wooden body made in Germany in the 1840s and is dressed in U.S. peddler tradition by Doris Hupp. (*Hupp Collection*)

Germany for centuries was considered the toy-making center of the world, and Nuremberg the principal toymaking place. At Christmastime a special open-air market called the Christkindlmarkt is held in the city. Here toys of all descriptions are sold, but the specialty is the little prune man.

Making these dolls is easy and inexpensive, and the fruit can be eaten later if so desired. The dolls might be hung on the Christmas tree, grouped on a mantel, or given as gifts.

To make the bases for the prune dolls, you will need pieces of ⅜″ plywood cut into 2½″ squares, nonlead green paint, and #17 gauge nylon or plastic-coated steel wire, which is sold in hardware stores. If you use nonlead paint and coated wire, the prunes and figs can be eaten later.

For the dolls, you will need walnuts, medium-size dried prunes, figs, scraps of gold foil from candy wrappers or aluminum foil if gold is unavailable, pins, red, black, and white paint to paint the features on the walnut heads, small red beads for noses, and thin wrapping wire.

For the man doll, you will need a small piece of print fabric for the shirt, a small piece of plain heavier fabric like corduroy for the vest, and scraps of cotton print fabric for the bow tie and kerchief tote. For the hat, you will need a section from a cardboard egg carton, and scraps of different colors of baby rickrack to decorate it. For a walking stick, use a twig or stick about ⅜″ in diameter and 6¼″ long.

For the lady doll, you will need crepe paper for her umbrella and skirt and a twig or stick about ⅛″ in diameter and 2½″ long. For her head scarf, apron, and kerchief tote, use scraps of cotton print fabric. For her shawl, use a scrap of white lacy fabric and a piece of satin ribbon for a bow. As equipment, you will need scissors, white glue, a ruler, hammer and nail or drill, and needlenose pliers.

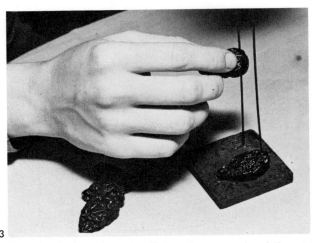

2

Slip the pieces of bent wire into the base from the bottom. Embed the wires into the underside of the base by tapping them with a hammer, and embed the ends of the wires into the top of the base again with the hammer.

3

To make the feet, choose two flattened prunes and push them on to the top of each wire. Push them on at the wider end of the prune just past the stone and bring them down on the wire to sit on the base.

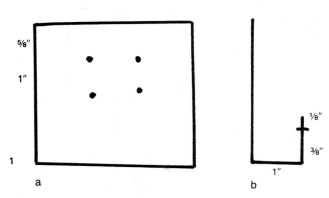

1

a   b

To make the base of a prune doll, paint a 2½″ square of plywood. Make holes just large enough for the wire to pass through, using a hammer and nail or a drill, if available, Place the holes as shown in (a). Cut two 12″ pieces of wire and bend them as shown in (b).

4 To make the legs, string on three more prunes on each wire. For the lower leg, push on the prune with the stone behind the wire. For the knee, have the stone in front of the wire, and for the upper leg, again have the stone to the back.

5 For the body of the man, push 5 figs onto both wires.

6 With the needlenose pliers, bend the wires at right angles toward and across the center. The wires should cross each other, then extend out on each side of the figure for arms.

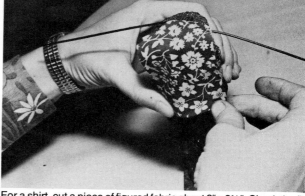

7 For a shirt, cut a piece of figured fabric about 2″ x 2½″. Check the fit on your figure as the sizes of figs vary. Turning under the raw edge of the fabric, attach it to the figure with pins at the top and bottom.

8

| 1″ | 1½″ | 2½″ | 1½″ | 1″ |

3½″

5½″

For the vest, cut a piece of fabric 5½″ x 3½″. If you want the doll for permanent display, and the fabric is one that ravels, you might allow ¼″ all around and hem it. Cut armholes as shown. Fold at the dotted lines at the underarms right sides together and stitch at the shoulder taking a ⅛″ seam. Turn to the right side.

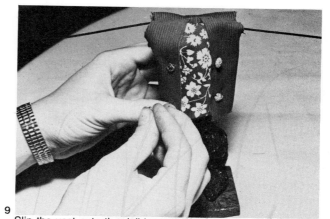

9 Slip the vest onto the doll by putting the wire arms through the armholes. You may have to bend back one wire arm temporarily. Cover the heads of four pins with foil. Press these into the figs holding the vest opened.

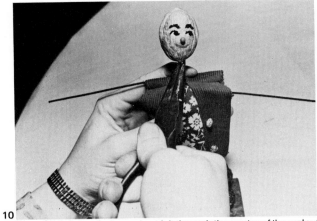

10 Cut a 2½″ piece of wire and push it through the center of the walnut at the wider, more rounded end. Secure with a bit of glue. With a fine brush, paint eyes, eyebrows, and a mouth on the walnut. Note that the eyes of the man should look to one side and the eyes of the woman to the other, so that when they stand together they will be looking at each other. Glue on a red bead nose. Force the wire from the head into the center top of the fig body.

11 String two prunes on to each arm and bend the arms toward the front.

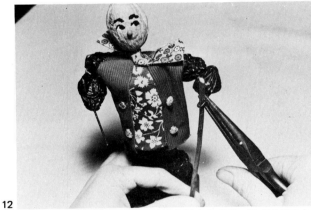

12 For the tie, cut a piece of cotton print fabric 1½″ x 5″. Fold it in half lengthwise. Lift up the walnut head temporarily and tie the tie around the wire, making a single knot at the center of the fabric. Cut off the ends if necessary. Twist the end of the wire arm into a circle cutting off any excess. Slip the walking stick into the wire circle hand and wedge it against the wooden base. For the other arm, make a handkerchief tote. Cut a piece of cotton-print fabric 2¾″ square. Cut a short piece of fine tie wire and insert it into each corner of the square. Bring the corners together and secure them to the doll's other hand. Cut a hat from the center partition of an egg carton where it sticks up between the eggs. Decorate as desired with strips of baby rickrack and put it on the man's walnut head to complete the doll.

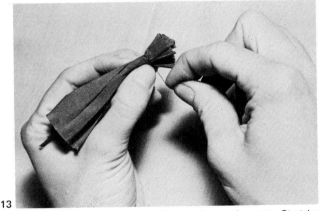

13 The woman is made in a similar fashion to the man. Start by making an umbrella or parasol for her. Cut a piece of red crepe paper 12″ x 2½″. Gather the paper slightly on one 12″ side, and wire it to the end of a 2½″ stick, allowing about ½″ of the crepe paper to extend below the wire. Turn this ½″ allowance upward so it covers the wire.

For the skirt, cut a piece of crepe paper 4″ x 21″. With matching thread, gather the crepe paper ¼″ in from one long edge, using a long sewing-machine stitch or a double-threaded hand-basting stitch. Gather the paper on the thread. **14**

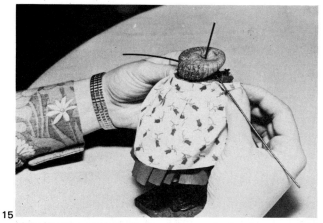

15

Make the legs and body for the woman as for the man, except put only 4 figs on the body before twisting the arm wires to the right and left. Add the fifth fig above the others, securing it the 2½″ piece of wire on which you will put the walnut head. Adjust the size of the skirt by gathering the crepe paper on the thread so that it goes around the doll just under the wire arms with a 1″ lapping behind. Fasten securely to the doll with pins. For the apron, cut a piece of print fabric 3½″ x 8½″. Make about five ¼″ tucks at the top of the apron; put it on the doll over the skirt and secure it in place with straight pins.

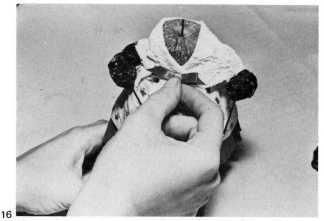

16

Make a small bow from satin ribbon, tying at the center with wire rather than knotting. Cover the head of a pin with gold foil and push it through the center of the bow. For the shawl, cut a lace triangle with a long side measuring 8″ and two short sides measuring 5½″ each. Turn under the longest edge and bring the shawl around the doll with the ends crossed in the front. Hold the shawl in place with the bow.

17

Paint the woman's features on the walnut head as for the man, but add a bit of black paint for hair. Attach the head to the doll on the wire coming out of the body. Cut a triangular head scarf with long edge 6⅜″ and two short edges 4½″ each. Turn under the long edge ¼″ and put it over the doll's head. Tie the ends of the scarf in a single knot under the chin and secure it to the body with a straight pin. Bend the arms as for the man. Make a handkerchief tote as for the man and put this in one of her wire hands. Put the parasol you have made in the other hand as Germaine Reusch is doing in completing her prune lady.

This 7½″ prune lady wears a red-print kerchief and a white shawl with a red ribbon bow. Her skirt is maroon crepe paper, and her apron is a piece of green-print fabric. She is carrying a maroon crepe-paper umbrella with a stick for the center. (*Made by Germaine Reusch; MacNeer Collection*)

18

The completed dolls made by Germaine Reusch look at each other. Germaine, who lives in the United States, learned to make the prune dolls by taking apart a set sent to her parents from Germany.

A 7″ pair of prune dolls made in Germany and purchased at the Christkindlmarkt in Nuremberg. The woman is wearing a green crepe-paper skirt and knit-fabric apron, scarf, and shawl. The man has a knit-fabric scarf, and both have small nails for noses. (*Author's Collection*)

ITALY

Italy has a dollmaking tradition that stretches back to ancient Rome. In those early times a child would be thrown into the Tiber River as an offering to the gods. Later on a doll was substituted for this sacrifice.

Some dolls, hand carved from bone or ivory, were made in Rome with elaborate headdresses. Jointed wooden dolls were also made, and one nearly 12″ tall was found in a Roman tomb with traces of gilding still on it. Dolls and other playthings were often buried with their young owners.

Romans observed various customs related to dolls. The Roman girl played with dolls until her marriage, perhaps at the age of twelve or thirteen, when she would solemnly consign them with other playthings to Venus or Diana. After her first child was born she would hang a doll with other offerings in the temple.

Dolls of ivory and bone have been found in the catacombs. The early Christians in hiding there might have carved such dolls for their children as a way of amusing them.

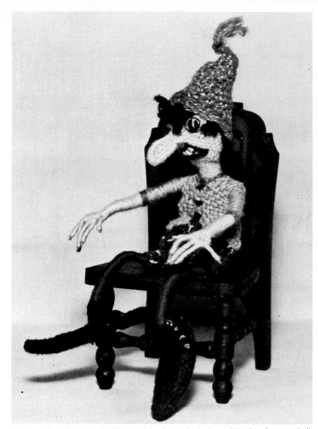

This delightfully ugly Pinocchio from Italy is a 9″ wire-frame doll. His limbs are wire wrapped with yarn, his hair is black yarn, and his features are stitched with yarn. His shoes are pieces of cardboard also wrapped with yarn. His yellow hat, pink face, brown pants, and blue jacket are pieces of woven yarn. His nose is a piece of wire with yarn woven over it. His long fingers are pieces of yarn-covered wire with painted ends. (*MacNeer Collection*)

These 11″ tall vegetable people were made in Italy. They have wire-framed bodies, mainly of stuffed felt. Both figures have big felt feet that keep them standing. The woman represents "three peas in a pod," with her three felt peas with painted faces looking out of the pea shell. She is wearing a red-print cotton dress with a red-striped apron. The man is a "bean head," representing the "tall stringbean," and wears a white-cotton shirt, with a red-felt collar and yellow satin-ribbon bow. His red-felt pants have a yellow waistband and yellow fringe. In his basket are some white-felt bean flowers. (*MacNeer Collection*)

This 10″ maharaja doll was not made in India but is an authentic Lenci doll from Italy. He has a pressed-fabric face, his features are painted, and his elaborate turban is made of felt. He is holding a painted wooden fan and has a wooden elephant on a string around his neck. Around his wrists are wooden bracelets, and hanging from his ears are painted wooden loop earrings. The rest of him is felt with a jacket beautifully embroidered and detailed. (*Hupp Collection*)

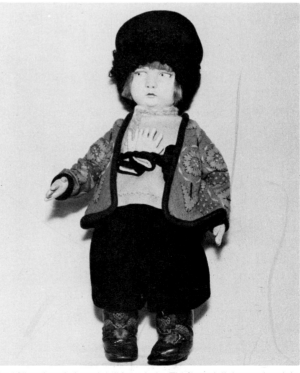

An 18″ authentic Lenci doll from Italy. This boy doll dressed mainly in felt is meant to be a Russian. He has a pressed-felt face, a black fur-and-felt cap, and green leather boots that are beautifully embroidered. He wears a felt jacket decorated with felt appliqués and embroidery stitches and full black pantaloons. Under his belt is a pair of beautifully detailed light brown felt gloves. (*Hupp Collection*)

A more modern doll custom of Italy is one that is practiced in Sorrento. There a wooden doll, known as a Lent doll, is made similar to the penny wooden but with her feet fixed into a wooden ball, apple, or orange. Feathers—six black and one white— are stuck in the ball and pointed downward. The black feathers represent the six weeks of Lent and one is pulled out each week. Finally on Easter Sunday the white feather is taken out. Dolls like this would be hung in hotels during the Lenten season, and as the feathers were pulled out, they would be burnt for luck.

A modern Italian doll that has become famous is the Lenci doll. Designed and made by Enrico Scavini of Turin, Italy, these dolls were first patented in 1921 and made until the mid-1930s. Made of felt and exquisitely clothed, these dolls had appealing and charming faces, with wide-spaced wistful eyes and small rosebud mouths.

The original Lenci dolls were expensive, but later less expensive imitations were made with cloth bodies and less elaborate costumes. The later Lenci-type dolls were often attractive, but they did not equal the charm and fine workmanship of the authentic Lenci dolls.

Lenci-type dolls, made in Italy, which were very popular in the 1950s. These are stuffed felt dolls with felt clothing. The 9″ boy skater doll has the tag "Original Eros, Florence." He wears wooden shoe skates and has on a green-and-gold-felt skating outfit with tiny buttons decorating the front. His white-felt neck scarf is decorated with pieces of felt. The girl is dressed in a skirt, blouse, apron, and hat, decorated with felt. (*Hupp Collection*)

In the early years in the United States and Canada the settlers sometimes made dolls using imported heads and homemade bodies. These dolls by Doris Hupp are contemporary examples of purchased heads and homemade bodies. Miss Hupp was given a couple of Lenci-like pressed-felt heads made in Italy meant to be label pins, out of which she made complete dolls. The bodies are stuffed fabric and the clothes are beautifully detailed. The boy is dressed in Alpine style, with petit-point shoulder straps and belt by Miss Hupp. He has a felt cap with feathers stuck in it and embroidered detail on his socks. The girl wears a dress of net decorated with embroidery cotton. Her weskit is velvet tied with a velvet ribbon, and her necklace of seed beads. (*Hupp Collection*)

From Italy Lenci-like, but not authentic Lenci, dolls of stuffed felt. The doll on the left wears a cotton-fabric skirt with a floral design painted on it, a puffed-sleeve blouse, and a typical Italian headdress. The 11″ doll on the right wears a blue skirt and vest decorated with felt flowers, held on with French-knot embroidery stitches and decorated with lazy-daisy embroidery stitches. Felt also decorates the edge of her skirt, and she wears a felt hat. (*Hupp Collection*)

SPAIN

The matador and the flamenco dancers are the most popular themes for Spanish dolls. The Spanish people, it would seem, are fascinated with their folk hero the matador and make many dolls with his traditional outfit complete from his black weighted cap to his firm leather slippers. They also have dolls of the picador, the banderillos, and other bullring characters—even the bull himself.

Though the costume of the matador varies slightly in style and color from one matador to the next, most doll matadors seem to be dressed in bright red. Red is also a popular color for the flamenco dancers, the women with their tight-fitting bodices, skirts with rows of frills, and black mantillas.

Because the matador and the dancer dolls are posed in graceful positions, many have wire frames covered with padding and then sewn fabric skin. Most of the matadors and dancers are thin, exaggeratedly so, as are many of the other Spanish dolls. In contrast are the plump character dolls made with felt skin. These satirically designed Spanish dolls began to appear in the 1950s and are dressed in both folk costumes and contemporary clothing. They are usually beautifully designed, with interesting accessories.

An 11″ toreador bought in Spain in 1936. This doll has a stuffed fabric body, and his face is pressed pink-knit fabric with hand-painted features and hair. He wears the traditional bullfighter's cap, shaped like a skullcap, with stubby horns that are weighted so that it is a heavy headpiece. At the center-back edge of the cap a queue, or braid, of black yarn emerges and falls down his back. His costume is of red satin decorated with woven braid and tube beads like that of his human counterpart, whose outfit is usually embellished with gold thread and colored stones. He wears the traditional slim cravat that reaches to his waistband, and over his shoulders is his *capa*, or "walking cape," and on his feet are firm leather slippers. (*From the Collection of the Forbes Library, Northampton, Mass.*)

A 5″ pair of dolls from Spain representing the matador and the señorita who has come to watch him fight the bull. They are wire framed and covered with thread and fabric. The features are embroidered on their thread-wrapped faces. The woman wears a black net mantilla decorated with black seed beads and a gold satin dress trimmed with black lace. She wears a red-thread flower in her hair and holds another to throw into the ring. The man wears a light brown jacket and pants decorated with embroidery, a red belt, and a black felt hat. He holds his red-satin cape ready to wave at the bull. (*MacNeer Collection*)

A 10" woman from Spain with a pressed fabric face and painted features. Her body is a wire frame covered with fabric. She wears a white-organdy skirt decorated with black lace, and her weskit is red velvet. She wears a black veil and has flowers in her hair. In her hands she has brown-felt castanets. (*Hupp Collection*)

A whimsical portrait of a hunter labeled "Nistis of Barcelona, Spain." This doll carrying a wooden gun has a wire-frame fabric body and wears a beautifully detailed felt outfit. He has on a brown coat, blue vest, and black pants, and around his waist is a red-and-yellow gun belt. An obviously empty pouch for his catch hangs from one shoulder. His features are painted on, and his hair is of black thread. His white-felt dog has black spots painted on him. (*Hupp Collection*)

This fisherman doll was bought in Barcelona, Spain, in about 1972. He has a wire-frame body, stuffed and covered with felt. His face is pressed felt, and his features are painted on. He is dressed in a knit shirt and woven cotton pants. He carries a wooden fishing pole and his prize catch, two felt fish. (*Hulsizer Collection*)

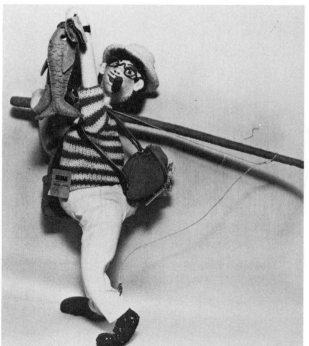

Dolls that show the Spanish talent for making stylized figures. These have stuffed felt bodies with wire frames. The 14½" gentleman has seed-bead eyes and a felt mustache and beard. He wears a brown-satin cape lined with purple, gray pants, and a green jacket. The lady wears a black-and-white houndstooth-weave skirt, black-net gloves, black-felt jacket with red edging and beads for buttons, and yarn hair. Feathers decorate her black hat, and she carries a felt suitcase and a felt umbrella. (*Hupp Collection*)

This 10″ felt doll from Spain is a caricature of the lady-about-town walking her dog and checking on her neighbors. The dog who is doing his own looking around is made of twisted pipe cleaners. The lady has a wire-frame body covered with felt and a pressed-felt face with painted features. Her clothing, pocketbook, and shoes are all felt. (*MacNeer Collection*)

The traditional types of Spanish town are represented in these 2″ clay dolls bought in Marbella. The flamenco dancers in matching costumes are at the left, and a flowerseller is at the far right. The policeman in the center is dressed exactly like the typical provincial policeman. The figures are formed completely of clay except for the cardboard brims on the hats. (*Hercek Collection*)

PORTUGAL

Beautifully worked, colorful, traditional wool embroidery is the hallmark of a doll made in Portugal. Portuguese women make dolls of fabric, some entirely of wool. These dolls representing flower, fruit, and vegetable sellers are often sold in pairs. The male is shown with a guitar; the female usually is dressed in a blouse, full skirt, and colorful apron, with a small basket of flowers or fruit on her head.

The women make and dress these yarn dolls during the winter months and sell them to the tourists who come to their town in the summer.

The wire-frame costume dolls in the folk dress of various parts of the country are another popular type of handmade Portuguese doll. These dolls, many of which were made in the late 1950s, have carefully detailed regional costumes. The large ones, over 7″ in height, often have hand-embroidered features and beautifully embroidered costumes. The smaller ones, each about 3″ tall, have hand-painted features and limbs made with wrapped wire.

Madeira, an island off the coast of Portugal, is a paradise of flowers and trees. Traders there sell dolls dressed in native costumes still worn by the local women and girls who sell flowers in the street. The local men wear white suits and straw hats.

These 10″ yarn dolls were made in Portugal. They have legs made from a tube of card and wrapped with yarn and shoes of vinyl scraps. The arms are all yarn, and their faces are a fabric ball wrapped with yarn, with features and hair of embroidery cotton. The man holds a wooden guitar made from a scrap of wood, with "Sintra, Portugal," printed on it. The woman has an embroidered apron, which also says "Sintra," and a basket on her head with crocheted red balls on it.

These 4½″ Portuguese dolls are made mainly from brightly colored yarn. The man has a wire-frame body with legs wrapped with blue yarn to represent pants. His shirt and face are white yarn, and he has a brown-yarn vest and a red-yarn waistband. His hat is a piece of red fabric, and his features are indicated with embroidery cotton. In one arm he carries a piece of wood, and under the other arm he has a bundle of straw.

The woman's legs are wrapped with white yarn, and her arms and face are formed with white yarn. She has a cotton slip, and over it a skirt made with green yarn caught in a braided band decorated with the herringbone stitch. Her apron is made of fabric decorated with yarn and embroidered with yarn French knots. Her features are embroidered with colored thread. Her brown hair is yarn, and she has yarn flowers in the straw basket on her head. (*Hupp Collection*)

Made in Portugal a 5½" pair of yarn dolls with white-yarn faces and embroidery-yarn features. The woman wears a red skirt and has white yarn wound around wire for her legs. The man is all in black with black yarn wound around his wire legs. He carries a mandolin made from a scrap of wood. (*MacNeer Collection*)

A 4½" Portuguese maiden in a blue yarn skirt. She is made with a wire-frame body, and her legs are wrapped with white yarn. She has a print-fabric bodice, yarn arms, and a white-fabric skirt under the yarn skirt. Her apron is decorated with yarn embroidery, and she has metallic-cord earrings and necklaces. (*Hupp Collection*)

A 7" boy doll from Portugal dressed as a fisherman and bearing the tag "Maria Helena." He has a wire-frame body stuffed and covered with pink cotton fabric. He is dressed in a red plaid outfit and he has brown yarn hair. His features are embroidered, and embroidery cotton stitches indicate his fingers and toes. He carries a net with tiny corks attached to it. (*Hupp Collection*)

These 7½" dolls made in Portugal have wire-frame stuffed fabric bodies. The female doll's legs are covered with yarn. The pair are dressed to represent people from Ribatejo, according to the explanatory tag on the dolls. People from that region are fond of colorful garments and wear feathers in their hats. They live on the lowlands that are often flooded by the Tagus River. The men are usually fishermen, wear no shoes, and love to dance during work breaks. The costumes of both these dolls are beautifully detailed. The male wears a Phrygian cap and a shirt decorated with cross-stitches. In one hand he carries a lantern made from felt. The female is dressed in a white blouse, plaid skirt, and has an embroidered apron. (*Hulsizer Collection*)

167

Handmade in Portugal, 7″ dolls bearing the tag "Maria Helena." The one at the far left is a fisherman with his net over his shoulder. The one at the far right is a friar, or priest, with a heavy missal with ribbon bookmarks hanging out of it. (*Mueller Collection*)

Made in Portugal dolls each only 3″ tall. Their faces are circles of stuffed fabric, with features painted on. Their bodies are pieces of wire wrapped with different colors of thread. Their colorful costumes are made with scraps of woolen and cotton fabric and woven bands. (*Mueller Collection*)

This 10″ fabric stuffed doll from Portugal has a fabric-molded face with painted features. Her hair is mohair, and she wears seed-bead earrings and a necklace. She has a black embroidered vest and a lace collar. She wears white-knit stockings, a print dress with a plain blue edge decorated with embroidery stitches. Over her dress is a print apron, and on her head is a print-fabric mantilla. (*Hupp Collection*)

A 16″ doll decorated with typical Portuguese wool embroidery was meant as a tea cozy. The stuffed fabric body reaches only to the waist, and the teapot would fit under her voluminous skirt. Her nose and mouth are stitched in embroidery cotton, and her hair, eyes, and eyebrows were made with brown yarn. She wears a white cotton blouse decorated with embroidery and a black woolen skirt and apron decorated with colorful yarn embroidered flowers in red, white, and pink. (*Hupp Collection*)

This family of dolls was bought in 1927 in Madeira, an island belonging to Portugal. The mother and father in the center are 10″ tall; the son and daughter are 9″. They all have stuffed bodies and embroidered features.

The men are wearing the Madeiran festival costume, which consists of a white linen shirt and baggy breeches with a fringed linen sash. They also wear the "pigtail" caps called "carapucas." The father's shirt and sash are embroidered, mainly with a featherstitch.

The females have red woolen outfits decorated with embroidery. The mother is wearing the traditional Madeiran festival costume for women, a red skirt and cape, and also a white blouse over which is a corselet laced in the front. She also wears a black pigtail cap like her husband's. (*From the Collection of the Forbes Library, Northampton, Mass.*)

This 14″ stuffed fabric doll, with embroidered features, was made in Madeira. She wears a white blouse beautifully detailed with feather-and-herringbone stitches. Her black hat is also decorated with embroidery as is her red skirt with its parallel lines of decorative stitching.

GREECE

Dolls have a long history in Greece—it was the center of the doll trade before the birth of Chirst. The oldest Greek toy doll found was a clay rattlebox in the shape of a woman. This was a discovery of the archeologist Schliemann who came upon this doll with missing head while excavating the lower strata of Troy.

The early Greeks made primitive images of bronze, terra-cotta, and wax. These images of both men and women engaged in useful work have been found in Greek tombs. These dolls probably served the same function as those in Egyptian tombs— replacing human victims, the wives and slaves who in earlier times were buried alive with the dead master to serve him in the afterworld.

Greek mothers after the birth of their first child consecrated a small doll in the Temple of Eileithyia. Dolls have been found in the graves of children, sometimes along with miniature objects that could be used in playing with the dolls. Greek girls of all ages enjoyed playing with dolls and dolls' clothes, and miniature clay furniture.

Dolls were popular at the time of Plato who mentioned them in his writings, comparing easily manipulated men with dolls whose par.. moved by pulling strings. Aristotle also referred to dolls in a similar way.

As far as modern-day Greek dolls are concerned, the most common handmade ones are those dressed in national costume, usually made with stuffed fabric bodies. Though Greeks may not wear their national dress as everyday clothing, many keep a full costume stored away for festive occasions. Nearly every region has its own distinctive style of costume so one of the best-known modern handcrafts in Greece is the making of dolls in native dress.

This Greek man and woman, made before 1927, have wire-frame bodies wrapped with yarn. Their arms and faces are pink cotton fabric, and they have hand-painted features and yarn hair. They wear leather shoes with black yarn pompons. The man is 15″ tall and wears the traditional short white pleated kilt, or fustanella, of white organza. This kilt is related to the one worn by the Scotsmen. Over 2,000 years ago the kilt was brought to Scotland by a Greek mountain warrior, and since then Greeks and Scotsmen have each had their own version of the kilt. This male doll wears a red Phrygian cap weighted with a large black cotton tassel, and his legs are wrapped with white yarn representing the white woolen stockings worn as part of the costume.

The woman doll is 13″ tall and has a woven woolen dress and coat. Each is richly decorated with red-and-black embroidery, gold sequins, and gold trim. Her legs are wound with blue-and-white yarn. (From the Collection of the Forbes Library, Northampton, Mass.)

Many of these are very beautiful and accurate in detail.

Probably the most common of the traditional Greek costume dolls is that of the evzone, a Greek highland soldier of light infantry who wears the short white pleated kilt, or fustanella, and a Phrygian hat. Women dolls in regional costumes of wool, beautifully detailed with wool embroidery, are also popular.

Made in Greece, a 12″ pair of stuffed fabric dolls with pressed-fabric faces. The man's modern uniform, based on the royal dress of the early nineteenth century, consists of a white linen shirt embroidered in blue and a white fustanella. His red Phrygian cap has a large black tassel on it. The woman's skirt and dress are beautifully embroidered. She wears a head scarf and woven apron. (*Hupp Collection*)

These dolls made in Greece have stuffed fabric bodies with pink pressed-cotton-fabric faces and painted features. The 8″ doll on the left has a tag that says she was made by the Near East Industries, Greek Refugee Work in Athens. She has a hand-embroidered green velvet vest, a red organza blouse, and a pleated purple brocade skirt. The 8″ doll on the right was made by the same refugee group. She wears a purple cotton skirt and a white hand-embroidered woolen vest. The boy doll in the middle wears a white organza fustanella, a white shirt, a purple vest, and leather shoes with pompons. (*From the Collection of the Forbes Library, Northampton, Mass.*)

This 5″ girl with a burro was made in Greece. She has a wire-frame body wrapped with yarn and a pressed-fabric face. She is wearing a blue coarsely woven woolen skirt and a green blouse and holds a bundle of straw. (*Weiner Collection*)

SCANDINAVIAN WOODEN DOLLS

The early dolls made in the Scandinavian countries were mostly carved from wood. The peasant brought in a block of wood from the forest and carved a doll from it while his wife embroidered clothing for it. In Norway in past centuries the peasants made a "house doll." Half the size of human beings, it was made of wood with long hair and a beard. In the summer it was given offerings of whey, and at Christmas time, beer.

In Sweden novelty dolls were made from birch bark while in Denmark wooden stump dolls were made. Today wooden turned dolls as well as carved dolls are still being made in the Scandinavian countries. Sometimes these are fishermen or peasants or other human figures, but sometimes they are trolls, humanlike creatures of the dark woods.

Norway and Denmark are known for their trolls. In fact, everywhere in these countries are reputed troll caves, peaks, and fjords. These dark shadowy places show clearly how troll legends grew up. A troll is usually described as a large old man, rather slow and stupid and often very hairy. Some trolls have a

A small 3″ Greek doll with a wire-frame body. He represents an evzone, and his fustanella is white yarn wrapped around a cotton base. (*Author's Collection*)

This 3½″ handcrafted doll from Norway represents a fisherman holding his catch. His body is carved from a single piece of wood and stained in muted colors. The fish is a separate piece of wood. (*Stukas Collection*)

sort of cow's tail, others multiple heads. Some have very ugly wives and large families of unpleasant children. Most trolls never wash, and there are some with trees growing out of their noses or the humps on their backs. They are said to own buckets of gold and keep bears instead of dogs. The rather harmless and disarming trolls, handcrafted today in Norway, are stained instead of painted to keep a natural woody look.

Wooden-carved dolls are also made in Lapland, which is the most northerly part of Sweden and Norway, and also in Greenland, which is related to Denmark.

This whimsical 5″ doll from Norway was carved by hand and represents a troll, a famous figure in Norwegian folklore. He is stained in forest colors and has a huge nose and a big white-painted tooth. (*Stukas Collection*)

A 9″ doll, on a wooden base made in Greenland, has huge leather boots topped with fur. This male figure wears a plaid shirt and fur pants, and his hair is tied in a topknot. (*Hupp Collection*)

A doll probably made between 1920 and 1940 in Lapland —the most northerly part of Scandinavia stretching across Sweden and Finland into northern Russia. An ancient people, the Lapps, unlike other Scandinavians, are a nomadic Mongolian race. They follow herds of reindeer, and because of their hard life in a very cold region their clothing is both practical and warm. This male doll from Lapland has a wooden carved face and a wooden base body. He wears the "cap of the four winds," or "sorcerer's cap," the traditional man's hat with four long points. He has on a reindeerskin tunic, called a *peski*, of thick natural fur. Bands of colored felt and rickrack decorate the front of the tunic. The figure also has a decorated belt and *mutukas*, the typical peaked and decorated reindeerskin boots worn by the Lapps. (*Hupp Collection*)

Made in Greenland, a primitive 9″ doll with a wooden base and hand-carved face. The figure is wearing a leather top and boots and bushy bearskin pants. (*Hupp Collection*)

These hand-carved trolls from Denmark are of stained wood and have a few dabs of white paint to accent their eyes and teeth. Several have fake fur as hair. These are woodland creatures that figure in the Danish folktales.

WOODEN TURNED DOLLS

Wooden turned dolls of high quality are made in both Sweden and Denmark. Even though they are mass produced by craftsmen, they are carefully made and show the Scandinavian genius for design. Danish craftsmen are known worldwide for their fine modern designs. Their furniture, textiles, dolls, porcelain, and ceramics are characteristically designed with simplicity, restraint, and elegance. The objects they design have clean lines, grace, refinement, and subtlety of design, and this is obvious in the whimsical dolls they create.

You can make your own wooden turned dolls, such as those produced in Scandinavia. If you have access to a wood lathe, you can make the body sections, or you can buy wooden balls and finials at a local hardware store. You can also buy these balls at a craft shop that sells supplies for macramé. You will also need acrylic paint, brushes, and glue as well as small amounts of yarn, felt, and burlap.

Pieces of turned wood can be purchased from sources such as Creative Playmakers, Inc., which offer this assortment, called "Bigger Guys," of turned pieces to simulate bodies, necks, hats, and so on. Combine these turned pieces to make interesting dolls in a variety of shapes.

1 With acrylic paints and a fine brush, paint features on a 1¼" wooden ball. Paint a wooden finial red. Glue the head on the wooden finial.

2 Cut 7 pieces of white knitting worsted-weight yarn 9" long. Make a slipknot at the center.

Place the yarn knot at the back of the doll's head near her neckline. Bring the strands up and around, crossing them at the front.

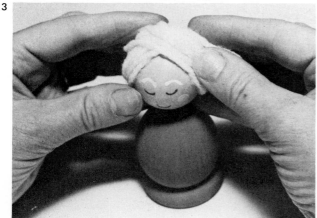

3

Cut a triangle of red felt 5½" on each side. Bring one side so it slightly overlaps a second side, forming a cone, and glue along the overlap. Glue the hat in place on the doll's head over the yarn hair. Bring the point down and glue it against the hat.

4

5
For the baby, paint features on a ⅜″ wooden ball. Cut a piece of red felt according to this pattern and glue it on the baby's head.

6
Cut a 1½″ square of white felt and wrap it around the baby for a bunting and glue in place. Cut a piece of brown burlap 1½″ × 6½″. Fringe it all around the edge. Bring it around the doll, fold over in front, and glue it in place.

7
The completed wooden turned doll holding a baby is joined by her partner, also a wooden turned figure but with a long fake-fur beard.

These wooden turned dolls are made like the ones above. The one on the left has a piece of fake fur for a muff and the one on the right is holding a paper bird and some grain for the bird's Christmas. In Scandinavian countries the people traditionally put out grain for the birds at Christmas. (*Author's Collection*)

From Sweden, a 3″ doll made of wooden balls and pieces of turned wood. This figure has a red-knitted cap and a flaxen mustache. His hands are wooden beads with holes drilled in the center. (*Schichtel Collection*)

This 4″ doll from Sweden is made with pieces of turned wood. He has a fake-fur beard, a knitted cap, and is carrying, in wooden bead hands, a wooden lantern and a ribbon-tied present. (*Schichtel Collection*)

From Sweden, a 7″ doll made with wooden dowels and balls. The features are painted on, and the nose is a small red ball. The hair is fake fur, and the arms are made from knitted tubing. He is carrying a square wooden lantern with a candle painted on it, and wears a red fabric hat with a large yarn pompon at the end. (*Schichtel Collection*)

This 7″ doll from Sweden was made from pieces of turned wood. He is painted mainly red and on the top of his red stocking cap is a red yarn tassel. In one hand he is carrying a little red wooden heart. (*Groszmann Collection*)

This little girl on a sled, made in Sweden, measures 5″ from the top of her knitted hat to the bottom of the wooden runner of her sled. She has a wooden-ball head and a piece of turned wood for a body, dowel legs, and big feet sawed from wood. She has yarn braids, a knitted hat, and a piece of woven band for a scarf. (*Schichtel Collection*)

A delightful 6″ doll from Sweden made with pieces of wood. She has flax hair and carries a bouquet of tiny pinecones in her wooden hand. Her face is natural wood with painted features. Her body is painted black with peach accents. (*MacNeer Collection*)

A wooden doll from Denmark, typical of those sold there. He is a Viking with a huge fake-fur beard that is red tipped with black. He wears a leather cape and carries a wooden sword and shield. (*Schichtel Collection*)

This 3″ wooden doll was made in Denmark from two pieces of turned wood. The features are hand painted, and the hair is made from yarn. (*Schichtel Collection*)

This 5″ wooden doll from Denmark has his rope arms full with a huge fabric sack. His body is turned wooden, and his face and nose are wooden balls. He has a felt hat and yarn beard. (*Schichtel Collection*)

A 6″ wooden doll made in Denmark. The head is a wooden ball, and the body is made from turned wood. She has cornhusk hair, and her simple body is painted red. She has paper flowers decorating her braids and in a garland around her head. No features are indicated on her wooden face. (*Hupp Collection*)

This roly-poly doll is made with a 2″ wooden ball flattened on the bottom. The hair is of flax, and the hat is red flannel. (*Author's Collection*)

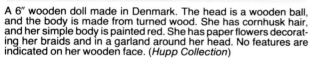

These tiny dolls are made with two wooden beads, ⅝″ × ½″ in diameter, and have tall red hats of red flannel fabric. (*Author's Collection*)

A 3″ wooden turned doll, painted white, with red yarn hair and a red flannel scarf. The figure holds a wooden racket in his pipe-cleaner hand. (*Author's Collection*)

COSTUME DOLLS OF SCANDINAVIA

Wooden dolls are not the only ones for which the Scandinavian countries are so famous; other types of dolls are also made there, including the straw doll. Straw is commonly used to make a variety of items, especially at harvest and Christmas time, and dolls are among them.

Another popular Scandinavian doll is the costume doll. Usually made with a wire frame, it represents some famous person, such as Hans Christian Andersen, or displays the contemporary or traditional clothing worn in a particular area.

Among the most famous costume dolls of Sweden are those made in the shop of Charlotte Weibull, where hundreds of thousands of dolls have been made by hand. Ms. Weibull got into her doll business through a costume business that was already in the family. In 1901 her grandaunt opened a shop selling Swedish national costumes in Malmö, and Ms. Weibull took it over in 1942. She found that when mothers came in to order traditional costumes for their little girls, the girls wanted to have identical outfits made for their dolls. She started making national costumes for dolls, and soon began to sell her

This 8″ doll made in Odense, Denmark, represents Hans Christian Andersen. This famous storyteller enjoyed making dolls as a young man and used them in his imaginative doll theater. This doll has a wire-frame body, and a face and hands formed from clay. He wears a black felt top hat and a brown felt coat and vest decorated with seed beads as buttons. He carries a plaid umbrella and a satchel with a hand-painted flower design on it. (*Weiner Collection*)

These dolls from Sweden were made with straw. Each 4″ figure wears a red flannel cap and is attached to his neighbors with red string at the wrists and ankles. (*Photographed at the United Nations Gift Center*)

Denmark is a country closely linked to the sea, one of the great seafaring nations of the world. Naturally fishing is one of her big industries, and fishermen are numerous in this country. Dolls dressed as fishermen, then, are typical. This beautifully made wire-frame doll has a hand-knit sweater and boots that extend above the knee, like those worn by Danish fishermen. His hands are made of pink felt, and he carries a gray felt fish. His face was modeled by hand from clay, and his features were painted. (Urdang Collection)

This beautifully detailed 5" doll of a mother and child from Denmark bears the label "Hedebo." The mother, dressed in a red plaid outfit, has a wire-frame body covered with a stuffed pink-knit fabric. Her features are drawn on her face, and she has yellow yarn hair and a red bow under her chin. She has a red felt underskirt and white pantaloons and black wooden shoes. In one arm she holds a baby with a stuffed pink-knit-fabric face and a lace bonnet. The baby wears a white cotton shirt, has hands molded from a claylike substance, and is wrapped in a blue wool blanket. In the mother's other hand she holds a "doll," a small replica of herself, which she is showing to the baby. The doll has wire arms wrapped with thread and is dressed in the same plaid outfit as the mother. (Hupp Collection)

From Denmark, an 11" boy on skis made of stuffed fabrics. His face is pressed felt with hand-painted features and hair. His body is stuffed purple velveteen. He is wearing a felt hat, scarf, and socks, and his hands are velveteen. He has wooden feet, skis, and ski poles. He was imported by Kimport before 1939. (From the Collection of the Forbes Library, Northampton, Mass.)

A beautifully finished 8" doll made in Norway. She has a pressed-fabric face and stuffed fabric body. She is wearing a light blue cotton blouse with seed beads at the neckline and a blue woolen hat. Her blue woolen skirt and vest are gorgeously decorated with hand-stitched embroidery with a flower design in brightly colored embroidery cotton. (Weiner Collection)

182

From Finland, 8″ dolls with clay hands, face, and feet and fabric bodies. They are dressed in felt and woven fabrics. The boy has a felt vest and pants, and a cotton shirt. Both girls have felt vests, cotton blouses, woven woolen skirts in bright stripes, and white cotton aprons. (*Photographed at the United Nations Gift Center*)

This beautifully made skier doll from Norway has a pressed-fabric face with painted features. Her tag says "Made in Norway—Vare Marke." She is a wire-frame doll wearing a red felt hat and mittens and an embroidered jacket and black felt pants. She carries wooden skies and poles. (*Weiner Collection*)

This 4½″ delightfully grotesque doll was bought in Iceland in the 1960s. She is sitting on a piece of lava stone. Her body is wire wrapped with yarn. She has a strip of unfinished dark blue cotton fabric with white dots gathered at the top for her skirt. Her hair is a vivid red-orange yarn, and on her head is a scarf made from a plaid fabric. She has a nut head and a bean nose, and her eyes and mouth are painted. Her tiny feet are cut from bits of black rubberlike material. She is knitting with a pair of nails and a ball of yarn. (*Stukas Collection*)

Swedish doll designer Charlotte Weibull is devoted to perpetuating knowledge of the national folk costumes of her country through the dolls she designs and her workers produce. She is also interested in how dolls are made by people in other countries. Here she shows just a few of the many dolls in her own private collection of dolls from all over the world, from which, of course, she has learned dollmaking techniques. (*Photo courtesy Charlotte Weibull*)

A delightful Swedish book *The Adventures of Nils Holgersson* tells the story of a boy who rode all over the Swedish countryside on the back of a goose and what happened on his journey. This is Charlotte Weibull's version of Nils the farm boy with his blond linen-thread hair and red cap. He is typical of the wire-frame dolls she designs. They are covered with flesh-colored jersey and dressed in beautiful handmade clothing. (*Photo courtesy Charlotte Weibull*)

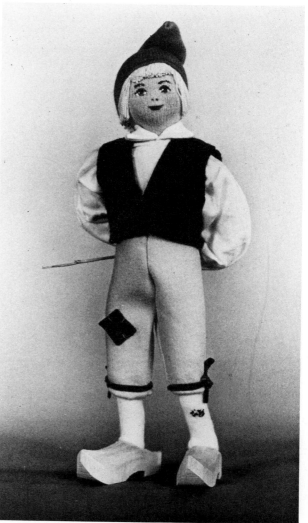

own handmade dolls in costumes representing thirty-two different districts of Scania, Sweden's most southern province. Tourists were especially attracted to her authentic dolls, and so her dollmaking business grew.

Today Ms. Weibull designs the dolls and has women making them in her shop. Craftspeople from all parts of Sweden are also employed in their own homes making various doll accessories which they ship to Malmö. They make wooden shoes, fiddles, rakes, pulpits, wheelbarrows, and so on, as well as tiny buttons and small pieces of jewelry, such as brooches and silver bridal crosses. About a hundred seamstresses also work in their own homes making the national costumes that the dolls wear. The dressed dolls are then sent to the main workshop in Malmö where the wooden shoes, headdresses, jewelry, and other accessories are added. These dolls, when completed, are sold not only in Scandinavia but all over the world.

Several women are employed full time in Charlotte Weibull's workshop making the bodies of dolls. The dolls are made with frames of annealed copper wire to make them strong but flexible. The faces are made with a plastic compound with the help of forms. The head is stuffed, and flesh-colored jersey is pulled over it and stitched in place. Prepared heads are visible on the table at the center of the photo.

The heads are then attached to the wire-body frames as shown on those on the table behind the pile of heads. The worker then winds strips of plastic foam around the body to shape it as she is shown doing. Wrapped doll bodies can be seen in the foreground of the photo. The next step is to add a covering of flesh-colored jersey. The hair, of wool or linen thread, is sewn in place, and the face painted on by hand. (*Photo courtesy Charlotte Weibull*)

Charlotte Weibull has a large collection of old costumes and parts of old costumes. She also collects information about the national costumes of Sweden—she has detailed descriptions of over 200 different costumes from all parts of Sweden. Her grandaunt started this archive before the turn of the century. With this vast store of information to draw on, Ms. Weibull designs such costumes for her dolls as the bridal pair of Skånskt shown here. (*Photo courtesy Charlotte Weibull, Malmö, Sweden*)

This lacemaker doll, handmade in the workshop of Charlotte Weibull, has a wire frame of annealed copper wire so she can pose in this lifelike position with her hands above her work. Her hair is made of linen thread, and her face is hand painted. On her feet are wooden clogs. Her apron is a beautiful piece of handwoven woolen fabric. She sits in front of her lacemaking cushion, which is on a wooden platform. The lace she is working on is held in place with tiny pins. (*Photo courtesy Charlotte Weibull, Malmö, Sweden*)

A 7″ pair of wire-frame dolls from Sweden made in the workshop of Charlotte Weibull. They have the typical hand-painted features and knit-fabric skin pulled over their padded wire frame. The female is dressed in a woven-wool magenta skirt, and a white cotton blouse edged at the collar and cuffs with embroidery. She also has a dark green felt corselet laced with red pearl cotton thread. Her hat is red taffeta with a white lace edge, and she has yellow thread hair. She also has a seed bead brooch at her neck and wears vinyl shoes. Her partner wears hand-carved wooden shoes, a red-knit-fabric liberty cap with a yarn pompon on the top. His waistcoat with double row of green seed bead buttons is blue felt. He is wearing yellow breeches with red garters and white hose. He is about to play on his wooden violin with his thin wooden bow. (*Weiner Collection*)

From Sweden, 6″ dolls by Charlotte Weibull. Their bodies are two balls of papier-mâché or a similar material. They have stockinette faces with features painted on them. Their bodies are covered with red stockinette. Both have yellow yarn hair and hats of red stockinette. The girl's body is covered with red stockinette, and she has a handwoven band down the front. The boy's body is covered with gray woven fabric with an insert of woven band. Seed beads and stitches represent buttons and buttonholes down the front of his jacket. (*Photographed at the United Nations Gift Center*)

A 7½″ doll made in Sweden by Charlotte Weibull, dressed in a regional costume. This woman has a woven band around her waist and a book in her hand to show she may be on her way to church. (*Photographed at the United Nations Gift Center*)

NORWEGIAN KITCHEN WITCH

Witches are usually thought of as ugly old women who put curses on people and generally bring bad luck to whoever crosses their paths. A different kind of witch is the Norwegian kitchen witch who, on the other hand, looks after the welfare of the family. If she's not on duty, toast burns, cakes fall, and the pudding boils over—nothing goes right. Once this little enchantress is in place, riding above all on her broomstick, her magic spell means the end of these disasters.

To make your own kitchen witch, you will need a 12″ piece of ⅛″ dowel, a white pipe cleaner, a piece of black, dark blue, or other dark color felt, a piece of fabric with a small print, bread dough (see page 249 for directions on making it) or self-hardening clay, a bit of cotton or fiber filling, grass, thread, black or dark blue seed beads. You will also need a needle, scissors, and glue.

3   Sketch a small boot outline and cut four copies from felt. Glue onto the ends of the pipe cleaner legs with one piece of felt on each side of the pipe cleaner. Glue a small amount of cotton or fiber filling on the witch's head for hair. For the dress, cut a piece of fabric 10″ x 5″. Hem one long edge. Match the two short edges, right sides facing together, and sew. Turn right side out. Turn down the top edge and put a gathering stitch along it. Slip it onto the doll, cut two tiny slashes, and pull the pipe-cleaner arms through. Pull the gathering stitch, adjusting the dress to fit and ending it off.

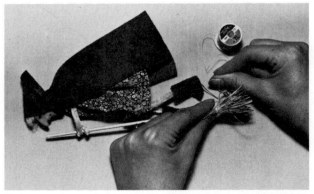

1   For the body, cut a piece of dowel 4½″ long. At the top, form a head with bread dough or some other self-hardening substance. Let the dough dry thoroughly. Protect with a spray fixative.

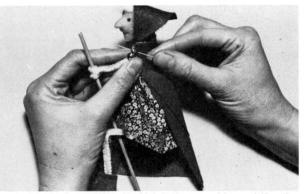

4   For the kerchief, cut a triangle of felt 2½″ on two sides and 4″ on the third. Glue the piece on her head, crossing the ends under her neck. Cut a 5½″ square for a cape. Put a gathering stitch along one edge. Gather and adjust to the doll around the neck and sew in place. Glue on seed bead eyes.

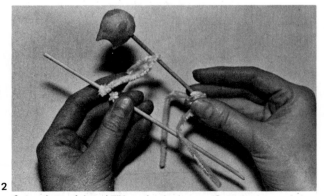

2   Cut a piece of dowel 7″ long for the broom. Cut two pieces of pipe cleaner, a 7″ piece for the arms and a 9″ piece for the legs. Twist the center of the 7″ piece around the dowel just under the head. Bring the ends around the broomstick piece and fold in elbows. Bring the longer piece of pipe cleaner around the shorter dowel, forming legs, and the skeleton of your witch is complete.

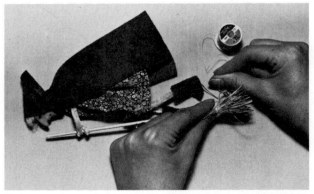

5   Get some pieces of straw or dry grass or similar natural material. Put a bunch around the end of the broomstick. Tie in place with string.

Add a hanging thread on the cape, and the kitchen witch is ready to take over her culinary duties.

POLISH DOLLS

In Poland today a variety of dolls are handcrafted using the skills that are a part of the Polish heritage. These crafts are still a vital and growing tradition in the country, partly because a market has been created for them by CPLIA, a nationwide organization that encourages the folk arts, with shops all over Poland and in foreign countries. By providing a large market for their work, CPLIA encourages the local craftspeople to practice their crafts at home.

Poland is outstanding for its wooden dolls, which have been exported all over the world. The dolls are made from wood, either hand carved or assembled from turned wooden pieces. In the mountainous regions of the country, especially where the people are snowbound for part of the year, the men cut wood in preparation for the long winter. When winter comes, they use their imposed time indoors to carve and turn the pieces of wood and to assemble and finish the dolls.

Some nesting dolls, often with a fairy-tale theme, are made in Poland. The turned dolls may be carica-

His tag says this 3½" whimsical all-wooden violinist was made by Brunon Nastaly in Zakopane in the southern part of Poland. The separate carved and turned pieces were glued together. The 7½" tree behind the violinist is wood burned to represent bark, and wooden leaves are glued onto it. (*Hercek Collection*)

These 6″ to 7″ Polish wooden musicians are hand carved. Parts of them are stained, but otherwise they are natural wood. (*Stukas Collection*)

A wooden figure from Poland, representing a swashbuckling soldier with a mug of beer in one hand and a long curved sword in the other. His rakish mustache and the crown of his hair encircling his bald head are separate pieces of darker wood glued into place. Each piece of the figure was cut out and finished separately, then glued together. (*Hercek Collection*)

This 3″ all-wooden doll was made in Poland. Each section of her body was made separately, painted, then glued together. (*Weiner Collection*)

Made in Poland, this 4½" whimsical lady is of wood with wire hair and spectacles and wire decorating her waist, parasol, and hat. (*Hercek Collection*)

A typical doll of Poland, this 9" wooden figure is dressed in the traditional costume of the Krakowiak region. He wears the traditional long blue felt vest decorated with brown fringe, seed beads, and sequins. His pants have the traditional red-and-white stripes, and his painted wooden feet and legs represent the traditional red boots worn with this costume. He has the typical four-cornered brown hat with a black velvet band and bright red feather. Around his waist is a wide leather belt with leather tassels. (*Hercek Collection*)

A delightful figure of a man on a horse made in Poland from pieces of turned wood. (*Photographed at the United Nations Gift Center*)

A set of musicians from Poland. Each part of their bodies is a separate piece of turned wood. Different woods were used to get different colors as each piece is the natural color of the wood. The pieces are glued together, assembled on a wooden base, and lacquered. (*Photographed at the United Nations Gift Shop*)

A pair of wooden figures from Poland. The tiny 2½" lady butter churner wears a skirt painted in the bright multicolored stripes woven into the woolen skirt, typical of those worn in the Łowicz region of Poland. Her body and that of her partner are all wooden pieces, cut, turned, finished separately, and glued together. The woman wears a blue bandanna and a white blouse with a black vest. The man wears a black vest and hat, and his shirt and pants are painted orange. (*Hercek Collection*)

tures of familiar characters, such as the diplomat, the coquettish girl, the dignified lady, and the swashbuckling soldier with his mug of beer. Some dolls are made with separately turned limbs that are connected through the body with elastic cord. These dolls typically have large wooden feet that let them stand up without falling.

Usually the wood for these dolls is left in its natural color and perhaps protected with lacquer. Sometimes it is painted or stained or even combined with another material like wire.

Certain parts of Poland are known for their weaving, especially the Łowicz region, which produces bright, multicolored, striped, handwoven woolen fabrics. Pieces of these fabrics are used in making dolls.

Many of the dolls made in Poland today are part of an effort to continue the rich folk heritage of the country through its peasant costumes representing the different regions. These colorful costumes are worn on festival days and when traditional dances are performed. Only a limited number are still being made today, and so prized are these costumes that authorities will not allow tourists to take them out of the country.

In preserving this tradition, craftsmen dress dolls in authentic traditional costumes. Many of these dolls are the typical wire-frame ones covered with fabric and stuffed (as discussed in Chapter 2).

The Russians are famous for their *matryoshkas*, but the Poles are also known for their nesting wooden dolls—made by turning wood on a lathe, then brightly painting the pieces. This set of fairytale figures represents Hansel and Gretel and the *baba,* or witch. The brightly painted gingerbread house stands 6″ high. Hansel and Gretel fit inside the witch, and she tucks neatly into the house. (*Hercek Collection*)

These 7½″ wooden figures, typical of dolls made in Poland, represent workers of the country. The millworker on the left is in a pink cotton-fabric uniform and hat with a red scarf and maroon vinyl belt. The bellboy in the middle is in a medium blue uniform decorated with gold braid. The nurse on the right wears a small white cap with a strip of black fabric and a black-and-white woven-fabric dress with white collar and cuffs. (*Hercek Collection*)

These 9″ dolls from Poland have wooden bodies with separate limbs that are movable, held together with elastic cord. Their faces have expressive features painted on, and they are shod in black boots also painted on. Their blond hair is flax. The female figure wears a black velvet blouse, and her skirt is made of the same heavy, woven, multicolored fabric used in the costumes of the Łowicz region. The skirt and blouse are both decorated with sequins and beads, and she wears a string of beads around her neck. She has a red scarf tied on her head, and under her skirt lace-and-cotton pants and slip. The male has on a black felt, yarn-trimmed hat, and a long black-felt coat decorated with trim, sequins, beads, and yarn. His pants are made from the same heavy multicolored woolen fabric used for her skirt. (*Weiner Collection*)

Polish wood-carvers delight in making dolls that are caricatures in wood of local townspeople. Popular subjects are the chimney sweep, who represents good luck. and the wise old diplomat, shown here. This 3½″ doll is made of wood with wire legs and wire handle for his umbrella. (*Hercek Collection*)

A beautifully detailed wire-frame stuffed cotton doll from a collector's series of dolls showing the regional costumes of Poland. This 9½″ doll is dressed in the traditional formal blue-and-red costume of the Kujawiak region of north central Poland. She is wearing a medium blue vest, a light blue skirt, and a lacy apron with a scalloped bottom edge. Her headgear is the traditional one of the region made with layers soft ribbon folded and formed into a crown. Flowing down her back are colorful ribbon streamers. She has a molded fabric face and braided brown vinyl hair. She wears orange beads around her neck and has black fabric boots with lacings made from red thread. (*Hercek Collection*)

A delightful 4½″ Polish doll with a wooden bead head and a wooden base body. Her hair is made of braided flax and decorated with bits of red yarn. Her skirt is a piece of typical woolen fabric—bright, multicolored, striped, and handwoven—used for the costumes of the Łowicz region. A purple velvet ribbon decorates the skirt. Her blouse is represented by a black velvet piece of ribbon and a small piece of lace at her neck. In front of the doll are two pincushions of the same type of woolen fabric as that of the doll's skirt. (*Hercek Collection*)

These two colorful Polish dolls were made with wood, straw, and thread. The 4½″ doll on the right has a body of dyed and natural-colored straw. The arms are straight pieces of straw tied together with thread near the ends. The head is a lacquered wooden ball with dots painted on for a mouth and eyes. The hair is pieces of natural straw tied together with yarn. The bodice and skirt are made of pieces of dyed and natural straw tied at the neck and waist.

The doll on the left has a similar wooden-ball head and hair of straw held together with a piece of orange yarn. She has a wooden base, and her wooden arms have white linen sleeves. She has a piece of white lace for a collar and a piece of green velvet ribbon over her shoulders. Her skirt is a piece of red woolen fabric with a black design woven into it. (*Hercek Collection*)

One type of doll, which is immediately recognizable as Polish, is a centaurlike figure, half man, half horse, representing a participant in the Pageant of Lajkonik, the Pageant of the Little Horse, which is celebrated every year in Poland. The pageant commemorates a skirmish that took place in the fifteenth century between the Christian boatmen of Krakow and an invading band of Tartar horsemen. The boatmen won the victory, and they dressed themselves in the clothes of their enemies. Their leader rode the Tartar chief's horse and entered Krakow in triumph.

This triumph is celebrated annually. A man, dressed as the Tartar chief, "rides" through the streets of Krakow carrying his own "horse," followed by a procession and accompanied by whistles and drums. Miniature wooden "Tartar chief" dolls painted in bright colors are sold during the pageant as toys for the children.

This 6½″ Polish doll is the type sold at the Pageant of Lajkonik, the Pageant of the Little Horse. The man has a carved wooden face and mohair beard and a stuffed fabric body. The horse is carved from wood; the trappings are satin with decorative trims. The man's feet are carved from wood. (*Stukas Collection*)

These 3½″ wire-frame dolls wear the traditional informal costume of the southern mountainous part of Poland. Both figures wear the typical laced shoes. The man is wearing the traditional woolen vest and pants and has felt hair and a white woolen hat. The woman wears a typical bright red shawl and a white peasant blouse. Lots of bright roses represented by tiny dots are on her skirt—decorative details typical of the dress of this region. (*Hercek Collection*)

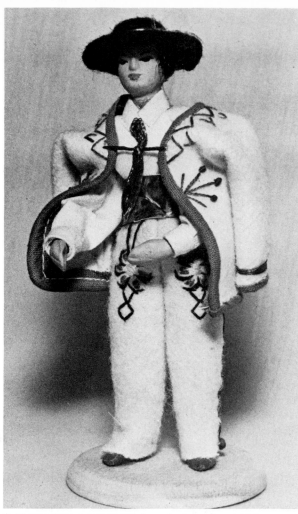

A 5″ wire-frame doll in the formal winter dress of the men of Zakopane, Poland. This man wears a white shirt and a ribbon tie. His long ivory-colored woven woolen pants are decorated with hand embroidery at the front and all the way down the outside of his legs. His jacket of the same fabric is bound with tape along the edge and decorated with embroidery stitches. He wears a wide belt to represent the wide, hand-tooled leather belts that are so useful to the mountain-climbing men of Zakopane. His shoes are leather moccasins, and his face and hands are hand-painted clay. In the summer these heavy woolen clothes are replaced by light fabrics decorated with rosettes and pompons. (*Hercek Collection*)

This 8″ wire-frame doll is dressed in the traditional costume of the Kujawiak region of Poland. She wears a white cotton blouse with full sleeves and a medium blue skirt with a large red cotton apron on which a white design is printed. Her vinyl synthetic braided hair is a grayish color, and she wears the traditional headgear made of layers of folded, colorful ribbon. (*Hercek Collection*)

These 12″ Polish dolls have pressed-fabric faces and wire-frame bodies. The girl's skirt is a floral cotton print, and her apron is made of net and decorated with ribbons. Her weskit is decorated with seed beads. The boy wears the traditional long blue vest, red-and-white-striped pants, four-cornered hat, and red boots worn in the Krakowiak region. (*Stukas Collection*)

DOLLS OF EASTERN EUROPE

Beautiful costume dolls are made in many of the countries of Eastern Europe. Dollmakers of Yugoslavia and Rumania produce wire-frame and fabric stuffed dolls in authentically detailed costumes, often with blouses and aprons richly decorated with embroidery. Dolls from these countries may also wear rawhide sandals.

Wire-frame costume dolls made in Hungary are known for their beautiful costumes, many with the black sateen apron colorfully embroidered and bordered with deep fringe, which is a distinctive feature of the Hungarian folk costume.

Among the most decorative and elaborate national costumes of Europe are those of Czechoslovakia.

This 5″ doll from Poland has a clay face, hands, and feet. She wears a white blouse with a floral design that is also on her weskit, and on a border around her skirt. She has a red head scarf and a single braid down her back. Her striped skirt is typical of the costume of the Łowicz region. (*Stukas Collection*)

This 4½″ Polish doll seated at a spinning wheel has a wooden head and body. Her wooden legs, connected to her body with pieces of wire, are painted red near the feet to represent the typical red boots worn in the Łowicz region. She wears the multicolored striped woolen skirt also typical of that region, a blue kerchief, white cotton blouse with very full sleeves, and a green vest. (*Hercek Collection*)

These 13½″ dolls from Yugoslavia bear the label "Narodna Radinost-Beograd." They are wire-frame dolls with felt hands, fabric faces, and embroidered features. Both have pointed rawhide sandals and woven belts.

The woman wears a black velvet corselet decorated with gold edging over a white blouse. She has a black embroidered apron and a pleated multicolored skirt. Her legs are wrapped with black yarn, and decorated near the shoes with embroidery stitches.

The man wears a white shirt decorated with embroidery, black wool jodhpur breeches, and a vest. Around his waist is a woven sash. He has a black wool crocheted hat and a black wool vest with a red lining. Attached to his belt is a woven fabric container. (*Stukas Collection*)

The most important piece in the costume of the Yugoslavian woman is her black apron embellished with brilliant embroidery. This close-up of the black velvet apron on the doll at the left shows the sequins and the flowers embroidered on it. The flowers are designed with satin embroidery thread, with the leaves in lazy daisy stitch and the stems in outline stitch.

These beautiful detailed dolls were made in Rumania. They have wire-frame bodies and felt hands. Their faces are molded fabric, and their features are stitched on with embroidery cotton. Their hair is mohair, and they wear leather shoes with curled and pointed tips.
The man has on felt pants and a vest and wears a black crocheted hat and a white cotton shirt embroidered down the front. The women wear white blouses embroidered with flowers and edged with lace. They have felt weskits edged in crochet and felt aprons also decorated with hand embroidery. (*Weiner Collection*)

This 6½" doll from Hungary has a pressed-fabric face and painted features. Her body is stuffed stockinette. She is dressed in a peasant costume with a pink brocade skirt with a red ribbon edge and a fringed apron, a white full-sleeved blouse, and a blue print shawl with a red fringe edge. She wears a headdress decorated with fabric flowers. (*MacNeer Collection*)

This 8" doll from Yugoslavia is beautifully detailed. She has a wire-frame body, a fabric face with embroidered features, felt hands, and legs wrapped with blue yarn. She wears laced leather shoes, a white skirt, and an elaborate apron. Her head scarf is decorated with sequins. (*Hupp Collection*)

A 2" doll made in Hungary. It was stitched to the end of a long piece of woven band and meant to be used as a bookmark. The doll has a wire body covered with fabric. Her face is white fabric with embroidered features. She wears a woolen apron edged with buttonhole stitch and decorated with a lazy-daisy-stitch flower. (*Groszmann Collection*)

These 13" Hungarian dolls are of stuffed fabric. Their faces, made of two pieces of fabric sewn down the profile, have embroidered features. Both wear leather shoes, with the woman's in red and the man's in black, and highly ornate black aprons embroidered with a typically Hungarian floral design in satin stitch. Also on the aprons are fringes and seed and tube beads. The man is wearing black trousers, a white linen shirt, with full sleeves decorated at the cuffs with a blue feather stitch and red crocheting. He is wearing a black felt hat and vest, and his hair and mustache are mohair. On the woman's head is a scarf with a typically Hungarian flower print. Pink and red yarn tassels decorate her head scarf. Her bodice is decorated with yarn and tube and seed beads. (*From the Collection of the Forbes Library, Northampton, Mass.*)

This 11″ Hungarian made doll is of stuffed stockinette. His features are needle sculpted and painted. Dressed in Sunday best, he has a black felt vest and a white shirt decorated at the front and on the sleeves with machine-embroidered trim. His embroidered apron covers white cotton trousers. His tall black felt hat is decorated with felt flowers. (*Hupp Collection*)

From Hungary, a 10″ doll with a body of stuffed stockinette. He wears a felt hat decorated with ribbons and fabric flowers. More ribbons and flowers are at his waist. His features are needle sculpted and painted. He wears a white shirt decorated with lace. Bead buttons adorn his jacket. (*Hupp Collection*)

The costume dolls of that country have the same colorful embroidery, ribbons, and flowers that people use in decorating their own costumes on feast days. Men as well as women wear the colorful costumes, and sometimes the boys even surpass the girls in the color of their clothes.

In past centuries the Czechs carved wooden dolls called *dziady,* or old men, which were kept in the home and used as part of the festivals at harvest and Christmas time. Czechs have also been very interested in marionettes and puppets, which are often used in school for teaching purposes.

The Czechs are also famous for their cornhusk dolls. These dolls are similar to those made in the United States, but usually have no features except eyes, designated simply by two dots, and sometimes flax for hair.

These 6″ stuffed felt dolls from Czechoslovakia have embroidered features and a bit of red paint to indicate rosy cheeks. Their clothes are beautifully embroidered. Both women have embroidery on the upper sleeves of their white peasant blouses. All three have felt shoes with thread to represent leather crisscrossing gaiterings on their legs. The man has a beautifully embroidered cotton shirt, and felt pants with pompons on the side seams. (*Photographed at the United Nations Gift Center*)

These 6″ stuffed dolls from Czechoslovakia have embroidered faces, felt shoes, and peasant costumes of both woven materials and felt. The man in the center wears an embroidered bolero with wool tassels, a white smock, and white felt pants decorated with embroidery and more tassels. His felt hat has various colored bands and a feather sticking out of it. The woman on the left wears a felt jacket with a fake-fur edging and embroidery. The woman on the right wears a skirt with an apron over it and a flower-print kerchief. (*Photographed at the United Nations Gift Center*)

From Czechoslovakia, 12″ simple, flat, stuffed dolls made from natural unbleached linen fabric. They have flax hair and their features are drawn on. The girl wears a cotton print dress, and the boy felt pants, shoes, and hat and a white cotton shirt. His vest is stiff fabric, trimmed with red fabric, cut with a pinking shears and glued in place. (*Photographed at the United Nations Gift Center*)

A 7″ baby doll with a simple egg outline made in Czechoslovakia from linen fabrics and stuffed. The face area is unbleached linen, and the bottom is linen woven with a design. The eyes and mouth are drawn on, and strands of flax are stitched onto the head for hair. (*Photographed at the United Nations Gift Center*)

From Czechoslovakia, a 5″ cornhusk doll. Though most cornhusk dolls are female, this one is an exception. The boy doll is accompanied by a lamb whose body is also made of cornhusks and whose legs are made of sticks. (*Groszmann Collection*)

This 6½″ cornhusk doll is from Czechoslovakia. She is sitting on a wooden bench with flax tied at the top. In her hand is a drop spindle which she is using to spin linen thread. (*Hupp Collection*)

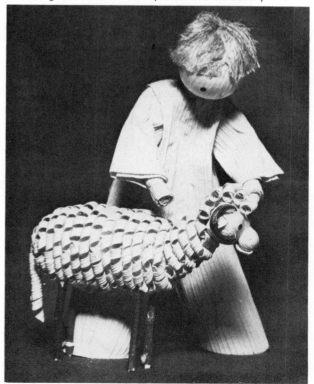

A 4½" cornhusk doll from Czechoslovakia. Both mother and child have flax hair braided and tied with red pearl-cotton embroidery thread. (*From the Collection of Nancy Ann Malik*)

These wooden dolls made in Bulgaria are similar to the taller ones shown below, but are only 8" tall. They have wooden cone bodies draped with woolen fabric clothing. Their heads are wooden balls and their features, hair, and hats are cut from scraps of woolen fabric. (*Photographed at the United Nations Gift Center*)

These 16" wooden dolls from Bulgaria are dressed in typical peasant costumes. The women are each wearing a *shamiya*, or headcloth. The woman in the center has coins dangling from a string attached to her headdress. (*Photographed at the United Nations Gift Shop*)

The people of Bulgaria, whose country borders on the Black Sea, are predominantly Slavic, and until fairly recently, wearing store-bought clothing there was a sign of laziness or lack of ability. Bulgarian women raised flax, spun and wove it, then made clothing for their family. Costume dolls from this country show some of the beautiful peasant costumes worn there.

These dolls, measuring about 16″ tall, were made in Bulgaria. They have wooden ball heads and wooden cones for bodies. Their costumes are made from woven woolen fabric, and their features are scraps of fabric glued in place. Their arms are wired through their fabric sleeves. The dolls wear costumes representing various regions of Bulgaria. (*Photographed at the United Nations Gift Shop*)

These rather strange-looking dolls are labeled "Made in Bulgaria." The smaller one is 11″ tall, and the larger one 17″ tall. They have wooden hands and face and wire bodies covered with fabric. Their feet are weighted with pieces of metal, and their wooden heads are decorated with different colors of felt and rickrack. The larger one has a leather three-dimensional nose. Both have large feather headdresses and fur coats with metal noisemakers hanging from the belts. They carry sticks with hanks of thread tied at one end and have leather shoes with ties crisscrossing their legs. (*Photographed at the United Nations Gift Center*)

In Lithuania, which has a wealth of customs and peasant traditions, dolls are often made of wood. Some are wood burned, others painted, and still others are wooden and dressed in fabric costumes.

Costume dolls made in Lithuania show off the beautifully hand-loomed fabrics made there. These dolls sometimes wear orange beads to represent amber or even real amber beads. This beautiful yellowish stone is a natural resource of Lithuania and is used for making jewelry and even dolls. Besides the costume dolls, Lithuanian dollmakers also make dolls of famous figures from Lithuanian folk literature, such as that of Joseph of Palanga.

These tiny 2¼" dolls, mounted on a piece of wood, were made in Lithuania. They have wooden balls for heads and vinyl fabric scraps for bodies. The man has a fake-fur mustache and hair and the woman's hair is made of thread. They have black-paper circles for eyes and mouth. Her body is made of two cones cut from vinyl and overlapped, her arms are represented by half circles of vinyl and her hands by two tiny circles. She is holding a little flower also made of vinyl. His body is a cone of vinyl with the same type of arms and hands as she has. His legs are represented by two cylinders of vinyl fabric twisted around and glued in place. On his head are three circles glued in place to represent a hat. She has a triangle of fabric glued on her head for a scarf. (*Stukas Collection*)

Lithuanian dolls made of wood. The brown lines are incised with a woodburning tool, and the designs are painted in. The 6" doll in the center wears a yellow apron, a puffed-sleeve blouse, and has a tall headpiece. The smaller pair of dolls are 3½" tall. (*Stukas Collection*)

This 5½" highly stylized doll was made in Lithuania. Her body is a graceful cone shape of wood, and her head is a wooden ball. She has blond vinyl hair with a woven band on it. Her features, arms, and dress are painted. (*Stukas Collection*)

These two 7½" dolls have what look like table tennis balls for heads. The balls are painted flesh color, and the eyes and mouth are circles of paper glued in place. The girls have hair of flax, which is sewn together at the center and then braided—they are literally examples of the Lithuanian ideal of beautiful girls having "flaxen hair." On their heads they have crowns, pieces of card twisted into a circle and covered with strips of handloomed band for which the Lithuanians are famous. Strips of band also fall from the crown behind the dolls to below their waists. The body of each doll is a cone made out of a piece of card. The card is covered with handloomed fabric to represent a skirt and a separate piece to represent the apron. The girls have a piece of handloomed band sewn in place at the top of the cone representing a vest. Their arms are pieces of wire covered with white cotton-fabric sleeves. Their hands are circles of leather glued on the end of the wire. The doll on the right holds a flower made of pieces of vinyl and a bit of yarn. The doll on the left is holding a piece of greenery probably meant to represent rue, the national flower of Lithuania and a symbol of virginity. (*Stukas Collection*)

Made in Lithuania, this 6" seated girl has a wooden head with features painted on. Her hair is of a synthetic material, worn in braids, and she has a crown, a lace-edged woven band, on top of her head. The head is attached to a wooden dowel that goes from the head down to the waist, where it is attached to a heavy card cone. The skirt, made of a woven handloomed material, is arranged over this cone. The vest is salmon colored, and the wire arms are covered with plastic. The doll is holding a tulip made of cardboard with yarn wrapped over it. The tulip is a very common motif in weaving and other handwork in Lithuania. Around her neck is a string of orange plastic beads to represent the amber beads for which Lithuania is so famous. (*Stukas Collection*)

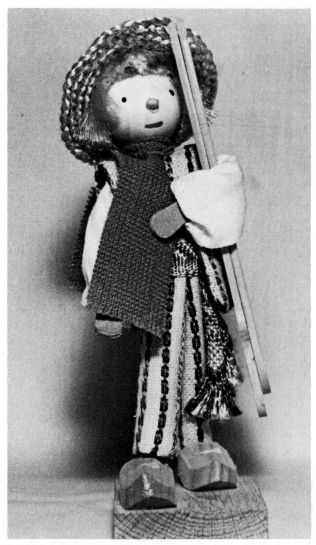

These three 4½" dolls mounted on a piece of wood are taking part in a traditional Lithuanian dance, called "Lenciugelis," or "The Little Chain." This dance is customarily performed with four girls and one boy who dances around and pretends to flirt with each one of the girls. The dancers here have leather shoes, wooden heads with painted features, and wire-frame bodies. The girls' wire legs are covered with fabric tubing. Their hands are vinyl, covering the ends of the wire arms that come through the puffed white-cotton sleeves. The girls have handloomed skirts, and the boy a hand-loomed belt tied around his waist. The girls have hair made from a synthetic material and braided, and the boy has the same type of hair cut short. On his head is a hat made from the same synthetic material as the hair, braided and stitched together. (*Stukas Collection*)

A 6½" doll representing "Palangos Juze," or "Joseph of Palanga," a famous figure from Lithuanian folk art. This character, a fiddler and barber who went from village to village to entertain, was created by Bishop Valancius, who wrote stories about him that taught the people both religious and patriotic lessons.

This representation of Palangos has a wire-frame body, hands covered with vinyl, and a wooden head with painted features and an extra piece of wood for the nose. He carries a huge pair of wooden scissors to show his profession as a barber. He has a white cotton shirt, white wool vest, wooden shoes, and a woven belt with the ends hanging from his waist. (*Stukas Collection*)

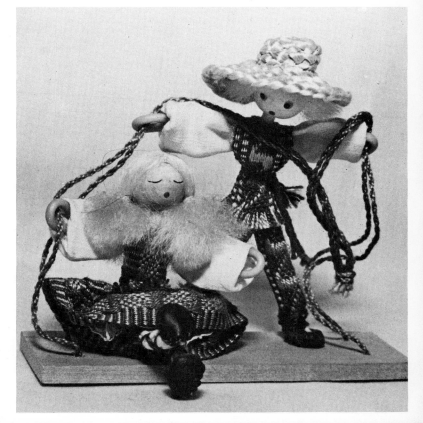

The man of this pair of Lithuanian dancers is only 3" tall. Both figures have leather shoes, wire-frame bodies, and wooden ball heads on which their features are painted. They have white cotton-fabric full sleeves, and the rest of their clothing is made of hand-loomed bands, predominantly green. (*Stukas Collection*)

This 3″ figure is made of amber, a fossiled resin found in abundance in Lithuania. This substance, which is hard and translucent, comes in yellow, brownish yellow, or orange and is used for jewelry and for ornaments, such as this whimsical figure of Joseph of Palanga, with his traditional barber scissors on his head. (*Stukas Collection*)

This 9½″ wood-turned figure from Estonia is flat at the back. A stylized doll, it is painted bright colors in a geometric design. (*Stukas Collection*)

THE DOLLS OF RUSSIA

In Russia the peasants have long made dolls during the cold winter months. They carved wooden dolls for their own children and made some to be taken to the market in spring. Probably the most distinctive type of wooden doll made in Russian is the *matryoshka,* which is a wooden turned, nested doll, but dolls of plaited straw, clay, fabric, and so on have also been made. The hand-shaped clay dolls from Dymkovo are outstanding, as are the Moss Men with wooden bases, with moss bound around them with string.

Fabric dolls with wire frames have also been made in Russia. These dolls often have pressed fabric faces made with knitted stockinette. They are usually dressed as peasants, often in authentic peasant costumes of specific areas. These dolls usually have either wooden feet or distinctive straw sandals on their feet. During the 1930s these dolls were made in quantity and exported. Other stuffed wire-frame dolls show in detail the peasant costumes with their beautiful embroidery.

This wooden doll was carved and painted in Russia. (*Hupp Collection*)

A small, 3½″ tall, doll from the USSR made of turned wood. She has yellow vinyl hair and a wooden-ball head with painted features. Her body, shaped like the top of an egg, is painted mainly in black. The top part of the body is painted white with a collar outlined in red. (*Photographed at the United Nations Gift Center*)

These tiny figures, each only 1″ to 2″ tall, were made in the USSR from wooden balls and pieces of turned wood that were painted, assembled, and lacquered. The dolls are supposed to be a family, with a bearded father, mother in a polka-dot dress, and daughter with a bow in her hair. Also included are the family cat, dog, mouse, and oversized mushroom. (*Photographed at the United Nations Gift Center*)

This all-wooden toyseller doll from the USSR is about 8″ tall. His body, which is made up of pieces of turned wood with designs burned on, is painted and lacquered. On his tray of merchandise is a matroyshka and also a boy and girl doll. (*Photographed at the United Nations Gift Center*)

An 8″ all-wood doll from the USSR. Each part of his body is a separate piece of turned wood. The circles for this boy's eyes, mouth, the lines that represent his hair, as well as all the other brown lines, are woodburned. His pants are painted blue and his hat red. (*Stukas Collection*)

Not only wood but other substances, such as walrus tusks, have been used by Russian artists to carve animal and human figures. (*Photo by Frederick G. S. Clow, Courtesy of Museum of Fine Arts, Boston, Mass.*)

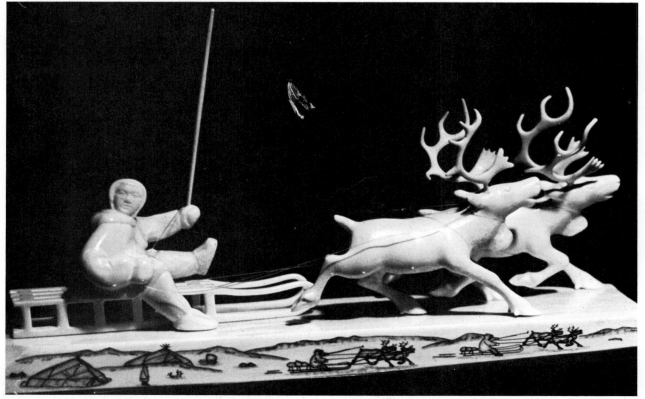

This 8" pair from Russia are wire-frame dolls. The female figure wears typical woven-straw sandals, and the male has carved wooden boots painted black. They have molded stockinette faces with painted features and wear white peasant blouses with full sleeves gathered at the wrist. He wears black pants, an organza waistband, and a straw hat. She wears a red skirt and a red-and-white tarboosh, or hat. (*MacNeer Collection*)

Russian dolls, 7½" tall, in peasant costumes. They are wire-frame stuffed dolls with stockinette bodies. Their molded stockinette faces have painted features. They both wear woven-straw shoes. The doll on the right is a "Mordvin" woman. She is wearing a white shirt and black coat with a red waistband. Her red tarboosh, cone-shaped hat, has painted stripes, and she is carrying a white fabric bag on her back. The woman on the left, from a Kazan village, wears a red print dress, red coat, and white print kerchief. (*MacNeer Collection*)

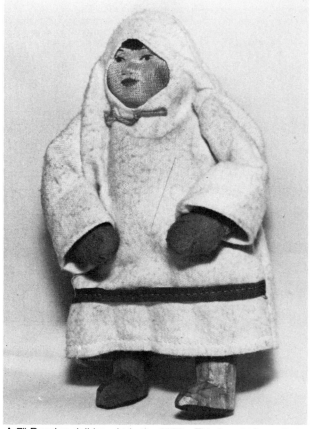

A 7" Russian doll bought in the 1930s. This female figure has a pressed-fabric face with painted features and wooden carved feet. The body has a wire frame, and the arms and hands are made of brown flannel. She is wearing a white flannel coat with a red fabric stripe. (*Hulsizer Collection*)

These 10½" Russian peasant dolls, bought in 1934, have stuffed cotton bodies, beautifully hand-painted faces and mohair for hair. The man is wearing a typically Russian fur cap and a white smock belted with a braided strip and topped with a Russian collar decorated with hand embroidery. He has on gray cotton breeches and shoes that are laced on with the strings twisting up his legs. The woman is wearing an orange kerchief and a long dress with cross-stitches on the sleeves. (*From the Collection of the Forbes Library, Northampton, Mass.*)

These 3½" stylized Russian dolls were bought around 1962. They are made with paper cones. Their features are inked on and their scarves and headdresses are made of paper. They are dressed mainly in bright red and represent different folk costumes of Russia. (*Groszmann Collection*)

A 6" Russian peasant girl with a cotton-fabric-wrapped wire-frame body. Her features are painted, and she has yarn hair. She is wearing a gray cotton skirt, white blouse, and an orange kerchief. On her feet are crocheted shoes, and her white apron is embroidered with a repeated cross-stitch design. (*From the Collection of the Forbes Library, Northampton, Mass.*)

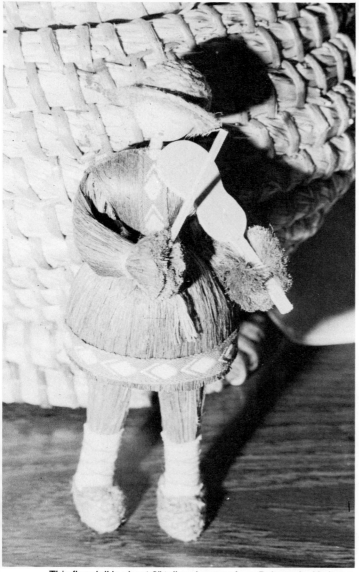

This flax doll is about 8″ tall and comes from Belorussia. He has a wooden ball for a head, with features painted on it. He has flax hair and a hat of flax. His arms and legs are hanks of flax tied together at each end. His tunic is decorated with woven trim, and he is playing a wooden violin.

Similar to the violinist at the left, this smiling flax peasant doll from Belorussia has shoes of flax. His legs are wound with fabric and are cross-gartered with thread.

NESTING MATRYOSHKAS

The matryoshkas, or nesting dolls, among the most famous Russian dolls, are wooden turned dolls that open in half around the waist revealing a slightly smaller doll inside. This doll again opens to reveal another, until the smallest doll, usually a half inch high, appears. The number of dolls in a set depends of course on the size of the first one. A set may consist of just three or five, or a dozen dolls. A set of fifty-six dolls has been recorded.

Matryoshkas can be used not only as display dolls, but also as real playthings that the child can disassemble and assemble endlessly. The word *matryoshka* means grandmother. The name may

have come from the fact that when a grandmother takes care of children she sometimes entertains them with these wooden dolls. Or the dolls may have been so named because they are painted and wear a babushka, a head scarf that grandmothers often wear.

Though the matryoshkas date back to the late 1890s and are usually thought of as Russian dolls, they actually originated in the Orient. However, the Chinese seem to have forgotten the nesting doll, and in Japan the *kokeshi* is only occasionally made in the form of a nesting doll.

The nesting dolls were originally hand carved often by the grandfather for his grandchildren. Today, however, they are made on a lathe. The wooden sections are turned from wood, painted, and varnished. They

A matroyshka set of six dolls that fit one inside the other. The largest is 6½″ tall, and the smallest 1¼″. They are painted in a floral design, predominantly red with yellow, green, and black. (*MacNeer Collection*)

Russian nesting dolls measuring from 7″ to 1¾″. These bearded men are similar to the typical female nested figures. The largest figure, as you can see, is ready to defend himself with his wooden club and shield. These dolls of turned wood have painted red hats and red bases. The circular designs were stamped on and, finally, lacquered. (*Photographed at the United Nations Gift Center*)

are usually painted in bright colors, with red, a favorite color of the Slavs, and black, the second favorite, predominating.

Usually the dolls are painted to represent peasant women with their kerchiefs tied under their chins. Some of the nested dolls, however, are men. Also, some Russian nested dolls instead of having one doll inside the other have a set of small dolls inside one large one—small tumbler dolls all the same size in one doll or a man doll containing a set of ninepins with two wooden balls.

DYMKOVO CLAY DOLLS

A distinctive type of doll made in the USSR is the gaily decorated Dymkovo ceramic doll fashioned by hand from clay, painted with tempera, and decorated with gold leaf. The dolls are made in the Dymkovo village in the Kirov region, a settlement on the outskirts of the city of Vyatka (now known as Kirov) in the Urals.

The Dymkovo dolls have a very interesting history, one worth recording in detail. The tradition of the clay figures is actually centuries old, having been traced back to pre-Christian Russia. The dolls were made for the festival holiday of the sun god celebrated on May 23. The two main figures produced for this celebration were the two- or three-headed horse, which was the symbol of the sun god, and a female figure, the Protectress of the Hearth.

When Christianity was introduced, these pagan images assumed the innocuous disguise of toys, thereby saving them from destruction and their owners from persecution by the Orthodox Church. Circles and rings painted on them in very bright colors symbolized the sun god. These same ornamental designs were often used on the kerchiefs, skirts, and scarves worn in Russia in the first half of the nineteenth century.

In addition to the two- or three-headed horse and the hearth goddess, other figures became traditional. They were all made with festive motifs because they were still sold primarily for the spring festival. The traditional dolls depicted mid-nineteenth-century urban characters, such as hussars, cavaliers, ladies, and wet nurses wearing the kokoshniki, a woman's headdress of old Russia.

Probably the most popular figure was that of the water carrier, a young woman in a broad traditionally bell-shaped skirt, set off by a frilly apron. This doll wears a bonnet and has several strands of beads around her neck. She wears a yoke studded with tiny squares of gold and from the yoke hang orange pails.

In the mid-nineteenth century the manufacture of these clay toys reached its zenith, and inhabitants of entire neighborhoods of Dymkovo were involved in molding, drying, and painting them. The secret processes used by the various families were jealously kept secrets handed down from one generation to the next.

The toys were made from red loam and fine sand, which members of the family collected during the summer in meadows, pastures, and from riverbanks. When collected, the loam had to be soaked in water, mixed with sand, and the whole mixture thoroughly kneaded by hand.

Once the summer harvest was in, the whole family, both young and old, would work on the toys in assembly-line fashion. If they were making a water carrier, for example, one member of the family would work continuously making bell-shaped skirts while another family member would be working on the arms and shoulders. A third person would be making bonneted heads, and a fourth would be fashioning yokes and pails. Still another family member might be joining the parts together, using a damp rag to rub the seams.

When all the dolls were completed, the whole batch would be set out to dry for several days. In the meantime the family would be making new batches

A recent exhibit of Soviet arts and crafts, which toured the United States, included contemporary clay dolls from Dymkovo. The woman with buckets and the rooster are two of the traditional figures made in this village in the Kirov region. (*Photo courtesy Museum of Fine Arts, Boston, Mass.*)

of figures, perhaps that of a nurse with a child, or a horseman. Once the dolls were dry, they were fired for three or four hours in an ordinary Russian kitchen stove. The family member who was watching the firing had to develop a keen sense of how long to allow each batch to be fired. If they were taken out too early the figures would crumble, but on the other hand if they were taken out too late, the ground coat of paint would not take.

After the dolls were successfully fired, they were bathed two or three times in a pail of crushed and sifted chalk dissolved in milk. Each figure then had a thin even coat of white over which the colors were painted. The next step was thoroughly coating the painted doll with egg white and gluing on tiny squares or lozenges of gold leaf for brilliance.

The peasants who made the Dymkovo dolls received very little payment for them—thirty or forty kopeks a hundred. If they tried to simplify the painting by making the designs on the dress less elaborate, the merchant who bought them would inevitably notice and pay less for the lot.

One day one of the shrewder dollmakers came up with a shortcut. He suggested, rather than doing all the hand modeling of the clay, why not make a mold and cast it in plaster of Paris. This worked for a while and the craftsmen were very happy, being able to get the same money for an item that took much less time to make. Though it seemed to work for a while, some customers stopped buying the dolls because the painted plaster of Paris dolls did not have the same lasting sparkle as did the clay ones.

Finally toward the end of the nineteenth century the making of Dymkovo dolls all but ceased. Only two or three old women continued to make them, and this was the situation until after the Communist revolution. If it had not been for A.A. Denshin, a writer who was a passionate and unselfish enthusiast of the Dymkovo dolls, they would have been completely forgotten. He wrote book after book to popularize them and even hand painted all the drawings that were pasted into his books. He went to Dymkovo to try to persuade the few craftswomen who still made the dolls to share and pass on their knowledge. This was accomplished, and the ancient craft experienced a revival. The dolls received worldwide attention when they were awarded gold medals at the 1939 World's Fair in New York.

Today the Dymkovo toymakers are still at work making the traditional dolls at the Artists' House in the center of Kirov. They use the traditional method of mixing red loam with sand and they still thoroughly knead it by hand as it has been done for centuries. The artists still use vivid colors to paint the figures in the traditional designs, and when finished, the dolls are shipped to shops in both the USSR and abroad.

Dymkovo dolls are painted in bright colors over a white base. Many are made in the form of women with bell-shaped bases. (*Photo by Lawrence Crump*)

RUSSIAN MOSS MEN

Another traditional type of doll made in Russia is the moss men. These dolls made by the peasants have carved wooden bases covered with moss and feet and legs covered with newspaper.

You can make your own version of these dolls. First buy spaghnum moss at the florist. Use any scrap of wood to carve the base. You will also need newspaper and string, and pine cones for arms. For hair, use a bit of grass or other natural material. If you wish, you can make a hat from two slices of birch wood—a very thin larger slice topped by a thicker one smaller in circumference. Add a walking stick and a hatchet made with a scrap of metal and a stick.

1 To make a moss man, use a piece of soft scrap wood (weathered wood if available) and carve a body, legs, and head. On the face, carve a nose and eyes.

2 Cut strips of newspaper 2″ wide and as long as possible. Fold the paper from each long side in toward the middle. Fold several layers of paper together and put them at the bottom of the doll extending them to the front for feet. Nail or glue to the wood. Wrap around the feet and legs with strips of newspaper and hold in place with string.

3 Take pieces of sphagnum moss and lay them on the wooden body starting near the feet. Tie on with a piece of string and keep wrapping the string around to hold the moss as you keep adding pieces to cover the whole body.

4 Pull off the petals of two pinecones almost to the end. Nail one cone in place at each shoulder for arms.

5 Glue on a small amount of frayed rope, dried grass, or any other appropriate material for the hair and beard.

6 Nail the moss man to a small square of wood. Give him a walking stick to hold in one hand. Make a hatchet with a small piece of metal and a scrap of wood and put it under the string at the waist.

6
Dolls of Latin America

This chapter on Latin American dolls will include those from Mexico, South and Central America, and also the islands of the Caribbean. Within this large geographic area the countries vary in many ways, but most have a dual heritage, that of the Europeans, mainly Spanish and Portuguese, who immigrated there, and that of the various groups of Indians who were there before the Europeans, including the Incas and Aztecs with their highly developed civilizations, and many other tribes.

A doll from a Latin American country then might be derived from the pre-Columbian culture, or it may show European influence, or be a combination of both. The dolls range from crude clay images to modern sophisticated dolls showing in exact detail traditional costumes of the country.

Many people in Latin America, especially the Indians, live very primitive lives. A much greater percentage of them live outside the cities compared to the populations of North America and Europe. Even today these people living on the land weave their clothing from the wool of their own llamas, alpacas, and vicuñas. They often make dolls to add to their meager income from the scraps of the same rough cloth they use in their own clothes. These dolls reflect the personalities of the people who made them. Other dolls, especially those made for the tourist trade, use modern manufactured materials and are more stylized and modernistic in appearance.

The Indians of Latin America have made bone dolls, crudely carved wooden dolls, and others from wax, dough, fiber, and straw. Clay ones are numerous, but cloth dolls are probably the most common type. Leather, straw, palm leaves, and other natural materials are also used for dollmaking.

Straw dolls similar to those found in Europe are made in parts of South America, and palm leaves are used by children to make dolls. In Bolivia and Chile, dolls are made with wire frames covered with woolen knitting and crocheting—often with real hair and glass bead ornaments.

In areas of Central and South America that are close to large cities, the dolls often represent ordinary people in ordinary costumes with street vendors being particularly popular. These dolls are made with wire, wax, clay, and fabric. They are usually made one by one so that each doll is unique and tells an interesting story about the time and place of the one who made it. Tourists often bring these dolls back from cruises to the West Indies and to Central and South America.

MEXICAN DOLLS

Mexico is a land rich in craft traditions, with many ancient skills used in dollmaking. There is such variety in Mexican dolls that complete coverage in this book would be impossible.

Mexican craftsmen use the materials nature provides and follow the traditions of their ancestors in working with clay, palm, and other natural materials. With the Spanish Conquest new methods and materials were introduced, enriching the range of Indian handcrafts. Blending the customs of Europe and of the Indians, Mexico has created a wholly unique, wholly Mexican craft tradition, and dolls are a vital part of it.

In Mexico crafts fulfill a spiritual as well as a practical need. The craftsman expresses his personal view of life and death. Potters, tinsmiths, and other craftsmen draw on their rich cultural heritage and produce a whole series of grimly humorous pieces with a uniquely Mexican view of life in death and death in life, making the dolls for the Day of the Dead a peculiarly Mexican vision.

Dolls have a long history in Mexico, dating back to the clay dolls of the Aztec civilization of 1000 B.C. These dolls, probably fertility figures, were made of clay. Their bodies had holes through which strings were passed to make the arms and legs movable.

Small dolls were found in excavations in Teotihuacán, but the purpose of these figures is unknown. Attributed to the Toltec people, they have realistic faces modeled from clay.

The Aztecs made large female dolls of pure gold and gold leaf, and male figures of pure silver. The Mayas used clay in making temple figures. According to legend, Cortez found Montezuma and his court playing with large dolls when he arrived there.

Today Mexican dollmakers use many different kinds of materials. The country is well known for its dolls made from wax, papier-maché, clay, palm leaves, and fabric. Also dollmakers use tin, cornhusks, tissue paper, and yarn. Mexican dollmakers are concerned with the accessories as well as the dolls themselves and take great care in making their costumes, including the usual hats and serapes.

This 5″ clay figure is a molded reproduction of a Toltec doll, with bell-shaped body but no arms or legs. The elaborate headdress perhaps represents magnificently plumed headgear worn by a warrior. (*Photographed at the International Craftsman, Flemington, N.J.*)

These 4½″ clay figures are reproductions of pre-Columbian Aztec dolls from Teotihuacan. The originals, whose purpose is unknown, date back thousands of years. (*Photographed at the International Craftsman, Flemington, N.J.*)

The Mexican government also tries to encourage craftsmen of the country to perpetuate the techniques and designs that they have learned and use the skills that they inherited from their ancestors. Dollmakers are encouraged to continue their craft, so in Mexican markets doll booths are fascinating places. Dolls representing people of the different parts of Mexico are popular with tourists and are also exported.

Among the most unusual dolls of Mexico are those made in Oaxaca for the annual feast held on December 23, called *Noche de los Rabanos* (Night of the Radishes). Extremely large radishes, grown specially for this occasion, are carved into human shapes and given arms and legs. With their ungainly size and strange forms, they look like macabre but humorous devils and demons whose evil powers are sheer pretense.

From Mexico, a 4¾″ clay figure in the natural light brown material from which it was formed. It is a reproduction of a Mayan temple figure. (*Hupp Collection*)

Made in Mexico, these 4″ cornhusk dolls have wire frames onto which the pieces of husk are tied. This technique in making cornhusk dolls is different from the one used in the United States and Czechoslovakia, where such dolls are also made. (*Photographed at the International Craftsman, Flemington, N.J.*)

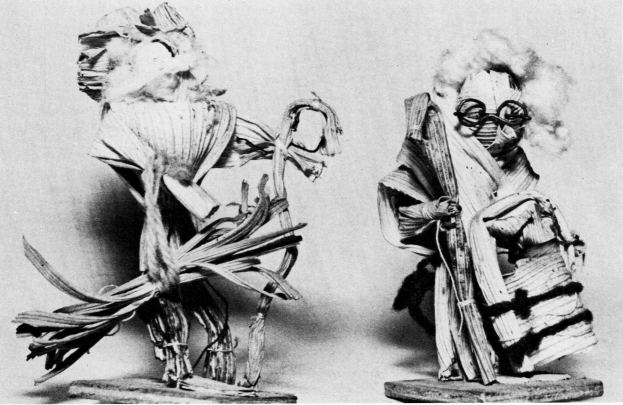

Another strange Mexican doll is the witch made of Spanish moss and fungus. Mexican dollmakers also make minute dolls that sit on the heads of pins. Another type of doll seen occasionally in Mexico is the cornhusk doll, which is somewhat different from that made in the United States. This doll has a wire frame over which the cornhusk is draped, and sometimes it is made with corn-silk braids entwined with pieces of bright yarn.

Mexican craftsmen are also known for the work they do with wax. They make dolls with faces from wax, bodies of fabric, and perhaps arms and hands also of wax. The Mexicans also make whole dolls of wax, with clothing of fabric saturated with wax. These dolls, often formed with great sensitivity and realism, usually represent peasants and peddlers.

Wood, too, is used by Mexican craftsmen, who make carvings of figures from their Indian heritage, using Aztec, Mayan, and other motifs. The Huichol Indians carve wooden offerings to their gods, and modern turned-wood dolls are sometimes seen in Mexico.

Wood is also used by Mexican mask makers, who double as santo-makers and carve these religious dolls from wood. Mexico is known for her santos in the tradition of her Spanish heritage.

Another natural material used by Mexican dollmakers is palm leaf. Mexico is a palm-growing area, and men, women, and even children braid palm leaves. While they are sitting or walking, their fingers move ceaselessly making one braided palm strip after another.

These Mexican dolls have wax faces and arms, wire-frame bodies, painted features, and red felt sandals. They probably represent peasants. The man, whose cotton-fabric clothes are patched, is about 10″ tall. He has on a straw hat and a serape, and on his back is a miniature lamb and a bundle of sticks. The woman carries baskets with flowers and fruit and has a bundle of sticks on her back. Shells hang on her arm and decorate her hat. (*Hupp Collection*)

These 6″ Mexican dolls were molded from wax. Their clothing is made of fabric impregnated with wax. The figures represent typical peasants. The women at either end carry baskets of vegetables. The woman in the center carries a load of wood on her back, and the man has a water jug. (*Hupp Collection*)

Molded from wax, these 4″ Mexican dolls are attractively detailed. Their clothing is fabric impregnated with wax. (*Hupp Collection*)

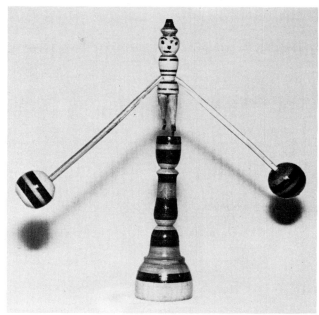

A balancing figure bought in Chiapas, Mexico. The figure itself is about 4″ high, and his stand about 6″. They were made from pieces of turned wood, dowels, and wooden balls, which were painted with bright stripes and lacquered. (*Photographed at the International Craftsman, Flemington, N.J.*)

Carved in Mexico, these 10″ wooden dolls are somewhat reminiscent of Mayan pottery figures. (*Photographed at the International Craftsman, Flemington, N.J.*)

This interesting wooden doll might be called Noah and his ark. The Huichol Indian who carved it during a dry spell made it as an offering to bring on the rains. He carved both the 5″ doll and the boat and decorated them with seed beads embedded in wax. He burned round holes in decorative lines into the doll. (*Photographed at the International Craftsman, Flemington, N.J.*)

These 10″ wooden dolls from Mexico are hand carved and painted in bright colors, mainly yellow and red. They are probably *santos*, religious figures. Each one wears a crown with a cross on the top. The ones on either side carry lilies made of wood. The one in the middle has what looks like wings on her crown, and painted in the front of her robe the image of an angel, a face with wings at the side. Separate pieces of wood were carved and glued in place to make these dolls. (*Photographed at the United Nations Gift Center*)

From Mexico, 8″ carved wooden figures called santos. The one on the right represents Saint Francis. (*Photographed at the International Craftsman, Flemington, N.J.*)

This 10″ Mexican man on a donkey is all palm leaf, left mainly in its natural color. The horse's bridle and the man's hat and features are magenta, and the grass protruding from the baskets is green. (*Weiner Collection*)

A 9½″ Mexican lady, woven from straw and palm leaf, standing on her hollow woven skirt. The natural materials are partly in their original colors and partly dyed. The skirt, for example, has dyed magenta, green, and purple strips. She has a magenta straw hat and yellow waistband, and even her features are of dyed straw on a woven palm leaf face. (*Weiner Collection*)

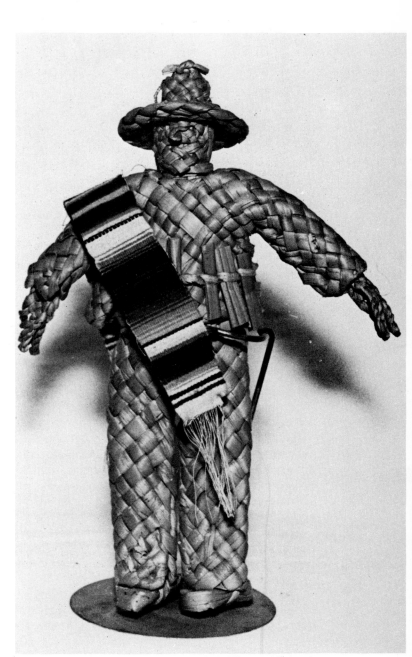

This 14″ Mexican straw man was bought in Tijuana, Mexico, in 1935. His body is made completely of woven palm leaf, and he wears a colorful woven serape (blanket) over his shoulder and a straw sombrero. (*Forbes Library Collection, Northampton, Mass.*)

These jute and rope figures are typical modern dolls from Mexico. The men and horses are made of rope, with wires through each piece to make them hold their shapes. The men dolls and the woman doll have straw over a ball for heads and scraps of felt glued on for features. The woman has a bell skirt of jute, decorated with rickrack. She wears a piece of lace for a shawl. The men wear woven straw hats and scraps of fabric for their shirts.

Hats, an essential feature of the Mexican male's attire, are made with braided palm strips, which are sewn together at special semi-industrial centers. Palm is used also to make baskets, floor mats, place mats, and even dolls. Mexican dollmakers also use such natural materials as straw and jute in making dolls.

A traditional craft for which Mexico is famous is the making of papier-mâché. In the Guanajuato state papier-mâché has been used, for example, to make dolls with articulated limbs and bright blue eyes, and in some villages dolls are modeled in papier-mâché and sold in the marketplace.

Today this craft has been revived and new methods of finishing have been introduced. Martin Renteria was a pioneer in putting this traditional craft to new and more artistic uses.

The dolls of Toluca are among the finest. They are constructed of cloth treated with glue and paste so they can be modeled when the glue is fresh—the

This man on a horse was made in Mexico. Both figures are papier-mâché painted in bright colors. (*Weiner Collection*)

A modern 15″ papier-mâché doll made in the state of Tonala, Mexico, by Jalisco Mateos. This girl doll has a cone-shaped body and braided string hair. Her features and the bird design on her dress are painted on. (*Photographed at the International Craftsman, Flemington, N.J.*)

A 16″ papier-mâché doll of a bird merchant, carrying cages with tiny birds in them on his back. This modern doll is in the style of Martin Renteria who put the traditional Mexican art of papier-mâché to new artistic uses. The doll is made of colored paper, draped artistically over a frame with a base probably of wire. The papier-mâché is antiqued and lacquered. (*Photographed at the International Craftsman, Flemington, N.J.*)

face is set when the glue hardens. The fabric base makes the faces as hard as papier-mâché and even more durable than composition. The faces are usually well-modeled copies of Indian or mestizo faces. The dolls are dressed in carefully made regional costumes, detailed with embroidery.

On market day villages in Mexico often have stacks of cloth dolls, most of which are the simplest kind of rag dolls. Many are made of manta, a coarse muslin that is stuffed with cotton. The doll's head is usually a round cloth ball with yarn hair sewn on, the face, painted or embroidered manta, and the clothing is scraps of leftover material sewn to represent the regional costume or peasant dress of the village where it was made.

A 10″ stuffed fabric woman doll, made in Toluca, Mexico, holding two woven palm leaf baskets. She has hand-painted exaggerated features and black braided embroidery-satin hair. She is dressed in the costume of the women of Tehuantepec, where probably the only matriarchal society in Mexico exists. The women are typically large and fat and have been compared to ships as they navigate through the town. Their husbands are typically small and slim. The women, called "Tehuana," usually have long black braided hair. (*Weiner Collection*)

This stuffed jointed 10″ doll was probably made in Toluca. The figure is dressed as a Huichol Indian. Much time and attention was lavished on this authentic costume with its beautiful cross-stitch embroidery. The doll is carrying a God's-eye, crossed sticks woven with yarn, which are made by the Huichols. He has a straw hat and two purses, one over each shoulder, with the straps crossing on his chest. These purses, typically worn this way by the Huichol men, are decorated with tiny cross-stitch embroidery. (*Photographed at the International Craftsman, Flemington, N.J.*)

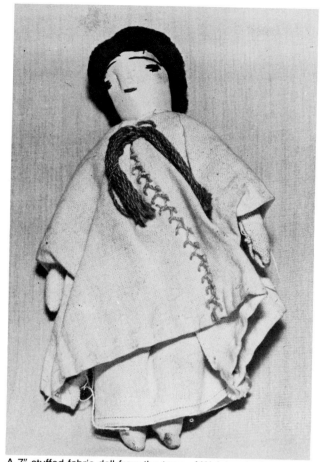

A 7" stuffed fabric doll from the town of Walalag, in the state of Oaxaca, Mexico. This female figure is made of muslin and wears the local ceremonial headdress of black yarn. Her eyes and mouth are embroidered on her rayon face, and her nose is needle sculpted. Her arms are stuffed white muslin, and her legs pink cotton fabric. Her huipil is decorated with a featherstitch in gold thread, with hanging fringe typical of costumes of this region. (*Photographed at the International Craftsman, Flemington, N.J.*)

These 9" Mexican dolls are named "Juan" and "Juanita," according to their tags. They were made in 1938 by Jane Mahoney in San Antonio, Texas. They are stuffed cotton figures with embroidered features. They have yarn hair sewn on their heads. The woman wears seed bead earrings and necklace. Her white huipil is decorated with green embroidery-thread stitches, and her red-and-green woolen skirt is decorated with sequins. The man has a serape over his shoulders decorated with a featherstitch, and his blue woolen pants are also decorated with featherstitch embroidery. (*Photographed at the United Nations Gift Center*)

Mexican dolls, 8" tall, of stuffed cotton, with pressed-felt faces and painted features. Their hair is black cotton thread, tied with a satin bow. The woman on the left, mounted on a piece of wood, has a black cotton skirt decorated with woven band. Her white huipil is edged with rickrack. The woman on the right has a red skirt decorated with sequins and a seed bead necklace. (*MacNeer Collection*)

These 12″ Mexican dolls are stuffed fabric and have embroidered features and yarn hair. Both are wearing felt sombreros decorated with crocheting around the edge. The man wears a black jacket and pants, decorated with sequins, crocheting, and embroidery stitches, and a colorful serape draped over his shoulder. The woman is wearing a cotton dress embellished with sequins and embroidery stitches. (*Photographed at the White Star Trading Co.*)

This photo of the back view of the dolls at left shows the detailing with sequins and seed beads on the woman's skirt, and so on.

Mexico is a land of potters. Even before the Aztecs, pottery was put to a variety of uses. Clay was used by the Aztecs to make water storage jars, pots, dishes, and to form idols and figures of human beings. These early craftsmen brought it to the status of great art. They made dolls, fashioning them by hand or using molds. For decoration they incised them with shells or sharp instruments, roller stamped them, or made textile impressions. Glazing was unknown and firing was haphazard.

Today Mexico is still a land of potters and pottery making continues to play an important role. Many of the Indian traditions are still carried on, with dolls being modeled from local clay and baked hard in the ashes of the open fire.

Each village of Mexico has its own distinctive kind of pottery. Indian girls of the Chipas highlands make their own dolls of clay and dress them in miniature *huipils* and wraparound skirts like their own. Today there are some potters, for example, Theodora Blanco, who have concentrated on making dolls and are known for their special skills.

Potters sometimes make a whole series of dolls, which when put together form a scene, which might be that of a wedding, a christening, or even a funeral. Potters also make special Christmas groupings.

Almost every Mexican family has a *nacimiento*, which is a crèche reproduced in clay. Some crèches are small and simple; others are very elaborate with a stable for the Holy Family, angels and shepherds, and all kinds of animals, including the whole village of Bethlehem, with tiny clay houses and shepherds' huts on country hills.

The markets of Mexico from early December until Christmas offer hundreds of clay dolls meant to be part of a nacimiento. Ranging in size from two inches to two feet, they are carefully modeled, with painted-on clothes of bright color.

These very primitive dolls were bought in San Cristóbal de las Casas in the state of Chiapas, Mexico. The 7" figure on the right has a crudely formed clay body. She is dressed in coarse brown wool fabric with green yarn tied at her waist and on her head. On her back is a baby, crudely made with a paper base. The 9" doll on the left has a body of fabric and wrapped with thread. On her head she has human hair and is dressed in a coarse fabric skirt and blouse. (*Photographed at the International Craftsman, Flemington, N.J.*)

A 5" Mexican clay figure with separate arms attached to the body with wires. The figure is clay colored with black-and-white lines painted on the arms and legs, and features painted on the face. The figure has a feather headdress and painted leather garment. He is probably a feather dancer from the state of Oaxaca. (*Hupp Collection*)

These 6″ pottery dolls very similar to each other were made by one of the finest artisans of Mexico, Theodora Blanco of Atzompa in the state of Oaxaca. Dolls such as these might be sold in local *tianguis*, or weekly markets. (*Photographed at the International Craftsman, Flemington, N.J.*)

Contemporary Mexican potters make whole sets of dolls to show groups of people at a christening, a wedding, or, as here, a funeral. These figures average about 5″ tall. The dolls in white beside the casket are angels. The grieving wife on the left, holding her baby in one hand and her handkerchief in the other, is being comforted by a friend. Despite death, life goes on, as shown by the woman at the far right who is nursing her baby. (*Photographed at the International Craftsman, Flemington, N. J.*)

DOLLS OF THE DEAD

The Day of the Dead is celebrated in Mexico on November 2. On that day both Indians and mestizos believe that the deceased are given celestial permission to visit relatives and friends on earth, where they are welcomed with ceremony. Tombs are made tidy, and living relatives get together to visit.

The rites for the Day of the Dead differ widely in various parts of Mexico. Usually the ritual involves the solemn feeding of the dead, according to the old Indian ritual of the region. Sometimes the food is offered in cemeteries, but usually it is set out on a special altar in the home.

This altar is decorated with papercuts, flowers, candles, and incense burners. Hot food is served to the ghostly guests in the best clay dishes. The aroma of the food is strong, and this is important because it is the aroma or essence of the food that the ghostly guests consume. The more mundane part of the food is consumed later by the living.

In some parts of Mexico the family spends the day or evening of the Day of the Dead in the cemetery. They decorate the tombs and light candles. The adults keep vigil while the children sleep rolled up in blankets. Special bread, called the Bread of the Dead, is baked throughout the country, and everyone must eat of this bread on the holiday.

The Mexicans eat cakes decorated with skulls and cut in the shape of men and animals on which the skeleton is outlined in sugar icing. There are also skulls, skeletons, and coffins made of sugar cake.

This bit of background information is necessary in order to understand the various dolls that are made especially for this unique feast. Though its name sounds solemn, the day is actually one of the gayest holidays of the year, and it seems to be a feast totally unique to Mexico.

The dolls and other toys created especially for the feast are made with what some would call a macabre sense of humor, which makes death seem to be a big joke. Skeleton dolls are made with limbs of coiled wire, and plaster heads, feet, hands, and bodies. About four inches tall, these strange figures are sold with tiny coffins.

There is a special jack-in-the-box, a little wooden coffin from which a white wooden skeleton doll jumps out. Wooden jumping-jack skeletons are made to dance madly when you pull the string. Clay dolls are also made, including whole families of skeletons lounging in a parlor or sitting at a table, or groups of musicians playing their instruments. The tin crafts-

men of Mexico also make their skeletal contributions to the Day of the Dead.

Among the metals worked in Mexico, tin is probably the most popular since it is inexpensive, light, and flexible. A soft metal, it can be cut, punched, and twisted easily in infinite ways into the shapes desired. It can also be embossed, engraved, left plain, or painted with translucent colors. Tin is used in making candelabra, mirror frames, lamps, tree ornaments, and even dolls.

This 14″ jumping jack of a skeleton playing a guitar was cut from wood, painted, and mounted on a stick. He was sold in Oaxaca, Mexico, for the Day of the Dead. Witches, and even a skeleton smoking a cigarette, are among the jumping jacks sold for this occasion. (*Photographed at the International Craftsman, Flemington, N.J.*)

Among the strange figures the Mexican craftsmen make for the Day of the Dead are clay skeletons portrayed in the midst of everyday activities. Grimly humorous, these figures might be those of wedding couples, women making tortillas or musicians playing in a band. Josephina Agular from Ocotlán, Oxaca, Mexico, made this skeleton band for the Day of the Dead. The skeleton dolls, each about 6″ high, were formed of clay and set on a clay bench. They were hand painted white and black, with their instruments in bright colors. (*Photographed at the International Craftsman, Flemington, N.J.*)

This spectacular skeleton lady is a 24″ tall candle holder made specially for the Day of the Dead. Of painted pottery, she was made in Izúcar de Metamoros in Puebla, Mexico. The potters of this town specialize in making ornate and colorful candlesticks for festive occasions and for the Day of the Dead. (*Photographed at the International Craftsman, Flemington, N.J.*)

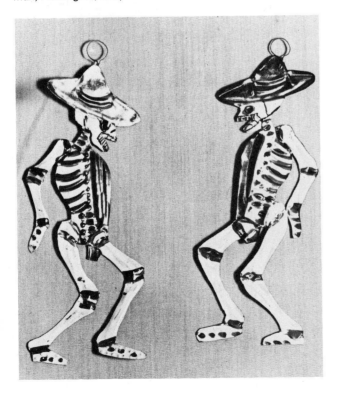

These 5″ skeletons were made in Oxaca, the center for tinwork in Mexico. (*Photographed at the International Craftsman, Flemington, N.J.*)

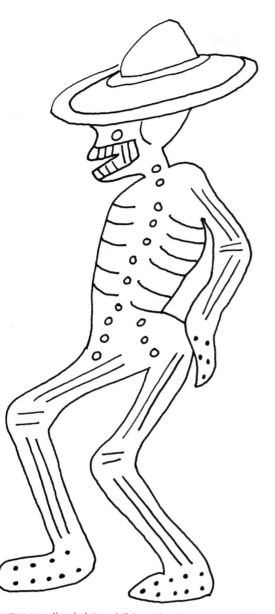

ZAPOTEC FEATHER DANCER

The Zapotec Indians in the state of Oaxaca, Mexico, are famous for their traditional feather or plume dance. The dancer wears a headdress reminiscent of the spectacular feather headdress worn by Montezuma, These Indians also make yarn dolls as colorful as the dancers themselves.

To make a feather dancer, you will need rug yarn—a skein of white, and small amounts of maroon, orange, green, and blue, or the other colors you wish to use. You will also need scrap cardboard, red and black embroidery cotton, a needle and strong thread, scissors, and a ruler.

1

To make a yarn doll, first cut a piece of cardboard 6″ x 2″ for the arms. Wrap the white yarn around it about 10 times. Cut the yarn at one edge and slip the cardboard away holding the yarn together. About 1″ from the cut edges, bring string around several times and tie off securely. Repeat at the other side, then cut open the loops.

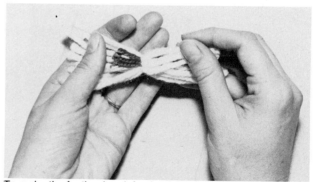

2

To make the feather brush for the right hand, cut pieces of green, gold, and magenta yarn each 5″ long and fold in half. Cut 12 pieces of white 5″ long. Hold the folded colored pieces inside and put the white pieces around them so that the white pieces extend approximately ½″ beyond the folded ends. Tie the whole bundle together about ¾″ from the loose ends of the colored yarn. Fold the white ends back on themselves so that the colored ones now show in the center. Bind the whole bunch together, starting about 2″ below the colored tops, with blue yarn winding it around for about 1″. Tie to the yarn arm and fasten off the blue yarn.

Make your own tin skeleton doll by using decorator craft foil, a heavy aluminum foil available in craft shops. If you cannot get it from this source, look for very thin aluminum sheets available in metal supply and hardware stores, You will also need transparent paint that will take on metal, such as glass-stain paint. Copy this pattern or make up one of your own. Cut out the paper pattern and draw around it on the foil with a pen. Run the point over the lines and circles on the pattern so that they show faintly on the foil. Remove the pattern and go over the internal lines with a pen (that has run out of ink) to indent them properly. Cut out the skeleton with sharp scissors. Paint the doll with transparent paint. Note that it is not necessary to cover every bit of space with paint—leave some silver showing. Your finished dolls should look something like the authentic ones shown at the left.

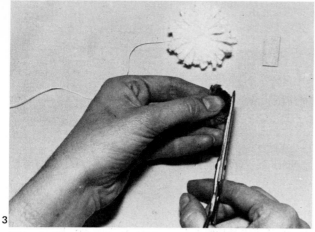

3

4

To make the rosette for the left hand, cut a piece of cardboard ¾" x ½". Wrap white yarn around it approximately 20 times, the short way. Slip a piece of yarn under the strands at one edge of the cardboard and tie this tightly, holding the wound strands together. Cut yarn at the other edge. Spread out the yarn into a rosette and trim the ends as necessary. Cut a piece of cardboard ½" x 1". Wrap magenta yarn around this piece 10 times. Tie with string at one edge, leaving ends of several inches of string. Cut at the other edge. Trim the rosette and put it at the center of the white rosette bringing the strings to the back of the white rosette. Tie both onto the left arm of the doll.

Cut a piece of cardboard 10" x 3". Wrap the white yarn around it about 40 times. Tie together at one edge of the cardboard and cut at the other edge.

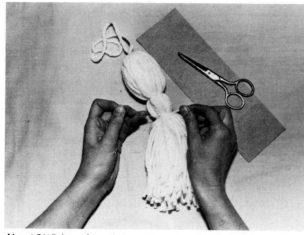

5

6

About 3¼" down from the tied end bring all pieces of yarn together and wrap a piece of thread or string around them several times. Tie together very tightly. This makes the top of the head. Tie all strands together again at about 4½" from the bottom of the head.

Insert the arm section and tie again for the waist about 6¼" down from the top. Below this, split the yarn and bring half to each side for the legs.

7

Cut four 8" pieces of gold, green, and magenta yarn. Take two of each color, fold them in half, slip a piece of string into the fold, and tie them securely at the back of the waist, bringing the ends over the doll's left shoulder across the chest and down the right leg. Tie the strands at the waist. Tie twice on each leg at about 8" and 9½" from the top. Trim off the excess colored yarn at the feet. Repeat the process with the second group of pieces of colored rug yarn, bringing them over the right shoulder and down the left leg.

8
With black embroidery cotton using all six strands make three straight stitches for the eyes and a long stitch above each eye for the eyebrows. With red embroidery cotton, make three stitches for the mouth. For the headdress, cut loops above the head and spread out the white yarn in a semicircle above the head. Cut six pieces of magenta yarn 12″ long and braid them, making the braid 8″ long and cutting off any excess yarn. Lay the braid on the spread-out headdress near the edge and sew there by machine or by hand. Trim the yarn above the braid making it even all around. Make a rosette like that made for the left hand, using magenta yarn with green for the center section. Sew it in the middle of the headdress.

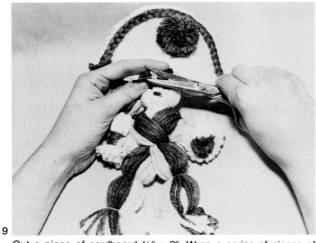

9
Cut a piece of cardboard ½″ x 2″. Wrap a series of pieces of different colors of yarn around it the short way, with each piece going around three or four times. Thread the string into a large needle and bring it under the yarn at one edge. Tie the string onto the doll above the head at the base of the headdress. Cut the yarn, remove the cardboard, and trim back the yarn.

This is the type of feather dancer doll made in Mitla, in the state of Oaxaca, Mexico. Made by the Zapotec Indians, these dolls represent the feather or plume dancers who do a traditional native dance wearing a headdress reminiscent of the spectacular feather headdress of Montezuma.

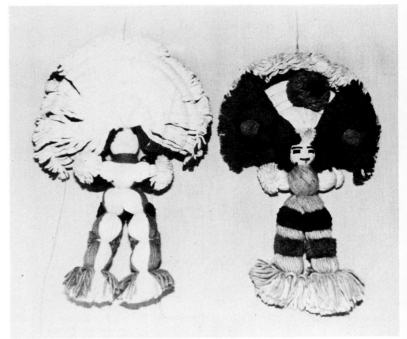

This feather dancer, shown back and front view, is an authentic doll made in Mexico and is decorated somewhat differently from the smaller sized doll above. It has three rosettes on the headdress and extra yarn where it is tied on the legs. (*Photographed at the International Craftsman, Flemington, N.J.*)

MEXICAN "SEED BAPTISM" DOLLS

The Otomi Indians of San Pablito, Pueblo, Mexico, make primitive paper idols. Originally they cut these paper dolls from bark paper that they made, but today they use tissue paper.

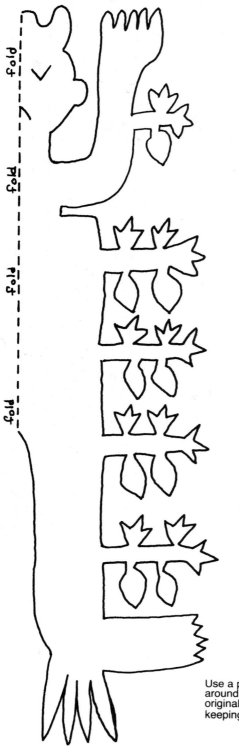

For the special "seed baptism" crop ceremonials, the Brujo and Bruja (male and female witches of the village) cut these paper dolls which show men with their arms raised in supplication. Sprouting from their arms and legs is whatever crop they are praying for: corn, peppers, sugar cane, peanuts, and so on. As part of the ceremony the witch doctor dipped the paper doll into the blood of a sacrificial animal and buried it in the field so that the spirit represented by the doll would ensure a good crop yield.

The figures are usually made by putting two layers of white paper between two layers of colored tissue. The layers are held together with thread. The paper is folded in half, and a design is cut so when the paper is opened the design is symmetrical. Both the color and the design are related to the crop to be planted in the field. A yellow figure with corncobs at the sides is meant for a cornfield, green for a field of peppers, and so on.

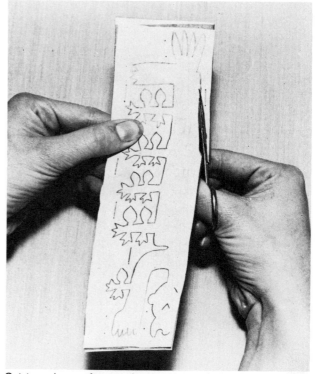

Cut two pieces of green tissue paper and two pieces of white typing-weight paper 9″ × 4″. Hold them together, with the white paper sandwiched between the layers of tissue paper, and fold them in half the long way. Place the half pattern along the fold line of the paper. Staple all the layers of paper together, putting staples in here and there only where the paper will be cut away. The staples will hold the papers tightly together, keeping them from slipping as you are cutting.

Use a piece of tracing paper or other lightweight paper and trace around the full-size pattern given here. If you wish to make an original design, study the one shown here and develop your own keeping the essential characteristics.

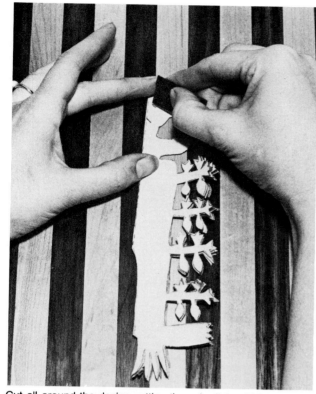

Cut all around the design cutting through all the thicknesses of paper. Do not cut along the fold line. Use a craft knife to cut along the lines for the eyes. Do not cut off the paper at the eyes and mouth, but leave the small flaps in place.

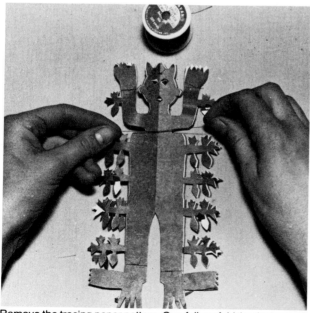

Remove the tracing paper pattern. Carefully unfold the design and lay it flat. Thread a needle with sewing thread to match the tissue paper. Make stitches here and there on the figure, tying off the ends of the thread. Tie the layers of paper together at the waist, ankles, and wrists. Pull forward the cut paper at the eyes and mouth. Spread out the paper at the feet and hands.

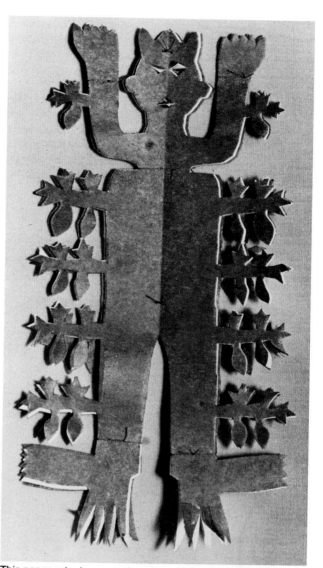

This paper cutout represents a man with his arms raised in supplication for peppers. Try another one, with a different crop growing from his arms and legs. Make him out of yellow tissue and have him begging for corn, or out of red tissue, begging for tomatoes.

GUATEMALA

Guatemala has a great variety of beautifully made hand-loomed fabrics and many dolls from this country are shown engaged in making the fabric— weaving or preparing the wool with a drop spindle. There are also Guatemalan dolls shown busy with other crafts. These dolls usually have wrapped wire bodies and faces of nylon stockings.

In contrast to these dolls dressed in hand-loomed fabrics are the modern-looking stuffed dolls also made in Guatemala; these are sometimes machine-embroidered, with the stitching done on the latest-model sewing machine with stitching attachments.

A scene from the Friday market in Chimaltenango, Guatemala. In many South American countries the local open-air market is still where goods are exchanged. Dollmakers sell their work in stalls beside farmers and other craftsmen. (*Photo courtesy of World Neighbors*)

These small 3½" dolls, made in Guatemala, have wire bases wrapped with brown tape. Their faces are covered with nylon stocking and are embroidered. Their clothing is small bits of hand-loomed fabric. The female has a bundle on her head made from a taffeta material, and the male carries cornhusks in one arm and sticks in the other. (*Imported by SERRV, from the Author's Collection*)

A 7" doll, made in Guatemala, with a wire-frame body, wrapped first with tape and then with nylon stocking. This man is dressed in scraps of handloomed fabric. His features are embroidered, and on his back is a wooden carrier with a length of rope, two woven strips, and pieces of cornhusk tied on. (*Imported by SERRV, from the Author's Collection*)

These musicians, made in Guatemala, stand behind a wooden marimba, which is like a small orchestra in itself. This primitive wooden instrument when skillfully played is exceedingly effective. The instrument is decorated with a strip of woven fabric. The dolls have wire-frame bodies, wrapped first with tape and then with nylon stocking. They are dressed in bits of colorful fabrics, and their hats are stitched by hand from pieces of burlap. They hold drumsticks made of small sticks tipped with balls of black wax. (*Imported by SERRV, from the Author's Collection*)

Indian women of Guatemala still use simple traditional backstrap looms, a method of weaving going back to pre-Columbian times, to make beautiful fabrics for themselves and occasionally to use in making dolls. This weaver, Margarita Alonzo, a Cakchiquel Indian and a weaver of the Ri-Ixoki Cooperative in San Jacinto, Guatemala, could be the real-life counterpart of the doll shown below. (*Photo courtesy of World Neighbors, Oklahoma City, Oklahoma*)

This woman weaver, with her loom and child lying under it, was made in Guatemala. The wooden platform on which she is sitting is 9″ long, and the figure is 7″ high. She is crudely made with a wire-frame body and has a stuffed stocking-fabric face with embroidered features. She wears handloomed fabric clothing, a predominantly green skirt and a red blouse, and has yarn for hair. The child, tucked under a handloomed blanket, is represented by a face made the same way as his mother's. (*Weiner Collection*)

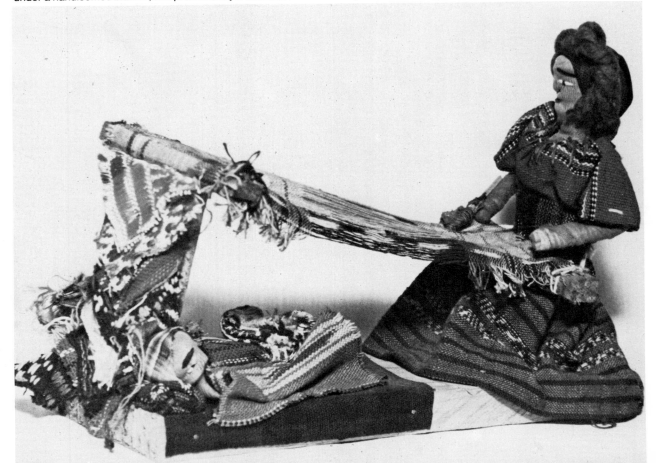

These 12″ dolls from Guatemala are firmly stuffed fabric. They have black yarn hair, red felt mouths, and black bead eyes with embroidered nose and eyebrows. Both wear sandals made of vinyl. The girl has a white blouse decorated with embroidery, a woven skirt, bead earrings, and a basket on her head. The boy is wearing a straw hat, black vest, and short pants decorated with machine embroidery and contrasting binding. (*Mueller Collection*)

Bought in Guatemala in the 1960s, this happy fellow playing the maracas is made with a wire-frame body. Made of modern materials, he has a very contemporary look. His hand, feet, and face are covered with a knit-stocking fabric over cotton filling. He wears brown velvet pants and a blue shirt with pink tassels. His hair is a strip of brown tassels, and his features are painted on his stocking-fabric face. His hat is made from a synthetic material that looks like straw. (*Weiner Collection*)

This unusual 11″ carved wooden doll from Guatemala has jointed legs and is dressed in fabric clothing. His huge hands are out of proportion to the rest of his body, and his features are painted on. (*Photographed at the International Craftsman, Flemington, N.J.*)

UCHUS AND REVERSE APPLIQUÉ

Off the coast of Panama in the Caribbean Sea is a string of over three hundred coral islands where the Cuna Indians live. The Cunas, a short, stocky, generally uneducated people, still observe the customs of their ancestors and work at the same crafts they have been engaged in for centuries.

The men are known for the carved dolls they make called *uchus,* wooden figures of men, women, and animals. The Cunas believe these dolls can trap the good spirits and appease or outwit the bad spirits. According to their ancestral beliefs, spirits exist, and both living and nonliving things, as well as the forces of nature, have spirits.

The women, on the other hand, are known for their beautiful needlework, on their blouses, or molas as they are called. A mola is a unique artistic creation that takes a month or longer to complete. It is made in layers of vividly colored cloth fragments to produce reverse appliqué designs of great intricacy. The predominant colors are red and black, but green, blue, yellow, and orange are also used. The designs can be anything, and are typically imaginative free forms but often realistic enough to be recognized. Common are complicated geometric designs, depictions of animals or fish, real or imaginary, and letters of the alphabet.

The women usually make rectangular panels about 24″ by 16″ and use them as part of their blouses. The women also use them on the dolls they make, perhaps from salvagable pieces of a mola they have worn out. Pieces of their appliqué work have been used to decorate the uchus.

You can make a piece of reverse appliqué as the Cunas have done to decorate a wooden figure or use it as part of a costume for a fabric stuffed doll, perhaps dressed exactly like the women of the tribe.

This young Cuna girl holds out examples of the craftwork done by her tribe. The men carve uchus, like the one she holds in one hand, and the women make molas, like the one she holds in the other hand. (*Photo courtesy of the Panama Government Tourist Bureau*)

The Cuna women wear straight skirts, and their blouses have intricately stitched panels on both the back and the front. They go barefoot, wear lots of golden jewelry, and live in thatch-roofed and stick-walled huts on small islands off the coast of Panama. (*Photo Courtesy of the Panama Government Tourist Bureau*)

Cuna women and girls sit outdoors on low stools or benches and carefully hand stitch molas for themselves or for use in dollmaking. (*Photo courtesy of the Panama Tourist Bureau*)

This wooden doll was made by the male Cuna Indians who live on the islands off the coast of Panama. This roughly carved wooden figure has a piece of fabric tied onto its head with feathers attached. Wrapped around the body is a mola, or piece of reverse appliqué work. (*Photographed with permission of the White Star Trading Co.*)

The Cuna women dress in brilliant red-and-gold costumes that rival the brilliance of their sunfilled landscape. This doll beautifully shows off their typical costume. They wear the family's wealth in their gold jewelry, including a gold nose ring, earrings, and as many necklaces as possible. The doll wears costume-jewelry substitutes. They also wear bands of colored beads on their arms and legs; the doll has bands of woven fabric to represent these. The Indians wear red-and-gold bandanna-like scarves on their heads, and their blouses are made using a panel of reverse appliqué for which the tribe is so famous. The doll's clothing is made from new fabric, except for the piece of reverse appliqué on her blouse. This piece was evidently cut from a blouse, which was probably worn out, except for a few areas perhaps around the edge. Her skirt is a piece of straight fabric, just as it would be for the Cuna woman. This 18″ doll is stuffed fabric. Her hair is black yarn with the typical eye-level black bangs of the Cunas, and her features are painted on her fabric face. (*Author's Collection*)

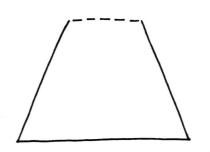

To make your small sample of reverse appliqué, copy this pattern on scrap paper, fold the paper on the dashed line, and cut out.

To make a panel, such as the one shown on the wooden uchu, cut three pieces of lightweight fabric 5″ × 7½″. Select three contrasting colors, for example, yellow, blue, and red. Pile them one on top of the other (red, yellow, blue, top to bottom) and baste them together all around the edge. Put your paper pattern in the center of the fabric and draw around it. Cut away the red layer on the penciled line. Cut away the yellow layer below even farther back. If you cut out these pieces very carefully, you can use them later for appliqué.

Turn under the edge of the red layer and sew it all around to the blue layer with small hemming stitches. Make small cuts into the corners to make turning under easier.

Turn under the edge of the yellow piece of fabric, which you had cut out, and appliqué it on top of the blue fabric. Cut off the points so you will not have too much bulk in turning under the corners. Appliqué the red piece in the center.

Make small diamond-shaped holes above and below the bow-tie shapes by cutting only the red, or top, layer. Stitch back to reveal the yellow fabric.

THE DOLLS OF ECUADOR

Ecuador is known for several different types of dolls. Probably the most famous type is the bread dough doll, shaped by hand from colored dough and lacquered. The woven straw doll made by the Otabolin Indians is another well-known type.

Ecuador, also produces fabric stuffed dolls and dolls made with wooden or wire frames, usually dressed peasant style and often sold in pairs. The woman doll usually carries a baby or a drop spindle and the man doll often carries a reed flute.

Stuffed dolls decorated with colorful embroidery are sold by dollmakers in the open-air markets of Ecuador. (*Photo courtesy of SERRV*)

A simple 9½" doll from Ecuador made of bone. It has not one but two heads carved in the Inca tradition. Black pigment was rubbed into the carved indentations to make them stand out. (*Photographed at the International Craftsman, Flemington, N.J.*)

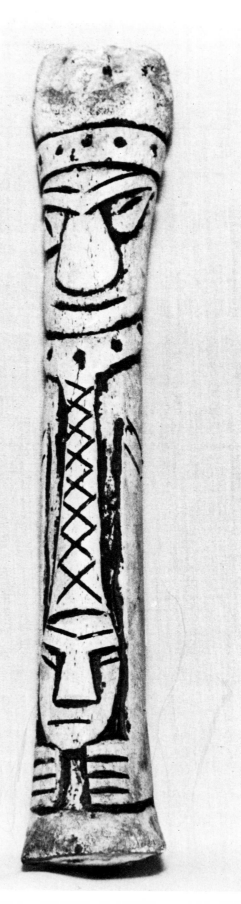

These 2" and 4" straw dolls were made in Ecuador. Weaving dolls from straw is a tradition of the Otabolin Indians who live there. (*Imported by SERRV, in the Author's Collection*)

These 7" dolls made in Ecuador have wooden bodies and fabric tube arms. A claylike substance was used to form the heads on top of the wood, and fabric was pressed over it. They are dressed in coarsely woven fabrics and have leather hats and black yarn hair. Carrying a flute made from straw the man wears a white shirt and pants and has a pink poncho over them. The woman has a wooden paddle baby tied to her back. (*Imported by SERRV, in the Author's Collection*)

This pair of 4" dolls from Ecuador was made there by Akios Industries. Their bodies have a wooden base and are attached to wooden platforms. Their arms are pieces of cotton fabric folded several times and stitched. Their faces are pressed-cotton fabric, and the features are painted on. Their hair is yarn, and their clothing is made from scraps of native materials. Both have molded leather hats. The man carries a flute of straw, and the woman wears silver bead earrings and carries a baby in a backpack. Her dress is decorated with sewing-machine embroidery. (*Weiner Collection*)

The Otabolin Indians of Ecuador used straw to weave this angel with her harp and wings. She wears a derby-type hat, like that worn by the Indians who wove her. (*Photographed at the International Craftsman, Flemington, N.J.*)

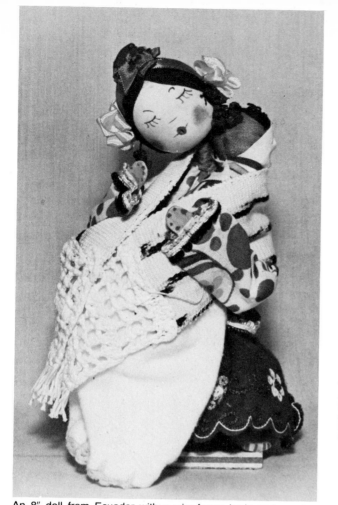

This pincushion with 2″ doll attached is from Ecuador. The doll is a simple long bean shape. Her features are embroidered, and she has braided black yarn hair. Her skirt is decorated with feather-stitch embroidery. The pincushion is beautifully decorated with hand embroidery. (*Imported by SERRV, in the Author's Collection*)

An 8″ doll from Ecuador with a wire-frame body and wooden hands, feet, and head. This female figure has painted features and black string hair decorated with ribbons and ribbon rosettes. Her skirt is machine-embroidered wool, and her blouse is printed-cotton fabric. She wears a shawl decorated with a wide band of hand crocheted lace. The baby she is holding has a stuffed fabric head and body and is dressed in a long white flannel dress edged with hand crochet, with the upper part of its body wrapped in printed-cotton fabric. (*Imported by SERRV, from the Author's Collection*)

A pair of dolls from Ecuador, bought in the early 1960s. Their wire frames are covered with a gray cotton fabric. The faces are painted on and embroidered, with the noses formed by fabric sculpture, that is, by pinching the fabric and holding it in place with stitches. Both have black yarn hair and felt hats. The woman wears beads at her neck, and a white blouse and red skirt, both decorated with machine embroidery. She carries a baby, whose face is made in the same way as his parents', and who is tightly wrapped in a blanket decorated with machine embroidery and pieces of yarn. The man wears white cotton pants and a handloomed multicolored serape and carries a black-and-white woolen scarf on his arm. (*Weiner Collection*)

ECUADORIAN BREAD DOUGH

The people of Ecuador have been making elegant creations from bread dough for hundreds of years. Originally they were made as offerings of food for All Saints' Day, and the tradition is still carried on today.

They make many different shapes, including stars, owls and other birds, llamas, horses, and other animals, and people. No two of these bread dough people or other shapes are ever exactly alike because each tiny piece is shaped by hand and carefully assembled. Natural dyes are used to color the pieces of bread dough before they are assembled into a single doll. After the dough doll has dried, it is always lacquered to preserve it.

Making bread dough items of all kinds has become a popular craft in the United States. Many different recipes are used to make the dough itself, but the only really necessary ingredients are white bread and white glue. White bread when mashed and squeezed makes an easily workable dough, and the white glue added to it gives it strength.

The usual proportion is a tablespoon of white glue to each piece of bread. To this basic recipe, some people add glycerine, lemon juice, liquid detergent, or white shoe polish. If you want to use any of these, experiment with them to see if they help make your dough any easier to handle and work with. None are really necessary, however.

Bread dough is very easy to work with. You can roll it into shape, and it will hold whatever shape you give it. It cuts easily, and you can make very small shapes with the dough, so it is very good for detail work. The floral designs on the bread dough doll, for example, are easy to make.

You can use all sorts of implements to help you work with dough, including scissors, knives, cookie cutters, toothpicks, and so on. When you are making small details to add to your doll, an easy way to handle these is with toothpicks. You can slip a toothpick under a small shape and pick it up easily. Or if you want the shape you have made to have a little circle or indentation in it, the toothpick can make it very easily for you. You can stick the toothpick into the small shape, pick it up, and put it in place, pulling out the toothpick and leaving the shape with a hole made by the toothpick.

Whenever you are putting a bit of dough in place on your doll, always put a bit of white glue either on the piece of dough or on the doll itself, whichever is more convenient. Since you are using white glue it will not matter if the glue shows now when it is wet because it will dry clear.

In working with the dough, remember that it can dry out very quickly. Keep it in a plastic bag when you are not using it. If you are working on a project and have to leave it temporarily on your worktable, cover it with plastic.

If you want to keep the dough for use later, tightly fasten the plastic bag and put it into the refrigerator. You can store it there for weeks. When you take it out, work it a little with your fingers. Add a bit of liquid detergent if necessary, work it in, and the dough will be ready for use.

The Ecuadorian bread dough doll was designed by the author who simplified somewhat the typical decoration of the figure.

A good surface for working with bread dough is a piece of waxed paper or aluminum foil, if you prefer. If the dough seems sticky, sprinkle a little flour on the paper.

For the bread dough, you can use slices of any of the white breads sold in the stores today. Use stale bread, or bread that has been marked down by the store because the freshness date has expired. Make as much dough as you wish at a time, but keep the ratio of a slice of bread to a tablespoon of white glue.

For the doll shown here, you would need five or six slices of bread.

The colored areas on the bread dough dolls are not painted on; the color is all the way through the dough, having been added to the dough before the doll was made. Many different types of coloring can be used, but probably the most convenient are acrylic or poster paints. You can also experiment with liquid and paste food colors, watercolors, or powdered dyes.

1

To make bread dough, first remove all the crusts from six slices of bread. Be sure to get off all the brown edges or they will show up as dark spots in your dough. Break the slices of bread into small pieces putting them into a bowl. Measure 6 tablespoons of white glue and pour it over the bread. At first mix with a spoon and then with your hands. You may think you will never get smooth clay as you work this mixture, but keep kneading. Work it with your hands for a good five minutes, until it is a velvety dough that no longer sticks to your hand. If it sticks just a little, try putting a little hand lotion or other lubricant on your hands. If this does not help and you have kneaded the dough for a full five minutes, add more bread a little at a time and work it in. If on the other hand, your dough has come out too dry, add a small amount of glue at a time and work it in thoroughly. When the dough is ready to use, it will be smooth and easy to work. Wrap it in a plastic bag and take out only that part of the dough you will be working with.

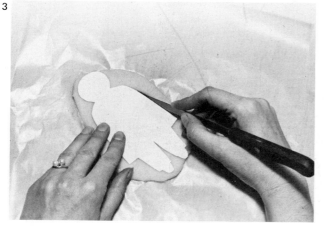

2

Choose several colors of paint and make a small ball of dough for each color. Keep a larger ball the natural bread dough color. Flatten out each ball, put a little paint directly on the dough, and knead it in well so the color is thoroughly distributed. Add more color until the dough is the shade you desire. Colors dry somewhat darker than the workable dough.

Lift up the feet and press them in place so that they are three-dimensional. Work the dough in the face area. If necessary, add more uncolored dough, putting some white glue on the face area before adding new dough. Form a nose and chin by pinching the dough with your fingers. Use a toothpick or other instrument to make the eye slits.

To make the white llama felt hat for your doll, take a piece of uncolored dough and flatten it out to an oval shape. Put some white glue on the head and put the hat in place spreading out the brim as desired. Flatten some pieces of colored dough and put at the sides of the head for hair. To make the eyes and eyebrows, take a very tiny amount of colored dough, roll it between your index finger and thumb to make a small thin line of dough. Put glue in the eye hole and put this small line in place. Repeat for the other eye, eyebrows, and for the mouth. Take a tiny ball of a different color of dough, work it into a miniature round ball, put it on a toothpick, dip it in glue, and place it on the eye, making sure the toothpick makes a hole at the center of the circle.

Take your ball of uncolored dough and flatten it out with your fingers, or if you wish, with a rolling pin. Smooth it out so that it is between ¼" and ⅛" thick. Make an oval at least 5" long and 3" wide. You can cut out your own outline or make a scrap paper copy of the outline given here for the bread dough man. Place the paper copy on the dough, and with a kitchen or craft knife, cut all around it. If necessary, smooth out the edges with your fingers.

3

4

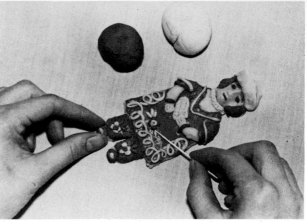

5

Dress your doll as desired. To make a shirt, take some colored dough, flatten it, and cut around it to make a shirt to fit your doll. Put glue on the doll and put the shirt in place. Repeat with a different color to make the trousers. To make arms, take some of the uncolored dough and make arm shapes and glue in place. With a toothpick, mark in the fingers. If you wish your doll to be carrying a flute, form this out of colored dough and slip it under one of his hands. Take a little more dough the color of the shirt, make sleeves, and glue them in place at the top of the arms. To make sandals, make a small oval of colored dough and glue it on the bottom of the foot. Make a small straight strip and glue this over the foot. Repeat for the second sandal.

6

Add whatever decoration you wish to the figure. To make lines, take some dough and work it back and forth on the waxed paper, rolling it under your palm so that it makes a long "snake." Use this to edge the top of his shirt and along the edge of his sleeves. Bring it around and around in a curlicue for the bottom of his shirt. To make the flowers, use colored dough. Make four tiny balls of one color, flatten them out, and glue them on around in a little circle. Take another color of dough, make a tiny ball, put it on a toothpick, dip it in glue, and put it in place at the center of the flower. For the leaves, work a small amount of dough with your fingers to make a teardrop shape and glue these in place next to the flower.

Bread dough figures made in Ecuador can be human representations, such as this doll, with a pointed hat and a bulbous nose, or they might be animals, such as this llama, or birds, insects, or objects. (*Photographed at the International Craftsman, Flemington, N.J.*)

Let your doll dry completely, then give it several coats of lacquer or spray fixative to protect it and make it shiny.

This large bread dough doll measures 14″ and is very elegantly decorated with ruffles and flowers in many bright colors. The face is clownlike with its bulbous nose and huge lips. (*Photographed at the International Craftsman, Flemington, N.J.*)

Bread dough figures made in Ecuador can be human representations, such as this doll, with a pointed hat and a bulbous nose, or they might be animals, such as this llama, or birds, insects, or objects. (*Photographed at the International Craftsman, Flemington, N.J.*)

PERUVIAN DOLLS

In Peru, dolls have been unearthed in ancient burying grounds in children's graves. In places like Ancón, these dolls have been discovered during excavations. Often dressed in fine Indian weaving, these dolls were buried along with their owners, sometimes with extra clothing and small utensils.

Since these grave dolls were buried in such dry soil—it contained a certain amount of saltpeter in this area—some of the dolls have been preserved almost perfectly. Some were even prepared as mummies, swathed in cotton in the same way as the bodies of the children with whom they were buried. Today reproductions of these grave dolls are often made to be sold at home and abroad.

Besides these grave dolls, Peru has other dolls in its Inca heritage. Dolls of brass, stone, and tapestry were found in the ancient Inca cities of Peru. Because the tapestry dolls are of fabric and therefore unbreakable, many have survived, although their woven features have often disappeared. Clay dolls made in molds—with painted faces, large heads, and small bodies—have also been found in Peru.

Today a variety of dolls are being made in Peru, using the traditional and modern craft techniques. The Peruvians are especially skilled in textiles and ceramics, a legacy of the early Indians. Certain towns and areas are known for their specialized handcrafts; for example, craftsmen in Huancayo, Puno, and Cuzco are famous for their dolls, toy llamas, and for textiles from the wool of the llama, alpaca, and vicuña.

Ceramic objects, such as bowls, utensils, and dolls, are made in almost every province of Peru, and those made in the Chaco territory are especially well known. Few wooden dolls are made, except those which some Indians have carried on their backs to represent an infant they have lost.

Peruvian dolls often wear handwoven llama wool and rough linen in their costumes, replicas often of the costumes worn by the people who live high up in the Andes. Peruvians are skilled knitters and make colorful hats with complex and colorful designs, some distinctive to a certain region. They also turn their knitting skills to dollmaking, sometimes making only the hat for the doll but sometimes making the whole doll, both body and clothing. Embroidery has also been used by Peruvian dollmakers.

Pre-Inca dolls, probably reproductions, sewn onto a fabric container with a fringed bottom. The dolls have stuffed fabric balls for heads and are made of primitive handloomed fabrics. Their features are embroidered, and their limbs are sticks, which have been wrapped with thread. (*Photographed with permission of Car-Be Associated, Fort Lee, N.J.*)

Primitive-looking pre-Inca dolls, probably reproductions of dolls found in Peru. Dolls like these were made by the Incas and buried with the dead. (*Photographed with permission of Car-Be Associated, Fort Lee, N.J.*)

These 4″ dolls, made in the Cuzco region of Peru, have clay heads and wire bodies wrapped with yarn. The man is wearing a multi-colored crocheted hat and a piece of handloomed fabric band for a poncho. He is holding onto a large staff, his symbol of authority as a headman. The woman is dressed in pieces of handloomed woolen fabric and is holding a drop spindle. (*Hulsizer Collection*)

These 7″ dolls from Peru are from the 1940s. They have leather sandals and big brown fabric feet with toes indicated with embroidery cotton. They are nailed to a wooden board and have light brown cotton stuffed bodies. Their heads are made of a clay substance, and their features are painted. The Incas' love for brilliant colors, with basic black, can be seen in the clothing of these dolls. Their favorite colors, red and deep yellow, predominate in costumes of primitive handloomed woolen fabrics.

The man wears black pants and a deep yellow jacket trimmed with red-and-blue rickrack. His red shirt is trimmed with pink rickrack. Painted on his head is a typical Peruvian knitted woolen hat with its multicolored stitch pattern. He has a colorful bag hanging on his back.

The woman is wearing a black skirt and jacket topped with a bright multicolored shawl. Her hat is a large round one, which is typically worn with a knitted skullcap. The slant of such hats varies, and they are usually picot edged. (*MacNeer Collection*)

These all-knitted 6″ dolls have knitted faces with features sewn on with yarn. Both have knitted bodies of brown yarn and stuffed. Both wear the typical sandals worn in Peru and the typical large round picot-edged hat—even the hats on these dolls are knitted and are decorated with seed beads and sequins. The Inca love for bright colors is shown in their costumes. The man has the inevitable red jacket, which is decorated with seed beads and sequins. He is wearing the typical black breeches, with yellow stitching and sequins along the bottom edge, and a green shirt, and is holding what looks like a white llama. The woman has a baby on her back and is dressed in multicolored clothing with the designs knitted into it. She has spinning equipment in her hand and wears a blue vest and shawl. (*Weiner Collection*)

A back view of the knitted Peruvian dolls, showing the attention to detail with which these dolls were made. Notice the sequins and seed beads sewn on the hats and the designs knitted into the pouch in which the baby is carried.

CHAIN-STITCH DOLL OF PERU

In Chijnaya, a small Indian village in the Peruvian Andes, boys and girls have learned to embroider, and they sit on ichu grass and work with a needle and vivid colors of yarn. They use their own designs and patterns. They might make a rainbow-striped llama, the sun, their homes, a church, or men fishing, working in the fields, or herding pigs, or girls leading a llama. They embroider all these designs "Grandma Moses style" on pieces of homespun, and their embroideries give their own free untaught vision of life in a Quechua Indian village.

The children were taught a few basic stitches by a Peace Corps volunteer. They had no prior experience with embroidery, but they were given needles, colorful yarn, and homespun wool from sheep and llamas to work with. They were left on their own as far as what design they were going to embroider and how they would arrange these designs.

Sometimes individually, but usually in a group, the children work on the embroideries after school. Working together is an important social function for the children, and they look on the project as play rather than work, but they are proud of the fact that their pieces of embroidery have been sold and exported and the money received for them has helped supply the village with books, shoes, and other necessities.

The designs by the young embroiderers have a charm and naïve beauty all their own. They have made both large and small tapestries. The children themselves are from the ages of 6 to 16, and most of them have never been outside their own small community.

These children also make simple dolls of their own. They make up the same human figures, embroider them in bright colors, and cut around the embroidery, allowing extra fabric for a seam. They cut a second piece of fabric the same size, sew the pieces together, then stuff them to make dolls.

Try completing a simple embroidered doll like the one shown here, based on a design used on one of the children's tapestries. The original inspiration was an old Inca design. The materials you will need are linen or similar fabric, and crewel embroidery wool, thread, and fiber filling. You will also need scissors, needles, and an embroidery hoop. To transfer the design to your fabric, you will need scrap paper, pencil, and dressmaker's carbon paper.

This 6" × 7" piece of homespun wool was made by a child from Chijnaya, Peru. Its chain-stitched design of a girl leading a llama is typical of the scenes embroidered by the children of the village. (*Author's Collection*)

A 9" doll was embroidered in a rainbow of colors by a child from Chijnaya, then cut out, backed, and stuffed. (*Author's Collection*)

Untrained in art, the children of Chijnaya make dolls, such as this one of a villager. (*Author's Collection*)

Try embroidering this simple design of the doll shown above.

This ancient Peruvian design was used by a child of Chijnaya to make a wall hanging. It could also be made into a chain-stitch doll.

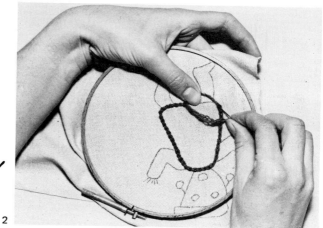

2 Put the fabric into an embroidery hoop. Using a double strand of crewel embroidery wool, chain-stitch all around the outside of each part of the design. After you finish the outside of each section, do the lines of stitches inside of the outline with each row a different color. If the area is to be filled in completely, keep going around and around with the rows of stitches until it is filled in.

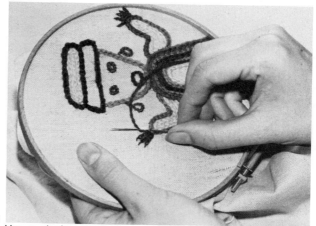

3 Use a single strand of crewel wool to complete the features, fingers, and toes. At the end of each finger, make a long tie-down stitch to represent a fingernail. Do the same with the toes, for toenails.

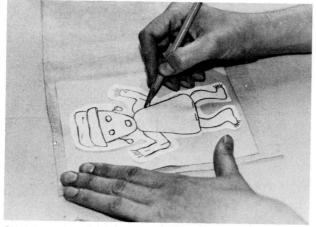

1 Copy the embroidery design for the doll on scrap paper or make up your own design. Pin the scrap paper on top of a piece of dress-maker's carbon paper, over your piece of fabric. Carefully draw over all the lines with a pencil or pen, being sure to bear down hard enough so that the design is transferred to the fabric.

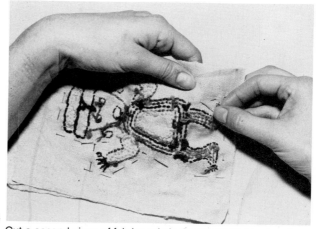

4 Cut a second piece of fabric and pin the two right sides together. Sew around the design, leaving an extra border all around it. Leave a space unsewn for stuffing.

5

Turn right side out and stuff. Sew up the hole you left for turning.

OTHER SOUTH AMERICAN DOLLS

The countries of South America are very different from one another in terrain, climate, people, and natural resources. Since the dollmakers use the materials available to them, the dolls they produce are *very different.*

The dolls vary from the peasant-type Bolivian dolls in dresses of hand-loomed fabric, similar to those made in Guatemala, Ecuador, and Peru, to the modern-looking felt dolls from Venezuela and the modern rope dolls from Brazil. Some are made with great care, such as the stuffed fabric dolls with beautifully detailed costumes from Argentina, and others are put together quickly to be sold as tourist items, such as the pair from Uruguay.

This chain-stitch doll was made by the author and based on a figure on a wall hanging made in Chijnaya. Figures, such as this one, reflect the interest of children in their Incan ancestry. Crewel wool and linen fabric were used.

These 8″ dolls were made in Bolivia. They have wire-base bodies filled out with straw and wrapped with heavy pink thread. Their faces are balls of cotton covered with white fabric over which a bit of nylon stocking is stretched. Their features are embroidered. On the woman's back is an infant, just a small head like those of its parents and wrapped in a piece of blue fabric. Their clothing is strips of fabric probably handloomed on a backstrap loom. The man, who is holding a straw flute, wears a hand-knitted hat. The woman, who has a drop spindle in her hand, wears a derbylike hat, made by pressing felt into the form desired. (*Imported by SERRV, in the Author's Collection*)

From Venezuela, 7½″ dolls with wire-frame bodies covered with brown felt and painted features. The girl is wearing seed bead earrings and a bright pink polka-dot dress edged with white lace, with a slip underneath also edged in lace. The boy is wearing a white felt outfit with seed beads as buttons on his jacket. He has a felt hat and is carrying a plastic guitar. They are both mounted on slices of wood. (*Weiner Collection*)

A 7″ doll from Venezuela of felt glued and sewed over a wire frame. This male figure is dressed in a red felt top and pants and wears a red cape. He has red felt horns and a yellow mask with scraps of felt for features. In one hand he has a flag, and in the other a maraca. Perhaps he is meant to be a devil or voodoo man. (*Author's Collection*)

This 12″ doll from Brazil has a body made from jute rope. Her face is jute with felt mouth and eyes of black vinyl with a white dot pupil. She has on a felt hat with fabric flowers on it and gold rings for earrings. She has a pink felt skirt decorated with satin bows and rows and rows of lace with some metallic threads. Under the skirt is a stiff crinoline petticoat that holds out the skirt. (*Stukas Collection*)

This set of modern-looking dolls was made in Venezuela. Each one is about 8″ tall and has a wire-framed body covered in felt, and stuffed as needed in the head and chest areas. Each one wears a pointed burlap hat and has black yarn hair and painted features. Most of the clothing was made from felt. The figure on the left wears a huge red poncho and holds a stick. The boy in the middle plays on a drum covered with felt. He has on a white felt outfit and wears a long fringed orange scarf. The girl on the right has a printed-cotton fabric skirt and wears a huge felt shawl. (*Weiner Collection*)

These 3¼″ dolls from Uruguay are obviously meant as souvenirs. Each one has a wooden ball for a head, wooden cone for a body, and two wedges of wood for feet. Their features are drawn on their wooden ball heads. They have beads for arms, yarn for hair, and scraps of fabric for their clothing. The girl has little red fabric bows in her hair and scraps of cotton fabric for her skirt and apron. The boy has a leather belt with a silver ornament and a piece of woven ribbon for a poncho. He carries a lasso of rope and has a triangle of fabric below his belt to represent a chiripa, a skirtlike garment worn by the cowboys of Uruguay. On his head is a white bandanna, made of a woven band. (*Stukas Collection*)

A beautifully detailed pair of 9″ dolls made by the Industria Argentina in Argentina. Their limbs have a wire base, padded with filling and covered with pink felt sewn in place with very tiny neat overcast stitches. Their bodies and heads are stuffed fabric. Their flat fabric faces have hand-painted features. The woman wears an orange print dress with two rows of flounce and a shawl. Her long black synthetic fiber hair is tied with ribbons.

The man is dressed as a gaucho, or Argentine cowboy, in full regalia. His *chiripa*, a square woolen blanket here made of black felt, is wrapped around his hips and held by a silver belt. His jacket is made with matching fabric, and both are decorated with colorful hand-embroidered flowers. He wears a white shirt and lace-trimmed pantaloons with flaring open bottoms. Over his shoulders he has a brown woolen poncho. He has a black felt hat and leather boots and carries a wooden guitar with thread strings. (*MacNeer Collection*)

From Paraguay, a pair of 3″ dolls with wire-frame bodies attached to a piece of wood. Their features are painted on their stuffed cotton-fabric faces. The man wears a straw hat, a white coarsely woven shirt, and black pants. His multicolored serape is predominantly green; the cotton neckerchief tied around his neck is red. The woman wears a coarsely woven white blouse and a pink skirt. They both wear scraps of woven ribbon around their waists and have hair that appears to be black crepe paper, probably wet while it was being applied to their heads. (*Weiner Collection*)

DOLLS OF THE CARIBBEAN ISLANDS

Though the islands of the Caribbean vary in their cultural heritage, they have a common denominator—the tourist trade. Many dolls are made in the islands to sell as souvenirs. Some are marked with the name of the island and are obviously intended to be sold to visiting tourists, though actually they were not even made there.

Many of these tourist dolls are hurriedly made in great numbers, but obviously some are constructed with great care and attention to detail, especially those from Barbados. Some are of wood and palm, but most are fabric stuffed—and female—made of manufactured materials and looking very modern. There are also dolls with a primitive appearance.

Though some Caribbean dolls are light skinned, most seem to have brown skin, ranging in tone from tan to blackish. They vary in style from those made with great attention to realism and detail to those that are almost caricatures. Practically without exception, every one of these dolls is wearing a head scarf or a straw hat.

The Caribbean dolls reflect the various skin colors in the population. Among the people of the Carib-

This doll on a donkey was made in Jamaica. The woman is evidently on her way to the market. Saturday is market day so the women flock to town, carrying their wares balanced on their turbaned heads. Others, as this doll shows, ride a donkey sitting between the loaded panniers. Since market day is the most exciting day of the week, the women would rather walk or ride all the way into town rather than sell their produce on the road. This doll and her donkey are both stuffed black taffeta. The woman's features are painted on her flat face. She has scrap-cotton-print clothing cut out with pinking shears. Her blouse and skirt are both brightly colored print-cotton fabrics, and she has a piece of scrap fabric as a bandanna. Straw baskets hang on the side of her donkey and contain crepe paper fruit. (*Weiner Collection*)

beans, almost every shade of skin color is found: black, brown, white, and even yellow, with mixed population including mulatto (half black and half white), quadroon (¾ white), octoroon (⅞ white), and so on.

The dolls from the Caribbean are usually dressed in bright colors. The love of bright colors can be seen in the clothes worn by the Caribbean women, as well as on the dolls in this section. The women wear colored turbans or madras wound around the head. The madras, in some islands, is fashioned on a stiff paper "shape," which can then be put on and taken off without disarranging its folds. Each island has its own style, and thus anyone who has lived in the Caribbean awhile can tell which island a woman comes from as much by the fashion of her headgear as by her dialect.

A 10½" crudely made stuffed fabric souvenir doll from Barbados, with black taffeta skin. The facial features of this female figure are painted on, and she is wearing metallic rings for earrings, a red blouse, and a print skirt cut with pinking shears. In the straw basket on her head she is carrying crepe paper fruit. (*Weiner Collection*)

These 12" dolls from Barbados are beautifully detailed with stuffed cotton bodies and embroidered features. They both have needle-sculpted faces and hands of light brown woven fabric. Their features are embroidered, and they have tiny beads for eyes. The man's ears are gathered pieces of fabric sewn in place. He wears a white head scarf and a white shirt with decorative stitching. A red handkerchief is sticking out of his pocket, and he wears a small brown bead necklace and bands on his ankles. His pants are one long strip of fabric twisted around his body. The woman has braided yarn hair, a multicolored head scarf, a pink figured dress with a ribbon at the waist and multiple white petticoats underneath. She has a seed bead necklace, bead earrings, a brown figured shawl, and a woven straw purse decorated with beads. (*Wood Collection*)

A pair of 14" dolls, probably made in Barbados or one of the other Caribbean Islands. These stuffed black-cotton dolls have fabric-sculpted faces with embroidered features, and each one is anatomically correct. Each finger is a piece of wire wrapped with black thread and with a piece of human fingernail at the end.

The man has on a brown cotton suit with matching hat. The woman is wearing a red cotton-print skirt and white lace blouse, a bandanna on her head and a serape-like piece of plaid fabric over her shoulder. This buxom lady's feet in fabric shoes seem small in proportion to her body. (*MacNeer Collection*)

This 8″ doll of stuffed fabric has "Jamaica" written on her belt. She is made exactly like dolls from Barbados, even to having her her clothes cut with pinking shears and carrying a basket with crepe-paper vegetables in it on her head. She has a multicolored skirt, green apron, and red blouse, all from scraps of cotton fabric and poorly finished. (*Weiner Collection*)

Made in the Virgin Islands, these 6″ dolls are of stuffed cotton fabric and have embroidered features and yarn hair. The man wears a straw hat, a red striped cotton shirt, and a tie or scarf around his neck. She is dressed in a green print cotton dress, with a plaid shawl over her shoulders and a plaid head scarf. (*Imported by Kimport; Mueller Collection*)

These three wire-frame stuffed fabric dolls are from Trinidad. The figures, about 9″ tall, are made of brown cotton fabric with pressed-fabric faces and painted features, and though they are attractively made, their clothes are poorly finished. They have brightly colored cotton-print dresses and shoes with cardboard bottoms and yellow fabric tops. Each one holds a pineapple, made from a tiny natural cone painted green with brown fabric leaves coming out of the top. (*Weiner Collection*)

A 5″ doll with the label "The French Doll Store, Havana, Cuba." This female figure is of stuffed fabric on a wire frame. She has embroidered features and wears a green taffeta dress with rows of flounce and a red ribbon bandanna. (*MacNeer Collection*)

A 9″ doll from Haiti with hand-carved wooden body painted dark brown. The features of this female figure are carved into the wood and painted. Her nose is a separate piece of wood glued on her face. White teeth are painted in her mouth, giving her a grotesque look. She has on a blue striped cotton dress and a brown plaid bandanna. (*MacNeer Collection*)

Different versions of the balancing toy can be found in many countries. The balancing figure usually represents a human being, perhaps an acrobat or a clown, but sometimes it is that of an animal. The balancing doll is usually attached to two long poles, one going out on each side of him, with weights on the ends. This warrior doll from Haiti is a balancing figure carved out of wood. He wears a feather on his head and a grass skirt. He is balanced by two pieces of wood on the ends of wires. He is balanced on another doll with two carved faces and a legless, armless body. The man who sold him to me claimed that he was a voodoo doll. (*Author's Collection*)

Stylized 11" carved wooden dolls made in Haiti. They portray a native woman with a bundle on her head and a man with a drum. (*Photographed at the International Craftsman, Flemington, N.J.*)

These whimsical 11" dolls are from St. Vincent. Their limbs are made with wire centers that are slightly padded and covered with tubes of brown cotton fabric. Their heads and bodies are stuffed brown cotton fabric, and their features are embroidered. The woman is dressed in a blue cotton-print dress and a red gingham apron and head scarf. On her head is a basket with fruit made of painted date pits and seed pods. She has on Jacob's-tears earrings. The man wears a cotton-print shirt, short gingham pants, and a straw hat. He carries a bamboo fishing pole and a straw basket with painted palm leaf "fish." (*Imported by SERRV, in the Author's Collection*)

This 6" tall wooden figure from Bermuda bears the label "Gombey Dancer." Pieces of wire hold his separate wooden sections together. He is colorfully painted with a white shirt, black face, and red-and-green pants. (*MacNeer Collection*)

These 6″ dolls from Dominica have painted features. He stands on a plaited straw mat. His body has a wire base and is covered with padding and brown cotton fabric. He wears a straw hat and cotton pants and shirt. Around his waist is blue straw, and on his back is a straw basket with a big red vegetable in it—maybe a tomato. She is made with a straw cone base. Her upper body is a wire frame covered like his with brown fabric. She has a white petticoat edged with lace, and her dress is a cotton-print fabric. She has a plaid head scarf and a yellow rayon shawl decorated with featherstitch embroidery. (*Imported by SERRV, in the Author's Collection*)

This 7″ doll was sold in the Bahamas as a souvenir. It is made of woven jute, dried palm leaf, and a papery material that looks like Swistraw. On the head and at the back are pompons of Swistraw; the rest is woven jute and palm. (*Author's Collection*)

An 8″ wooden doll with painted features and limbs, strung with elastic, and with "Puerto Rico" written on her straw hat. This doll was probably sold in Puerto Rico as a souvenir, but it is likely that she was made in Poland (she is exactly the type of doll made there) and dressed in Puerto Rico with fabric made in the United States. She has a pink-and-white-print skirt with the words "Hip Chick" on it. (*Weiner Collection*)

An 11″ wooden doll made in Honduras. Her arms and legs are attached with rubber bands. She has black jutelike material braided for hair, and her features are inked on. Her skirt, apron, blouse, and shawl are of a knit fabric. Her slip and pants are of muslin. On her head is a basket with painted clay vegetables. A centavo from the Republic of Honduras is sewn on her shawl. (*Imported by SERRV, from the Author's Collection*)

This 11″ wire-frame doll bears the tag "St. Lucia," but she is very similar to a type of doll made in Spain (see pages 164–65). She may have been made in Spain and imported to St. Lucia to be sold there as a souvenir. She has a pressed brown cotton fabric face with painted features. The rest of her skin is brown felt. She wears an orange cotton dress with blue trim and a cotton apron with a yellow bias binding. She carries a basket on her head, containing felt bananas and bead oranges. (*Weiner Collection*)

GRENADA STUMP DOLL

A stump doll is one that has no legs. This stump doll is from Grenada, one of the Windward Islands of the West Indies south of Puerto Rico. She has a stuffed circular base and is dressed in the typical Caribbean style, a blouse, skirt, apron, turban, and basket on her head.

The women of the Caribbeans carry almost everything on their heads, a habit that is said to make them stand straight and walk gracefully. The black stump doll is typical of the Caribbean Islands, since many of the inhabitants are black people, descendants of the slaves brought to the islands in the days of Drake and Hawkins before the slave trade was abolished in 1807.

1

To make a stump doll first cut a circle of black fabric 3″ in diameter and a rectangle 4″ x 13″ for the base. Match the short ends of the fabric right sides together and sew a seam. Set the fabric circle in the center of the fabric tube and pin one end of the tube to the fabric circle. Sew all around. Turn right side out.

2

Cut a 2¾″ circle of cardboard. Slip it into the bottom of the base. Run a gathering stitch all around the top edge. Fill the base with cotton or fiber filling.

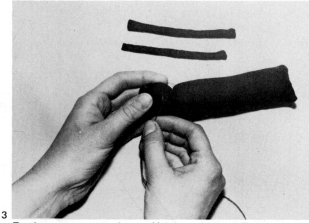

3

For the arms, cut two pieces of fabric each 4″ x 1″. Fold the fabric in half the long way and pin across one short edge and along the long edge. Sew and turn the tube right side out by pushing a paintbrush handle through it. Stuff both tubes with a little stuffing, pushing in a very small amount at a time with the handle of the paintbrush.

For the body, cut a piece of fabric 5½″ x 4¼″. Fold it in half matching the 5½″ sides, putting it right sides together. Sew a seam along one short edge and along the long edge. Turn right side out and stuff. Make a gathering stitch at the top and pull the thread closing the tube at the top. About an inch below the top, tie a thread tightly around the tube forming the head. Make a mouth by taking a few stitches with red embroidery cotton and sew on two sequins for eyes.

4

Sew the arms to the body below the head. Stick the body into the base, adding more stuffing as necessary. Pull the gathering thread to secure the body to the base. Take more stitches around to secure the two together.

5

For the blouse cut a piece of small print fabric 3½" x 4½". Match the pieces right sides together and sew seams along the longer sides sewing to within 1" of the top. Hem the last 1". Sew across the shoulder from each side for ½" and hem the bottom of the blouse. Turn right side out and slip the blouse on the doll. Turn under the raw fabric around the neck and run a gathering stitch, taking small stitches. Adjust to fit the neck and end off.

For the slip, cut a piece of fabric 3½" x 8". Sew a piece of trim across the bottom edge. Matching the short sides, right sides together, sew side seam. Turn right side out.

For the skirt cut a piece of striped fabric 4½" x 11". Hem one long edge. Match the short sides right sides together and sew the side seam. Turn right side out.

For the apron cut a piece of fabric 7½" x 6". Turn up the bottom edge (one of the 7½" sides) 2" and turn under. Sew down two stitchings to divide it into three pockets. Turn under both side edges and stitch down. Put a long gathering stitch across the top. Open a 12" piece of bias binding and put it around the top of the apron with even strings on each side. Sew in place. For the turban, cut a piece of solid color fabric into a triangle with an 8½" base and two sides of 6½".

Put a gathering stitch along the top edge of the slip. Put it on the doll and pull the gathering stitch so the slip fits, and end off the thread. Put a gathering stitch along the top edge of the skirt. Put this on the doll and pull the gathering stitch so the skirt fits, and end off the thread. Tie on the apron. Fold under the long side of the turban; bring it around the head from the back, adjusting it on top of the head. Pin or sew in place as necessary. Add a small basket on the top of her turban, if you wish, and fill it with miniature bread dough vegetables.

6

7
Dolls of North America

The dolls of North America include those made by the earlier inhabitants, including the various tribes of Indians living in the United States and Canada and also the Eskimos of Canada and Alaska. They also include the folk dolls of the United States, which are familiar to many, especially the cornhusk, corncob, nuthead, jigger, and two-headed dolls. In the United States and Canada, too, dollmakers today are producing artistic dolls, and some of these are of a historical or regional nature.

AMERICAN INDIAN DOLLS

Dolls made by the Indians and Eskimos of North America have been studied by anthropologists for the information they give about their makers. Some scholars maintain that only the Eskimos had dolls before contact with the white man. Other researchers claim that the Indians, mainly the Woodland tribes, were making cornhusk dolls that the settlers copied. And still others say it was the other way around—the settlers introduced cornhusk dolls and these were copied by the Indians. In either case, both groups, the Indians and early settlers, made cornhusk dolls.

The North American Indians used not only cornhusks but also a great variety of other materials in making their dolls, materials usually indigenous to the area where the dolls were made, leather, wood, and clay being among the most popular.

Earlier dolls were made from buckskin, which was once so plentiful. Later this material was in much more limited supply so few buckskin dolls were being made and rag dolls, instead, took their place. After the arrival of the white man, fabric and beads were popular materials for Indian dollmakers. If the doll

was clothed, it was usually in imitation of the clothing of its maker.

Today Indians make dolls for sale through their tribal cooperatives. They also sell them through reservation shops and in trading posts. The Indian Shop in the Department of the Interior Building in Washington, D.C., carries a line of dolls representative of the various tribes.

Indian dolls are usually dressed in the traditional tribal costumes depicting both earlier periods and present-day styles of costumes, and some of the dolls are in ceremonial dress. They are made with traditional craft techniques, which have developed over the years of contact with the white man. The dolls vary widely in workmanship.

Old dolls made by the Indians are in great demand today as collector's items, and the prices being paid for them are constantly escalating. The dolls are valuable as records of the costumes worn by the Indians and as samples of their craftwork. One of the most important collections of North American dolls is at the Museum of the American Indian Heye Foundation in New York City.

Among the Indians of the Southeast, dolls seem to be little used as toys or as fetishes. One group of Indians from this area, the Seminoles of Florida, developed dolls after long contact with the white men. They make palmetto fiber dolls dressed in traditional tribal costume. You will find more about them later in this chapter.

Quite a few of the Woodland Indian tribes have made dolls. Living in verdant areas, they had a wealth of natural materials from which to choose in making their dolls. Ojibwa Indians, for example, carved dolls out of wood and bark or made them from grasses, leaves, pine needles, or roots. They made very sturdy dolls from willow withes and spruce roots. They also made them from the roots

Beaded dolls were not made by the Indians until the white men brought glass beads to America. Some Indian tribes did use porcupine quills as decoration. This 5" beaded doll is of American Indian origin. The base is stuffed fabric over which the beads were sewn. The skirt hangs separately and is attached to the doll at the waist. Beads were used by many different Indian tribes. Today the beads are sewn together with a stout needle and a waxed linen or nylon thread. Originally, however, the Indians used sinew and an awl. (*Hupp Collection*)

As part of the midwinter festival, Iroquois Indians dress up, some wearing False Face masks, and others Husk Face masks. The Husk Face messengers race through to help the community ahead of the False Face dancers. Both have come to help the people. The False Face dancers scatter hot ashes on the people to help prevent illness. This cornhusk doll was made by an Iroquois craftsman from New York State, using cornhusks and pieces of leather. He is a Husk Face messenger, who represents the agricultural spirit. According to the Iroquois, such spirits taught them to hunt and grow crops.

This figure wears a miniature of the Husk Face masks worn by the Iroquois. These masks are made by drying cornhusks, cutting them into strips, then braiding them. The braids are then wound into coils and stitched together. Separate coils are added around the mouth, and each eye and straight strips are added for the nose. A fringe of cornhusk is added around the entire mask. The whole figure is wound with cornhusks and dressed in leather moccasins, breechclout, and a fabric shawl. (*Photo courtesy of the U.S. Department of the Interior, Indian Arts and Crafts Board*)

of the bulrush, which they tied with basswood fiber.

The early dolls made by the Ojibwa were crude and had no features. Later they made dolls in cotton costumes like those which the women were wearing at the time, decorating them with the prevailing type of bead ornamentation. Sometimes they wove dolls out of cedar bark as containers for wild rice.

One strange custom of the Ojibwa Indians involved the "doll of misfortune." At the death of her child the Ojibwa Indian woman made a doll out of feathers and laid it in a cradle. She took care of it for a year or more talking to it as if it were a real

American Indian tribes, such as the Mohawks, traditionally make cornhusk dolls. This simple but effective contemporary-looking 5″ Indian cornhusk doll has yarn braids, a leather deerskin headband with a feather in it, and a satin ribbon at her waist. Her arms are braided cornhusks. (*Photographed with permission of Mohawk Crafts, Malone, N.Y.*)

baby, giving it presents, and carrying it along on journeys until the baby was considered old enough to reach paradise on its own.

Wood was readily available to the Woodland Indians so the Chippewa made wooden dolls of those they wished to harm and pierced them to inflict pain on the enemy. Since deer roamed the forests buckskin was another material readily available to the Woodland Indians. It was used by the Iroqouis Indians who made buckskin dolls and dressed them in the same material decorated with beads. For hair they used braided horsehair. Cornhusk and corncob are the most distinctive types found in the eastern Woodland area. Some of these cornhusk dolls are used in medicine rites.

The Woodland Indians also made applehead dolls, with cornhusk or wooden bodies. To make an applehead, the Indian took a slightly green apple, peeled it and molded it with his hands, and hung it to dry. Each day the head was taken down and further shaped until it was dry.

In recent times the traditional Indian craft of making cornhusk dolls has been revived and revitalized by the Mohawk Indians who live on the St. Regis Reservation, which straddles the border of New York State and Canada.

A contemporary faceless corn-pounder doll, approximately 8″ tall. This Indian woman's body is made of cornhusks, and she wears a tunic, breeches, and moccasins of natural deerskin. Her hair is long braids of black yarn. She holds a large carved wooden mortar with which she is pounding corn in a tall wooden cylinder decorated with carving. The doll is mounted on a piece of birchwood. (*Photographed with permission of Mohawk Crafts, Malone, N.Y.*)

A large piece of petrified tree fungus is the base for this Mohawk drummer set. The dolls each have cornhusk bodies. They are decorated with yarn wrapped around their legs, arms, and chests, and each wears a breechclout of deerskin, decorated with seed beads. They have deerskin moccasins and strips of fringe on their legs. Each one has a deerskin headband decorated with feathers. At the center, with handcarved wooden drumsticks, two of the dolls are beating on a deerskin drum, which stands on sticks covered with yarn. (*Photographed with permission of Mohawk Crafts, Malone, N.Y.*)

Mohawk Crafts was organized in 1973 to reawaken interest in the traditional Mohawk Indian crafts and help make their handcrafted products economically rewarding. The Mohawk Indians who live on the St. Regis Reservation, straddling the borders of New York State and Canada, make baskets of black ash splints and sweet grass, such as the one shown in the background as well as such items as this papoose on its cradleboard. The doll, which is about 6″ tall, has a face of nylon-stocking material with embroidered features. The hair is yarn, and the body is stuffed cotton fabric, made like a bag. The cradleboard is a piece of wood with a wooden footrest and a fur headrest. The baby is lashed in with leather thongs, and a piece of leather holds her head from falling forward. (*Photographed with permission of Mohawk Crafts, Malone, N.Y.*)

The women of this reservation make cornhusk dolls but with a modern look. They often add deerskin clothing to their dolls and also beads and feathers to decorate them. They market these modern versions of their traditional cornhusk dolls as well as other native craft products through their cooperative, Mohawk Crafts of Malone, New York.

Though some Plains tribes may not have had toy dolls before contact with the white man, they certainly did soon after, often making dolls as sale items.

Among the Plains Indians, leather dolls were probably the most popular type. Those made by the Dakotas often had grotesque faces and were embroidered with glass beads, but sometimes they were a combination of fabric and buckskin.

The Blackfeet Indians had several different types of dolls. The simplest, made for young girls, were fashioned with a birch limb about a foot long and four inches in diameter. The doll's head was crudely carved with eyes, nose, and mouth, and then the wood was wrapped in buckskin or trade cloth.

More realistic dolls were made for older girls from skin or trade cloth and stuffed with grass. These dolls had arms, legs, and heads, and their features were marked with thread or with trade beads. On their heads they had human or horse hair. These dolls had human proportions and were dressed in miniature garments like those of the Indians who made them. They wore moccasins, leggings, dresses, and sometimes robes.

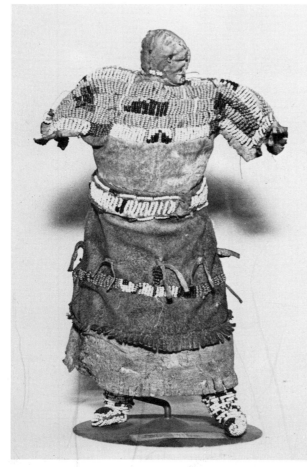

This doll made by a Blackfoot Indian is quite old and once belonged to an Indian child. It has a stuffed fabric body with a leather face. The clothing is all leather and is decorated with hundreds of blue, white, and red seed beads. The eyes and mouth are also indicated with seed beads. Bought in the West, in Montana or California, this doll was a gift to the Forbes Library, Northampton, Massachusetts, in 1921.

A 12″ Indian squaw doll, bought in 1944, made by a Blackfoot Indian of northwestern Montana. The Indians of this region wore very dressy garments, beautifully made of tanned skins, decorated with embroidery of beads and brightly colored porcupine quills. This doll has a stuffed cotton body, but her face, hands, and feet, as well as her clothing, are deerskin. She has seed beads for features and human hair for her braids. Her tunic is deerskin decorated with red and yellow seed beads. (*Collection Forbes Library, Northampton, Mass.*)

This 12″ all-leather doll was made by one of the tribes of Plains Indians, probably Cheyenne, and is about 100 years old. She has seed bead features and braids of human hair. Her ankle-length dress of soft tanned elk-skin has a beautifully beaded yoke, and fringe is cut at both the bottom of the skirt and the sleeves. The decorations on such dresses as these were originally made of porcupine quills, but with the influence of the white man seed beads replaced the quills. Eventually trade cloth was substituted for the elk-skin. (*Photographed at the White Star Trading Co.*)

A 9″ Blackfoot Indian doll, bought in 1921. It has a stuffed fabric body covered with leather and fur. The clothing is decorated with colorful seed beads and leather tassels, and the bottom edge is fringed. (*Collection Forbes Library, Northampton, Mass.*)

Some Indian tribes continue to make attractive leather dolls. This modern leather doll was made by Irene Devereaux, a member of the Blackfoot tribe, and sold through the North Plains Indian Craft Association and the Indian Arts and Crafts Board. The body is of stuffed fabric, and the hair and eyebrows are embroidery cotton. The dress and moccasins are all leather, decorated with seed beads. The eyes, nose, and mouth are indicated by seed beads. (*Hupp Collection*)

Leather Indian dolls are sometimes made as souvenirs. This 5"
leather doll, obviously made for sale in Niagara Falls, has a stuffed
fabric body, but the rest of her is leather, decorated with beads.
(*Author's Collection*)

The Cheyenne Indians made dolls with rag bodies
and horsehair wigs and decorated them profusely
with beads and small metal disks to represent
money.

The Sioux Indians made buckskin dolls and
dressed them in buckskin costumes like the ones
they themselves wore. They decorated the costumes
with fringe and beads and gave the dolls real hair or
hair made of strings of beads, making them as realistic as possible in detail.

The Indians of the Southwest have made a variety
of dolls, but probably the most famous are the kachinas made by the Hopi and Zuñi Indians. More
information is probably recorded about these than
any other type of North American Indian dolls. There
is more about them later in this chapter.

Among the other dolls from the Southwest are the
clay ones made by the Pima Indians. These were
made for play and were dressed in wool and decorated with beads. The Mohave made dolls from clay,
gave them fabric and yarn clothing, yarn wigs, and
beaded earrings, and necklaces.

The Jicarilla Apache Indians made leather dolls
decorated with seed beads and yarn hair. The Zuñi
have made dolls completely covered in beads with
the clothing, features, and hair all indicated by the
beading. The Papago Indians have cotton-stuffed
dolls, dressed in contemporary Indian clothes.

The Apache Indians made rag dolls that looked
just like themselves. Many years ago the women of
this tribe gave up their native dress and begn wearing

This 7½" pottery female figure, holding a child, was probably made
by a Mohave Indian from Arizona. Many tribes made pottery, with
each tribe using its own symbols. The doll is a natural light brown
clay color, painted with darker brown lines and dots. It has black
human hair and loops of seed beads attached to its ears. (*Hupp
Collection*)

Clay dolls made by Zuñi Pueblo Indians. Formed from native clay, they were fired in a beehive oven. They are painted a light brown color, with black markings on them. The larger doll is 3¼" tall. (*Photographed at the United Nations Gift Center*)

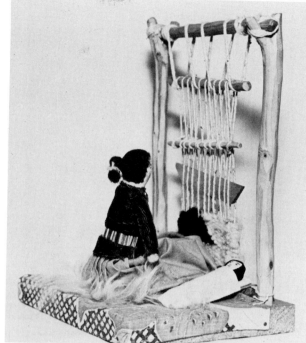

Among the Navahos, the women were the weavers, as shown by this doll, a Navaho weaver, sitting at her primitive loom. Weaving in wool began in the Southwest around 1600 after the Spaniards introduced sheep. The Navahos were well established as weavers by 1700. After their confinement at Fort Sumner, New Mexico (1863–68), they began to use commercial dyes, twisted yarns, and new designs. The whole family helps in shearing the sheep, but it is the woman who cards, dyes, and spins the wool, using a primitive loom that works from the bottom up to make exquisite rugs and blankets. This doll is sitting on a wooden base, covered with fabric and a fur rug. The loom, which is 8" high, is warped with string and has a wooden stick batten and needle. Some weaving with yarn is being done on the loom. The weaver is about 4½" tall and wears the typical Navaho costume. The baby, lying beside her, is just a face appearing out of the top of a stuffed white fabric bundle on a piece of wood, the cradleboard. (*Weiner Collection*)

that of the Spanish conquerors, so the dolls are in Spanish costume.

The Navaho have made sacrificial dolls in order to correct the damage done by the violation of a minor taboo. The Indians believed that an unborn child might be injured if its mother sees blood or a wounded animal while she is pregnant. If this happens, to prevent any injury to the child, the medicine man carves a human figure from wood during a brief ceremony and puts it near ancient ruins where it will be easily accessible to the supernaturals.

Found in many collections are the fabric stuffed dolls dressed in the traditional costume and made by the Navajo Indians. The costume of the Navajo woman has changed little over the years. Until recently most of the Navajo women and girls wore dresses in the style of the 1860s. At that time the Navajos were held captive by the U.S. government at Fort Sumner in New Mexico. At the fort the women and girls started wearing full skirts of calico or other bright material with a velvet or velveteen blouse. They also wore red woven belts and high-topped shoes or traditional moccasins of buckskin or cowhide.

Both men and women wore much jewelry, including silver and turquoise rings, bracelets, earrings, necklaces, pins and buttons, headbands, and even shoe buckles. Though a fully decked Navajo at a ceremony or other public gathering gave an appearance of wealth with his or her silver jewelry, these accessories were often borrowed.

Besides the genuine dolls made by the Indians, there have also been dolls made to look like Indians and sold by whites in Indian areas. These dolls, popular as tourist items, often portrayed the stereotyped Indian—inscrutable and blanket wrapped. Probably the most famous Indian-type dolls were the Skookum dolls designed and trademarked by Mary McAboy, and made from 1913 to about 1925. Her dolls had a bit of authentic Indian blanket wrapped around them. Early Skookums had dried appleheads, and later ones composition heads. The body was built over any oblong piece of wood and the hair was human hair. The dolls were made to resemble Indians of various tribes and were used in schools.

A 10½″ Navaho Indian woman with a stuffed fabric body and rubber hands. She wears a purple velvet blouse and a flowered cotton skirt. She has silver bracelets, buttons, and a belt. Her hair is mohair; her features are painted on her fabric face. She wears a necklace and earrings of seed beads. (*Hupp Collection*)

This Navaho woman doll is a stuffed cotton figure with features stitched in embroidery cotton and hair made of mohair. She is wearing a traditional Navaho velveteen shirt, sewn on a machine. Her shirt is decorated with seed beads; her green satin skirt has two flounces. Navaho women have been wearing full skirts, such as this one, since the 1870s, when they adopted the style of skirt worn by white women of the period. (*Photographed at the White Star Trading Co.*)

This Navaho doll is different from the typical dolls made by the Navaho tribe in that it has a smaller head than most of their stuffed fabric dolls. This figure has the typical velveteen shirt in dark green with sequins and seed beads to represent the beautiful silver buttons worn by the Navahos. She also wears an orange satin skirt and seed bead necklaces and earrings. Her mohair hair is in the style worn by Navaho women. (*Photographed at the White Star Trading Co.*)

These 11" Navaho dolls have stuffed cotton fabric bodies and features drawn in pen. The woman has leather hands and wears a red velvet dress with a belt of black-and-gold woven braid. She has sequins and seed beads on the front of her dress and wears a seed bead necklace. The man wears a green corduroy shirt and white cotton pants. He has a silver belt and wears a necklace of seed beads. (*MacNeer Collection*)

A 15" Skookum doll with a wooden base over which the Indian blanket is draped. Most likely this figure originally had a headdress of feathers. (*Luisi Collection*)

This Indian figure is not an authentic Indian-made doll, but looks like a Skookum doll. Dolls, such as this one, were not made by the Indians but by white men. This 8½" Indian figure with a wooden frame for her body has a bit of Indian blanket around her and is wearing a seed bead necklace. Her face is unusual in that it was made from crepe paper with features painted on it. (*Hupp Collection*)

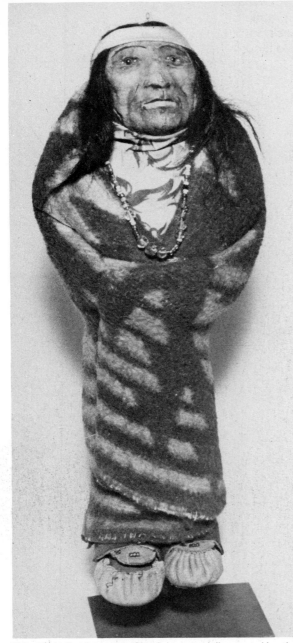

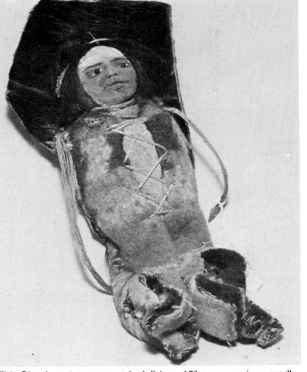

This Skookum-type souvenir doll is a 10" papoose in a cradle-board. Most Indian tribes of America used a cradleboard, or baby board, as a carrier for the restraint and transportation of babies. One of these consisted of a flat surface with padding or a pillow for the protection of the head and a footrest. They also had lashing and a device for suspension. The baby would be put into the cradleboard usually for short periods of time and strapped on the mother's back, hung in a tree, or on a horse when the tribe was on the move. To amuse the baby, trinkets and rattles might be added. This baby has a crepe paper face and human hair. The cradle-board is of animal hide with the hair left on, and the body is of stuffed fabric and lashed into a pocket made from an Indian blanket. (*Hupp Collection*)

This 10" Indian brave is a Skookum-type doll wrapped in a brown piece of Indian blanket. He is wearing leather moccasins deco-rated with seed beads and a string of beads around his neck. His crepe paper face is beautifully painted. (*Hupp Collection*)

A modern Indian-type doll made for the tourist trade by the Huala-pai Indians who live in Peach Springs, Arizona, on a reservation near the Grand Canyon. Called Tonita, she is a "Suzy Bell" doll, designed by Ruth Underwood. She is 17½" tall, made of cotton fabric stuffed with kapok. She has machine-embroidered features and black rug-yarn hair. She is wearing felt moccasins and a yellow gingham dress decorated with lace and rickrack. (*Mueller Collection*)

SEMINOLE PALMETTO AND PATCHWORK DOLLS

The Seminole Indians have lived in Florida for over two centuries. About the middle of the eighteenth century, after Indian troubles in the southeastern British colonies, Creek and Creek relations drifted south to Spanish Florida where they became known as *Se-mi-no-lee,* or "wild" (as the deer is wild).

The Seminole occupied good farmland that the white men soon wanted. The Indians after been pushed back finally refused to move again, and a seven-year conflict began, the most costly Indian war fought. Andrew Jackson marched on one of the campaigns against the Seminoles. The Indians put up fierce resistance under their famous chief Osceola, but eventually their strength was broken. Bands that refused to give up their freedom held out in the swamps and forests of Florida. The U.S. Army and Navy joined forces in a plan to kill all the free Seminoles, and though they murdered a lot of Indians they finally gave up.

The Seminoles, who live today mainly on small federal reservations in Brighton, Big Cypress, and Hollywood, Florida, have developed a highly decorative, unique type of patchwork, which has become their trademark. Woven-cotton fabric was once a luxury to the Indians who obtained it by trading with the Europeans, and so their patchwork may have been the result of a thrifty desire to use even the smallest scrap.

Their distinctive patchwork was not developed until the late 1800s after the Seminoles obtained hand-cranked sewing machines. To make the patchwork, the Indian woman uses solid color fabrics, which are cut or torn into narrow strips. She sews these together horizontally making striped bands and cuts the bands on the diagonal or vertically into many small equal size segments, which she then restitches together in a specific pattern. The segments might be turned upside down, or each one might be slipped up a half inch or so. Many different border designs are made by combining segments in different ways.

On larger items several different borders might be used and between them might be straight bands of fabric. In recent years the Indians have started using rickrack in place of the straight bands.

This pattern was made by sewing together four strips of fabric, two narrow and two wide. The strip was then cut on the diagonal, every other piece switched and then reassembled to make the zigzag shown.

To make a Seminole patchwork costume start with pieces of solid color fabric. For this patchwork pattern, two long pieces of fabric were sewn together, then cut vertically into narrow straight pieces. Every other one was switched around and sewn together, slipping each one up about ½".

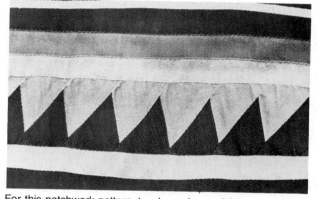

For this patchwork pattern, two long pieces of fabric were sewn together, then cut on the diagonal into narrow strips. They were sewn together, slipping each one up about an inch.

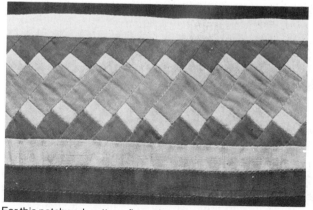

For this patchwork pattern, five strips of fabric were sewn together. The middle piece was wide, and on each side of it were two narrow bands and then two wider bands outside of these. The fabric was cut vertically into narrow straight pieces and sewn together, slipping each strip up about ½".

This beautiful patchwork is incorporated into the clothing worn by the Indians. The woman wears a long full skirt with bands of patchwork, and a poncho-like cape, often made with sheer fabric with a band of patchwork along the edge. On top of the poncho the woman wears as many strings of beads as she can afford. The Seminole men also wear patchwork decorating their shirts. They used to wear patchwork on their trousers, but that is not popular today. Seminole children wear clothing that is similar to that worn by their parents

The Seminole Indian women are fond of sewing, and most of them have sewing machines with which they make not only their own clothes but also dolls and dolls' clothes. To make the body of the doll the Indian goes out and collects fibers from the base of the palmetto fronds. Palmetto is the name given to several varieties of small palms that grow in the southern United States. Care is required in gathering the fiber because poisonous reptiles lurk in the plants.

The body of the female doll is made without arms or legs, and the features are sewn on with embroidery cotton. Male dolls are only occasionally made—and these with arms and legs. In dressing the dolls the Indians use their unique patchwork designs to make miniature versions of their own patchwork costumes. The female dolls usually have the traditional black hat worn by the Indians, but today modern versions are also made with yarn braids and with ponytails.

The Seminoles have a cooperative marketing enterprise, the Seminole Arts and Crafts Center, which was founded in the 1950s and today provides income for the older generation of Seminoles who still practice the traditional crafts. The cooperative markets not only dolls but also other patchwork items.

In addition to the palmetto dolls dressed as Seminoles, other dolls have been made in Florida with palmetto fiber. These dolls may also have been made by the Seminoles.

You can make a Seminole doll with a band of patchwork on her skirt. Like the Indian woman, use a sewing machine, if possible, to make the stitching go much faster. For the body, use palmetto fiber, if possible. If this is not available, a good substitute is felt.

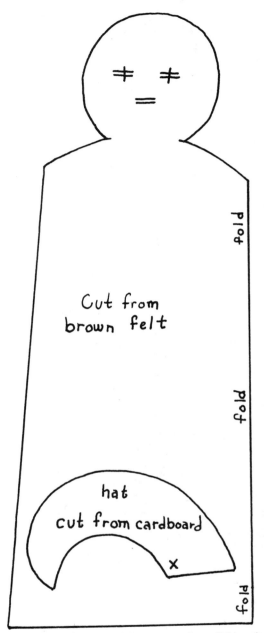

Make a scrap-paper copy of the pattern given. Fold a piece of brown felt (or palmetto if available) and pin the pattern on the fold line as indicated.

1 Cut out the pattern from felt and also cut a 1¾" circle from brown felt. Embroider the face, making straight stitches as shown on the pattern. Hold the layers of fabric together. Begin at the left shoulder by the fold, and with brown thread do the buttonhole stitch around the head and down the right side of the doll. Leave the bottom edge open.

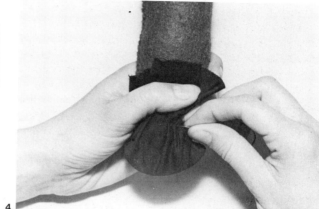

2 Pin the 1¾" circle of felt matching it around the bottom edge of the doll. Begin doing the buttonhole stitch to attach the circle base. When partway around, stuff the doll. Complete the stitching.

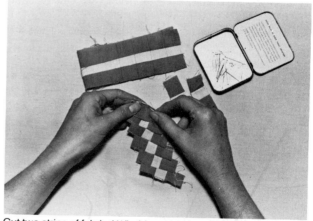

3 To make the hat, cut a copy of the hat pattern from cardboard. Cut a 6" circle of black cotton fabric. Hold the cardboard at the center of the fabric and draw the fabric over it. Begin stitching at the x mark on the pattern, drawing the fabric in to this point. Make several stitches here, then fit the hat over the doll's head, and attach it securely at the side of the head.

4 Holding the hat to the head, sew the hat on, gathering the hat fabric across the back, securing the hat at both sides of the head.

5 Cut two strips of fabric 1¼" wide and as long as your fabric allows. Cut one strip of fabric of a contrasting color 1" wide and as long as possible. Stitch the three pieces together horizontally with the contrasting piece in the center. With a ruler, draw lines ⅞" apart on the fabric, across all three colors. Cut the pieces apart. Reassemble the pieces, slipping each one about 1" up from the one before it, pinning them together wrong sides together as shown, and then stitching them in place.

283

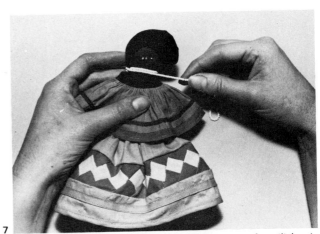

7 Put the skirt and cape in place on the doll and take a few stitches to hold them in place. Wind strings of seed beads around under the head to cover the raw edges of the cape and of the hat.

6 To make the cape, cut a shoulder piece about 1″ x 4″. Cut a second piece of fabric about 2½″ x 12″. Sew a piece of bias binding at the bottom edge, finishing it off and decorating it at the same time. Add another piece a little above this edge. Sew the back seam, then put a gathering stitch at the top and gather to fit the shoulder piece. Sew the two pieces together. For the skirt, cut a waist piece about 5″ x 1″. Make a piece of fabric that is decorated with patchwork or pieces of bias binding, or pieces of rickrack or a combination of these. The completed piece should be about 14″ x 3½″. Gather the top of the skirt so it fits the waistband, and stitch it in place.

8 Your completed doll is dressed in a simplified version of the patchwork costume of the Seminole woman.

Seminole craftswomen make their patchwork and palmetto dolls using hand-cranked sewing machines (one is shown at the right of this photo). This woman is working in her tent home (raised off the ground by posts) at the Seminole Indian Reservation in Hollywood, Florida. She is completing the head of a doll, while finished dolls are lying in front of her. Some palmetto fiber can be seen on the right. (*Photo courtesy U.S. Department of the Interior, Indian Arts and Crafts Board*)

The Miccosukee, as well as the Seminole, Indian women make beautiful machine-sewn patchwork from solid-color fabrics. They make patchwork skirts for themselves as well as such items as this pinafore by a Miccosukee Indian from Florida. (*Photo courtesy of U.S. Department of the Interior, Indian Arts and Crafts Board*)

The Seminole Indian women make not only patchwork skirts for themselves but also colorful shirts for their husbands and sons, using the same technique. (*Photo courtesy U.S. Department of the Interior, Indian Arts and Crafts Board*)

This small Seminole doll has a body made of traditional palmetto fiber. The eyes and mouth are of embroidery cotton; the earrings and necklace are of seed beads. The skirt and cape are made of sections of colored fabric, decorated with rickrack rather than the traditional Seminole patchwork. In the last few decades Seminole women have started to use rickrack to separate the rows of traditional patchwork. Here the rickrack is used without the patchwork. (*Photographed at the White Star Trading Co.*)

This 12″ Seminole doll has an interesting patchwork pattern on her skirt, made of four strips of fabric alternating with a piece of solid color. Note also her nose, which is made from an additional piece of palmetto stitched in place. (*Hupp Collection*)

An 8″ beachcomber from Florida with sponges on a string in one arm and driftwood in the other arm. This charming doll, a study in shades of brown, was made of palmetto fiber, the same material the Seminole Indians use to make their dolls. His features are painted on his palmetto face, and a palmetto hat is on his head. His hands and feet are leaves, or sections, of a large pinecone, with a wire through the center of his body and limbs to hold them in place. (*Hupp Collection*)

This beautiful doll was made by Mary Tiger, a Seminole craftswoman from Florida. Two different patchwork patterns are shown on her skirt. The lower one uses four different colors of fabric and the upper one uses only two. (*Photograph courtesy U.S. Department of the Interior, Indian Arts and Crafts Board*)

A pair of 7″ dolls, bought in a Seminole village in the 1930s. Female dolls, like this one, are very common, but male dolls are rare. This man doll is made in a similar manner to the woman doll, except that he has arms and legs of palmetto fiber rather than just a stump body like hers. He has also a multicolored shirt like, but much simpler than, the ones worn by the Seminole Indian men. (*Hulsizer Collection*)

A 16″ palmetto doll, bought in Deland, Florida, in 1942. This female figure is made almost entirely of sheets of fibers stripped from the palmetto plant. Some machine sewing went into the making of this doll, and the stitches can be seen especially on her skirt. Shells decorate the front of the doll's dress and ankles and are used for her earrings and eyes. Her mouth is embroidery cotton. Her fingers, which are clearly delineated, have bits of what looks like cuttings from human fingernails attached with wound thread. Each tip is painted with a dot of red. (*From the Collection of the Forbes Library, Northampton, Mass.*)

An 18″ doll of palmetto fiber, the same material the Seminole Indians use to make their traditional dolls. This figure, which dates from the 1930s, might have been made by a Seminole Indian. Made mainly of the palmetto fiber, the doll is stitched together with a sewing machine. The stitches can be seen on the skirt and hat especially. The eyebrows and mouth are thread, and the eyes are black buttons. The fingers have fingernails that appear to be cuttings from human fingernails. (*Photographed at the White Star Trading Co.*).

CHOCTAW APPLIQUÉ

The Choctaw is one of the tribes living in the Southeast that became known as the "Five Civilized Tribes." The white men drove the Choctaw out of their homelands and moved them to Oklahoma, but some of them eluded the troops and remained on scattered small tracts of land in Mississippi.

Some of the descendants of these Choctaws still live in Mississippi and have formed the Choctaw Craft Association of Philadelphia, Mississippi. This group produces a wealth of beautifully patterned river-cane basketry, delicately constructed beadwork, jewelry, clothing decorated with finely patterned bands of appliqué, and fabric dolls in the colorful traditional attire of the Choctaws.

The dolls they make are of simple stuffed fabric with embroidered features and yarn hair. What makes them totally unique is their clothing and accessories, including the beautiful beaded collars or necklaces that are reminiscent of the gorgeous beadwork done by the Zulus and other tribes of South Africa. A very unusual feature of the dolls is the zigzag appliqué work with colored and contrasting fabrics used to decorate their dresses.

The Choctaw Indians who live in Mississippi still wear their traditional dress on special occasions, so members of the tribe still make the costumes. They also make stuffed cotton dolls, like this one, with embroidered features and yarn hair, and dress the dolls in miniature versions of their traditional costumes. Using plain colored cotton fabrics, they cut each part and then trim it with bands of delicately patterned appliqué. This doll has three bands of appliqué on her skirt and a row on her apron. She wears the traditional seed bead necklace and earrings. On her collar she has a circular pin of seed and tube beads. This beautifully detailed doll was made by Rosalie Steve, a Choctaw Indian from Mississippi. (*Photograph courtesy U.S. Department of the Interior, Indian Arts and Crafts Board*))

To learn to do Choctaw appliqué, start with a test strip. Once you see how to do it, you can cut the necessary lengths of fabric to do whatever project you wish. To begin, cut a strip of black cotton or cotton-blend fabric 1½" × 12". Fold it in half and again in quarters and finally in eighths. Make cuts as shown to create a series of valleys and mountain.

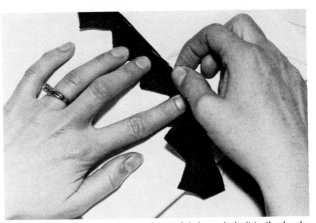

Turn under the straight edge of your fabric and pin it to the background fabric. Stitch along this seam by hand or by machine.

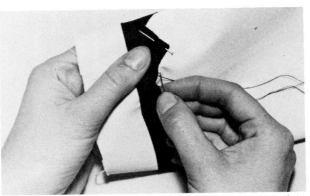

Turn under the jagged edge of your fabric. If you make some short cuts straight down in the centers of the valleys, these will help you turn the fabric under more easily. Do a small hemming stitch along the jagged edge. If you wish to complete the appliqué, as in the photos of authentic Choctaw appliqué, add a thin strip of fabric just above the mountaintops. If you have matching double-fold bias binding, use this to make the job easier.

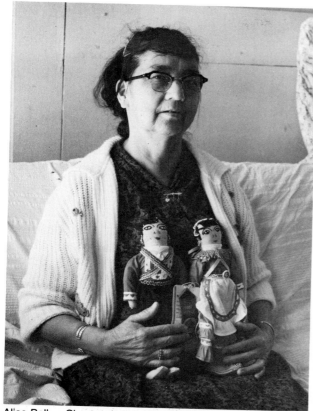

Choctaw Indian women use their sewing skills in making their own costumes and in dressing dolls, as well as in producing such items as blouses, dresses, and aprons for other women and children. This beautiful child's dress and apron, in traditional Choctaw style, shows the delicately patterned appliqué work for which this tribe is known. The costume, of cotton fabrics, is by Mary Ann Bell, a Choctaw Indian from Mississippi. (*Photo courtesy U.S. Department of the Interior, Indian Arts and Craft Board*)

Alice Bell, a Choctaw Indian from Mississippi, shows two of her prizewinning dolls. They are stuffed cotton-fabric dolls with embroidered faces, dressed in traditional Choctaw costumes. The woman wears an apron and dress, and the man a shirt, all with traditional Choctaw appliqué work. Both wear belts of seed beads, the woman a traditional necklace and the man two bands of beads crossing his chest. (*Photograph courtesy U.S. Department of the Interior, Indian Arts and Crafts Board*)

The Choctaw craftsmen are renowned for their beaded network necklaces as well as bracelets, pins, and belts. This typical bead network necklace of tube and seed beads was made by Elsie Jim, a Choctaw Indian from Mississippi. Note the miniature version of it on the doll shown above. (*Photograph courtesy of U.S. Department of the Interior, Indian Arts and Crafts Board*)

KACHINAS

Kachinas are dolls made by the Hopi Indians as well as several other tribes, included the Zuñis. These tribes, called the Pueblo Indians from the Spanish word *pueblo* meaning village, have lived on the sandstone plateaus of New Mexico and Arizona, in houselike dwellings for many centuries. They have a rich cultural heritage, and an important part of this heritage is the kachinas.

In 1894 J. Walter Fewkes of the Smithsonian wrote the first illustrated report on Hopi kachinas, and ever since then a growing number of people have been interested in them. Kachinas refer to (1) supernatural beings in which the Hopis believe; (2) the masked human impersonations of these beings; (3) the wooden dolls that depict the human impersonations.

THE SUPERNATURAL BEINGS

Among the American Indians who made dolls a few seem to be connected with religion. The kachina dolls are one example. These dolls represent the kachinas—chiefly the benevolent beings who, according to Hopi mythology, live in the ice and snow of the nearby San Francisco Peaks near Flagstaff, Ari-

zona. The main job of the kachinas is controlling the weather. They bring many blessings especially rain, good crops, and health. Though the kachinas, for the most part, are friendly spirits and givers of good things, some are demons or ogres who discipline those who break ceremonial or social law.

The Pueblo Indians are agricultural tribes, who engage in raising crops on the lower lands surrounding their mesas. In this rather dry climate, rain is absolutely vital to the success of the crops, so rain, wind, and sun play important parts in the lives of the Indians. The kachinas are thought to be the spirits who provide this necessary rain, and if they are properly petitioned, they will send it when it is needed. The kachinas, and there are hundreds, represent spirits of the water, sky, earth and so on. Kachina dances, songs, and ceremonials are all designed to petition these gods for rain, good crops, and health.

According to Pueblo legend, kachinas used to come to the people and dance for them and bring them gifts. They taught them arts and crafts and how to hunt. They also danced in the fields when rain was needed, and it always came.

Legend says that the kachinas and the people had a terrible fight. After that the kachinas refused to come back, but they did give the people permission to wear masks and costumes to represent the spiritual beings. The costumed men could then act as if they were the kachinas, and if they did this properly the kachinas would take possession of the masked dancer while he was dancing in his costume, and the rain would come.

THE DANCERS

The Hopis have kachina ceremonies from winter solstice until mid-July. During that time five major ceremonies of nine days each are held as well as some one-day dances.

Each of the ceremonies is a social occasion for the villagers. The men, in their kachina costumes and masks, keep time with their feet, dance, and sing. They distribute gifts to the children including the kachina dolls they have made.

The dancers wear sacred masks of deer or buffalo hide held in place by leather strings, and appropriate costumes and body paint. When a Hopi man is so attired, he believes he has lost his personal identity and receives the spirit or assumes the character of the kachina he represents. The Hopis believe that what happens is the gods borrow the bodies of the

men to come down to the village to distribute the presents and receive prayers.

The belief of the Hopi Indians in the kachinas goes so far back in time that usually not a word of the old songs used as part of the ceremonies is understood by today's Hopis. The Indians prepare for the ceremonies in underground rooms called *kivas.* There the fathers and uncles of the Pueblo children carve the kachina dolls, which they will give as gifts during the dances.

THE DOLLS

At the ceremonies the kachina dolls are given mainly to the girls while the boys receive small bows and arrows. They are not made as playthings, but the child may carry around a kachina in the same way a non-Indian would carry a doll.

The kachina dolls are meant to teach the child about the spirits, or gods, they call kachinas. The dolls are usually hung on the whitewashed walls of the home as a constant reminder of the "real" kachinas, those supernatural beings. The Hopi Indians make their kachina dolls not only for decorating the home and teaching religious beliefs to the children but also to sell to visitors. The dolls made especially to be sold as mementos are not used in religious rites. While the Hopis display their dolls, the Zuñis hide them away and refuse to sell them to strangers.

The kachinas are so well made and without precedent that they might be considered works of art. They represent almost every natural phenomenon as well as animals. They are very light in weight and so well balanced they can stand alone. Old kachina dolls are usually stiff looking, simply carved with mere stumps representing their legs, but today's kachinas more closely resemble the bodies of the human dancers. A doll's legs and arms stand out from the body, and knees and elbows are usually bent.

MAKING KACHINAS

Though both the Zuñis and the Hopi make kachinas, those of the Hopi are better known. The Zuñi kachinas are usually thinner and taller than those made by the Hopi, and their arms are carved separately, so they are articulated or movable.

To make a kachina, the Zuñi Indian uses the wood of the pine and the Hopi a solid piece of dried root from a dead cottonwood tree (wood that grows near the mesa or on the banks of the Little Colorado River). He saws off tree roots with a diameter of three to four inches.

The Hopi makes the body of the kachina from one solid block of wood; the horns, headdress, nose, protruding eyes, and ears are made separately and attached with tiny pegs. In carving the doll the Hopi simplifies, leaving out unessential details and including only those which are absolutely essential to identify the figure.

The Hopi uses a penknife, chisel, wood rasp, and a piece of sandstone. First he roughs out the figure with a saw and chisel. Then he whittles it into shape with a penknife, smooths it with the wood rasp, and sands it carefully with sandstone. Then he adds a nose, horns, tablita, ears, snout, or whatever extra parts must be whittled from wood and attached to the doll. This fastening is usually done with dowel pins a little larger than toothpicks; but glue is also used.

Once they are carved, the dolls are ready for painting. Before the color is put on, the Hopi covers the figure with a layer of kaolin for an undercoat. This undercoating is not bound to the wood, so it may peel off, which often makes old kachinas look shabby.

The dolls are then painted with the same substances that the Hopis use as body paints, including copper carbonate for green or blue, soot or corn smut for black, ground hematite for red, limonite for yellow, and kaolin for white. Today the Hopis often use poster paints instead of these traditional substances, and though the poster paints may adhere better to the wood and be much brighter, they fade much more quickly than the old native paints. After the doll is painted it is decorated with bright feathers from small birds.

The Hopi Indians today still observe their kachina ceremonies and still make the kachina dolls. Probably fewer than 1,000 new kachinas are made each year by the Hopis. Some of these find their way to trading posts and then into non-Indian homes, but the demand for kachinas is greater than this supply.

Senator Barry Goldwater is probably the most famous of the avid kachina doll collectors. An antique kachina doll, dating from 1870 to maybe 1920, can sell for as much as $10,000 today. A contemporary one might be bought for $50 or $100, but one by a famous kachina carver might sell for $5,000.

Kachinas are being made today by whites and being sold as authentic Indian products. Some are made by machine and painted by Indians, and thus the buyer must beware. Some kachinas are also being made and sold as "honest imitations," marked

as imitations of those made by the Indians.

Kachina dolls are usually made from dead cottonwood roots, but to make yours you might substitute balsa wood, which is easily obtainable, easy to carve, and takes paint easily. Or choose another soft wood that is easy to carve—a piece about 12 inches long and 3 inches in diameter, or smaller. The carving of the kachina is usually fairly simple, and the painting is done with symbolic designs. Look at the photos of authentic kachinas here to give you inspiration for your carving. For more information on the names and essential characteristics of the hundreds of kachinas that exist, see books listed in the bibliography.

This Hopi kachina, made by Ronald Honyouti in 1974, is of excellent workmanship. The figure, which represents the Hano Clown or Kashare, is called the Watermelon Eater, and around his neck a tiny shell is tied. The face mask of this kachina is always painted white with black eyes and mouth. On the top of the head are two black-and-white-striped horns. The clown's body is painted in black-and-white horizontal stripes, and he wears a breechclout. *(Photographed at the White Star Trading Co.)*

This ferocious-looking kachina, Awatovi Soyuk Wuti, was made by Bruce Auguah, a Hopi Pueblo from Arizona. The doll is mainly carved and painted cottonwood, with many details added with leather, yarn, and feathers. (*Photograph courtesy of the U.S. Department of the Interior, Indian Arts and Crafts Board*)

Kachina figures are usually males, but there are some female kachinas. This old-woman figure, called Piptu Wu-uti, is a kachina, dating from about 1910. The kachina makers do not protect the flat paint they apply to their figures, so old kachinas, such as this one often suffer from peeling paint. The white kaolin undercoat can be seen where the colors have chipped off. (*Photographed White Star Trading Co.*)

On the left is Patun, the Squash kachina, represented by a man whose body is painted green with black strips. He wears a mask of the same color, also with black strips. On the larger end of the mask is a representation of a squash flower made from a gourd. The figure also carries a yellow-squash-blossom gourd. On the right is a Tube Mouth kachina. He has rectangular eyes and symbols on his cheek, indicating he may be an Early Morning kachina. (Fisher Collection)

On the left is the Sun kachina, or Tawa kachina, probably one of the most familiar and easily recognized kachinas. This doll represents the spirit of the sun god and appears regularly in dances. He wears a yucca-basket mask with his forehead red and yellow and his mouth painted as a triangle. His face is completely surrounded by radiating eagle feathers. He wears a kilt and moccasins, and his body is painted with the forearms and lower legs yellow. He carries a flute and a rattle. On the right is a Black Ogre, wearing a black case mask with a large toothed snout and large movable jaws. (*Fisher Collection*)

On the left is the Hano Clown or Kashare. He has horns of soft material attached to the top of the mask. His face is painted white with black eyes and mouth and he has two soft black-and-white-striped horns on top of his head. His body is painted in black-and-white horizontal strips, and he wears a breechclout. He performs with similar clowns at the kachina dance ceremonies.

The kachina on the right is called Heheya's Uncle. This figure appears with the ogres, wearing a case mask painted white with vertical zigzag lines. He wears a breechclout, sheepskin belt, knitted leggings, and red moccasins. (*Fisher Collection*)

This kachina, called Ho-O-te or A-hote, is named for the sound he makes. Carved in the 1940s by Jimmy Kewanwytewa, this male figure appears in mixed kachina dances wearing a black case mask with a yellow top. He has pop eyes, feathers on his head, horns, and a snout. On his cheeks are the sun and moon painted in white. He has a Douglas-fir ruff, represented on this figure by green yarn, and wears a seed bead necklace. He wears a kilt, sash, and foxskin at the back. His body is painted red, with yellow shoulders, forearms, and lower legs. He carries a bow in one hand and a rattle in the other. (*Photographed at the White Star Trading Co.*)

This doll, a Hemis kachina, was carved in the 1940s by Jimmy Kewanwytewa. This figure is usually the principal character in the Niman Kachina Dance (Home Dance), which is the last dance of the year and so is sometimes called the Niman kachina.

He wears a case mask with half the face painted green and the other half pink. The mask is surmounted with an elaborate tablita (headdress), painted with phallic and cloud symbols and decorated with feathers. He wears a Douglas-fir ruff, represented by green yarn. His body is painted with black corn smut and decorated with light-colored half-moons.

The figure wears a kilt with large leaves, a woman's belt, a foxskin at the back, and red moccasins. He has a hank of yarn across one shoulder and around the chest. He is supposed to carry a rattle and also a sprig of Douglas fir, but these seem to be missing on him. (*Photographed at the White Star Trading Co.*)

This kachina is a Mudman. He wears a mud-colored mask and may also carry balls of mud to smear on his victims. He adds a comic note to the kachina dance ceremonies. (*Fisher Collection*)

This kachina has arms and features painted on a crudely carved piece of wood. Said to be the mother of all the kachinas, this type of flat kachina is given to Hopi infants. Such dolls are made of pieces of flat board, measuring about 3½″ × 8″. They are not realistic, with only the essential characteristics of the kachina being represented. They are roughly finished, with only crude touches of paint and perhaps a few feathers to decorate them. Despite this there is no doubt as to which kachina is being represented by them. (*Photographed at the White Star Trading Co.*)

These Indian dolls are very old. The 7″ doll on the left, named Horvila, was carried in the Snake Dance of the Hopi Indians. It was bought in Cedar City, Utah, and donated to the Forbes Library, Northampton, Massachusetts, in 1928. The 10″ doll on the right is a female Navaho spirit doll. It was left out of doors, and had to be repainted many times. Named Sotso, or Morning Star, this doll was bought in Cedar City, Utah, and was a gift to the Forbes Library in 1928.

This Zuñi kachina spirit doll, called Salimopia Kohana, dates from the 1950s. Note that it is taller and thinner than the typical Hopi kachina, but unlike the Hopi kachina, with clothing and accessories painted on, this Zuñi figure has a cotton-fabric kilt with appliqué and rickrack and wears a seed bead necklace. His body is painted dark red, and he has a green yarn ruff around his neck as well as around one wrist and both his ankles. In his hands he holds prayer sticks. (*Photographed at the White Star Trading Co.*)

Since the demand for kachinas exceeds the supply, some non-Indians have started making them. These kachinas, by Kachina Creations (Technigraphics, 7124 North 11th Avenue, Phoenix, Arizona 85021), are made not with wood but with fabric draped over a Styrofoam base.

A Hopi doll representing the highly popular kachina called the Butterfly Maiden kachina, or Polik Mana. This figure has a large tablita decorated with many feathers and a yarn ruff. It is not an authentic Hopi-made kachina but a reproduction, carved from wood and painted by a student of Indian culture.

ESKIMO DOLLS

Eskimos are thought to have made dolls as far back as their prehistoric culture and used them as charms, amulets, and fetishes. Dolls have been found in the graves of children. Some Eskimos, rather than burying the dolls with the children, built small wooden houses and put the dolls on the grave together with a cross. The house might be painted a bright color and be equipped with tiny tables, dishes, and other items besides the dolls.

Traditionally Eskimo dollmakers have used the natural materials available to them in their cold environment. In the most northern areas they made dolls from ivory, walrus tusks, and mammoth teeth. Further south they used wood in dollmaking. They might also use gut, feathers, stone, fishskin, bone, sealskin, rabbit skin, reindeer leather, and so on.

Basically the local environment determined the dolls that could be made; for example, on St. Lawrence Island girls caught mice in order to use their skins for dollmaking. They also used seal, cormorant, and weasel skins. Today many of the same natural materials are used, but others have been introduced, including dental floss to replace the sinew used for sewing and fabrics such as felt.

Traditions in dollmaking and doll use vary among the Eskimos in different geographic areas. Both boys and girls in the St. Lawrence Island and Bering Strait regions played with small dolls (one to three inches high) made of ivory adorned with beads or strips of cloth. These dolls are sometimes faceless, but if a face is carved, the sex is determined by the mouth. The male's mouth turns upward at the edges, and the female's turns downward. Sometimes whole families of dolls were made, including babies with their feet apart so they could be carried on the mother's back astride the neck, according to the custom of the area.

Many Eskimo dolls have hand-carved wooden bodies. The Eskimos are well known for their carving skills. Every Eskimo used to be able to carve to some extent, since this was the basic means of making tools.

In carving dolls the Eskimos use knives of iron or steel with curved blades. They used these so-called crooked knives to whittle wood, bone, and ivory. Today they have more modern tools.

A study of Eskimo dolls is essentially a study of Eskimo clothing because almost all that is visible of the doll itself is usually a face buried inside a furry hood.

Eskimo dolls are dressed typically in the type of garments worn where they were made. The basic costume of the Eskimo is almost the same everywhere in the polar world. Men and women wear similar clothing, and children wear costumes very much like those of their parents, except for babies who ride on their mothers' backs in pouches called *amuauts.*

Both men and women wear a knee-length fur jacket, or *parka,* with fur-edged hood to protect their eyes from swirling snow. They have mittens often made from caribou skins. For the summer they have a lighter weight seal coat.

The Eskimos wear sealskin boots called *kamiks.* The man wears his kamiks up to his knees and his bearskin trousers come down to the knee. Where the trousers and kamiks meet he often has a fox tail sewn around to keep the air from getting in. The woman's kamiks go higher on her legs before meeting her pants.

In a cold land where a rip in a pair of pants could cause someone to freeze to death, clothing is carefully made and taken care of. Though Eskimos often have very handsome clothing, their first concern is practicality. They have found that the fur of the animal skin must be worn on the outside to protect them against freezing winds.

Their overclothing must be loose with not too much overlapping. A tight jacket could make the wearer perspire, and the wet hide then would become frozen stiff when taken off. In the Arctic, practical, warm, useful clothing is a matter of life and death, and their dolls show what the Eskimos have found to be practical clothing for a very cold environment.

During the summer the Eskimo wears one fur suit, but in the winter he wears two, one next to his skin and the second turned out against the harsh cold Arctic wind. To get the fur the Eskimo must first trap and kill the animal, then skin, scrape, prepare, and sew it.

The clothing of the Eskimo can be very beautiful depending on the artistry of the woman who designed and made it. They know from long practice where to cut and sew without bothering to measure. These women cut and stitch without patterns. Originally the Eskimo woman used bone needles and sinew. They chewed the sealskin until it was soft enough for boots and they scraped caribou furs.

The Eskimo woman cuts with a curved knife called an *ulo*, then sews the hides together. The Eskimos used sinew, or dried meat fibers, for sewing but later replaced these with strong thread such as dental floss. In making their dolls the Eskimos have these same materials to work with that their own clothing is made from so that their dolls are usually dressed in replicas of their own costumes.

This 10″ Eskimo has a body carved from wood, and his happy-looking features are inked on the wooden face. He wears a fur parka, and his boots are made of felt, decorated with multicolored seed beads. (*Weiner Collection*)

A 12″ Eskimo doll with a wooden body. This male figure's rather woeful face is carved, and his eyes are inked on. He wears a fur parka, and his boots are decorated with multicolored seed beads. (*Weiner Collection*)

An 11" Eskimo doll with a wooden body, a carved wooden face with eyes drawn on it, and human hair on his head. This male figure has a wooden body and is wearing fur boots and an outfit with stitched detailing on the shoulders, the bottom of the coat, and at the knees. He is carrying a wooden bow and arrow, and on his back is a fur pack with more arrows. (*Hupp Collection*)

This wooden doll, which stands 14" high, has a carved face with the features inked in. He wears leather boots with fur trim and a fabric outfit. (*Hupp Collection*)

This 12" Alaskan doll has a stuffed fabric body. The face is leather with a leather nose and red felt mouth. The eyes were stitched with black embroidery cotton. The clothing is all fur, and leather and seed beads decorate the parka. (*Mueller Collection*)

An 11″ doll, bought in Fairbanks, Alaska, in 1970. This figure has a beautifully carved wooden head with a stuffed fabric or hide body. She is dressed in fur clothing. (*Hulsizer Collection*)

This contemporary 15″ Eskimo girl doll has a modern-looking felt face with stitched features. She has a stuffed felt body and wears red boots, tied at the top with strands of colorful yarn, and a fur parka with the hood tied under her chin with colorful pieces of yarn. (*Hupp Collection*)

REGIONAL AND HISTORICAL DOLLS

Many parts of the United States are famous for the regional dolls they produce. In some areas special dollmaking techniques are used, or the regional difference may lie in the character of the doll.

Typical of New England are fishermen dolls often sold at seashore resorts. In Maine dolls are made using lobster shells. Plymouth is famous as the place where the Pilgrims landed, so dolls sold there are dressed like these English settlers.

Dolls made in the South in the nineteenth century and early part of this century often present stereotypes of black people. The woman is usually dressed in a long cotton dress and an apron and has a bandanna tied around her head. She is portrayed as a mammy holding one or more babies, often white, or as a cotton picker with a bag of cotton, or a servant with a broom. The black man characteristically wears a cotton shirt, overalls, and often a felt hat. He is represented as a cotton picker or as a lazy fellow escaping work by going fishing or picking on a guitar.

Another type of regional doll is the hillbilly. These hillbilly dolls are typically fabric stuffed and have exaggerated features and limbs so that they are like caricatures or cartoons of the real hill folk. The dolls are typically dresssed in patched and ragged clothing. The men usually have pants held up by suspenders or even by rope.

Other parts of the country also have dolls representing typical characters; for example, Louisiana is known for its street peddler dolls.

According to their tags, these two dolls were handcrafted by Allison Hunt Studio on Cape Cod, Massachusetts. They have wire-frame bodies, and their hands and faces, beautifully sculpted and painted, are made of a papier-mâché-like material. They have hats and feet also made of the papier-mâché-like material, with the upper part of their black boots of painted cardboard. The 10″ fisherman on the left has a yellow oilcloth slicker, green jeans, and a green-and-black knit-fabric pullover shirt, and he is carrying a piece of fishnet.

The clamdigger on the right, shown opening a clam, is sitting on a piece of cork. In front of him is a bucket, silver-sprayed paper cup with a wire handle. It's filled up, perhaps with sand, and on the top are some small clamshells. The man is wearing a red-and-black-knit pullover shirt and gray-and-black tweed pants. (*Weiner Collection*)

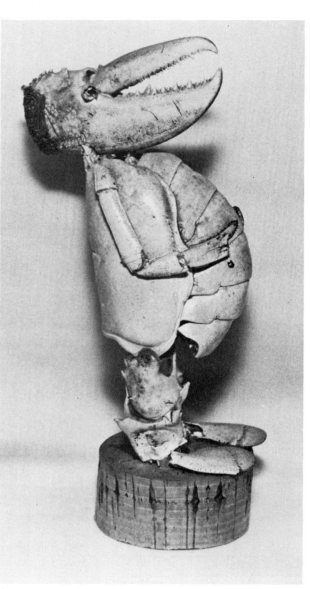

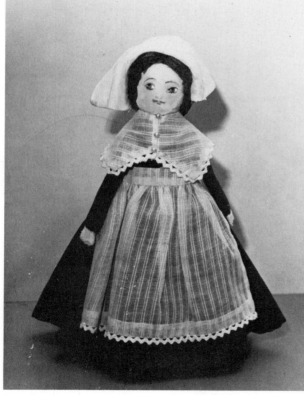

This Pilgrim doll has a corncob body, and her arms are tubes of white fabric. Her face is fabric, and her features are painted on. She has yarn hair, a white bonnet, and wears a black dress with a deep white collar and long apron, both edged with rickrack. Tiny pearls are sewn on the collar as buttons. (*Photographed at the Children's Museum, Boston, Mass.*)

An 8½″ doll, bought in Maine. This male figure, on a cork base, is made of pieces of lobster shell with a claw used effectively for his head. (*Stukas Collection*)

The corncob body is nailed into a piece of wood. A stiff crinoline slip holds the skirt flared out. (*Photographed at the Children's Museum, Boston, Mass.*)

A stuffed fabric doll, about 12" tall, made in 1874. Called Dinah, she wears a cotton-print fabric dress and gingham apron. She has black string braids, and her features are embroidered. She was donated by Clara Atwood Felts to the Children's Museum, Boston, Mass.

These 8" black dolls are from New Orleans. They are made of black cotton fabric and stuffed, their features are painted, and they have gray yarn hair. The man has a beard, a little mustache, eyebrows, and a fringe of hair around his head, all of gray yarn. He also wears a red felt hat, green fabric pants, and a red cotton-print shirt. The woman is wearing a red bandanna, a print dress, and a white cotton apron. Metal rings represent her earrings. (*Mueller Collection*)

These walnut-head dolls portray the stereotyped black family: the plump mother, the father playing the banjo, the daughter holding a doll, and the son eating watermelon. The dolls have wire frames, wrapped with black crepe paper, and black felt hands. They all have black painted walnuts for heads, with a side seam of the walnut in front for their noses. Their features are painted on, and all have numerous and predominant white teeth.

The 9½" father wears a brown felt hat, red-and-white cotton-striped shirt, and black pants and suspenders. The mother wears a black dress decorated on the bodice with white lace, a white dotted-swiss apron edged with white lace. The son, eating a wooden watermelon, wears a maroon felt hat, a blue print shirt, and black pants. The 5" daughter wears a blue print dress and a red bonnet and carries a piece of white felt rolled up with a face drawn on it—a simple doll perhaps? (MacNeer Collection)

Hillbilly dolls of stuffed cotton, with heads of knit fabric and bodies of woven cotton fabric. These figures have embroidered features and stuffed fabric balls for noses. They have yarn hair and patched clothes. (Author's Collection)

This 19" hillbilly doll is made of cotton fabric and stuffed. He wears a red bandanna-print shirt, blue jeans with suspenders and knee patches, and a hat of denim. He has black yarn hair and a beard. His features are embroidered, and he has a small piece of stuffed fabric for a nose and oversized feet. (From the Collection of Peg Cassott)

A 9″ black doll, bought in the South, in the 1930s or 1940s. Mounted on a piece of house shingle, this wire-frame figure has a stuffed cotton face with embroidered features. She is wearing a red cotton-print skirt, a white apron, red polka-dot bandanna, a cotton-print blouse, and a knit black-and-violet jacket. In one arm she carries a black fabric umbrella, and in the other a white bag stuffed with cotton. (*MacNeer Collection*)

This 12″ black stuffed fabric doll was made in the South. The figure has black yarn hair, a needle-sculpted nose, and embroidered eyes and mouth. She is wearing a maroon dress with white polka dots and a small printed-fabric apron. She is carrying a broom made from a piece of wood and string. (*Hupp Collection*)

These 15″ stuffed cotton hillbilly dolls have oversized feet and hands. Their faces are stitched in profile, and their features painted on. Their hands and feet have fingers and toes stitched in. The man has a black yarn beard, a black felt hat, and a plaid cotton shirt. His black woolen pants are held up with fabric and leather suspenders. The woman is wearing a blue cotton-print bonnet and maroon print dress. The child in her arms has a blue dress and a knit cap. (*MacNeer Collection*)

From Louisiana, 10″ dolls representing peddlers. The man carries a basket with loaves of fresh bread, made of light brown crepe paper. Dangling from the basket are sheets of newspaper with which he wraps the bread for his customers. He has a painted clay head with white hair painted on it, a wire-frame body, and wears blue-striped pants and a blue checkered shirt. The woman has a straw basket filled with painted clay fruits and vegetables. Her face was formed of clay and painted, and her white hair was made of mohair. Her body has a wire frame with fabric over it. She wears a stiff crinoline underskirt, which holds out her blue figured skirt. She wears a red dotted blouse with a white felt collar, a green dotted apron, and black stockings and shoes. (*Hupp Collection*)

A unique type of handmade doll that was made in the United States was the wax doll made by Francisco Vargas and his family. He came to the United States from Mexico in the nineteenth century and lived in New Orleans. From an old parish priest he got a secret recipe for wax that would harden and remain very hard. The recipe called for beeswax, as well as other ingredients.

Mr. Vargas started making lifelike statues of saints using the wax. Then he began making dolls, representing black people working in the fields or engaged in a trade. The dolls were made completely of wax with a wire frame, and the clothing was made of wax-impregnated fabric that was made to stick to the dolls with more wax.

Mr. Vargas worked quickly with pans on the stove, each containing different colors of melted wax. He had a patent on his wax technique and taught it to his children. After he died in the 1890s his children carried on the tradition. The art of sculpting in wax and the secret of making the dolls continued to be passed down in the family, but are now lost forever.

Dollmakers of the United States have also delved into history to find subjects for their dolls. The Bicentennial celebration in 1976 brought forth a rash of George Washingtons, Betsy Rosses, Ben Franklins, and other historical figures. Also common types, such as the spinner and the sailor, were made into dolls.

Dollmakers in the United States do not stick to their own historical past but look to the history of other countries for doll subjects. England's King Henry VIII has inspired many a dollmaker not only in his own country but also in the United States, where recent TV specials have thrust His Majesty into the limelight.

These two 8″ cotton pickers are typical Vargas dolls. Their bodies are all wax, and their clothing is fabric impregnated with wax before it was put into place. Both are mounted on pieces of wood and have sacks of cotton in front of them as well as on their backs. (*Hupp Collection*)

These Vargas wax dolls represent street criers of the period. Both bakers, the doll on the left has a basket of pralines made of wax and seeds. The one on the right carries wax rolls and pastry. (*Hupp Collection*)

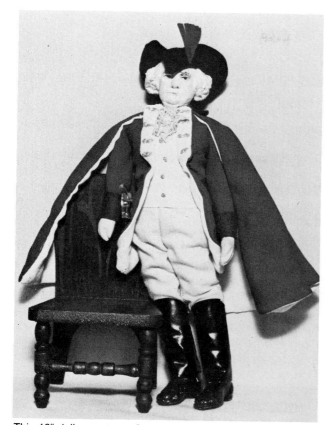

This 10″ doll represents George Washington. His head, hands, and feet are made of papier-mâché and painted. He is wearing a white shirt with a lace ascot and French-knot buttons of yellow embroidery cotton. He has a blue cape, lined in white, and a black felt three-cornered hat with red felt feather. (*MacNeer Collection*)

A 6½″ figure of Betsy Ross making the flag. This doll is wearing a blue dress and a white cotton shawl with a sequin at the neck. She sits on a piece of wood, covered with fabric. She has a papier-mâché head and arms and a white cotton mobcap on her head. (*Weiner Collection*)

A 6½″ woman sitting at her wooden spinning wheel. Her head is made of painted papier-mâché. Her hair is painted gray with white paint dry brushed over it. She is wearing a green figured dress decorated with white lace and black rickrack at the neck. (*Weiner Collection*)

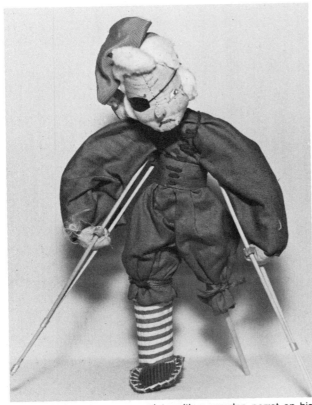

This 8½″ pirate comes complete with a wooden parrot on his shoulder. He is a stuffed cotton doll with his face sewn in profile. He has a blue suit, white cotton hair, and a red satin hat. His good leg is made from red-and-white-striped fabric, and a red ribbon ties down his pant legs. His shoe is corduroy, edged with a buttonhole stitch. (*MacNeer Collection*)

CORNHUSK DOLLS

Corn was an indigenous product of the New World. When the colonists arrived here, they found the Indians growing corn, and it was corn that induced the Indians who had originally been nomads to stay in one place. They built their communities around the cornfields and stayed at least until the fields were barren and they had to move on.

Corn was such a successful crop of the colonists that within one generation of the first settlers it was grown in Europe, and several generations later it was also grown in Africa. The corn, which was grown by the colonists and was an important resource in their lives, is very different from the corn we have today. Multicolored Indian corn, which is put up as a fall decoration on doors, is a healthy-looking descendant of what the colonists grew in the seventeenth century. Hybridization has produced a corn today that is much fatter, juicier, and longer than the corn the Indians raised.

Corn was an integral part of the lives of the colonists. They worked in the fields to raise it, made the shucks into rugs and baskets, slept on cornhusk mattresses, attended cornhusking bees, used corncobs for kindling, and when there was time they even made dolls and toys from the husks or cobs.

The cornhusk doll is probably the best known among the folk dolls of North America. One tradition, which may or may not be valid, holds that the American Indians taught the colonists how to make these dolls in return for the wooden dolls distributed by the English settlers. Certainly the making of cornhusk dolls is a traditional type of dollmaking done by the colonists as well as by the American Indians. Also making cornhusk dolls is a tradition in Czechoslovakia, Mexico, and other countries.

Cornhusk dolls made by the early settlers are found in many museums in New England. As the settlers moved south and west they carried the tradition of making cornhusk dolls with them and made dolls in the costumes of their own period and place. Dolls from cornhusk thus can be found in museums in states as diverse as Florida and Virginia and even Colorado. As time passed more sophisticated dolls were made, but the tradition continues and today cornhusk dolls are still made in the traditional way in places like the southern Appalachians and Ozark Mountains. Making the dolls has been revived as a contemporary craft, and supplies are sold for the cornhusk dolls in craft shops across the United States.

Cornhusks can be purchased in some craft shops and also in Mexican food shops, which sell them as wrapping for tamales. These husks are ready for making dolls. If you wish to prepare your own, ask a farmer if you can remove the dried husks from his feed corn. Or treat your family to corn on the cob and save the husks.

If you are buying corn to use for dolls, choose pieces that have not been ripped open, ones that still have corn silk on the top, which can be used in making the doll's hair. Also look for pieces that have as few black spots and blemishes on the outer shucks as possible.

If you are using field corn, you can harvest it late in the fall when it is already dried on the stalks. If you must dry it, lay the shucks singly out to dry on newspaper or cloth. Drying may take several days. Be sure that the husks are thoroughly dried, or you may have trouble later when your finished doll becomes moldy.

If you dry them in the sun, the cornhusks will be bleached to a light tan color. They can also be dried

To make a cornhusk doll, first shuck the corn, being careful not to tear the husk. Do not rip off the shucks, but cut them all around the ear of the corn at the top and bottom, then peel off the shucks one at a time.

indoors near a source of dry and constant heat. Save the corn silk also and dry it along with the shucks for the doll's hair. Discard discolored and very coarse husks and use the softer, lighter colored inner husks.

To save husks that are discolored or mildewed, bleach them before you use them by soaking them in water to which a half cup of laundry bleach has been added. Soak until the spots disappear. Though bleaching will soften the husk for use, do not allow this process to go too far or the husks will disintegrate. Be sure to wash the husks in water after bleaching.

For the most part you will probably use the cornhusks in their natural color. If you decide you want to have dyed pieces to add accents to your dolls, dye the shucks, using commerical fabric dyes, or if you prefer, use natural sources of color like onions, nuts, roots, and flowers.

Soak the pieces of shuck in the dye mixture long enough to get the intensity of color you desire. Rinse them in water and spread out singly to dry. You will notice when you are putting your doll together that, if the dyed pieces become too wet, the dye may run onto the pieces left the natural color, so be careful.

Cornhusks are usually dampened before use. To

begin, soak about a dozen cornhusks in water until they are soft and pliable. This may take less than ten minutes or up to a half hour, depending on how thick they are. You can put them into boiling water to rush the process. If the cornhusks seem very stiff, soften them by adding a tablespoon of glycerine or a bar of facial soap to the soaking water.

Once the husks are soaked, shake off the excess water and wrap them in a damp towel until you are ready to work with them. Remove each cornhusk from the towel as you need it, so the rest will stay damp and workable. If the husks are damp rather than soaking wet, there will be less shrinkage in drying. If you work on a bath towel, this will soak up any excess moisture.

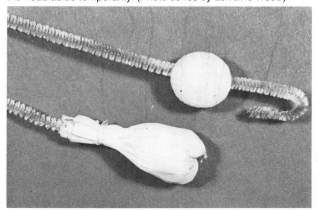

1

The materials you need for making cornhusk dolls are cornhusks, a Styrofoam ball 1″ or ⅞″ in diameter, a pipe cleaner or 18-gauge covered wire, and thread. The equipment you need are a pair of scissors, a ruler, thick white glue, a container of water, and absorbent bath towels. (*Photo by Lorraine Wood*)

As shown at the top, push a 6″ wire or pipe cleaner through the middle of the Styrofoam ball and form a hook with it at the top of the head. Then take a strip of softened cornhusk, about 5″ long and 2″ wide, and center it on top of the Styrofoam ball under the wire hook. Pull the hook down into the ball securing the center of the cornhusk at the top of the Styrofoam ball. Spread the cornhusk out all around the ball so that it covers the entire ball smoothly. Gather the husk where the wire comes out of the Styrofoam ball at the bottom. Cut a piece of very strong thread and hold one end of it against the cornhusk. With the other hand, wrap the thread a half-dozen times, at least around the cornhusk, pulling it very tightly against the head. Tie the ends of the thread tightly, and lay the head aside temporarily. (*Photo series by Lorraine Wood*)

2

3

To make the arms, cut a piece of wire or pipe cleaner 5″ long. Take a piece of cornhusk about 6″ long and lay the wire along one long edge. Wrap the cornhusk tightly around the wire, and keep rolling it tightly until you get to the other edge of the piece of cornhusk. Wrap and tie each end with pieces of strong thread about ½″ from each end to make wrists. Mark the center of the roll.

If you wish to make puffed sleeves, cut a piece of cornhusk about 3″ long and 4″ wide. Bring that piece around the end of the strip you have already tied just above the wrist, about 1″ from the end, so that it falls over the end of the hand. Wrap it with thread and tie it tightly. Fold the free end of the cornhusk back over itself toward the center of the arm strip, letting it puff into a sleeve. Gather it and tie it in place near the center line you drew. Repeat for the other sleeve.

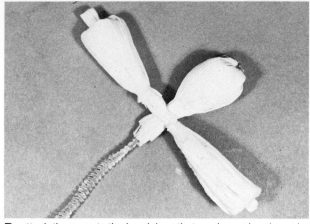

4

To attach the arms to the headpiece that you have already made, place the arms across the headpiece about ½″ below where you have tied it at the neck. Hold the arms and head so that the arms are at the back. Wrap thread around about ten times in a criss-cross manner so that the arms are firmly attached to the head and neck. Wrap tightly and tie off.

5

To fill in the chest, use another piece of cornhusk about 4″ square. Fold it in half, then again in half, so that it is 1″ wide. Fold this strip in half and hold the center of it near the neck of the doll. Bring the thread around the neck and over the padding strip at the center so that it is securely attached just below the neck. Bring the loose ends down to the waist, and if you wish, add a little cotton padding at the bustline. Tie very tightly so that the waist stays small, trimming away some of the husk at the waistline if necessary.

6

To make the bodice, use two strips of cornhusk about 6″ × 1½″. Bring each one from the waist in the front up and over the shoulders to the waist in the back. Bring the other piece over the other shoulder in a similar manner, arranging the pieces so that they cross both in front and in back. Wrap very tightly with thread at the waist.

7

To make the skirt, raise the arms. Overlap five or six wide pieces of cornhusk around the waist, with the ends about an inch below the waist, bringing them up over the head. Gather them and put them in place one at a time, and wrap with thread very tightly at the waistline. As you put each piece in place, overlap it halfway so the skirt is always a double thickness.

8

Bring the strips down and form the skirt. To keep it from spreading out too much, hold the pieces of cornhusk in place with a rubber band or a strip of soft cloth until they are thoroughly dry. Trim the skirt so that the figure is 7″ or the desired height.

9

If you want your doll to assume a particular posture, perhaps hold something like a book or a bundle, put her arms into that position before she dries. She can be made to look gentle, proud, flirty or take other humanlike poses. Experiment to get the expression and pose you want into your figure.

10

The details you add to your cornhusk dolls will give them personality. For the face, make two black dots for the eyes. You can add more elaborate features, but these must be done artfully. If you don't want to take a chance on your skill, stay with the two black dots, which are very effective. Make hair from cornsilk, embroidery cotton, yarn, or other fiber. Try adding a cap of cornhusk, lace, or trim, or use a small scrap of fabric for an apron. Make a miniature piece of embroidery for the doll to hold or make a cornhusk book or a basket filled with miniature dried flowers.

Martha Peters Garrott works on trimming one of her original corn-husk dolls, which she makes from shucks she has gathered, and dyed if necessary. She is an exhibiting member of the Craftmen's Guild of Mississippi, a nonprofit professional group organized to preserve and promote the crafts of the state. Travelers may observe Mrs. Garrott at work at the Mississippi Crafts Center in Jackson, a crafts shop that she manages. (*Photo courtesy of the craftsman*)

These beautifully crafted cornhusk dolls were made by Martha Peters Garrott. They are from 7" to 9" tall. Note that the doll on the right has a black face, which is not typical of cornhusk dolls. Mrs. Garrott comments: "As a Mississippian I think it appropriate to make about half of my dolls white and half black (brown literally)." (*Photo courtesy of the doll artist*)

Cornhusk dolls, 6" tall, made of natural and dyed cornhusks. The woman has a long red-dyed skirt and a green hat. The man has a blue-dyed jacket and pants, and his beard is cornsilk. He carries a hatchet, and she a broom, both of cornhusks. Their facial features are drawn on the cornhusk, except for their noses, which are separate pieces of cornhusk. (*MacNeer Collection*)

This cornhusk doll has a fabric flower on her hat and dried cornsilk for hair. Otherwise, she's completely cornhusk, including her stylish hat and the pocketbook or bag she is carrying. Made at least several decades ago, she has a shawl-like arrangement of cornhusk over her shoulders. (*Photographed at the Children's Museum, Boston, Mass.*)

A 5½" cornhusk doll made in the southern United States. The doll, made especially to be in a sitting position, is all cornhusk and is much thinner in the body than the typical cornhusk doll. Her horse is out of the ordinary in that it is made of cornhusks twisted and woven together. Note the use of dried cornsilk for the horse's mane and tail. (*Hupp Collection*)

An 8½″ cornhusk doll, probably made in North Carolina, This female figure is nicely detailed with cornhusk pieces dyed purple and narrow bands of red crossing at her waist. She holds a cornhusk baby. Her hat is crocheted from cornhusk fiber and decorated with dried flowers. Note the detailing on her skirt, which is sewn through with red-dyed cornhusk. (*Groszmann Collection*)

This beautifully made 8″ cornhusk doll is mainly of natural cornhusk, except for her blouse, which is dyed. Her features are delicately drawn, and she has a hat of cornhusk, decorated with natural miniature dried flowers. In her cornhusk basket are more dried flowers. She was bought at Auntie Peg's Country Crafts in Clarksdale, Arizona. (*Mueller Collection*)

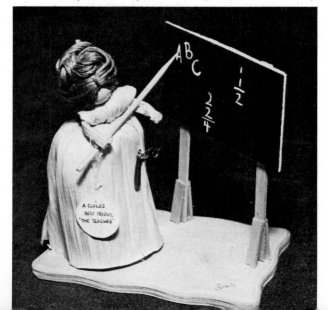

Rita Polchin added interesting accessories to this cornhusk doll to make her a teacher.

A cornhusk doll, cooking her family's meal in a metal pot, made by Rita Polchin of Crafts Keyhole, Allendale, New Jersey,

A mother and baby doll set, made completely of cornhusks except for the hair, which is of embroidery cotton. The dolls are by Rita Polchin of New Jersey.

CORNCOB DOLLS

Cornhusks are not the only part of the corn plant to be used in dollmaking. Cornstalks are made into doll bodies, and corn silk into hair. The cob is another useful part and has been made into doll bodies and heads. The U.S. dollmakers are not the only ones using corncobs for dollmaking. Their counterparts in Northern Rhodesia have been inspired by the same material.

There is a great variety of cornhusk dolls, but not such a diversity in the U.S. branch of the corncob family. The head of the corncob dolls is usually a slice of corncob fastened to the corncob body. The nose is usually a bean, and the features are drawn on with a pen or brush. Some dolls with corncob bodies have buckeye nuts for heads and are called buckeye dolls. Since the buckeye is a dark brown, the buckeye doll looks like a black person.

Corncob dolls have been made as folk toys in the Ozarks and in West Virginia, North Carolina, and neighboring states. The clothing has become more or less traditional. The women usually wear long dresses and bonnets and the men usually have print shirts, overalls, and a burlap hat.

To make a corncob doll, naturally the first material you will need is a corncob. If it is not corn eating season or if you do not want to take the time to dry a cob (from which you have eaten or scraped the corn), you can purchase prepared corncobs in craft shops. You will also need thread, a bean for the nose, pipe cleaners for the arms, a wooden matchstick or other small piece of wood, marking pens to draw on the features, and scraps of fabric from which to make the clothing. You will also need a saw, drill, scissors, glue, and a needle to complete your doll.

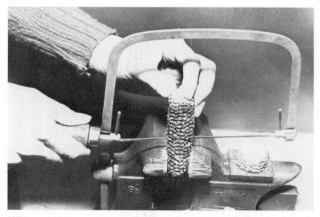

With a coping saw, saw off 1″ from the large end of your corncob for the head. If the doll is female, use the cob as is for the body, but if the doll is male, saw up from the bottom (the narrower end) about 3″ to separate the legs so that the pants can be put on.

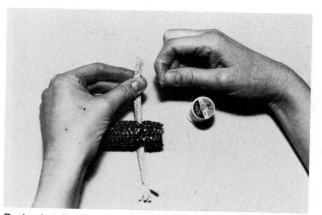

Push a bundle of five 6″ pipe cleaners through the hole you have made in the body and secure them in place with a bit of glue. About ½″ from the end of the arms, wrap a piece of thread around the pipe cleaners to hold them together and to mark off the hands.

About ½″ below the top of the corncob, drill a hole through which you can put the pipe-cleaner arms. Drill a small hole in the top of the corncob and in the head, so you will be able to insert the dowel at the neck. Also drill a small hole in which to insert the bean nose.

Put glue on the small piece of dowel and insert it into the head and the body at the neck. Put a little glue on the bean and insert in place as the nose. Use marking pen to draw on the eyes and mouth.

Dress the corncob doll any way you like. Corncobs vary in size, as do the dolls made from them, so you will have to custom-make your doll's clothes. To make the woman's bonnet, cut a circle about 3″ in diameter and put lace at the edge. Gather it by putting a basting stitch in a little way from the edge, pulling it to the right size, and adjusting it to the size of the head. Glue it in place. Make a slip and long dress for the doll, with the skirt of the dress about an inch longer than the corncob body, so it will flare out and help hold up the doll. Gather the skirt at the waist and make a bodice with long sleeves to fit over the pipe-cleaner arms. Trim the dress with lace and attach the bodice to the skirt. Put on the clothing, then fan out the doll's pipe-cleaner fingers, bending the pipe-cleaner arms into a graceful pose. Make the man's shirt the same way as the top of the woman's bodice, with a small calico print or gingham fabric. Use denim for his overalls. For his hat, cut a circle of burlap about 3″ in diameter. Put a running stitch about ¾″ in from the edge and gather slightly to fit the head. Glue in place. Put a stick about 5″ long in the man's hand, curving his pipe-cleaner fingers around it. The stick will help the doll stand up. (*MacNeer Collection*)

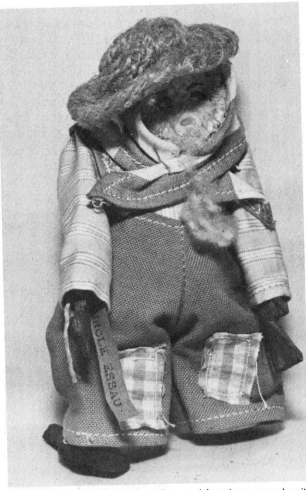

A 5″ corncob doll, different from the usual American corncob, with a label that says his name is "Uncle Essau." He has a corncob body and face with features drawn on. His arms are pieces of wood. He wears machine-stitched brown pants, a brown-striped shirt, and a hat of jute. (*MacNeer Collection*)

These 7″ dolls are Bea's Ozark Handmade Dolls. Both the man and woman have corncob faces, stuffed fabric bodies, and pipe-cleaner arms, hands, legs, and feet. They have mouths drawn on the piece of corncob and beans stuck in for noses. Each one is smoking a pipe—a wooden stick with a piece of dried corn glued on the end. The man sits an a piece of natural wood, holds a wooden gun, and has a burlap hat. The woman sits on a chair made with a wooden seat and cane basketry for legs and back. She has cornsilk hair, wears a cotton houndstooth print dress, and on her lap is yarn for braiding a rug. (*Photographed at United Nations Gift Center*)

APPLEHEAD DOLLS

The early colonists learned to make applehead dolls from the Indians who made bodies for their dolls from a bone or piece of wood. They used their own hair or hair cut from a horse's mane and a bit of buckskin tied on for clothing to complete the dolls. The Indians always made squaws, toothless old women. When the colonists learned how to make applehead dolls, they made mostly women and even called them "apple grannies."

The mountain women in Appalachia still make applehead dolls and it is a true folk art still flourishing in the Ozarks. Other dollmakers have also revived the art, having become fascinated with the possibilities that this type of doll offers.

Applehead dolls can be bought in gift shops and other stores catering to the tourist trade in the mountain sections. Also they can often be seen at craft shows where contemporary craftspeople have set up a whole display of applehead dolls, each one elaborately costumed and often with appropriate accessories like a rocking chair to sit in.

No two applehead dolls are ever alike, even though the same person does the carving from the same batch of apples on the same day. The appleheads can never be the same because each apple wrinkles differently as it dries. Part of the fascination of the craft is that in carving the apple you can try for a certain look, but you cannot be sure as to what kind of dried face will result. You may aim for a smiling face, but you may end up with a scowl on the dried applehead.

The applehead dolls made by the Indians and by the early settlers were much more primitive than today's. The early settlers did not have the materials that are available now, nor did they have the necessary time to devote to the dolls. And since the dolls were meant to be playthings, very little time was spent in making them.

At first the appleheads were not carved, but instead the features were pinched with the fingers. Daily the dollmaker would press and pinch the flesh of the apple until it was completely dry and hard. The head then was usually impaled on a pointed stick that was inserted into a stuffed cloth body.

Today's dollmakers usually find it helps to carve the features while the apple is fresh, and to use wire armature in place of the neckstick. No longer play dolls, present-day applehead dolls are usually character dolls meant as conversation pieces for display only.

MATERIALS AND EQUIPMENT

Each applehead dollmaker has his or her own preferences for the type of apple to be used. Most will agree you should use a fresh, firm, fully ripe apple without bruises. Among the varieties of apples that have been recommended are Winesap, pippins, Jonathans, Rome Beauties, Golden or Red Delicious, and snow apples. Almost any kind of apple can be used, but remember that the juicier the apple, the more it will shrink and wrinkle as it dries and the darker it will become.

Probably more important than the type of apple is its condition. The best time to make an applehead doll is in the fall or winter. Apples sold in the spring and summer may have been stored too long to give satisfactory results.

Size is important too in choosing an apple, if you are concerned about the size of the dried apple and therefore the body which you will make in proportion to it. Naturally you will choose an apple much larger than the head you wish to have. While it varies according to the type of apple and its moisture content, the apple will usually shrink to perhaps one third of its original size.

If you plan to make an applehead doll, don't carve just one head, because once you have waited out the drying period you may be disappointed with the result and have to start all over again. Instead carve perhaps a half dozen to a dozen apples to give yourself a better chance of ending up with a useful head. You can even carve one head on the front and one on the back of each apple and see which heads are best when they finish drying. Also carve more apple hands than you need. These can dry twisted, queerly, or otherwise unusable and can get broken easily.

You will also need an apple peeler or a paring knife to peel the apple. Use a sharp pointed paring knife to do the carving. For eyes, you might use beads, cloves, okra seeds, apple seeds, black-headed dressmaker pins, or whatever seeds or beads you have that are appropriate. Or you could make cardboard eyes or use inverted sequins.

For hair, use yarn, embroidery floss, cotton, white drapery cable, real hair (animal or human), or some long-haired fake fur, a doll's wig or any other appropriate material. To color the lips and cheeks, you can, if you wish, use watercolor or poster paints, or even lipstick and rouge.

If you want your doll to have teeth, you can use seeds, elongated pearls, or rice. Remember in choosing the teeth, they should be in proportion to the dried apple not the newly carved one. You will be putting the teeth in before the apple dries and whatever is put in will stay—once the carved apple is dried, it's almost impossible to perform dental surgery on it or to take out anything that was put into it.

For the body of your applehead doll, you can use a wire frame, as described on page 18. In making the wire frame, leave a piece of wire on the body that will slip up into the applehead and hold it securely to the body. Be sure to cover the wire with adhesive tape or it may blacken the apple.

Applehead dolls often have hands and even feet carved and dried like the heads. Or they might be made from felt, papier-mâché, clay, bread dough, or nylon-covered wire, to name a few materials.

Applehead dollmakers are probably in as much disagreement as to the best method to use in drying the apples as they are in the best type of apple to choose. Alice Miller who has had much experience in making appleheads says that she stores her carved apples in a cool place—the same way farmers store apples over the winter. She merely places her carved heads on a paper towel and puts them in a cool dark place. Every day she turns them so they will not flatten on one side.

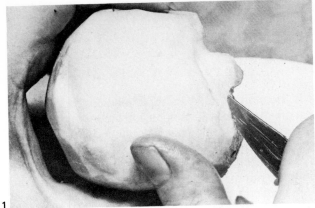

1 To make an applehead doll, first pare the apple and immediately get rid of any hard rims or ridges and any other imperfections on the surface. Some applehead dollmakers leave a margin of skin about the size of a nickel around both ends of the apple, to minimize shrinkage, and though this may make drying time a little longer, it is worthwhile. Alice Miller, who is carving this apple, advises that before you begin, inspect the apple, then choose the nicest-looking area or section of it. Let the shape of the apple itself suggest the kind of face you carve. Plan where the nose will be and begin to carve into the apple, removing some pulp below and some above the nose, then some to the right and left to make a high ridge for it and have it stand out from the face. It should not be exaggerated but should be in proportion to the whole face.

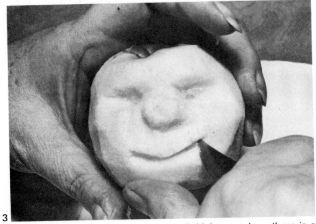

3 Form the mouth by making a long slit high enough so there is a chin underneath, forming it so the mouth is opened very little. Make a shallow cut, curving upward at each end, removing just a little of the apple. The upward curve of the line should result in a smiling mouth on the dried face, but there is no guarantee of this.

5 Once your apple is carved, you must wait until it is dried before you can continue to make the doll. To dry the head, run a piece of covered wire or pipe cleaner through the apple top to bottom. Make a hook at each end of the cleaner. Hang the apple from the upper hook in a warm place to dry, or suspend it from a string, or use one of the other methods described in this chapter.

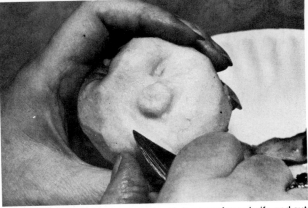

2 Once the nose pleases you, work with the top of your knife and cut out eye-shaped holes above the nose.

4 Once the facial features are completed, trim the apple back a little, forming and rounding the forehead, cheeks, and chin. Make sure the face is symmetrical and natural looking. Check that one cheek is not higher or rounder than the other. Smooth the face as necessary until you are pleased with the result. If you wish to insert teeth, put them in now and they will be held fast when the head is dry. Remember the number and placement should be in accord with the size of the dried head and not appropriate to the newly carved head. Some applehead dollmakers say at this point you should rinse the apple in lemon juice and sprinkle it with salt. This process will keep the face from turning too dark. As an alternative to lemon juice, you can use a solution of a tablespoon of powdered citric acid dissolved in a cup of water.

6 Every few days check the apple and smooth the face a little with your fingers if you want your doll to have a smooth face. You can do a limited amount of shaping while the apple is drying. Check the apple for mold and other problems. The amount of shrinkage and the drying time will vary from one type of apple to another and according to the humidity in the air. During humid weather it is much harder to dry an apple effectively and is not a good time to try. Be sure that the apple is completely dry before continuing to make the doll.

7

When the apple is dry, you can complete the face. Insert cloves, blackheaded dressmaker's pins, or whatever for the eyes. If you wish, you can paint the lips and cheeks very lightly with water-colors or poster paints, or apply a small amount of lipstick and rouge, depending of course on the character and effect you are aiming for. When the face is completed you can, if you wish, apply a coat of fixative. Now figure out what kind of body and costume goes along with the face you have created.

9

8

To make the hands and feet, cut an apple in half, with a larger half that has the core and a smaller half without it. Cut slices from the smaller half and carve the hands and feet from these slices. Shape the hands and make straight cuts between the fingers. Make very small cuts between the toes. When you have finished carving the pieces, dip the pieces into lemon juice and treat them with salt, if you wish. Put the carved pieces on a piece of covered wire or string and hang them up to dry, or lay them on a rack turning them occasionally until they have dried to the consistency of leather. After they are completely dried, it may be possible to use cuticle scissors to trim round them to improve the shape of the fingers and thumb or the toes. Be careful, however, as you may find that the apple is lighter in color inside, and this will show wherever you have trimmed the apple.

If you wish, you can add ears to your applehead. Cut them from thin apple slices as you did the hands. Cut slits at the side of the applehead and insert the ears. During the process of drying, the ears will become solidly fixed in the applehead. If they turn out poorly, you can always cover them with hair. Be sure your face and hands are made in proportion to each other.

They take longer to dry in a cool place, but she claims they never get moldly during the drying process or later after the doll has been made. She still has applehead dolls she made twenty-two years ago, and they have not rotted. Stored in a cool place, the apples take about three months to completely dry out. After that, they are never going to change, she says

Rather than keeping the apples in a cool dry place, many dollmakers prefer to dry their appleheads in a warm place, which makes the drying process faster. The apples can be suspended on a piece of wire or string, and the air circulating around them will dry them out. If you choose this method, remember it is difficult if not impossible to get the wire or string out of the dried apple, so insert into the apple only whatever can stay there. Another way to dry a carved apple is to insert a wooden stick into the blossom end of the apple. Stand it in a tall glass in a warm place, perhaps over a radiator.

Though most applehead dollmakers believe that drying the head is not to be rushed, some say that the applehead can be oven dried. After being dipped in lemon juice, it can be put into the oven at 150 degrees and kept at this low temperature for twenty-four hours, when the apple should be completely dried. Or the oven can be turned off at night and on again during the day for several days.

Once the applehead is dried, a dollmaker can apply a coat of shellac, varnish, matte spray fixative, watered-down white glue, clear nail polish, or resin spray in order to protect the apple and ward off insects. Some dollmakers feel this is unnecessary—after all, the Indians did not have these fixatives. The spray, too, gives the applehead a sheen, which may not be desirable. An effectively dried apple, according to Alice Miller, does not need a fixative and will last without it.

Half the fun of making an applehead doll is watching to see how the carved head dries. Until the apple is dry, you will not be able to decide exactly the character you wish to create. Because the apple usually dries to give a wrinkled caricature-like face, the most common applehead figures are those of grandma and grandpa. But there are many other possibilities, among them, the fisherman or sea captain, chef, happy tippler, farmer, golfer, preacher, businessman, scrubwoman, organ grinder, squaw, and even Mr. and Mrs. Santa.

Sometimes by chance the head may dry in such a way as to look somewhat like a famous person's and the doll can be dressed to further the illusion. Sometimes the apple dries with not too much wrinkling, so it is possible to make applehead figures of children—though these are rare.

A 9″ applehead doll, made by Alice Miller. The figure has plastic eyes, a doll's wig, and apple hands. She is wearing a gingham dress decorated with lace and embroidery and a pair of elegant felt slippers decorated with seed beads. She is holding a baby made with an applehead and a wire-frame body and dressed in an eyelet gown.

An 8″ applehead lady, made by Alice Miller. She has a wire-frame body, plastic eyes, and a doll's wig for hair. Her applehead, made about 1964, is still in excellent condition because it was well dried at the time. She is wearing a cotton-print dress, a hand-knitted shawl, and is holding a baby made from a peanut.

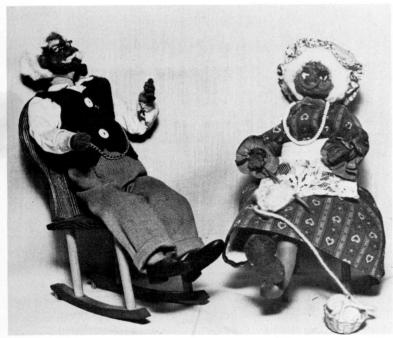

These applehead dolls, each about 7″ tall, were made by Alice Miller. They have wire-frame bodies wrapped with nylon stocking, apple hands, plastic eyes, and hair of cotton. They were made around 1956, and their appleheads are still in excellent condition. The man has a white cotton shirt, a felt vest, and carved wooden feet and wears eyeglasses of twisted wire. The woman wears a cotton-print dress, cap, and seed bead necklace. She has on felt slippers and holds her knitting on wooden toothpicks.

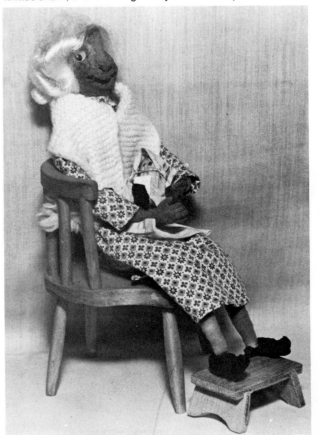

Sitting on a log, this amused and amusing applehead man looks at the harmonica he is about to play. His hands as well as his face are dried apples. He wears blue jeans, a red print shirt, and a black felt hat. (*MacNeer Collection*)

This applehead doll has a wire-frame body. Her hands are wire wrapped with tape, and her feet are bread dough. She has yarn hair and her clothes are made of tiny-print cotton fabric. Her blue dress has lace cuffs and collar, and her pink apron is decorated with lace and tiny rickrack. She is holding a piece of orange yarn knitting. She was made in the Appalachian Mountains of West Virginia by Patricia Tate of White Sulphur Springs and is dated Sept., 1971. (*Hupp Collection*)

These 11″ applehead dolls were made by Ann Hulsizer. Their hair is made from wool roving (carded wool before it is spun), and they have wire eyeglasses, which were dipped in liquid plastic. They have wire-frame bodies and felt hands. The woman is wearing an old-fashioned gray print dress and a shawl hand crocheted of Scotch-tweed yarn. The man has a hand-crocheted straw hat, a gingham shirt, and denim overalls.

Grandma and Grandpa are common subjects of applehead dolls because the carved apple dries naturally to a rather wizened look. This pair of dolls, made by Adele Moore, have cotton hair and wire-frame bodies, covered with stockinette and stuffed. Grandpa wears a woolen outfit with a cotton shirt, and Grandma is wearing a figured-cotton dress and a hand-embroidered shawl, and is holding a bouquet of dried flowers.

CLOTHESPIN DOLLS

Clothespins whittled from wood and made for drying clothes on the line have been used for making folk dolls for many years. This old form of dollmaking has been recently revived, and today's commercially made clothespins are so readily available and so inexpensive that making clothespin dolls has become a popular craft.

A clothespin doll is usually made using one wooden clothespin. Sometimes the doll's head is the rounded top of the clothespin left as is; other times this rounded top is sawed flat on one side, so it is flat-sided like nineteenth-century clothespins. The features are then drawn on this flat side.

These 4½″ clothespin dolls were made of regular clothespins—the rounded tops were sliced off to make flat faces, an which the features were painted. The arms are pipe cleaners, and the hair of each is yarn. He wears blue cotton pants, and a red shirt and hat of blue felt. She wears a red print dress trimmed with lace. At the bottom of the clothespin bread dough, clay or a material like it was used to fashion feet that were painted black. These feet allow the doll to stand. (*Weiner Collection*)

A 4½″ clothespin doll made by Ann Hulsizer. The nose is a separate piece of balsa wood glued in place, and the head was dipped in wax to give it texture. The doll has wire arms, brown paper hands, thread hair, and clothing of cotton fabrics decorated with lace.

The arms of the clothespin doll are usually made of pipe cleaners or wire. The wire is wrapped around the body section of the doll below the head and above the split for the legs. Another way of making a clothespin doll is to add a head above the round top of the pin. The arms then are placed just below the rounded top of the pin, and the doll is made in the usual way. (*Doll made by Helene Vosburgh*)

These three are clothespin dolls. The ones at either side are the traditional clothespin dolls, with the tops of the clothespins for the heads and pipe cleaners for arms. The doll in the middle shows an interesting use of clothespins. The head is a wooden ball, and the arms and legs are clothespins that have been cut as shown in the diagram. This doll has thread hair in braids and wears a yellow flannel nightgown. (Mueller Collection)

Clothespin dolls with faces painted on the top or head of the clothespin. They have pipe-cleaner arms and yarn hair. Their bonnets match their dresses, which have lace trim. Each one carries a broom, consisting of a thin dowel and string. (Weiner Collection)

A clothespin doll, made by Helene Vosburgh, with carved feet glued on at the base of the clothespin and hands of small pieces of wood glued into the fabric sleeves (instead of using wire arms). The female figure has mohair for hair, wears an off-white taffeta dress with a maroon edging, and carries a paper fan of pleated paper.

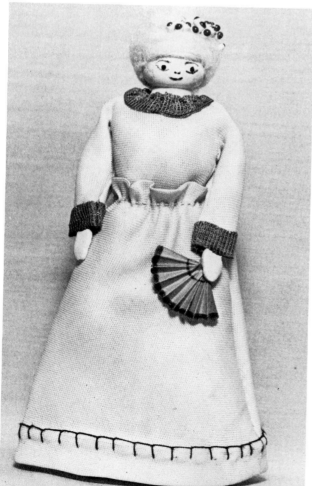

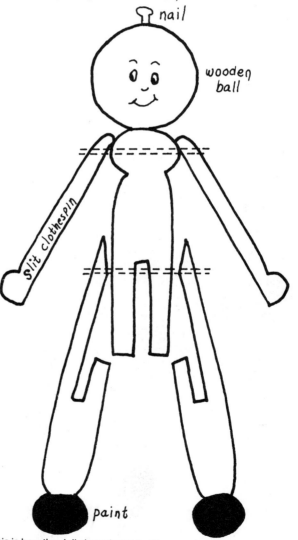

This is how the doll above is made. The arms are a clothespin slit in half and trimmed to size, and the legs are cut off as shown. The limbs are attached to the body with wire.

NUTHEADS

The nuthead doll is one of the most versatile folk dolls. It can be made in so many ways from the extremely simple to the quite elaborate, but choosing just the right nut and developing the proper body to go with it takes a bit of imagination.

A variety of nuts have been used in making the nuthead doll, including hickory, acorn, peanut, hazelnut, filbert, walnut, pecan, chestnut, and so on. Each type of nut seems to suggest its own type of doll. Walnuts, for example, usually have a wrinkled surface so senior citizen dolls are often made with them. Hickory nuts with their pointed ends suggest younger faces with predominant noses.

Nutheads can be given different types of bodies. They can be wire framed or made from twigs, attached to bodies made of dried prunes or carved from wood.

The nuthead might also have a body made from a clothespin. To make this type of doll you will need, besides the clothespin and the nut, a pipe cleaner for arms, a hammer and nail, and some cotton for hair. To clothe the doll, you will need a piece of cotton fabric with a small bright print for the dress, some white fabric for the apron, and a piece of flannel to match the print for the shawl.

2

Cut a narrow strip of print fabric and twist it around the pipe-cleaner arms and around the top part of the body, taking a few stitches as necessary to hold it in place. For the apron, cut a piece of white fabric 2½″ x 4½″, saw-toothing it around the edge with pinking shears. Cut a waistband 5″ x ⅞″. Sew a gathering stitch across the one 4½″ side of the apron. Gather the thread slightly and sew the waistband on it. Cut a 2¾″ circle of print fabric for a hat, one of a piece of solid-color fabric that is ½ of such circle. Glue them wrong sides together and pink them all around the outside edge.

Sew a gathering stitch along the top edge of the skirt. Pull the thread, adjusting it to fit the doll. Put it on the doll and secure the end of the thread. Tie the apron onto the doll with its strings. Glue a small amount of cotton on the doll's head for hair. Sew a gathering stitch around the edge of the circle made for the hat, stitching only where there is a single layer of fabric. Gather the hat to fit the head and finish off the end of the thread. Glue the hat in place. Put the shawl over the doll's shoulders and across the ends in the front and let her hold it in place with her pipe-cleaner arms. (*Wood Collection*)

3

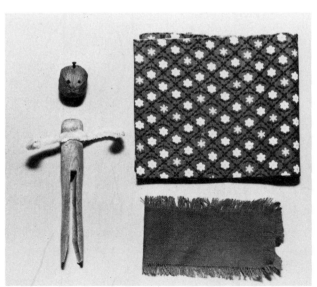

1

Draw or paint a simple face on the nut. Nail the nut to the top of the clothespin. Cut a 5″ piece of pipe cleaner, twist it around the clothespin to form arms, and loop the ends for hands. For the skirt, cut an 18″ x 8″ piece of fabric for the skirt and fold it in half, matching the 8″ edges right sides together. Sew the seam. Fold the fabric in half so that it is 4″ wide with the right side showing on both sides. For the shawl, cut a piece of solid-color flannel 7″ x 2″ and fringe it all around, removing threads for about ¼″.

At the center of this grouping of traditional American folk dolls is a primitive 5½" pecan-nut-head doll. The features are inked on the nut, and the hair is a bit of cotton. A scrap of bandanna fabric is tied on the head. The body is a stick of wood wound with gingham fabric. The wire arms are wound with the same fabric. The figure wears a green-and-white gingham skirt and a white apron, and a triangle of cotton fabric is her shawl.

On the left is a more modern pecan-head doll. This figure has a stuffed fabric body and pipe-cleaner arms and her features are painted on. Her dress is a red print fabric, and white bias tape was used for cuffs and over her shoulder as the top of her white apron.

On the right is a primitive 6" American hickory-nut doll. Her features are inked on her nuthead, which has on it a fabric bonnet tied with embroidery cotton. She has a stump body made from a piece of wood wrapped with fabric. Her arms are a bit of upholstery or slip-cover edging, and over her flower-print dress she wears a black felt shawl. (*Hupp Collection*)

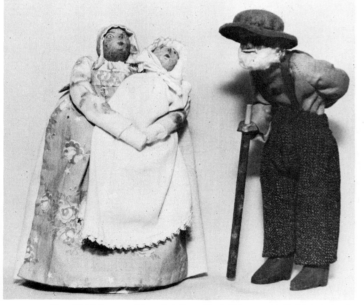

The 6" hickory-nut-head doll on the left has a stuffed fabric body with a cardboard base. The woman's dress is a yellow print fabric with a blue cotton-print apron. Her arms are pieces of fabric stitched together and stuffed. The baby she is holding has a white gown and a hickory-nut head. The old man has a hand-carved wooden body and fabric clothing. He wears a gray felt hat and brown cotton shirt, black and white tweed pants, and leather suspenders. (*Hupp Collection*)

These 9" hickory-nut dolls have bodies carved from wood and are jointed so that their arms can move. They are both mounted on slabs of wood and have hickory-nut heads with features painted on them and hair of cotton. They were sold in Isla's Doll Shop in Plainview, Nebraska. They are supposed to be mountain people, perhaps Appalachian hillbillies. The man wears gray-twill pants and a cotton-print shirt and carries a wooden jug with the words "Mountain Dew" on it. He has a pipe in his mouth consisting of a stick and a piece of pipe cleaner for the bowl. The woman wears a black print dress with a white lace collar and a white apron edged in rickrack. She is cooking some fish for supper while he sits contentedly with his pipe and bottle. (*Mueller Collection*)

This 11″ walnut-head lady doll has a wire body. Her arms are wrapped with yarn, her head is a walnut that has been painted, and her black hair is braided yarn. She wears a long red-print dress with lace at the collar, cuffs, and hem. (*Mueller Collection*)

An acorn-head doll, made with a pinecone body, is wearing a stiffened burlap skirt, cotton-fabric apron, and head scarf. She has pipe-cleaner arms and holds a natural bouquet of dried flowers and grass. (*Author's Collection*)

These primitive dolls have chestnut heads, felt features, and yarn hair. Their bodies are made with wire frames, covered with fabric. (*Author's Collection*)

A beautifully made walnut-head doll with painted features, white string hair, and small pearls for earrings. Her body is a wire frame, padded and wrapped with nylon stocking. (*Harp Collection*)

Made in the Ozarks, these dolls have carved wooden bodies. The 5″ nut head has a tag that says she's "Grandma Scott." This female figure wears a green cotton-print bonnet, blue cotton-print dress, and black apron. She has white pantaloons and a red slip. The male figure wears a brown shirt and black-and-white pants held up with leather suspenders. His beard is white cotton, and he wears a brown felt hat. (*MacNeer Collection*)

BEANHEAD DOLLS

The nuthead is a popular type of American folk doll, but an American dollmaker has gone beyond the usual hickory-nut and walnut heads and tried a different natural seed for the doll's head and come up with a unique type of doll—the beanhead.

A whole row of beanhead dolls made with just dried beans and scraps of fabric is the collection in the Children's Museum of Boston. The dolls, each only about two inches tall, are mounted on a piece of wood and look like a queue of ladies chatting as they wait their turn.

All you need to make such dolls are scraps of fabric, including a tiny piece of solid color fabric for the head scarf and a small piece with a tiny print for the dress. You will also need a bean for the head. You can use a dried lima bean, pinto bean, or any other appropriate bean you find in your cupboard.

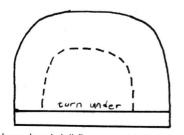

1   To make a bean-head doll first copy this hat pattern on tracing paper and cut a copy from fabric. Turn under as indicated along the straight line.

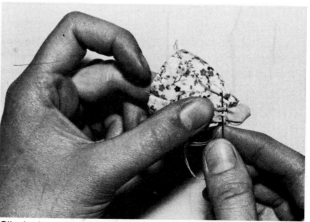

2   Bring the hat fabric around the bean so that one round end of the bean sticks out like a face where the fabric has been turned down. Stitch in the fabric as shown on the dashed line on the pattern, and gather it under the bean. Pull the thread tighter and anchor it securely with several stitches under the bean head.

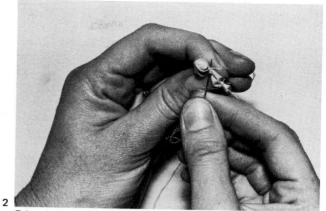

3   Cut a piece of fabric 2″ x 4″. Stitch a ¼″ hem along one long edge. Stitch the two short ends together holding the fabric right sides together. Turn the fabric right side out. Turn down the raw edge ¼″ to the inside and make a gathering stitch all along this edge.

4   Slip the bean head into the dress and let the head show above the top. Pull the gathering thread tight on the dress and fasten off.

Beanhead dolls like these are among the simplest of all fabric dolls. A whole collection can be made with small scraps of fabric and a handful of beans—dried limas, pintos, or whatever. (*From the Collection of the Children's Museum, Boston, Mass.*)

LIMBER JIM (JIGGER)

One of the oldest wooden dolls, popular even into the twentieth century, is the loose-jointed doll known as a jigger—Limber Jim or Limber Jack or Dancing Dan. This type of doll, which has been popular both in the United States and in Canada, has jointed arms and legs and is usually attached to a stick.

To make Limber Jim dance, the operator sits on a thin wood board and lets it extend out in front of him. He holds Jim above the board with the doll's feet just touching it. With the other hand the operator raps out a rhythm on the board. The doll's arms and legs, which are jointed, swing around and the feet clatter on the board in a dancing rhythm.

To make a jigger, you will need scrap wood and simple woodworking tools. Directions and exact measurements are given here, but you can change them as you wish to produce the Limber Jim you have in mind.

The jigger shown here in the step-by-step photos was designed by David Stuehler. Having seen a number of handmade traditional Limber Jims, he decided to try making his own version, using only scrap wood from his workshop and a few purchased dowels.

He offers some helpful advice on the project. He says that when inserting a dowel into a hole, whittle the top of it like a pencil point and it will go in much more easily than a blunt end. Also before inserting a piece of dowel into a hole of exactly the same size and gluing it to hold it in place, flatten the dowel just a little on one side to give the glue a little room. If you fail to do this, the wood may split.

To make a jigger, you will need scraps of wood, some ⅝" thick and some ¾" thick, also some ⅓" thick plywood, and pieces of ¼" and ⅛" dowels. You will also need a coping, jig, or band saw, drill, vise, quick-drying craft glue, paint and brush, fine and coarse sandpaper, and a hand or electric drill with a ⅛" bit.

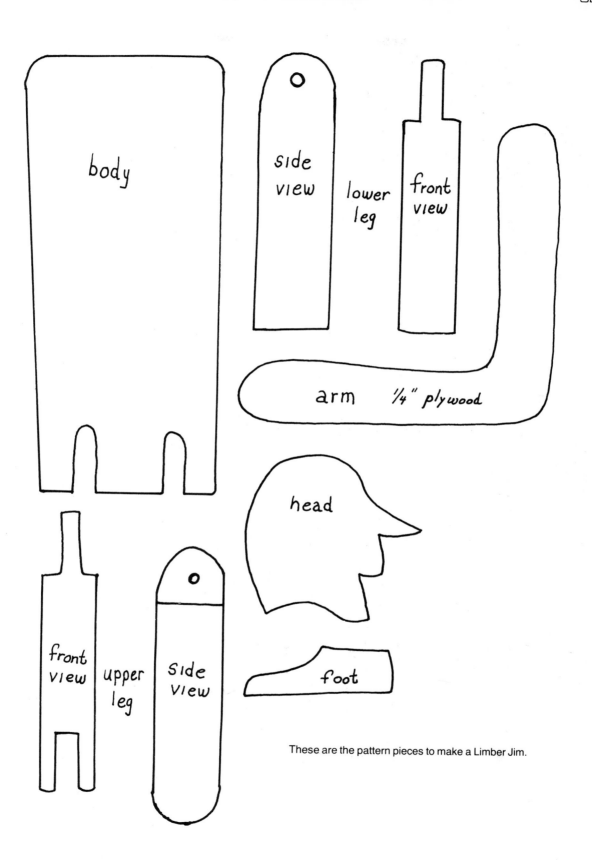

body

side
view

lower
leg

front
view

arm   ¼" plywood

head

front
view   upper
leg

side
view

foot

These are the pattern pieces to make a Limber Jim.

1

For the body, use a piece of wood that measures ¾" thick (your lumberman may call it 1" board). Copy the pattern onto the wood and cut it out with your coping, jig, or band saw. Notice that the body must be tapered so that the arms can swing freely from it. With a file, round off the body along the square edges.

2

At the bottom edge of the body, make cuts up into it, called mortises, where the tenons from the legs will be inserted. These cuts can be made before or after the hole for the dowel has been drilled. Drill a ⅛" hole through the bottom of the body.

3

To make the legs, use a 12" piece of wood that is ⅝" square. With a rasp or a file, round off the edges of the board along the whole length. With a coping or band saw, cut the wood into four 3" pieces and, with a rasp, round them off to the shapes shown in the diagrams.

4

The holes for the dowels that will connect the pieces can be drilled either before you complete the mortises and tenons or after. Copy the areas to be cut out for the mortises and tenons, as sketched on the diagrams, onto the pieces of wood and cut them out with a coping saw. Test the fit of the tenons into the mortises and cut off more wood if necessary.

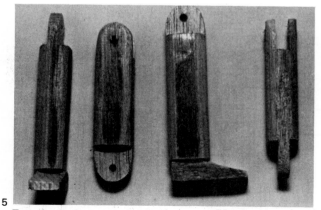

5

To make the foot, copy the pattern onto a piece of wood about ⅝" thick and cut it out with your coping or band saw. (Make two feet.) Drill a ⅛" hole on the top of each foot and at the bottom of each lower leg. Peg the two pieces together with ⅛" dowel, gluing them securely in place. This is how your leg pieces should look, ready to assemble.

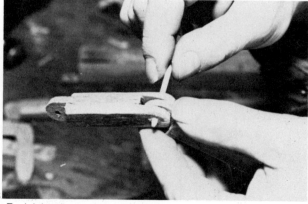

6

For joining the sections of the leg together and the legs to the body, you will need ⅛" dowels. The legs are supposed to swing freely, so the outer sections should hold the dowel tightly and the inner one should let the leg swing freely. To accomplish this, make the outer holes exactly ⅛" so they will hold the dowel tightly, and the inner ones a little more than ⅛". Drill holes in the sections of the leg accordingly.

7 Once you have inserted the dowel, cut off the excess. Check that the leg can swing loosely. You may need to file or sand a little more wood off to increase the swing.

8 Once the leg sections are joined together, use the same doweling method to join the legs to the body.

9 Copy the profile for the head onto a piece of ¾" wood. Cut it out with a coping or band saw. Put the head into a vise and carve it with a chisel. Shape the face, besides the nose, and round out the cheeks and chin. Round off the cap.

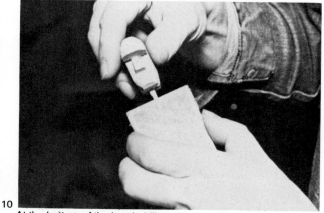

10 At the bottom of the head, drill a ⅛" hole and drill a corresponding hole at the top center of the body. Flatten a small piece of dowel slightly. Put glue on the dowel and slip it into the head, twisting as necessary. Put glue on the other end of the dowel and insert it into the body.

11 Drill holes at either side of the body where you will place the arms, making the hole just slightly smaller than the nail you will use.

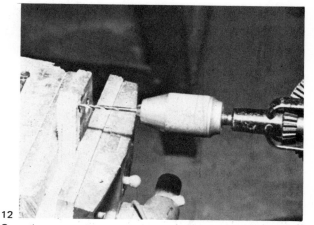

12 Copy the pattern for the arms onto ¼" plywood and cut them out with a coping or band saw. Drill holes through them where they will be attached to the body. Paint them the desired color.

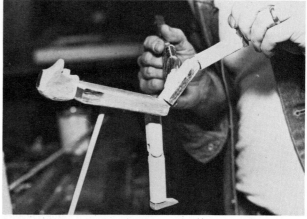

13 For the holder, use a 16″ piece of ¼″ dowel. Drill a ¼″ hole at the center back of the doll, drilling about halfway through the wood. Flatten the dowel a little on one side, put glue on it, and insert it into the hole, twisting it as necessary.

14 Sand and paint the Limber Jim. You can stick the end of his holder into a weighted can to hold him in the air while you paint him. Use any paint available, even latex house paint. Be careful not to get any paint into the joints. Paint his legs and partway up his body for his pants. Paint a shirt on the top half of his body. At his waist paint a belt, and also paint his hat. Glue on a small piece of yarn for his hair. Instead of painting him, you could stain him by dipping each piece of prepared wood into the solution or stain before assembling.

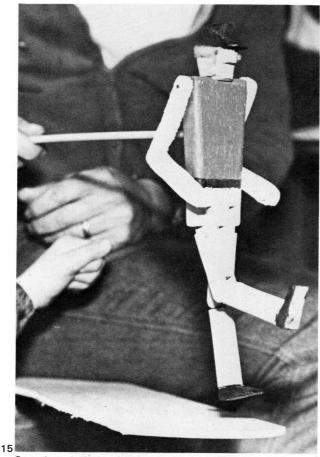

An antique carved wooden Limber Jim, varnished over the natural wood, held together with metal pins. Printed in black ink on his chest is "Sullivan County, N.Y." His face is hand carved, and his feet are separate pieces of wood pegged onto his legs. (*Hupp Collection*)

This wooden Limber Jim stands 9″ tall. The cutout sections of his body are held together with wires rather than wooden dowels. The pieces of wood are painted black with white areas silk-screened on. The figure has red crepe paper hair and a red bell attached to one foot. (*Hupp Collection*)

15 Once the paint is dry, nail the arms in place and Limber Jim is ready to dance. Get a piece of ¼″ plywood at least 5″ x 22″ for his dancing platform. Put the wood on a chair with the platform sticking out in front of the chair. Sit down so that the platform is in front of you and you are sitting on it to hold it in place. Hold the stick with one hand and knock on the board with the other, or have a friend rap out a rhythm on the board. (*Stuehler Collection*)

This Limber Jim was made in the Ozarks and sold through a craft cooperative called Ozark Opportunities. The body was made from cedar wood on a lathe. the nose is a peg, and the eyes and mouth are wood burned. As you can see, the pieces of the legs are joined a little differently from those of the Limber Jim shown in the step-by-step process. The legs and arms are cut out as silhouettes, and they are not carved or smoothed, but rather the edges are left square. Instead of having a dowel holder in his back, this jigger has a handle made from a coat hanger, attached with a screw to his hat. (*Author's Collection*)

TWO-HEADED DOLLS

A traditional American folk doll is the reversible two-headed, or upside-down, doll. Probably the most famous version of this doll is Topsy and Eva, a white doll with blond hair that reverses to become a black doll, and vice versa. Another version of the two-headed doll is a doll dressed in a pretty dress, with an awake face at one end, and, when turned over, a sleeping doll dressed in a nightgown.

Another type of upside-down doll is the storybook doll, for example, Little Boy Blue who reverses into his sheep, or Mary who reverses into her lamb, and Mother Hubbard who reverses into her dog. Sometimes these storybook dolls have even more than two heads. There might be three or even more; for example, a doll might have one head as Little Red Riding Hood, another as her grandmother, and the third as the wolf; or it might be Alice, the March Hare, and the Mad Hatter.

These storybook upside-down dolls have been made in the mountains of western North Carolina for many years. A cooperative, called Crafts Unlimited, in Lenoir, North Carolina, is a group of dollmakers who market their storybook dolls as a source of extra income for their families. Other cooperatives also in the Appalachian region have made this type of up-side-down doll.

Making a reversible doll with two flat faces is simple to do. Follow the same procedure as for a regular stuffed doll as described in Chapter 2. Draw a pattern for the body, such as the one shown on this page. Embroider the features, sew and stuff. Make two dresses for the doll and put them on. Blindstitch the hems of the dresses together, and you will have a reversible two-headed doll.

A 15″ stuffed cotton reversible doll, made before 1900. Both faces are painted. The white lady wears a lace bonnet and a blue dotted dress decorated with lace and embroidery at the cuffs. The black lady wears a bandanna and a red dress decorated with buttons down the front and embroidery at the cuffs. The name given the doll was "Topsy and Mamie." (*From the Collection of the Forbes Library, Northampton, Mass.*)

A modern upside down doll with a sleepy-face doll in a flannel nightgown on one end, and an awake doll in a gingham dress at the other. The doll is a simple flat-face stuffed doll with embroidered features and yarn hair. (*Author's Collection*)

This two-headed Topsy and Eva doll has Topsy with light brown skin and curly black hair at one end and Eva, with white skin and blond braided yarn hair at the other end. The doll is stuffed fabric with embroidered features, and the clothing is of cotton fabric. Topsy has a blue dress with white spots, a white apron, and red gingham bows in her hair, and Eva has a red dress with white dots. (*Wood Collection*)

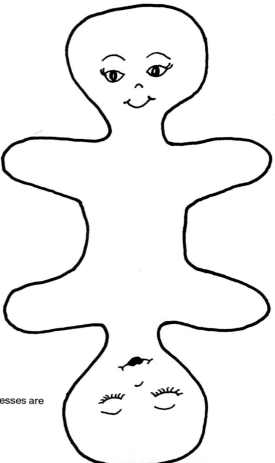

The body of a two-headed doll looks like this. The two dresses are stitched together at the hem.

CONTEMPORARY DOLLS OF THE UNITED STATES

Today in the United States there are many doll-makers and many more doll collectors. Some people who started out as doll collectors have also become makers; they became fascinated through their collections as to how dolls were made and began experimenting and making their own. Those who are dollmakers to begin with often become collectors because they appreciate the work of others and want to own samples made by them.

Doll collectors are basically interested in three types of dolls: the antique, foreign, and contemporary handcrafted. A market exists for quality handcrafted dolls among collectors and others interested in them as handcrafted items.

Today American dollmakers work in many different mediums. They have learned to make traditional and folk dolls, producing these or their own versions of the same in quantity for sale through craft shops or craft shows. Wood remains popular as a raw material for dollmaking, but there is a growing interest in making porcelain dolls—often with fabric bodies. These are usually reproductions of nineteenth-century dolls.

Among the most numerous modern dolls are those made with fibers. Some are knitted and others are crocheted or woven. Many are fabric stuffed dolls with needle-sculpted features. These dolls can be made to look humorous and appealing or grotesque.

Stuffed rag dolls of all kinds are still popular, and with the new interest in dollhouses, many people create not only the houses but also the small inhabitants to go with them.

There is such diversity in dollmaking in the United States today a book much larger than this one could be written on this subject. This section can only suggest the subject and tell you a little about the directions being taken by contemporary dollmakers.

Grass dolls were one type of early American doll made from natural materials on the spur of the moment to amuse children. Today they have made a comeback as door decorations. This grass doll has a body made of long pieces of dried grass and wears a patchwork print fabric dress, apron and bonnet tied in place with ribbons. (*Photographed at the Cricket Cage, Kingston, N.J.*)

A bread dough doll made by Dot and Joe Sinclair as a gift for Arthur Weiner from his wife, Ann. The figure of Mr. Weiner, shown at his desk in his real estate office, has a stuffed cotton wire-frame body and bread dough feet, hands, face, and pipe (see page 249 for more information on making bread dough). He is wearing brown knit-fabric pants and vest, a gingham shirt edged with bias binding, and a brown bias-binding tie. He is sitting at a miniature wooden desk with a pad, notebook, pens, and so forth. (*Weiner Collection*)

These attractive 5" dolls are signed "Emily of Florida." They have wooden-ball heads with painted features. Extending down from their heads are pipe cleaners, which are attached to stiff fabric cone skirts that hold the dolls up. The Spanish señorita at the left has a satin dress with lace flounces and a shawl with fringe. The peasant girl in the middle has an organdy apron. A lace dress and a feathery hat make an elegant outfit for the lady on the right. (*Weiner Collection*)

An attractive 6½" doll made in 1966 by Frances Bringloe, who is well known for her museum dioramas. Called "The Pioneer Girl in the Brown Dress," the figure is beautifully carved and fully articulated. Her dress, pinafore, and hat are all of tiny calico prints. Underneath she has three petticoats, one of which is red flannel, and holds a tiny wood-carved doll in her arms. The doll's costume is authentic pioneer tradition as researched by Ms. Bringloe. (*Groszmann Collection*)

This 12" wood-sculpted female doll was made by Helena Beachem of Lahaska, Pennsylvania. Her body is constructed of carved wooden sections, her features are delicately painted, and she is wearing a blue print dress, lace cap, apron, and shawl. (*Mueller Collection*)

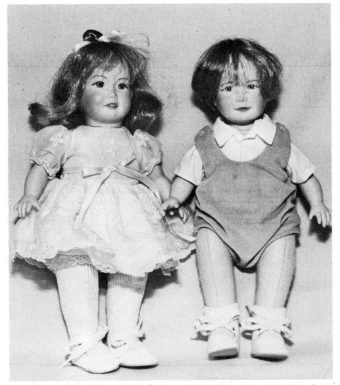

These 12″ dolls, called Becky and Ricky, were made by Astry Campbell. They have bisque heads and arms, with the rest of their bodies of stuffed felt. Both the boy and the girl are beautifully dressed in contemporary outfits and have vinyl wigs. He is wearing velvet overalls and a white cotton shirt, and she an organdy dress. (*Groszmann Collection*)

A stuffed cotton-fabric character doll, named Mrs. Abernathy, with a needle-sculpted face of a knit material. Her eyes and mouth are painted, and she wears a black felt hat decorated with feathers, a cotton-print dress, a fur stole, and muff. (*Photographed at the Children's Museum, Boston, Mass.*)

Dolls of recent vintage made in the United States by Jane Beckett. Their faces were hand carved, and the eyes and mouths were painted on. The baby is about 7″ tall, and the girl about 12″. Both have soft fabric bodies. The girl wears red flannel pajamas and the baby has on a white cotton dress. (*Mueller Collection*)

Today, along with dollhouses and miniatures, miniature dolls are very popular. This tiny 1½″ figure has a wooden-bead head with hand-painted features and yellow embroidery-cotton hair. Her limbs are made of toothpicks, and her toothpick legs are wound with lace to represent lacy pantalets. She wears a red dress trimmed with lace. (*Weiner Collection*)

These three dolls by Edith Flack Ackley, the author of *Dolls to Make for Fun and Profit*, are made according to the directions in her book. Each one is only 4½″ tall and beautifully detailed. They are stuffed cotton figures with embroidered features and dressed in calico prints. Each dress is a little different, with exquisite decorations. (*Groszmann Collection*)

Stuffed dolls are still as popular today in the United States as they have been in the past. These contemporary black stuffed dolls, made by Janet Spring, have bodies of brown cotton fabric, black yarn hair, and embroidered features. The girl wears a print dress, and the boy has denim overalls and a gingham shirt. (*Photographed at the Cricket Cage, Kingston, N.J.*)

A 13″ doll, made in the United States by Helen Jane Biggart, with a clay face and wire-framed, stuffed fabric body. This figure is dressed as a pirate with a red felt jacket, wire earrings, and black leather boots. He is well armed with a dagger, knife, and gun. (*Hupp Collection*)

These 17″ stuffed stockinette Revca dolls have beautifully detailed needle-sculpted faces, finished with oil paints. They have fabric clothing and carved wooden shoes. (*Hupp Collection*)

These 9″ stuffed fabric dolls with embroidered features were made by Teressa Mobry of Fullerton, California, a contemporary doll-maker who designs original dolls and sells patterns for them. (*Mueller Collection*)

DOLLS OF CANADA

Like the United States, Canada has a great diversity in its heritage of dollmaking traditions. It has those of the native Indians and Eskimos as well as those of the French English, and other Europeans who migrated there. The Indians of Canada make beautiful carvings from soapstone—including complete dolls as well as doll heads, for which they have made fabric-stuffed bodies.

Canada also has wire-frame and stuffed dolls, often attired in beautiful knitted or homespun fabrics, and both traditional and contemporary dolls are among those created in the country.

An issue of *Canada Crafts* magazine was devoted to dolls and surveyed dollmakers of Canada. The magazine concluded that cloth, applehead, and porcelain and every other kind of doll you can imagine are being made in Canada today. The magazine featured photos of woven, crocheted, and china dolls and also fabric dolls with needle-sculpted faces and appleheads made to look like specific people such as Winston Churchill, David Ben-Gurion, Pierre Trudeau, and others.

The Indians of Canada are famous for their soapstone carvings, such as this one. They carve complete dolls from soapstone as well as doll heads, which are attached to fabric bodies. (*Photographed at the United Nations Gift Center*)

An 11″ doll, with hand-carved soapstone head, made in Canada by an Eskimo and bearing the tag "Port Harrison Handicrafts." This male figure has a solidly stuffed fabric body, green fabric pants decorated with rickrack, and a white jacket trimmed with strips of green and blue bunting. He wears a multicolored belt and fur collar. (*Hulsizer Collection*)

These 7″ dolls, from New Brunswick, Nova Scotia, have wire-frame bodies covered with fabric. Their fabric faces have painted features, and they both have black woven-wool boots. The woman has white wool hair, wears a handloomed skirt and hand-knit sweater, and carries a large knitted muff. The man has a white wool beard and is wearing a black knitted hat, brown knitted sweater with red buttons, red knit mittens, and brown handloomed woolen pants. (*Hupp Collection*)

Made in Canada, 7½″ dolls, with wire-framed, stuffed cotton bodies. The woman has a fabric face with painted features and wears red knitted mittens, a knitted black wool skirt and hat, a green knitted shawl, and a black wool muff. The man has a pressed fabric face and wears a black wool jacket, white wool pants, and a black-and-white-striped vest with seed bead buttons. (*MacNeer Collection*)

This 9½″ pair of dolls was bought in Montreal in 1942. They have stuffed cotton bodies and very simple embroidered features. The woman is wearing a brown woolen coat with a real-fur collar. Her knitted hat has a crocheted edging. The man is wearing a red knitted stocking cap and a black woolen coat with a fur collar. (*Photographed at the Forbes Library, Northampton, Mass.*)

Bibliography

A wide variety of books on dolls are available. Some relate the history of dolls and dollmaking and others tell you how to make them. A list of these books follows.

Besides reading about dolls, you may want to research the costumes of specific dolls or look up background information about them. If you are planning to make dolls, you may want to find out about specific craft techniques you will be using. A complete list of books with such information would be impossible to compile. However, a partial list follows the list of doll books here.

DOLL BOOKS

Bachman, M., and Hansmann, C. *Dolls the Wide World Over.* New York: Crown, 1973.

Benbow, Mary; Dunlop, Edith; and Luchen, Joyce. *Dolls and Doll Making.* Boston: Plays, 1968.

Brinley, Rosemary. *Dolls and Stuffed Toy Making.* New York: Dover, 1952.

Christopher, Catherine. *Doll Making and Collecting.* New York: Dover, 1971.

Desmonde, Kay. *All Color Book of Dolls.* New York: Crescent Books, 1974.

Eaton, Faith. *Dolls in Color.* New York: Macmillan, 1976.

Fawcett, Clara Hallard. *Dolls: A New Guide for Collectors.* Boston: Branford, 1964.

Fletcher, Helen Jill. *The See and Do Book of Dolls and Doll Houses.* New York: Stuttman, 1959.

Fox, Carl. *The Doll.* New York: Abrams, 1973.

Gaylin, Evelyn. *Doll Repair.* Clackamas, Oregon: Gay World of Dolls, 1967.

Glubok, Shirley. *Dolls, Dolls, Dolls.* Chicago: Follett, 1975.

Gordon, Lesley. *A Pageant of Dolls.* New York: A. A. Wyn, 1949.

Gray, Else. *Designing and Making Dolls.* New York: Watson-Guptill, 1972.

Greenhowe, Jean. *Making Costume Dolls.* New York: Watson-Guptill, 1972.

Heady, Eleanor. *Make Your Own Dolls.* New York: Lothrop, 1974.

Hillier, Mary. *Dolls and Dollmakers.* New York: Putnam, 1968.

Hoke, Helen. *The First Book of Dolls.* New York: Watts, 1954.

Ives, Suzy. *Making and Dressing a Rag Doll.* New York: Drake, 1972.

Jacobs, Flora Gill. *A World of Doll Houses.* New York: Rand, 1965.

Johl, Janet Pagter. *Your Dolls and Mine: A Collector's Handbook.* New York: Lindquist, 1952.

Johnson, Audrey. *Dressing Dolls.* Newton, Mass.: Branford, 1969.

———. *How to Repair and Dress Old Dolls.* Newton, Mass.: Branford, 1967.

Jones, Iris Sanderson. *Early North American Dollmaking.* San Francisco: 101 Productions, 1976.

Jordan, Nina R. *American Costume Dolls: How to Make and Dress Them.* New York: Harcourt, Brace, 1941.

———. *Homemade Dolls in Foreign Dress.* New York: Harcourt, Brace, 1939.

Kelly, Karin. *Doll Houses.* Minneapolis, Minn.: Lerner, 1974.

Laury, Jean Ray. *Doll Making: A Creative Approach.* New York: Van Nostrand, 1970.

Lori. *Kachina Creations.* Phoenix, Ariz.: Techni-Graphics, 1977.

Mills, Winifred H., and Dunn, Louise M. *The Story of Old Dolls and How to Make New Ones.* New York: Doubleday, Doran & Co., 1940.

Mitts, June, and Johnson, Ginger. *Clothespin Dolls and Furniture.* Rosemead, Calif.: Hazel Pearson Handicrafts, 1974.

Moloney, Joan. *Dolls.* London: Wardlock, 1971.

Noble, John. *Collectors' Blue Books: Dolls.* New York: Walker, 1967.

Roberts, Catherine. *The Real Book about Making Dolls and Doll Clothes.* Garden City, N.Y.: Garden City Books, 1951.

Rogowski, Gini, and DeWeese, Gene. *Making American Folk Art Dolls.* Radnor, Pa.: Chilton, 1975.

Roth, Charlene. *Dressing Dolls.* New York: Crown, 1976.

———. *Making Dollhouse Accessories.* New York: Crown, 1977.

St. George, Eleanor. *The Dolls of Yesterday.* New York: Scribner's, 1948.

———. *Dolls of Three Centuries.* New York: Scribner's, 1951.

Schauffler, Grace L. *How to Make Your Own Dolls for Pleasure and Profit.* New York: Hobby Book Mart, 1948.

Schnacke, Dick. *American Folk Toys: How to Make Them.* Baltimore, Md.: Penguin, 1973.

Singleton, Esther. *Dolls.* New York: Payson & Clarke, 1927.

Tyler, Mabs. *The Big Book of Dolls.* New York: Dial Press, 1976.

Von Boehm, Max. *Dolls.* New York: Dover, 1972.

Wendorff, Ruth. *How to Make Cornhusk Dolls.* New York: Arco, 1973.

White, Gwen. *Dolls of the World.* Newton, Mass.: Branford, 1962.

Witzig, H., and Kuhn, G. E. *Making Dolls.* New York: Sterling, 1969.

Worrell, Estelle Ansley. *Americana in Miniature.* New York: Van Nostrand, 1972.

———. *The Doll Book.* New York: Van Nostrand, 1966.

Wright, Dare. *A Gift From the Lonely Doll.* New York: Random, 1968.

Young, Helen. *The Complete Book of Doll Collecting.* New York: Putnam, 1967.

———. *Here Is Your Hobby: Doll Collecting.* New York: Putnam, 1964.

BACKGROUND READING

Bahti, Tom. *Southwestern Indian Arts and Crafts,* Flagstaff, Ariz.: K.C. Publications, 1966.

———. *Southwestern Indian Ceremonials.* Flagstaff, Ariz.: K.C. Publications, 1970.

———. *Southwestern Indian Tribes.* Flagstaff, Ariz.: K.C. Publications, 1968.

Bradshaw, Angela. *World Costumes.* New York: Macmillan, 1952.

Cooper, Edmund. *Let's Look at Costume.* London: Frederic Muller, 1965.

Creekmore, Betsey. *Traditional American Crafts.* Long Island City, N.Y.: Hearthside Press, 1968.

Cummings, Richard. *101 Costumes for All Ages and Occasions.* New York: McKay, 1970.

Evans, Mary. *Costumes Through the Ages.* New York: Lippincott, 1930.

Foley, Daniel. *Toys Through the Ages.* Philadelphia: Chilton, 1962.

Fox, Lilla M. *Folk Costumes of Western Europe.* Boston: Players, 1971.

Haire, Frances. *The Folk Costumes of Europe.* New York: Barnes, 1927.

Holz, Loretta. *Teach Yourself Stitchery.* New York: Lothrop, 1974.

Hunt, W. Ben. *Kachina Dolls.* Milwaukee: Milwaukee Public Museum, 1957.

LaFarge, Oliver. *The American Indian.* Racine, Wis.: Western Publishing, 1960.

Leeming, Joseph. *The Costume Book.* New York: Lippincott, 1938.

Lyford, Carrie. *Ojibwa Crafts.* Washington, D.C.: U.S. Department of the Interior, 1943.

Minor, Marz and Nono. *The American Indian Craft Book.* Lincoln, Neb.: University of Nebraska Press, 1972.

Ross, Patricia Fent. *Made in Mexico.* New York: Knopf, 1952.

Sandford, Lettice. *Straw Work and Corn Dollies.* New York: Viking, 1974.

Sayer, Chloe. *Crafts of Mexico.* Garden City, N.Y.: Doubleday, 1977.

Shishido, Misako. *The Folk Toys of Japan.* Rutland, Vt.: Japan Publications Trading Co., 1963.

Stribling, Mary Lou. *Crafts from North American Indian Arts.* New York: Crown, 1975.

Tanner, Clara Lee. *Southwest Indian Crafts.* Tucson, Ariz.: University of Tucson Press, 1968.

Werner, E. T. Chalmers. *Myths and Legends of China.* London: George C. Harrap, 1922.

Whiteford, Andrew Hunter. *North American Indian Arts.* Racine, Wis.: Western Publishing, 1970.

Wilcox, R. Turner. *Folk and Festival Costumes of the World.* New York: Scribner's, 1965.

Williams, C. A. S. *Outlines of Chinese Symbolism and Art Motives.* New York: Dover, 1976. (Republication of 1932 edition of *Outlines of Chinese Symbolism*)

Wright, Barton, and Roat, Evelyn. *This Is a Hopi Kachina.* Flagstaff, Ariz.: The Museum of Northern Arizona, 1965.

Periodicals

Magazines are an excellent way of learning more about dolls and dollmaking and of finding out what is new in the world of dolls. Here is a list of doll and miniature magazines and some general craft magazines that often include articles on dolls. If you are interested in subscribing to one of these magazines, write directly to the publisher and ask the price of a sample copy and subscription.

Bernice's Bambini
Rt. 2A
Highland, Ill. 62249

Berryhill News
Elizabeth Berry, Editor
P.O. Box 1308
Bozeman, Mont. 59715

Crafts 'n Things
Clapper Publication Co.
14 Main St.
Park Ridge, Ill. 60068

Creating in Miniature
Grueny's Inc.
Box 2477
Little Rock, Ark. 72203

Creative Crafts
P.O. Box 700
Newton, N.J. 07860

Decorating and Craft Ideas
P.O. Box C–30
Birmingham, Ala. 35223

The Doll Artisan
Doll Artisan Guild
35 Main St.
Oneonta, N.Y. 13820

Doll Castle News
Edwina Mueller, Editor
RD 1, Brass Castle
Washington, N.J. 07882

Doll House Knitting Club
P.O. Box 367
Norquay, Sask.
Canada SOA 2VO

Doll News
Willma Jaxtheimer, Editor
P.O. Box 209
Wilsonville, Ala. 35186

Doll Reader
Paul Ruddell
4701 Queensbury Rd,
Riverdale, Md. 20840

Doll Shop Talk
Shirley Puertzer, Editor
Rt. 1, Box 100
Evanston, Ind. 47531

Doll Talk
Kimport Dolls
P.O. Box 495
Independence, Mo. 64051

Doll World
Tower Publications
P.O. Box 428
Seabrook, N.H. 03874

Dollcraft Club
11813–95A St.
Edmonton, Alberta
Canada

The Dollhouse and Miniature News
Marion O'Brien, Editor
#3 Orchard Lane
Kirkwood, Mo. 63122

The Dollmaker
P.O. Box 247
Washington, N.J. 07882

Ella's Doll Publication
Box 308
Fallbrook, Calif. 92028

Fantasy World
Cresco, Calif. 18326

Lanette's Dollogy
P.O. Box 1207
Summerville, S.C. 29583

McCall's Needlework and Crafts
McCall's Christmas Annual
230 Park Ave.
New York, N.Y. 10017

Midwest Paper Dolls and Toys Quarterly
Jane Varsolona, Editor
Box 35
Galesburg, Kans. 66740

Miniature Collector Magazine
Acquire Publishing
170 Fifth Ave.
New York, N.Y. 10010

The Miniature Entrepreneur's Newsletter
11 Brighton Terrace
Brooklyn, N.Y. 11235

Miniature Gazette
The National Association of Miniature Enthusiasts
Box 2621, Brookhurst Center
Anaheim, Calif. 92804

The Miniature Magazine
Box 700
Newton, N.J. 07860

Miniature Makers Journal
Fred Diedrick
409 S. First St.
Evansville, Wis. 53536

Miniature World
P.O. Box 337
Seabrook, N.H. 03874

Mott Miniature Workshop News
Box 5514
Sunny Hills Station
Fullerton, Calif. 92635

National Doll World
Barbara Hall Pederson, Editor
Box 337
Seabrook, N.H. 03874

Nutshell News
Calther MacLauren
1035 Newkird Drive
La Jolla, Calif. 92037

Paper Doll and Paper Toys Quarterly
Barbara Jendrick, Editor
495 Mendon Rd.
Pittsford, N.Y. 14534

Paperdoll Gazette
Shirley Hedge, Editor
Route 2
Princeton, Ind. 47670

The Pattern Book
2631 Curve Rd.
Delaware, Ohio 43015

Pixie Fashion Gazette
Deane Fenchel
204 S. Fourth Ave.
Miamisburg, Ohio 45342

The Scale Cabinet Maker
Dorsett Miniatures
Box 87
Pembroke, Va. 24136

Small Talk
JoAnn Jones
Box 334
Laguna Beach, Calif. 92651

Wee Sew
Rt. 1 Box 92
Armstrong, Mo. 65230

Supply Sources

Your local craft, hardware, dime, department, and fabric stores may have available all the materials and equipment you will need for making dolls. If you have trouble finding supplies locally, here is a list that may help you. Some of these companies have mail order catalogs. Others would be glad to give you the names of local distributors from whom you can make your purchases. Some have their own local retail outlets.

Beads

Bead Game
505 N. Fairfax Ave.
Los Angeles, Calif. 90036

Northeast Bead Trading Co.
12 Depot St.
Kennebunk, Maine 04043

Walco Products
1200 Zerega Ave.
Bronx, N.Y. 10462

Clay

American Art Clay Co.
Indianapolis, Ind. 46200

Stewart Clay Co., Inc.
400 Jersey Ave.
New Brunswick, N.J. 08902

Westwood Ceramic Supply Co.
14400 Lomitas Ave.
Industry, Calif. 91744

Craft Supplies (General)

American Handicrafts
P.O. Box 791
Fort Worth, Tex. 76101

Dick Blick
P.O. Box 1267
Galesburg, Ill. 61401

Boin Art and Craft Co.
87 Morris St.
Morristown, N.J. 07960

Holiday Handicrafts
Apple Hill
Winsted, Conn. 06098

Hazel Pearson Handicrafts
4128 Temple City Blvd.
Rosemead, Calif. 91770

S & S Arts and Crafts
Colchester, Conn. 06415

Lee Wards
1200 St. Charles St.
Elgin, Ill. 60120

Zim's
240 East Second St.
Salt Lake City, Utah 84111

Doll Parts and Patterns

Antique Doll Reproductions
Box 103
Montevallo Rt.
Milo, Mo. 64767

Aunt Hattie's Doll Cupboard
109 Walnut Ridge Rd.
Wilmington, Del. 19807

The Doll Maker's Gallery
681 Greenbrook Rd.
N. Plainfield, N.J. 07063

Doll Pattern House
100 Summit St.
Orange, Maine 01364

Doll Repair Parts
9918 Lorain
Cleveland, Ohio 44102

Dollspart Supply Co., Inc.
5–06 51st Ave.
Long Island City, N.Y. 11101

Mark Farmer Co., Inc.
11427 San Pablo Ave.
El Cerrito, Calif. 94530

Teressa Mobry
1250 Longview
Fullerton, Calif. 92631

Standard Doll Co.
23–83 31st St.
Long Island City, N.Y. 11105

Indian Craft Supplies

Grey Owl Indian Craft
Manufacturing Co.
150–02 Beaver Rd.
Jamaica, N.Y. 11433

Roberts Indian Crafts and Supplies
211 W. Broadway St.
Anadarko, Okla. 73005

Leather

Berman Leather Co.
23 Union St.
Boston, Mass. 02123

Tandy Leather Co.
1001 Foch St.
Fort Worth, Tex. 76107

Papier-Mâché (Instant)

Activa Products, Inc.
582 Market St.
San Francisco, Calif. 94104

Fibre-Craft Materials Corp.
7301 Cicero Ave.
Chicago, Ill. 60646

Straws (Long Craft)

Sweetheart Cup Corp.
Straw Division
Owings Mills, Md. 21117

Tapa Cloth

S. T. Foukimoana
1424–148 S.E.
Bellevue, Wash. 98007

Tools

Dremel Manufacturing Co.
Racine, Wis. 53406

PO Instrument Co., Inc.
13 Lehigh Ave.
Paterson, N.J. 07503

Wood (Turned Shapes, Etc.)

Colonial Craftsman, Inc.
Box 1644
Wayne, N.J. 07470

Albert Constantine & Son, Inc.
2050 Eastchester Rd.
Bronx, N.Y. 10461

Craftsman Wood Service Co.
2727 South Mary St.
Chicago, Ill. 60608

Creative Playmakers, Inc.
Box 904
Easthampton, N.Y. 11937

Gwenith Gwyn
P.O. Box 297
Park Ridge, N.J. 07656

JB Wood Products
Box 84
South Attleboro, Maine 02703

O-P Craft Co., Inc.
425 Warren St.
Sandusky, Ohio 44870

Doll Sources

The following is a list of sources from which you can buy authentic dolls. If you wish to make a purchase, write to the address and ask for information on the dolls currently available, and if a price list is available. BE SURE TO ENCLOSE A SELF-ADDRESSED STAMPED ENVELOPE. I have collected these addresses over a period of time. Addresses do change, and companies and individuals go out of business so that inaccuracies may have already crept into the list. If you have any corrections or additions to the list, please write directly to me at 97 Grandview Ave., N. Plainfield, N.J. 07060.

Many of these sources have only one or a few types of dolls that can be purchased, but SERRV, which is part of the Church World Service and sponsors self-help programs, has available for sale dolls from all over the world. The organization works on a nonprofit basis and will be glad to send you a copy of the current price list. The Mennonite Central Committee runs a similar program. Another excellent source of dolls is Kimport's, which issues a newsletter, *Doll Talk*, with information on international dolls and a description of those available for sale.

Aguilar Shop
St. 1, Box 318 C
Santa Fe, N. Mex. 87501

Alaska Native Arts and Crafts
4190 Aircraft Drive
Anchorage, Alaska 99503

Alaska Native Arts and Crafts
Cooperative Association
Box 889
Juneau, Alaska 99801

All Saints Home
Industries
P.O. All Saints
Transkei, South Africa

Allegheny Indian Arts and
Crafts Cooperative
Haley Building
Jimersontown, Salamanca,
N.Y. 14779

Apache Arts and Crafts Bead
Association
Box 1026
Whiteriver, Ariz. 85941

Arctic Trader
Dept. 1A, Box 4–MM
Spenard, Alaska 99509

Art Originals, Ltd.
43 Marshall Ridge Rd.
New Canaan, Conn. 06840

Artistic Siam, Inc.
512 Millburn Ave.
Short Hills, N.J. 07078

Helena Beachem
Honey Hollow Road
Lahaska, Penn. 18931

Blackfeet Crafts Association
P.O. Box 326
Browning, Mont. 59417

Blue Ridge Hearthside Crafts
 Association, Inc.
P.O. Box 96
Sugar Grove, N.C. 28679

Car-Be Associates
3031 Edwin Ave.
Fort Lee, N.J. 07024

Cherokee Arts and Crafts Center
P.O. Box 807
Tahlequah, Okla. 74464

Chief Ojibway Original Products
Box 97
Cass Lake, Minn. 56633

Chief Poolaw Teepee Trading Post
1 Center St.
Indian Island
Old Town, Maine 04468

Chief White Bird's Indian Store
Houghton Lake, Mich. 48629

Choctaw Craft Association
Philadelphia, Miss. 39350

Christmas Dove
P.O. Box 297
Rockport, Mass. 01966

Colorado River Indian Tribes
 Library Museum
Rt. 1, Box 23–B
Parker, Ariz. 85344

The Doll Maker's Gallery
681 Greenbrook Road
N. Plainfield, N.J. 07063

Dolls International
412 Southwood Drive
Kingston, Ontario, Canada

Wendy Ellertson
80 Thorton St.
Roxbury, Mass. 02119

Fine Apache Arts
P.O. Box 57
San Carlos, Ariz. 85550

Four Continent Book Corp.
156 Fifth Ave.
New York, N.Y. 10010

Gallery Shop
The Brooklyn Museum
Eastern Parkway
Brooklyn, N.Y. 11238

Gila River Arts and Crafts Center
Box 457
Sacaton, Ariz. 85247

Greek Island, Ltd.
215 East 49th St.
New York, N.Y. 10017

Ester Hills
Lincolnville, Maine 04849

Hopi Silvercrafts and Arts and
 Crafts Coop.
P.O. Box 37
Second Mesa, Ariz. 86043

Hopicrafts
P.O. Box 37
Oraibi, Ariz. 86039

International Craftsman
123 Main St.
Flemington, N.J. 08822

International Gift Shop
703 Watchung Ave.
Plainfield, N.J. 07060

Iroqrafts
R.R. #2 Oshweken
Ontario, Canada

Jo Dot Creations
848 Woodmere Drive
Cliffwood Beach, N.J. 07735

Kimport Dolls
P.O. Box 495
Independence, Mo. 64051

The Kiva Shop
112 Don Gaspar
Santa Fe, N.M. 87501

Lani Lei
1386 Akalani Loop
Kailua, Hawaii 96734

Lelooska Northwest Carvings
5618 Lewis River Rd.
Ariel, Wash. 98602

Elisa Lotter
427 10th St.
Santa Monica, Calif. 90402

Marlinda Dolls
Box 611
Wrangell, Alaska 99929

Mennonite Central Committee
 Self-Help Program
21 South 12th St.
Akron, Pa. 17501

Lois Morrison
105 Palmer Place
Leonia, N.J. 07605

R. C. Morrison
2815 Woody Drive
Billings, Mont. 59102

Museum of Navaho
 Ceremonial Art, Inc.
P.O. Box 5153
Santa Fe, N.M. 87501

Museum of the Plains Indian
 and Crafts Center
P.O. Box 400
Browning, Mont. 59417

Museum Shop
Museum of African Art
316–318 A. Street, N.E.
Washington, D.C. 20002

My Irish Cottage
61 Floral Ave.
Murray Hill, N.J. 07974

Native American Center for
 the Living Arts
466 Third St.
Niagara Falls, N.Y. 14301

Navajo Arts and Crafts Guild
Drawer A
Window Rock, Ariz. 86515

Navajo Tribal Museum
Box 418
Window Rock, Ariz. 86515

Norsk, Inc.
114 East 57th St.
New York, N.Y. 10022

Northern Plains Indian Crafts
 Association
P.O. Box E
Browning, Mont. 59417

Oke Oweenge Arts and Crafts
P.O. Box 925
San Juan Pueblo, N.Mex. 87566

Oklahoma Indian Artists and
 Craftsmen's Guild
c/o Nabel Harris, President
832 N. Warren
Oklahoma City, Okla. 73107

Gerryann Olson
Box 462
Sebastopol, Calif. 95472

Onondaga Indian Trading Post
Nedrow, N.Y. 13120

Organization of the American
 States Gift Shop
Washington, D.C. 20005

Papago Arts and Crafts
 Cooperative Guild
Box 837
Sells, Arizona 85634

Polish Cultural Foundation
851 18th Ave.
Irvington, N.J. 07111

Praphaphorn
20 Waterside Plaza 10D
New York, N.Y. 10010

The Primal Arts Center
33 East 68th St.
New York, N.Y. 10021

Qualla Arts and Crafts Mutual, Inc.
Box 277
Cherokee, N.C. 28719

J. Ragsdale
186 Fifth Ave., Room 405
New York, N.Y. 10010

Geraldine Robertson
P.O. Box 313
Washington, La. 70589

Seminole Indian Village and
 Crafts Center
6073 Stirling Road
Hollywood, Fla. 33024

SERRV
c/o William D. Nyce, Director
Church World Service
New Windsor, Md. 21776

Myrna Shiras
6441 Via de Anzar
Rancho Palos Verdes,
 Calif. 90274

Shopping International
Norwich, Vt. 05055

Sioux Indian Museum and
 Crafts Center
P.O. Box 1504
Rapid City, S.D. 57701

Southern Plains Indian Museum
 and Crafts Center
P.O. Box 749
Anadarko, Okla. 73005

Swedish Book Nook
235 East 81st St.
New York, N.Y. 10028

Thai House
Box 35
Essex, Mass. 01929

Tiger's Miccosuke Indian Village
Box 44021
Tamiami Station
Miami, Fla. 33144

Treasure House of Worldly
 Wares
Calistoga, Calif. 94515

United Nations Gift Shop
New York, N.Y. 10037

White Star Trading Co.
46 Green St.
Northampton, Mass. 01060

Wohali Traders
Box 45A, Rt. 1
Cherokee Indian Reservation,
 N.C. 28719
(US 19 in Birdtown)

Index